by their financial resources, they could thus obtain all the fighters required. During the fifteenth century when money had outmoded feudal custom and thinking, the *fief-rente* was gradually displaced by the indenture system, and from here it was but a step to the permanent armies that developed toward the end of the fifteenth century.

Here is a truly valuable comparative study of feudalism and of the financial, administrative, and military institutions of the principal feudal states. Because at least half of the book has been written from records in the archives of England, France, Belgium, and Holland, it presents much new material. To supplement the text there is an appendix of thirty documents, hitherto unpublished, containing important information on the *fief-rente*. Scholars and students of medieval history, as well as all college and university libraries, will find this a welcome — and necessary — addition.

Mr. Lyon is an associate professor of history at the University of Illinois. Harvard Historical Studies, 68.

HARVARD HISTORICAL STUDIES

Published Under the Direction of the
Department of History

From the Income of
THE HENRY WARREN TORREY FUND
VOLUME LXVIII

Oscar Handlin, Editor

FROM FIEF
TO INDENTURE

*The Transition
from Feudal to Non-Feudal Contract
in Western Europe*

By

BRYCE D. LYON

HARVARD UNIVERSITY PRESS

Cambridge, Massachusetts

1957

Library of Congress Catalog Card Number A 57-8618
Printed in Denmark
Vald. Pedersens Bogtrykkeri
Copenhagen

To the memory of
CARL STEPHENSON

Preface

The present book had its beginnings in a thesis completed in 1949 under the direction of Professor Carl Stephenson of Cornell University. It was at that time, while investigating the role of the *fief-rente* under the English kings, that I felt the need eventually to expand the study to include all western Europe. A cursory examination of the continental records had shown that the *fief-rente* was a prominent institution in France, Germany, and the Low Countries. In an excellent work, M. Sczaniecki had clearly defined the *fief-rente* in France, but its place in the rest of western Europe had been mainly neglected. When the conclusions I drew from the English records, as set down in an article in the *English Historical Review*, differed sharply from those of Sczaniecki, it was evident that the next step should be a study of the German and Low Country sources in addition to a more extensive examination of the English and French evidence. This project received the warm support of Professor Stephenson who, in the tradition of Henri Pirenne and Charles Homer Haskins, believed that medieval institutions could be better understood when viewed not as national but as western European.

During 1951–52 I was fortunate in having the opportunity to work in the national and provincial archives of Belgium and France, as well as in the Public Record Office and the British Museum. The material collected at that time has resulted in this book. It is regretted that time did not permit working in the German archives, but most of the pertinent records have already been so well edited that I feel the uncovering of a few more would have resulted in little new information. I have attempted throughout to maintain a balanced account of the *fief-rente* in France, Germany, the Low Countries, and England; if at times it seems that I have put more stress on the French, Low Country, and English evidence than on the German, it is only because the *fief-rente* never obtained the prominence and flexibility in Germany that it did in the other countries.

Within the past several years I have published in various journals articles dealing with certain aspects of the *fief-rente* in England and the Low Countries,* but in no respect has this book been built around them or the thesis; it is an attempt, where the articles were not, to study the *fief-rente* throughout western Europe and to place it in the stream of feudal history. I can think of no better device than the *fief-rente* to show how the reviving money economy ceaselessly chipped away at feudal institutions from the tenth to the later fifteenth century. In this respect I have gone beyond the problem of the *fief-rente* and have endeavored to explain how changes, principally military and economic, gradually made useless the practice of requiring homage and fealty with military and political contracts and antiquated paying a man for his services with a fief, either of land or of money. A study of the *fief-rente* is actually a study of the transition from fief to indenture in western Europe.

With printed sources I have given complete bibliographical information when referring to a work for the first time and have thereafter used short titles. Abbreviations have been used for material cited frequently. I felt it unnecessary to include a bibliography of the printed works, which would only repeat the data contained in the notes; for the unprinted records there is an extensive bibliography. I hope that the reader will benefit from the brief index of topics, names, and places.

When quoting Latin, French, German, and Flemish documents, I have reproduced them exactly as they were edited, changing no spelling, punctuation, capitalization, or extensions. A standardization of these documents could never have been wholly achieved. Editorial practice in Germany, France, Belgium, and England is so different and even varies so much with editors that to impose, for example, the Belgian canons of editing upon French and German documents could only be arbitrary. Where record type has been used, as with

---

* "The Money Fief under the English Kings, 1066–1485," *English Historical Review*, LXVI (1951), 161–93; "Le fief-rente aux Pays-Bas: sa terminologie et son aspect financier," *Revue du Nord*, XXXV (1953), 221–32; "The *Fief-Rente* in the Low Countries: an Evaluation," *Revue Belge de Philologie et d'Histoire*, XXXII (1954), 422–65; "The Feudal Antecedent of the Indenture System," *Speculum*, XXIX (1954), 503–11.

the English records, I have taken greater freedom with the texts, standardizing extensions, spelling, punctuation, and capitalization. I have always used *e* for *ae, v* for *u,* and *i* for *j* in the Latin records. In the documents where I have extended endings and in those which I have transcribed, pounds, shillings, pence, and marks have been consistently denoted by *l., s., d.,* and *m.* ; the lesser known currencies have not been abbreviated. To achieve any uniformity with proper names has been impossible ; in most cases Christian names have been put into familiar forms, but the surnames have generally been left in the French, German, and Flemish.

The documents in the Appendix are from the French, Belgian, and English archives ; to my knowledge they are here published for the first time. They serve to illustrate points made in the text and are arranged chronologically. With these documents there is not the critical apparatus that accompanies, for instance, the French *Documents inédits* ; I have included only the information necessary to make the document meaningful to the reader—a brief heading summarizing the content, the date of issue, and the archival source. To make the documents more readable, I have standardized capitalization and have inserted punctuation when it seemed essential ; I have not modernized the spelling or applied accent marks. Dubious readings are in italics.

In conclusion I wish to thank the Deputy Keeper of the Public Record Office of London, the *Archiviste Général* of Belgium, and the *Directeur des Archives* of France for allowing me to reproduce the six documents appearing at the end of the book, and to acknowledge the kindness of the editors and publishers for granting me permission to use portions of the articles referred to above. Without the help of the Belgian American Educational Foundation, which granted me a C.R.B. Fellowship for study and research in Belgium, France, and England, and without the financial assistance of the Harvard Foundation for Advanced Study and Research, this book would not have been possible ; to these foundations I am deeply grateful.

For assisting me with paleographical problems and for providing microfilm and photostats of various documents, I am indebted to M. Jacques Bolsée, *Conservateur-Adjoint* of the *Archives Générales du Royaume à Bruxelles* ; M. Jean Bovesse, *Conservateur* of the *Archives de l'Etat à Namur* ; MM. Carlos Wyffels and Maurits

Gysseling, *Archivistes* of the *Archives de l'Etat à Gand* ; and M. Piétresson de Saint-Aubin, *Archiviste en Chef* of the *Archives du Nord à Lille.*

And finally, I want to express my gratitude to Professors François L. Ganshof, Paul Bonenfant, and Jean de Sturler for their expert and friendly advice, and to my wife, whose blue pencil, typewriter, and constant encouragement made my task easier and the result better. To the one to whom this book is dedicated my debt will remain forever unpaid and my gratitude, inadequately expressed.

BRYCE D. LYON

Harvard University
September 1955

Contents

CHAPTER III

CHAPTER VI

THE DECLINE OF THE *FIEF-RENTE*: THE *AR-
RIÈRE-BAN*, THE INDENTURE SYSTEM, AND
Sczaniecki's explanation for the decline of the *fief-*

rente; contradictions to Sczaniecki's explanation; the *arrière-ban* and the decline of the *fief-rente*; the indenture system and the decline of the *fief-rente*; English military indentures; French military contracts; military contracts of the Low Countries; German military contracts; the *fief-rente* as the feudal antecedent of the indenture system; the *fief-rente* and its dependence upon feudalism and the money economy; contractual military service superseded by standing armies

CHAPTER VII

THE SIGNIFICANCE OF THE *FIEF-RENTE*: SUMMARY AND CONCLUSION 270–273

The juridical peculiarities of the *fief-rente*; the flexibility injected into feudal relations by the *fief-rente*; the procurement of military service as the principal use of the *fief-rente*; a thriving money economy essential for the *fief-rente*; a strong feudalized area essential for the development of the *fief-rente*; the relation of the *fief-rente* to the decline of feudalism

PLATES

following page 312

FROM FIEF TO INDENTURE

Abbreviations

A. D. N.	Archives Départementales du Nord à Lille.
A. E. G.	Archives de l'État à Gand.
A. E. N.	Archives de l'État à Namur.
A. G. R.	Archives Générales du Royaume à Bruxelles.
A. N.	Archives Nationales à Paris.
B. C. R. H.	*Bulletin de la Commission Royale d'Histoire.*
C. Ch. R.	*Calendar of Charter Rolls.* Rolls Series. London, 1903 ff.
C. Cl. R.	*Calendar of Close Rolls.* Rolls Series. London, 1892 ff.
C. L. R.	*Calendar of Liberate Rolls.* Rolls Series. London, 1916 ff.
C. P. R.	*Calendar of Patent Rolls.* Rolls Series. London, 1893 ff.
C. C.	*Chambre des Comptes.*
Cl. R.	*Close Rolls.* Rolls Series. London, 1902 ff.
D. K. R.	*Deputy Keeper's Reports.*
E. H. R.	*English Historical Review.*
H. Z.	*Historische Zeitschrift.*
I. R.	*Issue Rolls.* Record Commission. London, 1835–37.
L. I.	*Lists and Indexes of the Public Record Office.*
Pat. R.	*Patent Rolls.* Rolls Series. London, 1901 ff.
P. R.	*Pipe Rolls.* Record Commission and Pipe Roll Society.
P. R. O.	Public Record Office at London.
R. B. P. H.	*Revue Belge de Philologie et d'Histoire.*
R. G.	*Rôles Gascons.* Documents inédits sur l'histoire de France. Paris, 1885–1906.
R. S.	Rolls Series.
Rot. Chart.	*Rotuli Chartarum.* Record Commission. London, 1837.
Rot. Claus.	*Rotuli Litterarum Clausarum.* Record Commission. London, 1833–44.
Rot. Lib.	*Rotuli de Liberate.* Record Commission. London, 1844.
Rot. Mis.	*Rotuli de Misis.* Record Commission. London, 1844.
Rot. Norm.	*Rotuli Normanniae.* Record Commission. London, 1835.
Rot. Pat.	*Rotuli Litterarum Patentium.* Record Commission. London, 1835.
Rot. Praest.	*Rotuli de Praestitis.* Record Commission. London, 1844.
Trés. Fl.	*Trésor de Flandre.* Série I. Archives Générales du Royaume à Bruxelles.

I

Terminology Identification and Chronology
of the Fief-Rente

1. INTRODUCTORY REMARKS

At least since the time of Montesquieu feudalism has fascinated those engrossed in the study of the Middle Ages. Their approach, whether primarily political, legal, economic, military, religious, or sociological, has inevitably centered around the skein of relations arising from the fief—that land given by lord to vassal for military and political service. So closely has feudalism come to be associated with the natural economy out of which it developed that thriving feudal institutions have been thought incompatible with a money economy. This impression has, until recently, deflected attention from an important feudal institution made possible by the returning money economy —what, for reasons to be given later, is here called the *fief-rente*. Unlike the classic fief, the *fief-rente* usually consisted of money paid in annual installments by a lord to a vassal in return for homage and fealty, military service (customarily knight service), and various other feudal obligations; it could, however, consist of natural produce such as grain, wine, chickens, and wood paid in annual installments.

Since the seventeenth century various scholars of law and of history throughout western Europe have referred to the *fief-rente*.[1] It has been regarded as a tool of the great lords for acquiring vassals, for converting simple to liege homage, for procuring fighters for service in the field, for securing castle-guard, for obtaining rights to land, for concluding international treaties, for gaining allies and insuring benevolent neutrality, and for aiding commercial and political relations. It was only recently, however, that Michel Sczaniecki wrote

[1] For a review of the pertinent literature see the discussion on terminology where most of the important works are cited and also my articles in *E.H.R.*, LXVI (1951), 161–93; *Revue du Nord*, XXXV (1953), 221–32; *R.B.P.H.*, XXXII (1954), 422–65; *Speculum*, XXIX (1954), 503–11.

the first book on it, a study limited to medieval France. Basing his research on most of the relevant records, he concluded that it was unimportant as a military institution and consequently ascribed its pronounced development in the thirteenth and fourteenth centuries to its usefulness as a political and diplomatic weapon. It was the *fief-rente* that forged French spheres of influence beyond the borders of France. And within France it enabled the kings to convert simple homage to liege homage and for the first time to acquire as vassals numerous lords, simple knights, and *alleutiers*. Through the *fief-rente* the Capetians and early Valois were able to expand the royal domain and knit together the loose conglomeration of petty feudal units to form a greater France.[2] With Sczaniecki, then, the *fief-rente* was finally given the attention it deserved as an important medieval institution. His view accorded with the remarks already made by such German scholars as Walther Kienast, Heinrich Mitteis, and Ernst Clason, but ran counter to those of the French and Belgian historians who looked upon the *fief-rente* as essentially a device for obtaining military service.[3] Whatever ultimately may be decided with regard to these opinions, our first task is to concentrate upon the terminology and identification of the *fief-rente*.

2. TERMINOLOGY

Because no one prior to Sczaniecki had made a comprehensive study of the *fief-rente*, scholars, meeting cases in the records where annual incomes of money or kind were granted by lords to men in return for homage, fealty, and feudal services, came to call this type of fief by whatever term, however incorrect, seemed to them most descriptive. Obviously it is now time that it be known by one name. I have chosen, therefore, to call it the *fief-rente*—the term that most accurately describes it—and shall so refer to it throughout the present study; the reasons for this choice will become evident as we proceed.[4]

Unfortunately such early medievalists as Du Cange and Spelman never vernacularized their expression *feudum de camera* and we do

---

[2] M. Sczaniecki, *Essai sur les fiefs-rentes* (Paris, 1946), pp. 73, 75–103.
[3] *E.H.R.*, LXVI, 162–63; *R.B.P.H.*, XXXII, 463–65.
[4] For some of the problems of terminology see *Revue du Nord*, XXXV, 221–32.

not know what term they might have seen fit to use. But we do know that most seventeenth- and eighteenth-century French scholars agreed that the term *fief en l'air* best described incorporeal objects enfeoffed. A fanciful expression, it was not at all descriptive. Both money and kind are as corporeal as the classic object of enfeoffment —land. And furthermore, could not the so-called *fiefs-offices* and the variety of tolls and revenues, or the rights to them and such other profits as those of justice, be considered *fiefs en l'air?* They could indeed; yet they were certainly not *fiefs-rentes. Fief en l'air* was a term chosen without adequate knowledge of feudal institutions or of the phraseology of the documents themselves. It denoted only that this fief was not the traditional one of land.[5]

The many expressions employed somewhat later were no more accurate. A popular one was *pension* or variations of it—*pension en argent, pension annuelle,* and "money pension."[6] All can be immediately discarded. They do convey the idea of a yearly income, in most cases an income in money, but none designates an income of

[5] E. de Laurière, *Glossaire du droit français* (Paris, 1704), pp. 230, 240; C. de Ferrière, *Corps et compilation* (Paris, 1714), p. 46; H. de Pensey, *Traité des fiefs de Dumoulin* (Paris, 1773), p. 31 ; F. Hervé, *Théorie des matières féodales et censuelles* (Paris, 1785), I, 130–31 : "La concession en fief d'objets incorporels, a donné l'idée d'une classe de fiefs qu'on appelle *fiefs en l'air.* Ce sont tous ceux qui ne sont attachés a aucun corps d'héritage, et qui ne consistent qu'en droits incorporels."

[6] E. Boutaric, *Institutions militaires de la France* (Paris, 1863), pp. 120, 251, and *Saint Louis et Alfonse de Poitiers* (Paris, 1870), p. 268; A. Luchaire, *Louis VII – Philippe-Auguste – Louis VIII (1137–1226),* in E. Lavisse, *Histoire de France* (Paris, 1901), III, i, 172–73; F. Lot, *Fidèles ou vassaux?* (Paris, 1904), p. 23; A. Dumas, "Encore la question: fidèles ou vassaux?" *Nouvelle Revue Historique de Droit Français et Étranger,* XLIV (1920), 222–23; C. Seignobos, *Le régime féodal,* in Lavisse et Rambaud, *Histoire générale* (Paris, 1893), II, 83; H. Malo, *Un grand feudataire Renaud de Dammartin et la coalition de Bouvines* (Paris, 1898), pp. 60, 136 ; J. M. Toll, *Englands Beziehungen zu den Niederlanden bis 1154,* in *Historische Studien,* Heft CXLV (Berlin, 1921), 42–43, 48, 53–54; W. Stechele, "England und der Niederrhein bei Beginn der Regierung Eduards III., 1327–1337," *Westdeutsche Zeitschrift,* XXVII (1908), 103; H. Hallam, *View of the State of Europe during the Middle Ages* (New York, 1899), I, 108; F. Palgrave, *The History of Normandy and of England* (London, 1864), III, 494; F. M. Powicke, *The Loss of Normandy* (Manchester, 1913), p. 141 ; Seignobos, *The Feudal Régime,* ed. and trans. E. W. Dow (New York, 1902), pp. 50–51 ; J. E. A. Jolliffe, *The Constitutional History of Medieval England* (London, 1937), pp. 281, 424–29.

money or kind that is feudal. Pensions, numerous in the Middle Ages, were most often yearly salaries granted by princes to ecclesiastics working perhaps for the princely interest at the papal court, such as cardinals, notaries, deacons, and canons.[7] They could also be salaries to functionaries, administrative agents, or mercenary captains for military service.[8] They were nothing other than what one meets in the sixteenth and seventeenth centuries, especially during the Thirty Years' War. The financial records always made a sharp distinction between the fiefs and the pensions paid;[9] the documents of concession did likewise. This does not mean that the records never used the words *pensio* and *pension* when referring to a *fief-rente*, but that when so doing they qualified the pension as feudal by

[7] In 1319 "a discreet man staying at the court of Rome for conducting the king's business there" was granted a pension of 25 *m*. (*C.P.R. 1317–21*, p. 343). See also J. P. Kirsch, "Andreas Sapiti, englischer Prokurator an der Kurie im 14. Jahrhundert," *Historisches Jahrbuch*, XIV (1893), 582–603; W. Kienast, *Untertaneneid und Treuvorbehalt in Frankreich und England* (Weimar, 1952), p. 164: "Dieses immere Pensionssystem, ein Gegenstuck zu den Geldrenten für Kardinale, fremde Staatsmänner und Fürsten (vornehmlich deutsche) ist in seiner Bedeutung noch nicht entfernt richtig eingeschatzt und bedarf dringend näherer Untersuchung."

[8] In 1363 William Egrick rendered account for the lands of Ath, Flobecq, and Lessines in Hainaut. Under the rubric "Pencions a heritage et a vie" are listed payments to the various functionaries of the count (A.G.R., *C.C.*, no. 8254, fols. 6ᵛ, 11ᵛ, 16ʳ, 23ʳ). See also *Extrait des comptes de la recette générale de l'ancien comté de Hainaut*, in *Le cercle archéologique de Mons* (Mons, 1885), I, Supplément, 38–39, 48–49, 63, 95–96, 169–73. A similar list of pensions is found in the "Comptes des recettes et dépenses du receveur de Flandre, Thomas Fin, 25 décembre 1308 à juin 1309," A.G.R., H. Nélis, *Inventaire des comptes en rouleaux* (Bruxelles, 1914), no. 1. For the year 1364–65 the *bailliage* of Menin in Flanders paid from its receipts a sum to the "portière de Mâle pour son pensioen" (A.G.R., Nélis, *Inv.*, no. 121, Domaines du bailliage de Menin). In France the "Compte du trésor Saint-Jean 1316" has listed under "Parisienses ad Voluntatem": "Magister Radulphus de Praelis, pro pensione annua ad voluntatem: 100 *l*." (R. Fawtier, *Comptes du trésor*, 1296, 1316, 1384, 1477, Paris, 1930, II, no. 753).

[9] In the account of Thomas Fin cited in note 8 above, the fiefs are clearly separated from the pensions. The same is true for the French *Comptes du trésor*. Usually the Issue Rolls of the English exchequer followed the same practice. In the Issue Roll of 41 Henry III, Countess Margaret of Flanders received payment for her fief of 500 *m*. In the Roll of 42 Henry III, Finato, the king's proctor at the court of Rome, was paid for his pension of 20 *m*. (F. Devon, *Issues of the Exchequer*, London, 1837, pp. 32, 40). See Appendix, no. 7, and Plate III.

stipulating homage and fealty, or performance of feudal service.[10] To use *pension*, then, in context and when qualified as feudal would not be wrong, but it is obviously an unsuitable term when speaking of the *fief-rente* in general.

Most of the difficulties of *pension* are encountered also in *rente* and its variations—*rente annuelle, rente perpetuelle, rente en argent, Jahrerente,* "annual rent," and "annuity."[11] In French, German, and Dutch it means literally an annual income and nothing else. If properly qualified, it could refer to a *fief-rente* but when used in the records it ordinarily carried the meaning of a non-feudal *rente*; in the records of payment it was sharply differentiated from the *fief-rente*. Although it was frequently the yearly salary received by civil servants, more often it was the annual income paid by a town to an investor under a system of medieval urban finance not far removed from our modern bond and stock issues. To secure money for urban projects unable to be financed adequately by the normal tax receipts, the town would sell *rentes* (annuities) for a lump sum. The buyer would thereafter receive a yearly income much as one does today

---

[10] In 1440 Henry VI of England granted Diedrich, archbishop of Cologne, a "pensionem annuam 600 m." and Diedrich became Henry's "vasallum" and performed "homagium atque fidelitatem" (*Foedera,* 1704–35, X, 834–40). In 1395 Charles VI of France gave Count Adolf of Cleve a pension—"pensionis titulo mille libras . . . ex quibus homo noster ligius effectus est et homagium nobis fecit" (T. J. Lacomblet, *Urkundenbuch für die Geschichte des Niederrheins,* Düsseldorf, 1853, IV, no. 1006). Especially in the fourteenth century did the records of the Low Countries and France use "pension."

[11] N. Brussel, *Nouvel examen de l'usage général des fiefs en France pendant les onzième, douzième, treizième et quatorzième siècles* (Paris, 1750), I, 44–45; Boutaric, *Saint Louis et Alfonse de Poitiers,* p. 268; J. Viard, "La France sous Philippe VI de Valois," *Revue des Questions Historiques,* LIX (1896), 386; P. Viollet, *Histoire des institutions politiques et administratives de la France* (Paris, 1898), II, 435; E. H. J. Le Glay, *Histoire des comtes de Flandre* (Paris, 1867), pp. 79–80; C. Verlinden, *Robert Ier le Frison comte de Flandre* (Anvers, 1935), p. 109; L. Pabst, "Die aüssere Politik der Grafschaft Flandern unter Ferrand von Portugal (1212–1233)," *B.C.R.H.,* LXXX (1911), 81–82; O. Oppermann, *Holland unter Graf Florens V.,* in *Studium Lipsiense* (Berlin, 1909), p. 19; H. Obreen, *Floris V Graaf van Holland en Zeeland Heer van Friesland, 1256–1296* (Gent, 1907), pp. 152–53; S. A. W. Zeper, *Jan van Henegouwen Heer van Beaumont* ('s-Gravenhage, 1914), pp. 95–96; L. Landon, *The Itinerary of King Richard I* (London, 1935), p. 83; N. Denholm-Young, *Richard of Cornwall* (Oxford, 1947), p. 19; H. S. Lucas, *The Low Countries and the Hundred Years' War, 1326–1347* (Ann Arbor, 1929), pp. 207, 354, 551.

from stocks and bonds. Because these *rentes* were commonly transferred or alienated from bourgeois to bourgeois, to feudal lord, or to
feudal prince, they skipped about in the records—a circumstance
which has caused scholars to confuse the non-feudal variety of *rente*
with the *fief-rente*. There was also a *rente* assigned on a house.
According to H. Pirenne, if "a householder wanted to borrow for a
long term, he sold a rent on the house, that is to say, engaged to pay
the moneylender a rent, which was sometimes permanent but more
often redeemable, and which represented the interest on the capital
borrowed on the security of the house property."[12] The word annuity (*annuus redditus*) presents similar problems. From the treatises of medieval English lawyers we learn that it had a different
connotation in England from that on the Continent. Appearing
some time during the thirteenth century it was considered as "issuing out of" the grantor's chamber, "the place where he keeps what
treasure he has," and so was considered an incorporeal object as
distinguished from the "rent" (*redditus*) which was considered
thinglike and "issuing out of" the land.[13] If properly qualified, "annuity" like *rente* can refer to a *fief-rente*, but it does not meet the
requirements for use as a general term.

The word rent is perhaps one of the most inaccurate suggested.
It represents, as we now understand it, the return or payment made
by a tenant to an owner or landlord at a certain specified or customary time for the use of land and other material objects. In medieval
England it had a like meaning; it was, as F. W. Maitland points out,
the rent service, the rent payable by tenant to landlord. Not then
or ever has it been the English equivalent of *rente* which has no
suitable translation in English. In England "rent" appeared in the
records as *redditus* or rent; on the Continent, as *census, cens,* or

---

[12] G. Des Marez, *Étude sur la propriété foncière dans les villes du moyen
âge* (Gand, 1898), pp. 303–56; C. Lefebvre, *Observations sur les rentes perpétuelles* (Paris, 1914), pp. 72 ff.; P. Petot, *La constitution de rente aux
XIIe et XIIIe siècles dans le pays coutumiers,* in *Publications de l'Université
de Dijon* (Dijon, 1928), I, 59–81; H. Pirenne, *Economic and Social History
of Medieval Europe* (New York, 1937), pp. 137–39; G. Espinas, *Les finances de la commune de Douai des origines au XVe siècle* (Paris, 1902), pp.
321 ff.; W. Arnold, *Zur Geschichte des Eigentums in den deutschen Städten*
(Basle, 1861).

[13] F. Pollock and F. W. Maitland, *History of English Law* (2d ed., Cambridge, 1899), II, 133.

zins.[14] Those who have used "rent" for *rente* and then applied it to a *fief-rente* have been badly confused.

When describing the feudal treaties concluded by means of the *fief-rente* to provide military service, H. Delbrück used the expression *Soldvertrag.* Closely related to it are *Jahrgeldvertrag* and *Pensionvertrag.* If studied in context these are often found to describe a treaty or agreement in which was granted a fief in money involving the performance of homage and fealty. The terms by themselves, however, do not denote a *fief-rente*; in actual practice they usually referred to non-feudal military treaties. A feudal lord or mercenary captain would contract to supply a stipulated number of men in return for a subsidy in the form of a lump sum or a yearly cash income. In addition, of course, the men were paid wages.[15] Such treaties, often called "military subsidy treaties" by English historians, were not far removed from the English "treaties of retainer" which, along with the phrase "exchequer retaining fee," have been used to designate a *fief-rente*.[16] Such use is definitely inaccurate, for these two phrases actually refer to the English system of military indenture whereby a contract bound the recipient by a non-feudal fee to supply the grantor with a stipulated number of fighting men. The indenture system, although closely related to the *fief-rente,* was non-feudal; to see the *fief-rente* in the hundreds of retaining fees is to misunderstand it completely. Equally wrong are those English scholars who have made the *fief-rente* the retaining fee of the indenture system.[17]

[14] *Ibid.,* pp. 129–31. See also W. S. Holdsworth, *A History of English Law* (5th ed., London, 1942), III, 151–53, 262.

[15] H. Delbrück, *Geschichte der Kriegskunst im Rahmen der politischen Geschichte* (Berlin, 1907), III, 328; Kienast, *Die deutschen Fürsten im Dienste der Westmächte bis zum Tode Philipps des Schönen von Frankreich* (Utrecht, 1924), I, 40, 148–49. In 1103 Count Robert II of Flanders promised military assistance to Henry I of England for a *fief-rente*; Delbrück called this a *Soldvertrag.* In 1294 Philip the Fair of France donated a *fief-rente* to Henry VII, count of Luxemburg, in return for military support. This has frequently been referred to as a *Soldvertrag* (F. Kern, *Acta Imperii,* Tübingen, 1911, no. 92). On the other hand, in a treaty of 1197 Richard I of England granted a subsidy in the form of a lump sum of 5,000 *m.* to Count Baldwin IX of Flanders. This is a real *Jahrgeldvertrag* or "subsidy treaty" (Ralph of Diceto, *Opera Historica,* R.S., London, 1876, II, 152–53; *Foedera,* I, i, 67–68).

[16] J. H. Ramsay, *The Angevin Empire* (London, 1903), pp. 35–36.

[17] *Speculum,* XXIX, 509. A. E. Prince made the error of confusing *fiefs-rentes* with the non-feudal retaining fees ("The Indenture System under Ed-

In the French financial records the custom of including under the rubric "Fiefs et aumônes" entries pertaining to the annual payments of both led P. Viollet to coin the word *fief-aumône* to describe the *fief-rente*.[18] But the countless annual sums of money and kind granted to pious institutions were not fiefs; they were, as the records said, alms. Their being frequently lumped together with fiefs makes it often impossible to distinguish one from the other. Yet we may be sure that in the minds of the medieval grantors and grantees the distinction was clear. More exact, but still misleading, is *fief de soudée*, the term assigned to the *fief-rente* by historians of the Latin States of the Crusaders. So frequently did it secure military service that they thought it was actually the payment for the service rendered, as in the case of wages to mercenaries. In reality, its function was but the establishment of a feudal bond setting up the obligation of military service which, when performed, was to be paid for by wages. Only if properly qualified could *fief de soudée* refer to a *fief-rente*.[19]

Let us now consider those terms which convey the idea of a *fief-rente* somewhat more accurately. Those scholars first to deal with the *fief-rente* knew it in Latin as the *feudum de camera* and, like Du Cange, Spelman, and others, tended to identify *camera* as the medieval treasury. All fundamentally agreed with Du Cange's definition: "FEUDUM BURSAE, Idem quod *Feudum de Camera*. Ut enim *Camera* dicitur Thesaurus Regius ita *bursa* pro fisco usurpatur."[20] Consequently they translated *feudum de camera* into

---

ward III," *Historical Essays in Honour of James Tait*, Manchester, 1933, pp. 285–86, and in *The English Government at Work, 1327–1336*, ed. J. F. Willard and W. A. Morris, Cambridge, Mass., 1940, I, 347, 354).

[18] Viollet, *Histoire du droit civil français* (Paris, 1905), p. 689. There are extracts of such financial records in Boutaric, *Saint Louis et Alfonse de Poitiers*, pp. 267–68. In the "Compte du roi au trésor de 1226 à 1477" found in Fawtier, *Comptes du trésor*, the account for 1238 indicates that 15,930 *l.* 2 *s.* 5 *d.* were paid for what the rubric calls "Feoda et elemosine" (p. xlv). In the financial records of all the states on the Continent similar examples can be found. See Plate III.

[19] A. A. Beugnot, *Assises de Jérusalem* (Paris, 1841), I, 384–85 ; G. Dodu, *Histoire des institutions monarchiques dans le Royaume Latin de Jérusalem 1099–1291* (Paris, 1894), p. 206. Boutaric also used the expression at times (*Institutions militaires*, pp. 120–21).

[20] C. D. Du Cange, *Glossarium mediae et infimae Latinitatis*, ed. G. A. L. Henschel (Paris, 1844), III, 261.

Kammerlehen, fief-boursier, fief-boursal, fief de bourse, and *fief de chambre.*[21] One can accept these terms only upon the supposition that *fiefs-rentes* were always paid out of the princely treasury and that the term *camera* was always synonymous with treasury in all western Europe. But this is not upheld by the evidence. Without doubt more *fiefs-rentes* were paid out of the treasuries than any other source, but method of payment varied from region to region. Whereas in England most fiefs were paid by the exchequer, in the Low Countries they were generally paid directly from such revenues of the princes as the issues of the administrative districts, tolls, and duties.[22] In Champagne the brunt of the financing was borne by the fairs; in France, by the royal treasury at Paris.[23] To pay *fiefs-rentes* in Germany, all sorts of financial sources were tapped.[24] Unless referring to specific cases, it is thus obviously erroneous to label the fief we are dealing with as a fief paid only by a treasury. A second difficulty stems from the fact that *camera* did not mean *the* treasury throughout all western Europe. We need not concern ourselves in this study with the technical differences between *camera* and *thesaurus,* but it should be emphasized that they were two distinct financial departments in some areas of western Europe.

[21] J. Schilteri, *Codex Juris Alemannici Feudalis* (Frankfurt und Leipzig, 1728), p. 48; J. C. Lünig, *Corpus Juris Feudalis Germanici* (Frankfurt und Leipzig, 1730), III, 636, 642; G. A. Jenichen, *Thesaurus Juris Feudalis* (Frankfurt und Leipzig, 1750–54), II, 4; III, 60; E. Clason, *Die Pensionsverhältnisse deutscher Fürsten mit fremden Mächten* (Bonn, 1905), pp. 8–9; De Ferrière, *Corps et compilation,* p. 46; De Pensey, *Traité des fiefs,* p. 32; Hervé, *Théorie des matières féodales,* p. 382; De Laurière, *Glossaire du droit,* p. 230; A. Chéruel, *Dictionnaire historique des institutions, mœurs et coutumes de la France* (Paris, 1865), I, 427. The expression *fief de bourse* has been used almost exclusively by Belgian historians. See, for example, J.-B. de Marne, *Histoire du comté de Namur* (Liège, 1754), pp. 305–6; Pirenne, *Histoire de Belgique* (5th éd., Bruxelles, 1929), II, 101; E. Poncelet, *Les feudataires de la principauté de Liège sous Englebert de la Marck* (Bruxelles, 1948), pp. 25–26. M. Bloch has preferred *fief de chambre* (*La société féodale,* Paris, 1939, I, 268).

[22] *E.H.R.,* LXVI, 170–74, and *Revue du Nord,* XXXV, 223–26.

[23] Ample evidence on the fairs is found in the documents published by L. Chantereau le Febvre, *Traité des fiefs* (Paris, 1762), Preuves, pp. 17–18, 33–34 ff. See also F. Bourquelot, *Étude sur les foires de Champagne,* in *Mémoires présentés par divers savants à l'Académie des Inscriptions et Belles-Lettres* (Paris, 1865), 2e sér., V, 183–84. For France see Sczaniecki, *Essai,* p. 115.

[24] For example, the *camera* ; revenues of administrative districts ; tolls from roads, bridges, and gates ; tithes and other such revenues.

Within Germany and the Low Countries, *camera* and its vernacular equivalents could mean the treasury, but one finds, in the Low Countries at least, that *bourse* was more commonly used in the records.[25] In England during the twelfth century the *camera* came to be separated from the *scaccarium* and was henceforth more of a semi-private financial department of the king, while the exchequer became the state treasury and thus more responsible to the financial interests of the realm.[26] From the twelfth century to 1295 the treasury of the French kings was the Temple of Paris operated by the Knights Templars. As a result of the financial innovations of Philip the Fair, it was removed from the Temple to the Louvre and was called either the *Louvre* or the *trésor*. Later it was moved back to the Temple and from then on was known as the *trésor de Paris* or the *trésor du roi*. *Fiefs-rentes* when paid by the royal treasury were said to be paid by the *trésor* and not the *chambre*, which was a sort of private treasury of the royal household as it was in England.[27] In those instances where the records specifically state that *fiefs-*

---

[25] The expression *camera* appearing in the German records so often meant treasury that most earlier scholars called the *fief-rente* a *Kammerlehen*. In 1248, for example, Frederick II granted to Guy, dauphin of Vienne, "de annuo feodo trecentarum unciarum auri percipiendarum de camera nostra" (J. L. A. Huillard-Bréholles, *Historia Diplomatica Friderici Secundi*, Paris, 1861, VI, ii, 665–66). See also G. Doenniges, *Acta Henrici VII Imperatoris Romanorum* (Berlin, 1839), p. 185 ; G. Waitz, *Deutsche Verfassungsgeschichte* (2d ed. by G. Seeliger, Berlin, 1896), VI, 30. Around 1350 Arnold de Haycrusse held from Duke John III of Brabant "X libras parisienses in bursa annuatim" ; Giles de Hertsberge held "L libras annuatim in bursa" (L. Galesloot, *Le livre des feudataires de Jean III, duc de Brabant,* Bruxelles, 1865, pp. 10, 37). Similar entries are found in all the so-called *livres des fiefs* of the Low Countries. In 1277 Count Henry VI of Luxemburg gave quittance to Count Guy of Flanders "de nostre fief de burse que nos avons chascun an" (A.G.R., *Trés. Fl.,* Sér. I, no. 2067).

[26] The separation of exchequer and chamber and the latter's successor, the wardrobe, has been studied by T. F. Tout, *Chapters in the Administrative History of Mediaeval England* (Manchester, 1937), I, 44 ff., and in the succeeding volumes. See also Jolliffe, "The Chamber and the Castle Treasuries under King John," *Studies in Medieval History Presented to Frederick Maurice Powicke* (Oxford, 1948), pp. 118 ff., and "The *Camera Regis* under Henry II," *E.H.R.,* LXVIII (1953), 1–21, 337–62 ; Lyon, *E.H.R., LXVI,* 171–73.

[27] Borrelli de Serres, *Recherches sur divers services publics du XIIIᵉ au XVIIᵉ siècle* (Paris, 1909), III, 5–45. See also Sczaniecki, *Essai,* p. 115 ; Viollet, *Histoire institutions,* II, 123 ff.

rentes were paid by the *camera,* it would not be wrong to call them
fiefs de chambre and *Kammerlehen* ; similarly, fiefs paid by the treasury could be rightly called *fiefs de bourse.* None of these terms,
however, are comprehensive enough for general and unqualified
usage. In this same category are *Geldlehen,* "money fief," *fief-argent,*
and *fief-pécuniaire.*[28] These terms, though suitable for referring to
fiefs paid in money, do not embrace those, numerous throughout
the Middle Ages, that were paid in kind. As for *fief-argent,* E. Chénon's criticism that it was not a juridical expression and that, being
movable (*meuble*), it could not be enfeoffed seems rather super-
ficial ;[29] indeed, the documents show that practically anything of
value could be enfeoffed. Surely cords of wood, sacks of wool, all
sorts of measurements of beer, wine, cheese, and cloth were movable ; yet they were enfeoffed. Whatever Chénon may think of money
juridically or in the sense of movable property, he cannot deny that
money was enfeoffed.

We come finally to those terms that accurately describe an annual
income of money or kind that has been granted in fief—*Rentlehen,
renteleen,* and *fief-rente.*[30] To the German, the Dutch, and the

[28] Kienast, "Lehnrecht und Staatsgewalt im Mittelalter," *H.Z.,* CLVIII
(1938), 24 ; H. Mitteis, *Der Staat des hohen Mittelalters* (2d ed. rev., Weimar, 1944), p. 389 ; L. König, "Die Politik des Grafen Balduin V. von Hen-
negau," *B.C.R.H.,* LXXIV (1905), 210 ; J. Johnen, "Philipp von Elsass,
Graf von Flandern," *B.C.R.H.,* LXXIX (1910), 408–9 ; Lyon, *E.H.R.,*
LXVI, 162 ; S. Painter, *William Marshal* (Baltimore, 1933), pp. 202–3 ;
J. L. La Monte, *Feudal Monarchy in the Latin Kingdom of Jerusalem 1100–
1291* (Cambridge, Mass., 1932), pp. 139, 146–47, 150 ; P. W. Topping,
Feudal Institutions as Revealed in the Assizes of Romania (Philadelphia,
1949), p. 139 ; F. L. Ganshof, *Feudalism* (London, 1952), pp. 100–1 ; Lu-
chaire, *Manuel des institutions françaises* (Paris, 1892), p. 160 ; J. Declareuil,
Histoire générale du droit français des origines à 1789 (Paris, 1925), pp.
236–37 ; G. G. Dept, *Les influences anglaise et française dans le comté de
Flandre au début du XIIIᵐᵉ siècle* (Gand, 1928), p. 59 ; G. Smets, *Henri Iᵉʳ
duc de Brabant* (Bruxelles, 1908), p. 67 ; E. Varenbergh, *Histoire des relations diplomatiques entre le comté de Flandre et l'Angleterre au moyen âge*
(Bruxelles, 1874), pp. 90–91 ; Kervyn de Lettenhove, *Histoire de Flandre*
(Bruges, 1853), I, 233, 236.
[29] E. Chénon, *Histoire générale du droit français public et privé des origines à 1815* (Paris, 1929), II, 149–50.
[30] Kienast, *H.Z.,* CLVIII, 25, and *Untertaneneid und Treuvorbehalt,* p.
163 ; Mitteis, *Lehnrecht und Staatsgewalt* (Weimar, 1933), p. 476, and *Der
Staat,* pp. 292, 328, 498–99 ; *Algemene Geschiedenis der Nederlanden,* ed.
H. Van Werveke *et al.* (Antwerpen, 1950), II, 97 ; Chénon, *Histoire du droit,*

French scholar these terms say only that an annual income has been granted in fief; they are thus explicit without placing limitations upon the source of payment or upon the type of income granted in fief. Such scholars as Mitteis, Chénon, N. Didier, and C. Cahen had used these terms prior to Sczaniecki, but it was the latter who, for many of the same reasons discussed above, ruled out all the other expressions in favor of *fief-rente*. He saw no difficulty in placing the *fiefs-rentes en argent* on the same plane with the *fiefs-rentes en nature* and defined a *fief-rente* as "a fief of which the object constitutes a yearly income assigned on a source of revenue other than an estate of land and of which the installments are actually paid in kind or in money by the lord of the fief."[31] Although, for reasons that will be given later, I do not completely accept this definition, I am in accord with Sczaniecki's choice of *fief-rente* and have adopted it from lack of an English equivalent. Unlike Dutch and German, English has no one word which will translate *rente*. "Fief-in-income" and "annuity-fief" are clumsy renditions. The English word "fief" has been taken over from the French, and therefore it seems logical to borrow another expressive French word when lacking its counterpart in English.[32]

3. IDENTIFICATION

To distinguish between *fiefs-rentes* and non-feudal yearly incomes is imperative if one would obtain a true picture of the former. To Sczaniecki, the ambiguous, inconsistent terminology and the incompleteness of the records were most perplexing, being often responsible for his inability to determine whether the annual income under

I, 746; N. Didier, *Le droit des fiefs dans la coutume de Hainaut au moyen âge* (Paris, 1945), pp. 56, 181, and "Les rentes inféodées dans le comté de Hainaut du XIIᵉ au XVᵉ siècle," *Revue du Nord,* XVII (1931), 265–83; C. Cahen, *Le régime féodal de l'Italie Normande* (Paris, 1940), pp. 48–49, and *La Syrie du nord à l'époque des croisades et la principauté franque d'Antioche* (Paris, 1940), pp. 528–29. Terms such as *rente féodale, fief de revenu, fief pension,* and *rente inféodée* are fairly accurate but not as expressive as *fief-rente*.

[31] *Essai,* pp. 2–7.

[32] Since my article of 1951 in the *E.H.R.* further study of the *fief-rente* has convinced me that "money fief" is not accurate enough when dealing with the *fief-rente* on the Continent as well as in England. See also my discussion on terminology in *Revue du Nord,* XXXV, 221–23.

question was feudal. From a thorough examination of the matter he concluded that "the feudal character of an annual income is not in the least in doubt if the charter of concession speaks *expressis verbis* of the performance of homage, or better, of feudal and noble services produced by the constitution of an annual income."[33] These requisites for judging a *rente* feudal or non-feudal must be expanded if, in addition to the difficulties in the French records, those in the German, Low Country, and English records are to be unraveled.

Like Sczaniecki, I have found that the appearance of *feudum* or its vernacular derivations in a document does not always guarantee a *fief-rente*. It can usually be relied upon to do so in the tenth, eleventh, twelfth, and part of the thirteenth century, but not thereafter.[34] In its decline, more rapid in some areas than in others, feudalism left everywhere in its wake many remnants, among which was *feudum* and its vernacular equivalents. We are thus faced with deciding whether in an age progressively less feudal the word *feudum* is feudal or non-feudal. In England it becomes impossible to use *feudum* as a reliable criterion already in the second half of the thirteenth century; more and more it manifested an amoebic nature, its meaning ever changing to meet new demands quite unrelated to feudalism. The difficulty here is that *feudum* came to be used for both feudal and non-feudal incomes. As the English kings accelerated and expanded their practice of cash payment for service to the royal government, and as the new system of military indenture became the principal method of recruiting fighters for the royal service, so *feudum* was increasingly used to signify a non-feudal income such as a retaining fee or an annual salary. Non-feudal *feoda* were granted to the king's bannerets and knights of the household, to men having indentured for military service, to royal officers of the household and the administrative system, to the pettiest of functionaries serving the crown. This constant use of *feudum* resulted finally

---

[33] *Essai*, pp. 9–10.

[34] In the following documents, for example, it is safe to conclude that *feudum* designates a *fief-rente*: "Henricus Dei gratia Dux Lotharingie etc. Noverint universi, quod nos Domino Waltero de Ligne et fratri ejus Fastrado viginti marcas Colonienses concessimus in feodum [1224]" (F. C. Butkens, *Trophées tant sacrés que profanes du duché de Brabant,* Den Haag, 1724–26, Preuves, p. 70). "Rex etc. Sciatis quod concessimus Henrico Bailloil 50 *l.* sterlingorum de annuo feodo ad scaccarium nostrum Londonie [1203]" (*Rot. Pat.,* p. 32 b).

in its meaning simply a yearly salary not unlike the retaining fees now given to lawyers. In this sense it was the equivalent of the Old English *feo* meaning money, just as was its English counterpart "fee" which has since the Middle Ages signified money paid in one form or another.[35] In England, then, we dare not trust *feudum* to signify a *fief-rente* after the middle of the thirteenth century unless specifically qualified by other terms or subject matter.

On the Continent the problems connected with *feudum* are far more thorny because they are grafted to the classic problem of the decline of feudalism in western Europe. If we are willing to admit that real feudalism still existed in France, the Low Countries, and Germany in the late fourteenth century and throughout the fifteenth, then *feudum, Lehn, leen,* and *fief,* appearing in the records clear down to 1500, still signified a *fief-rente* because, in contrast to England, care was taken never to apply them to non-feudal incomes and salaries.[36] When *rente* was used it generally was designated feudal or non-feudal.[37] But if, on the other hand, we believe feudalism

---

[35] In the Wardrobe Book of 28 Edward I, the only account published, is a long list of household knights and bannerets receiving yearly fees in lieu of daily wages. They also received food and clothing and were remunerated for horses lost (T. Topham, *Observations on the Wardrobe Account of the 28th Year of King Edward the First,* London, 1787, pp. 188 ff.). Most of the unpublished Wardrobe Books have a similar list of *feoda*: P.R.O., E. 36/202, fols. 24–35; E. 101/354/5, fols. 13–14; *Wardrobe Book, 25 Edward I,* British Museum, Add. MS. 7965, fol. 59ᵛ. For examples of non-feudal fees paid to royal justices see the memorandum of judicial appointments for 1278 printed in Palgrave, *Parliamentary Writs* (London, 1827), I, 382. For the retaining fees of the indenture system see *Speculum,* XXIX, 503–11; Prince, *Tait Essays,* pp. 283–97, and *English Government at Work,* I, 347–55. Bloch has pointed out that in Italy officials and magistrates received a *fio* (*Société féodale,* I, 259–60).

[36] It is especially in the Low Countries that *feudum* or its vernacular derivations appear late into the fifteenth century. In 1459 Philip the Good, duke of Burgundy, confirmed the right of Renaud de Rouvreux to a fief of 50 florins which Renaud had come to possess by marriage with the heiress of John de Hertoge who had received the fief from Antoine of Brabant in 1415 (A.G.R., A. Verkooren, unpublished inventory of charters of Brabant). In the expense account of the receiver general of Limburg for 1499–1500 appears the rubric "Uutgeven—ierst in erflicken leenen." Then follow payments for five fiefs (A.G.R., *Recette générale Limbourg,* no. 2451, fol. 33ʳ–34ᵛ).

[37] In 1302 John I, count of Namur, granted to Roelof de Reifferscheid "hondert pont jaerliker renten suarter tornoyse" with the proviso "dat heer Roelof die houden sal van ons ende van onsen rechten erfnamen te rechten

to be practically dead by the late fourteenth century, then *feudum* is but a false façade, a term still used because the dead hand of custom or the inability to substitute more expressive and correct terms dictated its survival. If we apply the criteria of Sczaniecki, we should supposedly be able to determine when the men concerned with the *feudum* considered it feudal. But can we? If feudalism is dead, then homage and feudal and noble services, like *feudum*, are meaningless labels for something belonging to a more modern age. Later when we probe deeper into the problem of terminology as related to the decline of feudalism, reasons will emerge as the basis for what is now offered merely as assertion. Until the middle of the fifteenth century, it seems to me, the records describing *rentes* as feudal mean exactly that. This is to say that Sczaniecki's criteria, as well as *feudum*, are considered valid for signifying *fiefs-rentes* whether or not in the heyday of feudalism. Where it would be only folly to accept the evidence of *feudum* in England after the middle of the thirteenth century without additional proof showing it to be feudal, in the rest of western Europe it is necessary to rely often upon the sole evidence of *feudum* if we are to arrive at any figures closely approximating the number of *fiefs-rentes* existing during the different periods of the Middle Ages. To insist upon the appearance of homage or noble and feudal services in the records in the period down into the thirteenth century would be to ignore hundreds of *fiefs-rentes*. In this period and even longer on the Continent, *feudum* meant what it said. Although after the thirteenth century it must be regarded with caution, especially in England, never should it be considered a hollow expression.

We are further hampered in distinguishing *fiefs-rentes* by brevity of content in the records. The most informative documents are the

leene" (P. P. Brouwers, *L'administration et les finances du comté de Namur. Chartes et règlements,* Namur, 1914, II, no. 363). In his account of 1335–36 Nicolas Gaidouche, receiver of Flanders, made various payments which appeared under the rubric "Primierement as fiefs et rentes heritaules." Among them was a *rente heritaule* to "monsigneur de Hale," and a *rente* to "messire Flamenc de Canny ... dont il est hom monsigneur de Flandres" (A.G.R., Nélis, *Inv.,* Compte des recettes et dépenses du receveur de Flandre, no. 5). In the *Compte du trésor 1384* in France appears the heading "Redditus ad Vitam ad Omnes Sanctos et Nativitatis Domini Anno MCCCIIII^{xx} et Quarto." Then follow such entries as the following: "Bernardus de Bourgavalle in Brebancia, miles, pro medietate Nativitatis Domini, in homagio ligio domini Regis: 250 franc. auri" (Fawtier, *Comptes du trésor,* no. 1459).

3*

original concessions; lacking them, we often have the confirmations
and other acts pertaining to the original grant. Fortunately a large
number of such documents are so detailed that one immediately
knows he is dealing with a *fief-rente*.[38] But an almost equal number
lack the essential data. There is no mention of homage, fief, or the
type of service to be performed; they merely state that a certain
lord has granted a specified annual income to a certain individual.[39]
If one cannot find other evidence showing this income to be feudal,
it has to be ignored. Happily, other evidence frequently enables one
to establish the concession as feudal. Let us examine a case from the
English records. In 1220 Henry III ordered his treasurer and chamberlains of the exchequer to pay Engelard de Cigogné 25 *l.* in part
payment of 50 *l.* that Engelard received "per annum ad se susten-
tandum in servicio nostro." This entry can only mean that Engelard
was to receive 50 *l.* yearly for his maintenance; it cannot be inter-
preted as a *fief-rente*. It appears in the Close or Liberate Rolls twice
yearly without interruption until 1242. At this time Henry ordered
the treasurer to pay Engelard 50 *l.* yearly, 25 *l.* at two terms "de
annuo feodo suo 50 *l.*" We now know that this 50 *l.* was a fee, but
was it a *fief-rente* or just a yearly salary? Evidence of homage and
feudal service is still missing; it never appears. But from other records of a biographical nature we learn that Engelard was a trusted
councilor and soldier in John's service, a position he held for many
years under Henry III despite the fiftieth clause of Magna Carta
ordering him removed from any office in England, and we can

---

[38] The following are typical examples: "Nos Theodericus dictus Luf filius
nobilis viri domini Theoderici comitis Clivensis salutem. Notum facimus universis, quod illustris princeps ... Henricus dux Lotharingie et Brabantie pro
fidelitate et ligio homagio, quod sibi fecimus contra omnes homines ... nobis
dedit in feodum et concessit quinquaginta marcas Coloniensis" (T. Ilgen,
*Quellen zur inneren Geschichte der Rheinischen Territorien. Herzogtum
Kleve*, Bonn, 1921, I, ii, no. 13). In 1332 William I, count of Holland and
Hainaut, granted to Godfrey of Juliers, lord of Berghes, 200 *l.* of Tours "pro
fidelitate et homagio" (F. Van Mieris, *Groot Charterboek der Graaven van
Holland*, Leyden, 1754, II, 538). In 1254 Henry III of England "concessit
Johanni de Castilune, pro servicio et homagio suo, sexaginta marcas annui
feodi" (*R.G.*, I, no. 4001).

[39] The English records, especially the chancery enrollments, are brief. The
following entry is typical: "Sciatis nos dedisse et concessisse et presenti carta
nostra confirmasse dilecto et fideli nostro Gaufrido de Cella C libras sterlingorum annuatim recipiendas ad scaccarium nostrum. Teste etc. [1199]" (*Rot.
Chart.*, p. 11).

therefore justifiably conclude that the 50 *l.* was a *fief-rente*.[40] Countless other such grants of yearly incomes can be classified as *fiefs-rentes* because of additional biographical information proving that they were granted for the performance of feudal or noble service. Occasionally when such a concession of a yearly income is located among others which are feudal, as for example in a cartulary, register, or enrollment, one can conclude with relative safety that it also was feudal. It is commonly known that medieval chanceries tried to abbreviate their records as much as possible and for various reasons the scribe may have seen fit to include but a minimum of information. He may have thought it superfluous to include all such facts as that the recipient had done homage and had promised to render feudal services when he and all the interested parties knew them perfectly well. It is usually wise, however, to ignore a concession of an annual income when no additional information can be found to establish it as feudal; only by dealing with *rentes* known for certain to be feudal can we hope to arrive at valid conclusions. Because we are thus forced to disregard many concessions which doubtless were feudal,[41] any figures on volume of *fiefs-rentes* cannot hope to be exact.

In the financial records the data concerning payment of annual incomes is minimal. Seldom included were any facts stipulating the payment to be for a fief or by reason of homage done;[42] there were

---

[40] *Rot. Claus.*, I, 410 b, 415, 445 b, 447, 486, 488, 539 b, 581 ; II, 15, 18 ; *C.L.R. 1226–40*, pp. 12, 29–30, 64, 75, 115, 143, 172, 195, 204, 210, 253, 263, 277, 295, 363, 450, 456 ; *C.L.R. 1240–45*, pp. 21, 109 ; *Cl.R. 1237–42*, p. 397.

[41] Cf. Sczaniecki, *Essai*, p. 10 : "Mais, parmi une quantité très considérable de rentes d'un caractère douteux elle nous a certainement conduit à négliger aussi de nombreux fiefs-rentes."

[42] In a financial memorandum of 1242 the receiver of Frederick II of Germany noted that "recepit in vino XVI carratas quas assignavit duci Brabantie." One would not know that this was a fief if it were not for other documents showing that a fief of wine had been granted to the dukes of Brabant by Philip of Suabia. Under *exitus*, however, the annual payments for fiefs are described as follows: "Item dedit Johanni Bono de feodo Castelli VIII marcas. Item Everhardo de Mendorp de feodo Castelli VI marcas" (Huillard-Bréholles, *Hist. Dip. Friderici Secundi*, VI, ii, 832–33). In the account rendered for western Flanders (1473) by the receiver Walter Poulain appears the following entry: "Au seigneur de la Marbbeide et de Stam homme liege de monseigneur pour LX livres tournois quil tenoit et tient heritablement en fief sur la recepte generale de Flandres du don de feu le conte

as a rule only rubrics separating the issues into different categories. When fiefs alone were grouped under a single rubric one cannot fail to identify them.[43] When alms were bracketed with fiefs under the same rubric, it is not too difficult to separate the pious and charitable recipients from the others.[44] When, however, life and heritable *rentes*, as well as pensions, were listed under the same rubric as fiefs, no distinction is possible.[45] Nor is it possible when the only word in the rubric is *rente* or *redditus*. When, as frequently happens, one is confronted in the records with merely a list of annual payments with no comment and under no rubric, he can sometimes ascertain what annual incomes were feudal only by crosschecking with the concessions and similar records if they are available.[46] All

Guy" (A.G.R., *C.C.*, no. 2705, fol. 72ᵛ). Such entries as the following are scattered about in Viard, *Les journaux du trésor de Philippe VI de Valois* (Paris, 1899), no. 5362: "Thomas de Septem Fontibus miles, pro duobus terciis de dono Regis moderni consideratione fidelitatis, legalitatis et servicii per eum domino Regi et duci Normanie, ac eorum successoribus promissarum, de quo jam fecit homagium dicto domino Regi, 53 *l.* 6 *s.* 8 *d.* p.; habuit 26 *l.* 13 *s.* 4 *d.* p. xxiiᵃ Aprilis, et xvᵃ Junii, totum." In the Liberate Roll of 1295 a writ of *liberate* directed the treasurer and chamberlains of England to pay "nostro dilecto et fideli nostro Walramo, domino de Montioie et de Faukemount, ad valorem trescentarum librarum turonensium nigrorum in sterlingis ... de annuo feodo suo" (P.R.O., C. 62/71, m. 3). Similar entries are in the Wardrobe Books and Issue Rolls.

[43] The accounts of receipts and expenses of the county of Guelders for 1294–95 listed *fiefs-rentes* separately: "Exposita eius feodatis et aliis: Domino Godefrido Birch ex feodo suo ... 25 *m.* Item Willelmo Poet ex feodo ... 4 *s.* ... etc." (L. S. Meihuizen, *De Rekening Betreffende het Graafschap Gelre 1294/1295*, Groningen, 1953, pp. 23–24). The accounts of the receiver general of Limburg are similarly arranged: "Despenses a cause des fiefs heritables: Premiers au seigneur de Gronsvelt et de Renberch qui tient en fief de monseigneur XXX florins de Rin ... etc. [1411–1412]" (A.G.R., *C.C.*, no. 2441). See also Lot and Fawtier, *Le premier budget de la monarchie française. Le compte général de 1202–1203* (Paris, 1932), p. cxxxix.

[44] For example, D. de Wailly, *Recueil des historiens des Gaules et de la France* (Paris, 1865), XXI, 267: "Feoda, elemosinae et aliae expensae per praepositus Franciae" (Account of *prévôts* and *baillis*, 1248). See also pp. 277, 279, 518.

[45] In the *Compte des briefs de Flandre, fiefs-rentes* are lumped together with simple *rentes* and *pensions* (A.D.N., *Comptes des briefs et espiers*, B. 4240, fols. 1–2ᵛ, 4–5, 14ᵛ, 16ᵛ ff.).

[46] It is characteristic of many of the French records to mix payments of *fiefs-rentes* with all sorts of non-feudal annual payments. For example, among payments of all types in the *Journal du trésor* for 1298 appears the payment

these difficulties involved in distinguishing *fiefs-rentes* from other types of annual incomes increase as the Middle Ages run toward their end and we become less and less certain that anything was feudal. We shall probe deeper into this problem when we come to study the documents in detail, but for now let us sum up the various means by which a *fief-rente* can be identified. Throughout the Middle Ages evidence of homage or of feudal and noble service points definitely to a *fief-rente*. Not always as conclusive but almost as reliable is the presence of the word *feudum* and its variants. This word is almost always valid down into the middle of the thirteenth century; after that it must be regarded with caution although it continues to hold much validity, especially on the Continent, into the fifteenth century. Sometimes biographical data and the location of doubtful concessions in the source material provide the supplementary evidence needed for distinguishing a *fief-rente*. With these criteria in mind, let us now trace the *fief-rente* from its emergence to its decline and eventual disappearance.

4. CHRONOLOGY

The *fief-rente* first appeared in the region that had been feudalized earliest and most fully—those lands lying roughly between the Loire and Rhine Rivers. Wherever found beyond the borders of this hard core of feudalism, it is in a region that had known feudal custom. It did not appear in England until the Normans conquered it;[47] of the few *fiefs-rentes* in southern Italy and Sicily, none appear until the area had been conquered and organized by the Normans;[48] when the Crusaders from western Europe took the coastal strips along the eastern Mediterranean away from the Turks, the *fief-rente* was exported to the Near East.[49] But only in lands that were highly

---

of 80 *l.* to Fastré, lord of Ligny (Viard, *Les journaux du trésor de Philippe IV le Bel,* Paris, 1940, no. 933). Only by tracking down other evidence is one able to determine that this is a *fief-rente*. See also Fawtier, *Comptes royaux (1285–1314). Comptes généraux* (Paris, 1953), I, 251, 256 ff., 283–84.

[47] *E.H.R.,* LXVI, 161–93. See also C. H. Haskins, *Norman Institutions* (Cambridge, Mass., 1918).

[48] Cahen, *Régime féodal,* pp. 48–49. See also Haskins, *The Normans in European History* (Boston, 1915).

[49] La Monte, *Feudal Monarchy,* pp. 139 ff.; Cahen, *Syrie du Nord,* pp. 516, 528–29, 534, 654.

feudalized was the *fief-rente* prominent; in lands never or only slowly and partially feudalized it was insignificant if, indeed, it appeared at all. The Scandinavian peninsula did not know it, in central and eastern Europe it was all but unknown, and any knowledge of it in Spain and the Byzantine Empire has yet to be unearthed.[50] Secondary works dealing with Byzantium indicate that it was never used in this area—a conclusion not illogical in the face of general agreement that the so-called feudalism which developed in the Byzantine Empire lacked the basic characteristics of western feudalism, and never became as entrenched as in the West.[51] Constantinople and the neighboring region closely resembled southern Italy and Sicily; a money economy prevailed here even during the darkest days of western Europe. There was, then, no reason for the development of feudalism and the *fief-rente*. It is likely that the *fief-rente* was introduced into Spain by the feudal adventurers of the eleventh and twelfth centuries who started the *reconquista* of Moorish Spain, but as in Italy and Sicily it probably never attained real importance.

Yet there is another prong to the development of the *fief-rente*—

[50] See especially Bloch, *Société féodale*, I, 271–92. He traces the spread of feudalism from France throughout western Europe, to the Mediterranean basin, and to the Near East. See also II, 241–52. For further references see L. G. de Valdeavellano, "Les liens de vassalité et les immunités en Espagne," *Revue de l'Institut de Sociologie*, XXII (1936), 91–95; C. Sánchez-Albornoz, *En torno a los orígenes del feudalismo* (Mendoza, Argentine, 1942), vols. I–III.

[51] On the problem of feudalism in Byzantium see particularly E. Stein, "Untersuchungen zur spätbyzantinischen Verfassungs- und Wirtschaftsgeschichte," *Mitteilungen zur Osmanischen Geschichte*, II (1923–25), 1–62, and "Paysannerie et grands domaines dans l'Empire byzantin," *Recueils de la Société Jean Bodin* (Bruxelles, 1937), II, 122–33; A. A. Vasiliev, "On the Question of Byzantine Feudalism," *Byzantion*, VIII (1933), 584–604; G. Ostrogorsky, "Agrarian Conditions in the Byzantine Empire in the Middle Ages," *Cambridge Economic History* (Cambridge, 1941), I, 194–223, and "La Pronoïa. Contribution à l'étude de la féodalité à Byzance et chez les Slaves du Sud," *Byzantion*, XXII (1952), 437–518. For Russia see G. Vernadsky, "Feudalism in Russia," *Speculum*, XIV (1939), 300–23; A. Eck, "La vassalité et les immunités dans la Russie du moyen âge," *Revue de l'Institut de Sociologie*, XXII (1936), 103–18, and "Le grand domaine dans la Russie du moyen âge," *Recueils de la Société Jean Bodin* (Bruxelles, 1949), IV, 51–114; P. Struve, "Medieval Agrarian Society in its Prime. Russia," *Cambridge Economic History*, I, 418–37.

its dependence upon a money economy. That it reached its greatest extension in those regions which returned earliest to and benefited most from a money economy will be seen as we trace its development region by region. Almost invariably a late return to the money economy and a lag in trade and commerce is reflected in the number of *fiefs-rentes* granted. Always it was the economically backward areas such as Burgundy and the lands to the east of the Rhine that saw a late rise of the *fief-rente*. This emphasis upon the necessity of a money economy should not cause us, however, to look upon it as a *sine qua non*. Fiefs in kind appeared as early as fiefs in money. These grants in kind, more numerous in the early Middle Ages, declined as the money economy grew stronger but never completely disappeared. If there had never been a money economy the *fief-rente* in kind would no doubt have developed just as did other varieties of fiefs not of land. Circumstances such as a lack of land or a matter of convenience would have eventually compelled the feudal lord to enfeoff all sorts of objects and incomes in order to acquire the vassals needed.[52]

In France the earliest known concession of a *fief-rente* occurred in the duchy of Normandy in 1079. In his *Historiae Ecclesiasticae,* Ordericus Vitalis relates that a certain knight, the son of Richard de Hugleville, granted to the priory of Aufai "unum modium [of wine] ad celebrandas missas perenniter" out of "duas quadrigatas vini de principe Normannorum in feudo tenebat singulis annis." This donation was confirmed by Duke William the Conqueror.[53] In 1093 the monk Sevinus handed over to the abbey of Saint-Père de Chartres for the souls of his father, mother, and two brothers the "feodum" formerly granted to him by the abbey; it consisted of "duos . . . annonae modios, panem unum quotidianum et quartam partem sextarii vini."[54] Some time between 1101 and 1129 a certain Fouchard with the consent of his wife, daughter, and granddaughter sold to a person named Christian for 6 *l.* 12 *s.* "suum fevum panis et vini et annone" which he had held from the abbey of Saint-Père. Christian transferred his right to the wheat back to the abbey; in turn the abbey freed him of the "servicium istius fevi" with the

---

[52] The use and value of the *fief-rente* are treated in later chapters.

[53] *Historiae Ecclesiasticae,* ed. A. le Prevost (Paris, 1845), III, 37.

[54] B. Guérard, *Cartulaire de l'abbaye de Saint-Père de Chartres* (Paris, 1840), II, no. 58. For his comments on these fiefs see pp. xxv–xxvi.

stipulation that the whole fief would return to the abbey after the death of Christian and his wife.[55] Between 1119 and 1128 the abbey of Saint-Père granted to the knight Paganus and his heirs "duos annone modios in Loen annuatim in feodum"; Paganus and his heirs were to provide a horse ("unum caballum in servitium") for forty days in return for the fief.[56] In this same period two other fiefs in kind were granted, and then some time between 1130 and 1150 there was a document drawn up with the following rubric: "Quid feodatis ecclesie nostre a nobis, et quid ab ipsis nobis debeatur." There follows a list of twenty-four men receiving fiefs in kind, but undoubtedly some of the so-called fiefs were alms.[57]

The earliest record of a fief granted in money is of the year 1107. At that time an agreement was concluded between Bertrand-Aton, viscount of Béziers, and Richard, archbishop of Narbonne, whereby Bertrand surrendered his pretensions to the lands of Capestang and did homage and fealty to Richard who agreed to give him more money than his grandfather and predecessors had received. It was stipulated that Bertrand and his heirs should always do homage to the archbishop and live up to the conventions "propter fevum et propter talem pecuniam quam dedit Guifredus Petro Raimundo avo eius." Learning from the document that Bertrand's grandfather was Pierre-Raimond and knowing that he was the count of Carcassonne about the middle of the eleventh century, we can state with assurance that this fief had been in existence since some time in that century.[58]

There are no concessions of *fiefs-rentes* by the French kings until 1155–56. Then in a complicated feudal transaction Louis VII gave his brother, Count Robert, a fief of 50 *l.* from which Robert granted 30 *l.* "in feodum et in homagium" to William de Mello, who in turn transferred it to Guy, the royal butler, by a somewhat devious process. William placed the fief of 30 *l.* in Robert's possession, Robert

---

[55] *Ibid.,* no. 32.

[56] *Ibid.,* no. 62.

[57] *Ibid.,* nos. 141, 143, 167.

[58] C. Devic and J. Vaissete, *Histoire générale de Languedoc* (Toulouse, 1875), V, no. 427. Kienast (*H.Z.,* CLVIII, 26) and Ganshof (*R.B.P.H.,* XXVII, 1949, 241–42) do not believe that this grant is a *fief-rente*; I, however, concur with Sczaniecki that it is (*Essai,* p. 19). The document states that the sum of money has been paid at least several times previously; it consequently could not be a lump sum.

rendered it to Louis VII and he in turn invested Guy with the fief.[59] The next evidence for royal grants is in 1185 when Philip Augustus granted Jacob of Avesnes, councilor of the count of Flanders, a fief of 100 *l*. That same year he permitted Count Robert to grant in alms to the Temple or *Hôpital* a fief of 30 *l*. which Robert held from him on the *prévôté de Poissi*. In 1192 Philip conceded to a certain John le Noir a fief of 20 *l*. of Paris; in 1195–96 he gave to Richard de Vernone and his heirs 800 *l*. of Paris "in feodum et hominagium ligium."[60] These along with a few other concessions represent all that were granted by the French kings until the thirteenth century.

A similar pattern emerges in the large French principalities. There is no evidence of any *fiefs-rentes* until the middle twelfth century and only toward the end of this century is there a perceptible climb in the number granted. As would be expected the early grants are found in those regions enjoying a brisk economic life. In 1158 Count Henry I of Champagne made known that his father Count Theobald II had granted to Archibald de Souillac "120 libras Pruuinensium monetae singulis annis in feodum."[61] That such fiefs became more numerous as the century progressed is evidenced by the so-called book of the vassals of Champagne dating from the reign of Count Henry I (1152–81).[62] In Pontieu the first grant is of the year 1195. Count William II conceded to Peter "de Poestisiaco" in recompense of his services 20 *l*. of Paris "in feodum et homagium." [63]

The evidence summarized above is all that exists for France down to 1200. Beginning in the early thirteenth century, however, the concessions steadily increase. The kings now become the grantors of most fiefs and remain so down into the fifteenth century; their

---

[59] Luchaire, *Études sur les actes de Louis VII* (Paris, 1885), no. 353.

[60] Gislebert de Mons, *Chronicon Hanoniense*, ed. L. Vanderkindere (Bruxelles, 1904), p. 184; Kienast, *Deutschen Fürsten*, I, 114; H. F. Delaborde, *Recueil des actes de Philippe-Auguste* (Paris, 1916), I, no. 43; L. Delisle, *Catalogue des actes de Philippe-Auguste* (Paris, 1856), nos. 136, 358; A. Teulet and H. F. Delaborde, *Layettes du trésor des chartes* (Paris, 1863), I, no. 441.

[61] Chantereau le Febvre, *Traité des fiefs*, Preuves, p. 4.

[62] It contains such entries as the following: "Comes Suessionensis; feodum est xxx^lib. in theloneo et pedagio Castri Theodorici" (H. d'Arbois de Jubainville, *Histoire des ducs et des comtes de Champagne*, Paris, 1860, II, Documents, v ff.).

[63] C. Brunel, *Recueil des actes des comtes de Pontieu (1026–1279)* (Paris, 1930), no. 139.

grants can be found all over France. Following their example were the great feudal princes led by the counts of Champagne. The number of *fiefs-rentes* increases so greatly in the thirteenth century that one loses count of them; there are literally hundreds in existence throughout the thirteenth and fourteenth centuries. A marked decrease in grants begins around the end of the fourteenth century and continues into the fifteenth century. By 1500 the *fief-rente* has lost all importance in France.[64]

In Germany the *fief-rente* is found earlier than in France. In 1048 Egbert, abbot of Fulda, and a certain lord Wernhard reached an agreement whereby Wernhard surrendered to the abbot all his rights to a certain *beneficium* consisting of "xxx hubae" in area in return for eight talents yearly *pro beneficio* from the abbot's chamber; he promised to serve Egbert just as "alii milites seruiret abbati et in expeditionibus cum sex scutis militaret."[65] In 1073, according to Cosmas of Prague, Archbishop Gebhard of Ratisbonn granted to one of his knights in "beneficium xxx marcas argenti."[66] In 1092 Gerhard von Stumpenhusen handed over to Archbishop Liemar of Bremen all his holdings in land, houses, and other appurtenances such as mills, streams, and woods. Liemar made known that Gerhard had become "homo noster" and had accepted "de camera nostra octo libras denariorum Goslariensium" granted as a benefice. It was expressly stated that after Gerhard's death the benefice should not pass on to either his son or his heirs.[67]

In the twelfth century grants of *fiefs-rentes* probably increased, but the evidence remains scant. Although there may have been other documents like the following, it is the only one extant. Among the records of Goslar is a list, compiled about 1244, of all those "qui recipiunt annuatim feodum de advocatia Goslariensi." Well over a hundred names are included in the list. Many of these fiefs were *Burglehen* granted in the twelfth century by Frederick I, as well as by Philip of Suabia and Otto IV.[68] Only two other fiefs from the

---

[64] Sczaniecki, *Essai,* pp. 167–75.

[65] E. F. J. Dronke, *Codex Diplomaticus Fuldensis* (Cassel, 1850), no. 749.

[66] B. Bretholz, "Die Chronik der Böhmen des Cosmas von Prag," *Monumenta Germaniae Historica, Scriptores* (Berlin, 1923), New Series, II, ch. 28.

[67] J. M. Lappenberg, *Hamburgisches Urkundenbuch* (Hamburg, 1842), I, no. 119.

[68] G. Bode, *Urkundenbuch der Stadt Goslar* (Halle, 1893), I, no. 606. The document reads as follows: "Hec sunt nomina illorum, qui tenent feodum de

twelfth century are known. In 1182 Frederick I granted to Count Otto II of Guelders "in feodo" 300 *m.* of money of Cologne; Otto performed homage for himself and heirs. In 1190 the archbishop of Mainz granted "quinquaginta carratas vini ... in feodo" to Henry, the son of Duke Godfrey III of Brabant.[69]

In the thirteenth century *fiefs-rentes* became more numerous; yet it was the last quarter of the century before the German sovereigns, such as Rudolf of Hapsburg and Adolf of Nassau, granted many. The fourteenth-century rulers did not grant as many as their thirteenth-century predecessors, and in the fifteenth century the number of concessions becomes negligible. The records show that the German emperors were far surpassed in the granting of *fiefs-rentes* by the secular and ecclesiastical princes generally concentrated along the Rhine.[70] The foremost grantors were the archbishops of Cologne and the counts of Cleve. Many *fiefs-rentes* were granted by towns of this region, notably Cologne. Though numerous in the mid-thirteenth century, grants of *fiefs-rentes* are even more frequently found from the last quarter of that century on through the fourteenth. There are a few grants in the first years of the fifteenth century; then they become scarce and disappear after 1450. The inescapable conclusion is that the German princes granted considerably fewer *fiefs-rentes* than their French contemporaries.

In the Low Countries, with but one exception, *fiefs-rentes* were not granted until the late eleventh century. The exception is a fief of 12 *l.* given about 996 to a certain knight Frethebald in return for ceding his goods in Teisterbant to the church of Utrecht; this concession was confirmed in 1010.[71] We have no evidence of other such

---

eisdem: Bertoldus de Gowische VIIII marcas ... etc." For the comments of Bode see pp. 35–36.

[69] P. Bondam, *Charterboek der Hertogen van Gelderland en Graaven van Zutphen* (Utrecht, 1789), II, no. 64; Lünig, *Codex Germaniae Diplomaticus* (Frankfurt, 1733), II, 1739; Butkens, *Trophées*, Preuves, p. 44; A.G.R., Verkooren, *Inventaire des chartes et cartulaires des duchés de Brabant et de Limbourg et des Pays d'Outre-Meuse*, Deuxième partie (typescript copy), p. 24; A. Wauters, *Table chronologique des chartes et diplômes imprimés concernant l'histoire de la Belgique* (Bruxelles, 1868), II, 697.

[70] Between 1263 and 1325, for example, there are forty entries relating to *fiefs-rentes* granted by the archbishops of Cologne (L. Ennen and G. Eckertz, *Quellen zur Geschichte der Stadt Köln*, Köln, 1863–70, vols II–IV).

[71] S. Muller and A. C. Bouman, *Oorkondenboek van het Sticht Utrecht* (Utrecht, 1920), I, no. 145. There are many references to the earliest *fiefs-*

fiefs until 1088. Then a fief of 20 s., granted by Baldwin II, count of
Hainaut, to Guideric, *avocat* of Hautmont, and paid annually from
the income of Hautmont, was donated by him to two of his knights.[72]
Better known perhaps are the *fiefs-rentes* granted by the abbey of
Saint-Bertin. In 1087 the brothers Arnold and Gerbodo became the
men of the abbey and each received 2 m. of silver "in benefitium."
In 1093 two knights, Baldric and Eustace, each received a fief of 5 s.
payable by the *camera* of the abbey. And in 1096 an agreement between Baldwin de Salpervinc and the abbot Lambert indicates that
Baldwin and some of his family had held a fief of 3 l. some time
before this date.[73] These are the only *fiefs-rentes* known for this
century.

In the twelfth century *fiefs-rentes* become more prominent, especially in the last quarter of the century. Contained in the famous
charter granted by William Clito, count of Flanders, to Saint-Omer
in 1127 is the well-known entry referring to the *fiefs-rentes* in kind
received by those men performing castle-guard at Saint-Omer. For
his service each received "feodum suum et prebendam sibi antiquitus
constitutam in avena et caseis et in pellibus arietum."[74] Valuable
for its evidence of *fiefs-rentes,* particularly those emanating from the
counts of Hainaut, is the *Chronicon Hanoniense* of Gislebert de
Mons, the chancellor and loyal servant of the counts. In 1184, for
example, by means of the *fief-rente* Baldwin V recruited a group
of distinguished knights from Flanders, Brabant, and France for
service in his *mesnie.*[75]

rentes of the Low Countries in Ganshof's review of Sczaniecki's work
(*R.B.P.H.,* XXVII, 237–43). See also Kienast, *H.Z.,* CLVIII, 25.

[72] C. Duvivier, *Recherches sur le Hainaut ancien du VIIe au XIIe siècle*
(Bruxelles, 1864), p. 447; Didier, *Revue du Nord,* XVII, 266.

[73] Guérard, *Cartulaire de l'abbaye de Saint-Bertin* (Paris, 1840), Simon I,
nos. 28, 30; Simon II, no. 32.

[74] A. Giry, *Histoire de la ville de Saint-Omer et de ses institutions jusqu'au
XIVe siècle* (Paris, 1877), p. 373.

[75] To Baldwin Caron, who had fled to Hainaut because of a quarrel with
the count of Flanders, Count Baldwin granted "600 libras in feodo ligio."
The Flemish knight Baldwin de Neuville-Vitasse received a fief of 300 l.
Three French knights were granted fiefs of lesser value (Gislebert de Mons,
Chronicon, pp. 174–75). In 1185 Gosuin de Wavrin, brother of the seneschal
of Flanders, killed a serjeant of the count of Flanders and took refuge in
Hainaut where he became a member of Count Baldwin's *mesnie* with the
title of *commilito.* The count assigned him 60 l. "in feodo ligio" (*Ibid.,* p.
180). For other examples see pp. 182–84.

Turning to other records, we find evidence in the charters of the abbey of Saint Pierre at Ghent that it granted various small fiefs in kind. Some time in this century the abbey of Saint-Vaast at Arras granted several *fiefs-rentes*.[76] And scattered about in various cartularies and charters of Flanders, Hainaut, and Brabant are four or five more *fiefs-rentes* granted by ecclesiastical and secular lords.[77] Finally, in a military alliance concluded at Dinant on 26 July 1199 between Theobald, count of Bar and Luxemburg, and Baldwin IX, count of Flanders and Hainaut, appears the largest *fief-rente* granted by a prince of the Low Countries before 1200. Theobald promised to aid Baldwin against Philip Augustus of France. Baldwin granted 500 *l.* "in feodum" to Theobald who took some of his lands lying along the Meuse in fief from Baldwin and became his liege man. Furthermore, Baldwin, having recently entered into close political relations with King John of England, promised that he would persuade John to grant Theobald lands equal to those lost to the count of Namur in a dispute; this grant would be a fief for which feudal service was to be rendered. If, however, John was unwilling to make this concession, Baldwin promised that he would then give Theobald 200 *l.* yearly to be held in fief along with the 500 *l.*[78]

This examination of the eleventh- and twelfth-century evidence has shown that numerically the *fiefs-rentes* granted in the Low Countries down to 1200 greatly exceeded those in France and Germany. What was more natural than within a small area that

[76] In 1163 Robert, *châtelain* of Aire, gave in free alms to the abbey "duos modios frumenti" which he had formerly held "feodali iure" from the abbey. A document of 1168 states that a certain Eustace de Afsna held in fief from the abbey "X halsteria siliginae" (A. Van Lokeren, *Chartes et documents de l'abbaye de Saint-Pierre, Gand*, 1868, I, nos. 283, 313). For Saint-Vaast see M. Van Drival, *Cartulaire de l'abbaye de Saint-Vaast d'Arras rédigé au XIIᵉ siècle par Guimann* (Arras, 1875), p. 241.

[77] In 1191 Otto, lord of Cuyk, took his allod of Herpen and all its appurtenances in fief from Henry I, duke of Brabant; in return Henry granted him a fief of 40 *m.* of Cologne (F. Foppens and A. Miraeus, *Opera Diplomatica*, Louvain, 1723, I, 555). In 1197 Gerard de Saint-Aubert, with the consent of his wife, promised to give Conon de Béthune a fief of 45 *l.* yearly until land could be provided (*Inventaire analytique et chronologique des archives de la chambre des comptes, à Lille*, 1865, I, no. 211). See also Wauters, *Table chronologique*, III, 29, 69.

[78] C. Wampach, *Urkunden- und Quellenbuch zur Geschichte der altluxemburgischen Territorien bis zur burgundischen Zeit* (Luxemburg, 1935), I, no. 550. See also Kienast, *Deutschen Fürsten*, I, 155.

had greatly profited from trade and industry, the local rulers should have used the *fief-rente* to advance their feudal relations. Limited in this early period almost exclusively to Flanders, Hainaut, and Brabant, the *fief-rente* spread in the following centuries to all the neighboring principalities—Namur, Liège, Guelders, Holland, Looz, Limburg, and Luxemburg. Here, as in France and Germany, it was at its height in the thirteenth and fourteenth centuries; the fifteenth century saw its decline.[79] Throughout these centuries the total of *fiefs-rentes* in the Low Countries, grant for grant, is far greater than that in Germany. And, by taking into account the difference in area, it can be said that proportionately there were more *fiefs-rentes* in the Low Countries than in France. This is not surprising; for, in addition to being the hub of northern European economic life, the Low Countries were also important as a buffer region between France and the Empire and as a potential reservoir of military support for England in its struggle with France.[80] No region of Europe was more conducive to the growth of the *fief-rente* than this economic, political, diplomatic, and military crossroads.

The English kings, nevertheless, were the feudal princes who gave to their vassals the most valuable, if not the most numerous, *fiefs-rentes* in the eleventh and twelfth centuries. Indeed, a study of the *fief-rente* in England is actually restricted to royal grants, for the available records provide no example of such enfeoffment by a baron. Soon after coming under the efficient rule of the Norman duke in 1066, England could boast of the best organized and most highly centralized government of western Europe. Because of scrupulous management of their finances and because of the thriving economic life in England, as well as in their continental possessions, the kings had at their disposal more money than most of the feudal princes. They were consequently among the first to adapt money to feudal custom.[81] Able even in 1066 to grant a large *fief-rente*, they continued such grants throughout the twelfth century. It was almost a hundred years later before a French king granted a *fief-*

---

[79] *R.B.P.H.*, XXXII, 424–27.

[80] Though the works of Pirenne emphasize the economic and political importance of the Low Countries, those of Dept, De Sturler, Kienast, and Lucas treat in detail the economic, political, and military relations of the Low Countries with France, England, and the Empire.

[81] Lyon, *E.H.R.*, LXVI, 161–93.

rente, and it was not until the reign of Philip Augustus in the early thirteenth century that the grants of the French kings approximate those of the English. As for the enfeoffments of the German emperors, not even during their peak between 1275 and 1300 did they approach in value or number those of the English kings. Only in the Low Countries does one feel that the *fief-rente* attained the prominence it had under the English kings.

If the account of William of Malmesbury can be trusted, the first concession of a *fief-rente* by an English ruler occurred in 1066. In this year William the Conqueror, duke of Normandy, granted a *fief-rente* of 300 m. to Baldwin V, count of Flanders, in return for the count's homage, counsel, and military aid in the projected invasion of England.[32] Although Malmesbury is the only one to mention the granting of this fief in 1066, references by other chroniclers to its payment in the years following the Conquest support his account. Baldwin VI and Arnold III, the successors of Baldwin V, apparently received the fief without any interruptions or serious altercations; but upon the usurpation of the Flemish countship in 1071 by Robert the Frisian, the peaceful relations of the counts with William the Conqueror were abruptly severed and the *fief-rente* terminated. Robert the Frisian, resenting the intervention of his brother-in-law, William, in behalf of Richilde, adopted a hostile attitude toward the Conqueror and even co-operated with the two Danish attempts to invade England.[33] In the year 1093 before his death, Robert, less wary of the English power on the Continent now that William II did not possess Normandy, met that king at Dover, made his peace, and was permitted to receive the fief of 300 m. His successor, Robert II, eager to continue on the same friendly basis, was rebuffed by Henry I who, during the first three years of his

[32] William of Malmesbury, *De Gestis Regum Anglorum* (R.S., London, 1889), II, 478: "Baldewinus senior, huius Roberti avus, Willelmum in Angliam venientem, arguto quo pollebat consilio, et militum additamento, vivaciter juverat. His ille illustres crebro retributiones refuderat, omnibus, ut ferunt, annis 300 m. argenti pro fide et affinitato socero annumerans." See also Dept, *Influences,* p. 18; Toll, *Englands Beziehungen,* pp. 42–43; Kienast, *Deutschen Fürsten,* I, 44–45.

[33] *The Anglo-Saxon Chronicle* (R.S., London, 1861), II, 181–85; Malmesbury, *Gesta Regum,* II, 317; *Annales Monasterii de Wintonia,* in *Annales Monastici* (R.S., London, 1865), II, 34. See also Dept, *Influences,* pp. 18–19; Kienast, *Deutschen Fürsten,* I, 44–47; Palgrave, *History,* III, 494.

4

reign, haughtily refused to pay the *fief-rente,* declaring that it was not the custom of the English kings to pay tribute for allies.[84] Up to the twelfth century, then, only one *fief-rente* was granted by the English kings—that conceded by William the Conqueror in 1066 to the Flemish counts.

Only three years elapsed before Henry I reconsidered the advantages of a Flemish alliance; he was influenced, perhaps, by the bitter struggle with his brother, Robert Curthose, which was to culminate in the Battle of Tinchebrai (1106). At Dover on 10 March 1103 Robert II and Henry concluded the first Anglo-Flemish alliance of which there is official record. Robert agreed to aid Henry in the defense of England, Normandy, and Maine with a stipulated number of knights and "propter praedictas conventiones et praedictum servitium dabit rex Henricus comiti Rotberto unoquoque anno CCCCC libras anglorum denariorum in feodo."[85] This agree-

[84] Eadmer, *Historia Novorum in Anglia* (R.S., London, 1884), p. 39; Malmesbury, *Gesta Regum,* II, 478–79: "Verum Henricus majori pondere rem ventilans, ut nec indebite adunaret pecunias, nec nisi debite dilapidaret habitas, Roberto ab Jerosolima reverso, et quasi pro imperio 300 m. argenti exigenti, inhanc respondit sententiam: Non solitos reges Anglie Flandritis vectigal pendere, nec se velle libertatem majorum macula sue timiditatis fuscare: qua propter, si suo committat arbitrio, libenter se quod opportunitas siverit ut cognato et amico dare; si vero in exactione permanendum putaverit, omino negare." See also Dept, *Influences,* p. 19; Kienast, *Deutschen Fürsten,* I, 47–48; Varenbergh, *Histoire diplomatiques,* pp. 61–62; Ramsay, *The Foundations of England* (London, 1898), II, 270.

[85] F. Vercauteren, *Actes des comtes de Flandre* (Bruxelles, 1938), no. 30. This agreement is also printed in *Foedera,* I, i, 7, which makes use of a different text and states that "400 m. argenti" was the fief. The text used by Vercauteren is the better. He is supported by Kienast, *Deutschen Fürsten,* I, 49–54. The treaty printed in *Foedera* is incorrectly dated as 1101; it was confused with a later treaty of 1110. This mistake was repeated by Varenbergh, *Histoire diplomatiques,* pp. 61–62, and by W. Farrer, "An Outline Itinerary of Henry I," *E.H.R.,* XXXIV (1919), 309–10. J. Flach has questioned the authenticity of the treaty of 1103 as well as of another of 1110 ("Le comté de Flandre et ses rapports avec la couronne de France du IXᵉ au XVᵉ siècle," *Revue Historique,* CXV, 1914, 254–56, and note 2 on pp. 255–56). Contrary to Flach, Kienast has argued that these treaties are authentic; his view has been accepted by Vercauteren in his edition of the *actes* and by L. Vercauteren-Desmet in her essay "Étude sur les rapports politiques de l'Angleterre et de la Flandre, sous le règne du comte Robert II (1093–1111)," *Études d'histoire dédiées à la mémoire de Henri Pirenne* (Bruxelles, 1937), pp. 413–23.

ment, with some revision in terms, was renewed at Dover on 17 May 1110. Henry granted Robert a ficf of 400 *m.* of silver and reduced the contingent of fighters to be supplied by Robert.[86] For the remainder of Henry I's reign and the years of civil war, 1135–1154, there are no references to the Flemish fief. It is known only that the succeeding four counts—Baldwin VII, Charles the Good, William Clito, and Thierry of Alsace—maintained friendly relations with Henry as well as with his daughter Matilda, first in her capacity as German empress, and then as queen of England. Although numerous Flemish mercenaries helped Stephen of Blois in his fight against Matilda, Thierry of Alsace apparently remained loyal to her. We can only assume that Henry I continued to pay the fief of 400 *m.* and that Matilda, during the internecine struggle, followed suit whenever possible.[87] The only other *fief-rente* in this period was one of 100 *m.* granted by Henry I to Count Baldwin IV of Hainaut. Our authority for this statement, Gislebert de Mons, does not give a date for the concession but it was some time after Baldwin IV succeeded to the countship in 1120, probably in the year 1127–28.[88]

With the accession of Henry II there are fewer gaps in our knowledge. The Pipe Rolls for the first years of Henry's reign reveal that he granted Count Thierry sizable sums of money from the issues of various counties and manors in England. Though there is no evidence that these issues were given to Thierry as payment for the *fief-rente* of 400 *m.,* such may have been the case.[89] This suggestion

---

[86] Vercauteren, *Actes,* no. 41 ; *Foedera,* I, i, 6. See also Kienast, *Deutschen Fürsten,* I, 54–57 ; Dept, *Influences,* pp. 19–20 ; Ramsay, *Foundations,* II, 270.

[87] Dept, *Influences,* pp. 19–21 ; Varenbergh, *Histoire diplomatiques,* pp. 73, 76 ; De Lettenhove, *Histoire de Flandre,* I, 221 ; Norgate, *Angevin Kings,* I, 319, 326–27, 342 ; Ramsay, *Angevin Empire,* p. 4 ; A. L. Poole, *From Domesday Book to Magna Carta* (Oxford, 1951), pp. 131–66.

[88] Gislebert de Mons, *Chronicon,* p. 109 : "Ei super 100 marchis sterlingorum magno pondo annuatim habendis hominium fecit, et sicut ejus [Baldwin V] pater ab ipso rege et ab ejus avunculo Henrico rege Anglie infeodatus fuerat." See also Kienast, *Deutschen Fürsten,* I, 59–60.

[89] The yearly payments surpass 400 *m.* but this may be explained by the fact that the kings habitually granted the counts extra sums for traveling expenses and as remuneration for various services. For the year 1155–56 the count of Flanders received 200 *l.* blanch from Lincoln, 76 *l.* blanch from Benton (Bampton), 100 *s.* from Wike in Oxford, and 60 *l.* blanch from Dunham in Nottingham. In 1156–57 he received approximately the same amount, but

4*

receives more support when one takes into account the meeting of
the two princes at Dover on 19 March 1163 where they and their
sons, Philip of Alsace and the Young Henry, renewed the previous
Anglo-Flemish *ententes* of 1103 and 1110. In return for a fief of
400 m. Thierry and Philip agreed to supply the two Henrys with a
thousand knights for the defense of England, Normandy, and Maine,
and to defend them against all men save Louis VII, king of France.
It was at this same meeting that an unspecified number of vassals
of Thierry made formal recognition of the military service owed
to Henry II for their *fiefs-rentes*.[90] Scattered entries in the Pipe Rolls
down to 1173 indicate that, for the most part, the annual installments of the comital fief were paid.[91] Meanwhile in 1166 Henry II
granted a fief of 1,000 l. to Count Matthew of Boulogne and one
of 500 l. to Count Theobald of Blois.[92] And, then, in 1172 the new
count of Hainaut, Baldwin V, met Henry II in Normandy and there
received the fief of 100 m. that his father had possessed. At the same
time six of Baldwin's vassals received fiefs of lesser value.[93]

in 1157–58 he received an additional 65 l. by tale from Exning in Suffolk.
The total of these issues was 419 l. 16 s. or about 399 l. blanch (*P.R. 2–3–4
Hen. II*, pp. 36–37, 39–40, 82–83, 89, 91, 136, 149, 152). See also *P.R. 5
Hen. II*, pp. 8, 34, 51, 64; *P.R. 6 Hen. II*, pp. 1, 8, 43, 45; *P.R. 7 Hen II*,
p. 30; *P.R. 8 Hen. II*, p. 26; Robert of Torigni, *Chronica*, in *Chronicles of
the Reigns of Stephen, Henry II, and Richard I* (R.S., London, 1889), IV,
182; Kienast, *Deutschen Fürsten*, I, 64.

[90] L. Delisle, *Recueil des actes de Henri II* (Paris, 1916), I, no. 152. See
also *Foedera*, I, i, 23; Kienast, *Deutschen Fürsten*, I, 68–71, and *Untertaneneid und Treuvorbehalt*, p. 50; Dept, *Influences*, p. 21.

[91] Often the issues of the counties designated as payment to Thierry and
Philip do not total 400 m. but the balance was likely made up by payments
directly out of the exchequer (*P.R. 14 Hen. II*, p. 95; *P.R. 15 Hen. II*, p.
60). As far as we know there were at this time no enrollments of the issues
of the exchequer. This may explain why our only references to payment of
the Flemish *fief-rente* by the *scaccarium* or *thesaurus* come from the chroniclers. Surely many such payments were made but unfortunately the writs
directing payment by the exchequer and the receipt made out by the counts
are not extant.

[92] *P.R. 14 Hen. II*, p. 95; *P.R. 15 Hen. II*, p. 60; *Materials for the History
of Thomas Becket* (R.S., London, 1875), VI, 73–75; R. W. Eyton, *Court,
Household, and Itinerary of King Henry II* (London, 1878), pp. 102–3;
Kienast, *Deutschen Fürsten*, I, 73–76; Ramsay, *Angevin Empire*, p. 90;
Johnen, *B.C.R.H.*, LXXIX, 390; Gervase of Canterbury, *Opera Historica*
(R.S., London, 1879), I, 203.

[93] Gislebert de Mons, *Chronicon*, p. 109. Kienast points out that Count

Philip of Alsace, who succeeded his father Thierry in 1168, began his countship by reversing the traditional pro-English policy and turning toward Louis VII. He befriended Thomas Becket in his dispute with Henry II and actively allied himself with Henry's sons who revolted in 1173 under the leadership of the Young Henry. Henry II immediately suspended the fief granted in 1163, but the Young Henry handsomely rewarded Philip for his support with a fief of 1,000 *l.* yearly, plus the county of Kent, with Dover and Rochester castles. Theobald, count of Blois, also went into the camp of the rebels and was rewarded with a fief of 500 *l.* of Anjou.[94] After the revolt was suppressed in 1174 and peace concluded, the two Henrys received Count Philip at Caen in April 1175 and again established friendly relations. Philip surrendered his claims to the *fief-rente* granted by the Young Henry, as well as to the conquests made during the revolt; the two Henrys, in turn, gave back to Philip his *fief-rente* of 400 *m.* and increased it to 1,000 *m.* annually.[95] There is every reason to believe that this fief was

Baldwin IV of Hainaut had already received from Henry II in 1167 or 1168 the fief of 100 *m.* granted him by Henry I. Gislebert's use of "fuerunt recognita et reassignata" would seem to indicate that the six knights were also granted their fiefs at this time. See Kienast, *Deutschen Fürsten,* I, 76–78, and König, *B.C.R.H.,* LXXIV, 210.

[94] Benedict of Peterborough, *Gesta Regis Henrici Secundi* (R.S., London, 1867), I, 44–45: "In eodem concilio juvenis rex recepit homagium et fidelitatem a Philippo comiti Flandrie, et dedit ei pro homagio et fidelitate sua 1,000 *l.* redditus in Anglia per annum, et totam Cantiam, cum castello de Duvere, et castello Rofensi. ... Similiter recepit fidelitatem et homagium comitis Theobaldi, et concessit ei 500 *l.* reddituum andegavensium." See also Roger of Hoveden, *Chronica* (R.S., London, 1868), II, 46–47, 63–64, 72; William of Newburgh, *Historia Rerum Anglicarum,* in *Chronicles of Stephen, Henry II, and Richard I* (R.S., London, 1884), I, 171; J. Brompton, *Chronicon,* in *Scriptores X* (London, 1652), p. 1084; Kienast, *Deutschen Fürsten,* I, 85–86; Johnen, *B.C.R.H.,* LXXIX, 408–9; C. E. Hodgson, *Jüng-Heinrich, König von England, Sohn König Heinrichs II, 1153–1183* (Jena, 1906), pp. 23–24.

[94] Benedict of Peterborough, *Gesta Regis Henrici Secundi* (R.S., London, confirmaverunt predicto comiti, cartis suis, redditum quem ei dederant in Anglia, scilicet (mille) marcas argenti recipiendas ad scaccarium Anglie." Roger of Hoveden, II, 72: "Comes Flandrie tradidit in manu regis patris cartam regis filii, quam habuit de supradicta conventione. Et ipsi confirmaverunt predicto comiti redditum quem ipse annuatim percipere solebat in Anglia ante werram." See also Walter of Coventry, *Memoriale* (R.S., London, 1872), I, 238; John Brompton, p. 1101; William of Newburgh, I, 196.

paid regularly by Henry II until his death in 1189.[96] It is the only fief of which there is continuous record up to the reign of Richard I.

Richard, captured and imprisoned by the emperor Henry VI while on his journey back from the Third Crusade, was finally released after some two years of captivity on 4 February 1194. On the next day, prior to his departure from Mainz, he concluded military alliances with ten princes of Germany, the Low Countries, and Italy against his old enemy Philip Augustus, and granted all of them *fiefs-rentes*.[97] Meanwhile Baldwin VIII of Flanders and Hainaut continued to receive the fief customarily paid to the Flemish counts; when he died in 1194, his son who succeeded him as Count

Kienast feels that these chronicles are wrong in stating that the fief was increased to 1,000 m. Later under Richard I, John, and Henry III the fief was 500 m. It is quite possible, however, that Henry II, to win Count Philip away from Louis VII of France, was willing to increase the fief to the amount received by Philip from the Young Henry. See Kienast, *Deutschen Fürsten*, I, 88–89; Johnen, *B.C.R.H.*, LXXIX, 416; Varenbergh, *Histoire diplomatiques*, p. 85; Ramsay, *Angevin Empire*, p. 206.

[96] Benedict of Peterborough, I, 246–47; Roger of Hoveden, I, 197; Kienast, *Deutschen Fürsten*, I, 101–2.

[97] These princes were the archbishops Conrad of Mainz and Adolf of Cologne; Bishop Simon of Liège; the dukes Henry III of Limburg, Henry I of Brabant, and Conrad of Suabia; Count Diedrich VII of Holland; Conrad, count palatine of the Rhine; the marquis Boniface of Montferrat; and Baldwin, son of Count Baldwin VIII of Flanders and Hainaut (Roger of Hoveden, III, 234: "Rex Anglie promisit, et cartis suis confirmavit, quibusdam archiepiscopis et episcopis, et ducibus et comitibus, et baronibus multis de imperio, redditus annuos pro homagiis et fidelitatibus, et auxiliis eorum contra regem Francie." Gislebert de Mons, *Chronicon*, pp. 284–85: "Cum autem ipse rex Anglie, finitis omnibus erga dominum imperatorem, ad propria reverteretur, ipse in transitu suo Coloniensi archiepiscopo et Symoni Leodiensi electo et duci Lovaniensi et duci de Lemborch feoda in argento annuatim persolvenda dedit ... et omnes infeodati ab eo auxilium ei promiserunt contra regem Francorum"). See also Kienast, *Deutschen Fürsten*, I, 136 ff.; König, *B.C. R.H.*, LXXIV, 378–79; Smets, *Henri I*, p. 66; Clason, *Pensionsverhältnisse*, pp. 39–40; A. L. Poole, "Richard the First's Alliances with the German Princes in 1194," *Studies in Medieval History, Powicke*, pp. 90–99. Hoveden states that Leopold V of Austria received a *fief-rente* but it hardly seems possible that Richard would so have rewarded his captor. Apparently at the same time Richard granted a fief of 38 *l.* to Adam Pincerne, the butler of the archbishop of Cologne, and a fief of 20 *l.* by tale yearly to a certain Lambert of Cologne (*P.R. 6 Ric. I*, p. 76; *P.R. 7 Ric. I*, p. 118; *P.R. 8 Ric. I*, p. 275; *P.R. 9 Ric. I*, pp. 77, 167; *P.R. 10 Ric. I*, p. 161).

Baldwin IX came into its possession.[98] The Pipe Rolls of this period show various amounts paid by the sheriffs to Flemish lords for their *fiefs-rentes*.[99]

This account of the *fief-rente* under the English kings must terminate with the death of Richard in 1199, because in the last decade of the twelfth century there was an increase so sudden and swift in the number of *fiefs-rentes* granted that it renders impossible a detailed history after that year. In studying the *fief-rente* in the thirteenth century one deals with figures close to one thousand. Though this number decreases in the next century, the grants retain their importance because of their size and because of the stature of the men possessing them. Declining noticeably in the last quarter of the fourteenth century and in the first years of the fifteenth, the *fief-rente* disappeared from English history by the year 1450.

5. CONCLUSIONS

By the eleventh century all western Europe saw the emergence of a new feudal institution—the *fief-rente*. There were features of its development common to every region where it took root: a gradual and spotty beginning; an increase in the number of grants in the twelfth century so swift that, except in Germany, *fiefs-rentes* become too numerous to follow in detail after 1200; a retention of prominence until the end of the fourteenth century, when signs of decline become apparent; and finally, in the fifteenth century, its end as a significant institution. Emphasis has been put upon the close relation between the economy of a region and the development of the *fief-rente*. Nowhere did it appear until the chaos of the ninth and tenth centuries had been checked and some degree of political

---

[98] The Pipe Roll of 1197 shows that the *châtelain* of Ghent and other Flemish envoys received 20 m. from Yorkshire and 44 l. 10 s. from London and Middlesex for their expenses incurred while negotiating for the arrears of the count's *fief-rente* for three years (*P.R. 9 Ric. I*, p. 164). See also p. 62 where the envoys received another payment.

[99] The following entries are typical of those for the year 1198: Derby—"Flandrensibus 40 s. de feodis suis in Anglia"; Leicester—"Flandrensibus 105 s. 9 d. de feodis suis"; Lincoln—"Flandrensibus 31 l. 12 s. 10 d. de feodis suis . . . per breve Galfridi f. Petri quod attulit de computandis sibi 60 l. quas predictas Flandrensibus liberavit de predictis feodis" (*P.R. 10 Ric. I*, pp. 44, 115, 153). See also pp. 121, 154.

stability established. With this accomplished, trade and commerce were able to revive and so to introduce a money economy into western Europe. It was then that the *fief-rente* first appeared— always to show greatest vitality in those areas of northwestern Europe where a money economy early became dominant. With regard to the number of *fiefs-rentes* granted, England and the Low Countries led most parts of France; Germany, with the exception of the Rhineland, trailed behind. Thus the chronological pattern of the *fief-rente* was basically the same in all western Europe. The *fief-rente* was not indigenous or peculiar to any region; it was a feudal institution found throughout western Europe in the eleventh and twelfth centuries.

II

The Fief-Rente and Feudal Custom

Despite the development of certain feudal practices peculiar to each state there was general uniformity of feudal custom throughout western Europe. We now know that the ordinary fief was a fairly standard institution; to receive it a man had to become the vassal of the donor, participate in an investiture ceremony, and enter into mutual obligations with the donor.[1] Was this true also of the *fief-rente*? Was it, like the ordinary fief, basically the same in all western Europe or did it vary from state to state? The answer lies, not in its origin and chronological development traced above, but rather in its relationship to the ordinary fief within the framework of feudal law. Only when the juridical nature of the *fief-rente* is understood can one gainfully approach the study of its functions in medieval society.

The great feudal princes, inevitably the richest beneficiaries of the revived money economy, were responsible for nearly three-fifths of the total of *fiefs-rentes* granted. The rest were granted by such spiritual and secular lords as the archbishops of Cologne and bishops of Liège; the sons and close relatives of the French kings; and the counts of Pontieu, Hainaut, and Namur; and by such lesser lords as the counts of Guelders, Holland, Cleve, and Looz; the dukes of Luxemburg and Limburg; the bishops of Mainz, Trier, and other western German bishoprics; and the petty princes along the Rhine, in the Low Countries, and in France.[2] With little exception, however, none of these lesser lords granted more than a few fiefs; they comprised rather the principal class of recipients.

Although in all regions the donors insisted upon the performance of homage for *fiefs-rentes,* the type of homage varied. In France, where the concept of liegancy had been known since the middle of

[1] See especially the remarks of Ganshof, *Feudalism*, pp. xv–xvii, 59–62.
[2] For a list of the French lords who granted *fiefs-rentes* see Sczaniecki, *Essai*, p. 98.

the eleventh century, a large proportion of the *fiefs-rentes* found in the royal donations and in the records of the counts and lesser lords were held in liege homage. In 1203, for example, Philip Augustus granted to Ralph de Lovain 100 *l.* of Paris; in return Ralph did "hominagium ligium contra omnes homines." In 1287 Philip IV gave Ferri, duke of Lorraine, 300 *l.* of Tours "in feodum et homagium ligium." In 1347 Philip VI granted William I, count of Namur, a fief of 1,000 *l.* "dont il est devenu nostre homme lige."[3] In the great collection of documents listed under *Série* J. of the *Archives Nationales* pertaining chiefly to the relations of the kings with other princes and with the homages done to them by their vassals, the number of *fiefs-rentes* held in liege homage is so enormous as to prove beyond doubt, it seems to me, that the kings so granted the majority of their *fiefs-rentes*.[4] Liege homage also predominates in the grants of the other French lords.[5]

As in France, so in the Low Countries liege homage was more prevalent than simple. The one exception is Hainaut where Didier found that *fiefs-rentes* were given in liege homage in the twelfth and most of the thirteenth century, but in simple homage (*en fief ample*) from the late thirteenth century on.[6] For the rest of the Low Countries liege homage prevailed from the twelfth through the fifteenth century.[7]

[3] Delisle, *Cartulaire normand de Philippe-Auguste, Louis VIII, Saint Louis et Philippe-le-Hardi* (Paris, 1852), no. 67; Kern, *Acta Imperii,* no. 303; Delisle, *Mémoire sur les opérations financières des Templiers* (Paris, 1888–89), no. 26; J. Bovesse, "Actes originaux inédits de souverains de France et d'Allemagne conservés aux Archives de l'État à Namur (1281–1373)," *B.C.R.H.,* XIV (1949), no. 18. See also *Layettes,* II, no. 4429; Kern, *Acta Imperii,* no. 90.

[4] J. 620/10–11, 32, 37, 39, 45–46, etc.; J. 621/69, 82, 88; J. 622a/34; J. 622b/49, 51, 69, etc. For other such references see Viard, *Revue des Questions Historiques,* LIX, 351–55.

[5] In 1200 Hugh, count of Vaudémont, became the "homo ligius" of Count Theobald III of Champagne for a fief of 60 *l.* (Chantereau le Febvre, *Traité des fiefs,* Preuves, pp. 17, 102, 201, 207, 212). In 1260 Albert de Couzan did liege homage to the count of Forez for "xv sol. redditus" and "xv bichet avene" (G. Guichard *et al., Chartes du Forez antérieures au XIV*e *siècle* (Mâcon, 1938), IV, no. 467). See also Brussel, *Nouvel examen,* I, 45 ff., and Brunel, *Actes de Pontieu,* no. 309.

[6] Didier, *Revue du Nord,* XVII, 282; *Droit des fiefs,* pp. 29–37.

[7] In September 1202, for instance, Count Philip I of Namur received from Duke Henry I of Brabant a fief of 100 *m.* and did "ligium hominium" (M.

It is well known that the concept of liege homage never took root in Germany. It scarcely spread, in fact, further east than Lotharingia and even among the princes of the Empire under Frederick I the *homo ligius* was rare. That none of the *fiefs-rentes* granted in Germany were held in liege homage is therefore not surprising. The records state merely that the *rentes* are held in fief, in homage, or by feudal law. In 1212, for example, the emperor Otto IV granted to William Pusterla 25 m. "in rectum feudum" and in 1293 King Adolf granted to Godfrey von Eppenstein 25 m. "de liberalitate regia ... iusto feodali titulo." [8]

In England, by the reign of Henry I, every ordinary fief granted by the kings was held in liege homage ; this homage was a monopoly of the crown. That liege homage was also extended to include the *fief-rente* is borne out by numerous documents. In 1212, for example, John recognized "quod Adam de Wallencourt devenit homo noster ligius pro feodo 140 l." In 1337 Everhard, son of the count of Limburg, did "homagium ligeum" for a fief of 100 florins granted by Edward III.[9] But such cases of liege homage, though fairly numerous, are far outnumbered by *fiefs-rentes* granted simply "pro homagio" and "in feodum." [10]

We have now seen, so to speak, both sides of the coin. On one side is the concept of liege homage, that which governed the majority of *fiefs-rentes* granted by continental lords ; on the other, the concept of simple homage, that which governed the majority of *fiefs-rentes* granted by the English kings. It is strange, however, to find the English kings granting most *fiefs-rentes* in simple homage when ordinary fiefs were granted in liege homage. A possible explanation seems to hinge upon the fact that virtually all the *fiefs-rentes* granted by the kings were to men on the Continent. The kings realized that they

Walraet, *Actes de Philippe Ier, dit le noble, comte et marquis de Namur (1196–1212)*, Bruxelles, 1949, no. 23). In 1273 Countess Margaret of Flanders and her son Guy de Dampierre granted Jakemon Louchard, citizen of Arras, 200 l. "iretablement et franchement en fief 'et en houmage lige" (J. de Saint Genois, *Inventaire analytique des chartes des comtes de Flandre*, Gand, 1843, no. 175). For the Louchard family see J. Lestocquoy, "Deux familles de financiers d'Arras, Louchard et Wagon," *R.B.P.H.*, XXXII (1954), 51–76. See Appendix, nos. 1, 6, 15.

[8] J. F. Böhmer, *Acta Imperii Selecta* (Innsbruck, 1870), no. 256 ; Böhmer, *Urkundenbuch der Reichsstadt Frankfurt* (Frankfurt, 1836), I, 280–81.

[9] *Rot. Pat.*, p. 94 ; *Foedera*, II, ii, 972.

[10] *Rot. Pat.*, p. 12 b.

had little to gain by granting *fiefs-rentes* in liege homage to men who were in most cases already the holders of landed fiefs and the liege men of continental lords. A bond of simple homage seemed the most satisfactory relationship between the kings and the recipients of *fiefs-rentes*. In some instances, however, it would seem that the kings attempted to establish a closer feudal tie by granting *fiefs-rentes* in liege homage, but in view of the status of such homage on the Continent their goal was not attained. By the middle of the twelfth century it was common for a vassal on the Continent, especially in France and the Low Countries, to have any number of liege lords, and by the thirteenth century there was so much liege homage that it came to be graded. The highest liegancy was reserved for one lord and the other liege homages were scaled according to the value of the fiefs and to the length of time held. The result was that in reality many of these liege homages were equivalent to simple homage. If the kings of England granted a *fief-rente* in liege homage to a man already the liege man of the king of France, only exceptional circumstances could force him to reserve his highest loyalty for the English kings. We are thus led to suggest that, in spite of whatever concept of liegancy governed the ordinary fief in England, it did not govern the *fief-rente*; and when a *fief-rente* was held in liege homage, it actually had the force of simple homage.

To examine the actions of men holding *fiefs-rentes* is to understand better the complications arising from the type of homage performed. If a man held an ordinary fief in liege homage and a *fief-rente* in simple homage, according to established feudal custom he owed his highest loyalty and first services to the liege lord. In the treaty of 1163 between Henry II of England and Count Thierry of Flanders wherein Thierry promised military service to Henry for a fief of 400 *m.*, it was provided that Thierry, who had done simple homage to Henry, should never have to fight against his liege lord, Louis VII of France. Thierry was therefore insured against being forced into some overt act that would cause his French lord to confiscate Flanders, a fief assuredly more valuable than the one of 400 *m.* But to provide for those occasions of hostilities which inevitably would break out between Henry II and Louis VII, a further clause was inserted: "Et si illo tempore rex Lodovicus super regem vel Henricum filium suum in Normanniam intraverit, comes Theodoricus vel comes Philippus ad Lodovicum regem Francie ibit cum

XX militibus tantum, et omnes alii predicti milites remanebunt cum rege vel cum Henrico filio suo, in servitio et fidelitate sua." [11] We have occasion to see the efficacy of these provisions when war broke out in the Norman Vexin in 1187 between Henry II and Philip Augustus. Thierry's successor, Philip of Alsace, along with a token contingent followed his liege lord ; but, as the chroniclers record the event, he sent to Henry some hundreds of men who went first to England and later embarked for Normandy where they saw service against Philip Augustus and Philip of Alsace.[12] Thus did the counts of Flanders meticulously fulfil their obligations so as not to upset the delicate feudal relations existing between them and Philip Augustus. It was not long, however, before the expansionist policy of Philip Augustus forced Count Ferrand into open defiance and led him to stake his survival upon a close military alliance with King John. Ferrand then transferred to John his first allegiance.[13]

When a man holding fiefs of land in liege homage received also a *fief-rente* in liege homage, elaborate precautions were taken to grade the liegancy and to prescribe the obligations in time of war, particularly war between the liege lords of the vassal. In 1219 Guy de Montréal and his brother Andrew became the liege men of Blanche of Navarre, regent of Champagne, and her son Theobald "salva ligeitate fratrum nostrorum, ducis Burgundie, comitis Willelmi et domini de Sauz" ; they were granted a fief of 30 *l*.[14] In 1294 Humbert, dauphin of Vienne, received a fief of 500 *l*. from Philip IV of France and did liege homage "salvis fidelitatibus et homagiis domi-

---

[11] Delisle, *Recueil des actes Henri II*, I, no. 152.

[12] Gervase of Canterbury, I, 347 ; Benedict of Peterborough, II, 48–49. In his review of Kienast's *Deutschen Fürsten*, C. Petit-Dutaillis has drawn attention to this interesting point : "En 1186 Philippe-Auguste se prépara à envahir le Vexin normand et convoqua son vassal flamand, celui-ci consentit à remplir le devoir d'ost, mais en même temps il envoya quelques certaines de guerriers en Angleterre, pour la défendre soi-disant contre une invasion ; en réalité, le contingent flamand, arrivé en Angleterre, fut embarqué et alla servir Henri II en Normandie" (*Bibliothèque de l'École des Chartes*, LXXXVIII, 1927, 99–105). See also Kienast, *Deutschen Fürsten*, I, 106 ff. ; Dept, *Influences*, pp. 22–23 ; Varenbergh, *Histoire diplomatiques*, p. 87.

[13] Lyon, *E.H.R.*, LXVI, 177.

[14] *Layettes*, I, no. 1355. See also L. P. C. Van Den Bergh, *Gedenkstukken tot Opheldering der Nederlandsche Geschiedenis* (Utrecht, 1849), I, no. 41 ; F. de Reiffenberg, *Monuments pour servir à l'histoire des provinces de Namur, de Hainaut et de Luxembourg* (Bruxelles, 1844), I, no. 23, p. 116.

norum suorum imperatorum, regum Sicilie, archiepiscopi Viennensis, Aniciensis, Gratianopolitani episcoporum."[15] In an agreement of 1296 between Count Guy of Flanders and Walter, lord of Waës, whereby Walter received a fief of 60 *l.*, the obligations owed to his liege lords are concisely stated:

Promet d'aider le dit comte contre tous seigneurs, excepté contre le comte de Luxembourg, le comte de Namur, dont il est homme avant tous autres seigneurs, et contre les comtes de Chiny et de Looz, de Viane et monseigneur Jean d'Agimont, dont il est homme et qu'il doit défendre, même contre le comte de Flandre s'il entrait dans leurs terres à ost et à chevauchée; si au contraire ces trois comtes et le seigneur d'Agimont attaquaient le comte de Flandre, Watier s'oblige de le défendre.[16]

Such cases are rare in the German records. There is one instance contained in an act of the emperor Henry VII whereby in 1312 he gave Manfred de Claromonte, count of Mohac, a fief of 200 *m.* for which Manfred promised to be his man and the man of his successors "contra omnem hominem, excepto dicto domino Frederico rege Trinacrie."[17]

It is clearly evident from the preceding examples that the *fief-rente* promoted the practice of multiple lordship.[18] For a man who needed to supplement his income and had certain services to offer, the number of *fiefs-rentes* he could hold was virtually unlimited. And gone forever was the day when the amount of land at a lord's disposal and geographical location could dictate the number of vassals a man might have. Such petty lords of the Low Countries as those of Cuyk, Montjoie and Fauquemont, La Mark, and Petersheim held *fiefs-rentes* from many Low Country princes, as well as from some Rhenish princes and from the kings of France and England; the pattern was the same for the great Low Country princes such as the dukes of Brabant and the counts of Hainaut. A few of the German princes held *fiefs-rentes* from the kings of France and England. The petty French lords held *fiefs-rentes* from the French kings and also from the greater French lords, who in turn held them from the kings; in addition, both lesser and greater French lords held them

---

[15] Kern, *Acta Imperii,* no. 307.

[16] M. J. Wolters, *Codex Diplomaticus Lossensis* (Gand, 1849), no. 316. For other examples see Appendix, nos. 5, 12, 19.

[17] Doenniges, *Acta Henrici VII,* p. 185.

[18] For other examples see Sczaniecki, *Essai,* p. 99.

from the English kings and from some of the Low Country rulers. So overwhelming is the evidence of multiple lordship in all the regions that only a few examples have been selected to show how many men, like the artist on the tightrope, managed to balance their way through complicated feudal relations and awkward situations so as to retain all their fiefs. Receiving in 1289 a fief of 40 *l.* from Guy, count of Flanders and marquis of Namur, the lords of Blankenheim were still holding a *fief-rente* from the counts of Namur in 1360. Meanwhile they were acquiring others. The archbishop of Cologne granted them one in 1300; in 1308 Count Henry VII of Luxemburg gave Gerard, lord of Blankenheim, a fief of 100 *l.* of small money of Tours; in 1322 John the Blind, king of Bohemia and count of Luxemburg, conceded Arnold of Blankenheim a fief of 40 *l.* of small money of Tours; and in 1326 the town of Cologne granted a fief of 40 *m.* to the lords of Blankenheim.[19] Recipients of even more fiefs were the lords of Montjoie and Fauquemont. In 1267 they received a fief of 200 *l.* from the dukes of Brabant which continued to be paid through the rest of the century; in 1286 the town of Cologne granted them a fief of 100 *m.*; in 1295 Walerand, lord of Fauquemont, received from Edward I of England a fief of 300 *l.* which was still being paid in the fourteenth century and was increased by Edward III in 1346 to 1,000 *m.*; Count Guy of Flanders donated a *fief-rente* to the lords in 1296; three years later the archbishop of Cologne gave them one of 300 *m.*; some time early in the fourteenth century the counts of Hainaut added another to the impressive collection; and finally, in 1372 the dukes of Guelders gave Walerand of Fauquemont a fief of "mille vies escus de boin or et juste de pois."[20]

---

[19] C. Piot, *Inventaire des chartes des comtes de Namur* (Bruxelles, 1890), no. 209; Lacomblet, *Urkundenbuch,* III, no. 4; Verkooren, *Inventaire des chartes et cartulaires du Luxembourg* (Bruxelles, 1914), nos. 481, 521; Wauters, *Table chronologique,* IX, 66; Ennen and Eckertz, *Quellen Stadt Köln,* IV, nos. 131, 214.

[20] Verkooren, *Inv. Brab.,* 2d pt., pp. 97, 145; Ennen and Eckertz, *Quellen Stadt Köln,* III, no. 265; *Foedera,* I, ii, 820; *C.P.R. 1343–45,* p. 49; *C.P.R. 1345–48,* p. 61; Wauters, *Table chronologique,* VI, 536; Lacomblet, *Urkundenbuch,* II, no. 1034; III, nos. 25–26; De Reiffenberg, *Monuments,* III, no. 265, p. 287; A.D.N., B. 276/10552. For other examples see Chantereau le Febvre, *Traité des fiefs,* Preuves, p. 196; Wauters, *Table chronologique,* IV, 481; V, 649; Van Den Bergh, *Gedenkstukken Nederlandsche Geschiedenis,* I, no. 41; De Reiffenberg, *Monuments,* I, no. 23, p. 116; *Foedera,* I,

For Flanders Dept's study has shown that numerous Flemish lords held *fiefs-rentes* from both the French and English kings in the years prior to the Battle of Bouvines (1214).[21] The counts of Namur typify the greater Low Country princes holding *fiefs-rentes* simultaneously. In 1202 John of England conceded Count Philip I of Namur a fief of 100 *m*. In the same year Duke Henry I of Brabant granted him one of 100 *m*. A fief of 100 *l*. came to Philip in 1204 from the bishop of Liège; it was reduced to 50 *m*. as a result of a subsequent agreement, but was still being paid in 1297. In 1327 William I, count of Hainaut and Holland, granted a fief of 600 *l*. to Guy, future count of Namur. Three years later Count John I of Namur was given a fief of 300 *l*. by Louis de Nevers, count of Flanders. In 1335 Count Guy II of Namur received a fief of 400 *m*. from Edward III of England. And in 1347 Philip VI of France granted a fief of 1,000 *l*. to Count William I of Namur.[22]

---

ii, 820; II, ii, 1102, 1104; *C.Cl.R. 1330–33,* pp. 354, 495; *C.Cl.R. 1333–37,* pp. 5, 31, 217, 264, 392, 428, 446, 573, 610; *C.Cl.R. 1341–43,* pp. 393, 606.

[21] Dept, *Influences,* pp. 52 ff.

[22] *Rot. Lib.,* p. 29; Verkooren, *Inv. Brab.,* 2d pt., p. 38; Wauters, *Table chronologique,* III, 179; VI, 589; IX, 369; Poncelet, *Actes des princes-évêques de Liège Hugues de Pierrepont* (Bruxelles, 1941), nos. 23, 58, 59; S. Bormans and E. Schoolmeesters, *Cartulaire de l'église Saint-Lambert de Liège* (Bruxelles, 1893), I, nos. 98–101; Walraet, *Actes de Philippe Ier,* nos. 7, 17–18; De Reiffenberg, *Monuments,* I, no. 55, p. 76; *Foedera,* II, ii, 920 –21; Bovesse, *B.C.R.H.,* XIV (1949), nos. 18, 20. The following evidence is for other Low Country and French nobles. Luxemburg: Wauters, *Table chronologique,* IV, 226 and V, 41–42; J. de Saint-Genois, *Monuments anciens* (Paris, 1782), II, 673; Chantereau le Febvre, *Traité des fiefs,* Preuves, p. 267; Kern, *Acta Imperii,* no. 90. Limburg: Ennen and Eckertz, *Quellen Stadt Köln,* II, nos. 205, 456. Guelders: Ennen and Eckertz, *Quellen Stadt Köln,* II, no. 481 and III, no. 485; Kern, *Acta Imperii,* nos. 28, 80; Van Den Bergh, *Gedenkstukken Nederlandsche Geschiedenis,* I, nos. 38, 40; De Saint-Genois, *Monuments,* II, 854; Lacomblet, *Urkundenbuch,* III, nos. 830, 839; *Foedera,* II, ii, 1090. Hugh le Brun XI, count of La Marche and Angoulême, held a fief of 60 *l*. from Alphonse of Poitiers in 1249. He also had a fief of 300 *m*. from Henry III of England which had been granted to his father Hugh X in 1224. Geoffrey of Joinville, receiving a fief of 200 *l*. from Louis IX of France in 1252, also acquired one of 60 *m*. in 1254 from Henry III of England (G. Thomas, *Cartulaire des comtes de La Marche et d'Angoulême,* Angoulême, 1934, no. 13; *Pat. R. 1216–25,* p. 436; *C.P.R. 1247–58,* p. 35; *R.G.,* I, nos. 321, 3897; *C.L.R. 1245–51,* pp. 263, 268, 279, 287, 447; J. J. Champollion Figeac, *Documents historiques inédits,* Paris, 1841, I, 620; *R.G.,* I, no. 4143; *C.P.R. 1247–58,* p. 544; *Cl.R. 1254–56,* pp. 211–

It would be wrong to assume from the foregoing evidence that the multiple holding of *fiefs-rentes* worked smoothly; it did so only during the infrequent periods of peace. In many instances the very nature of the obligations imposed by some *fiefs-rentes* forecast that the vassal could never live peaceably with his lords; more often than not he found himself having to make a reservation of his loyalties and having to lose one or more of his fiefs. If forced to choose between a *fief-rente* and a fief of land, he usually considered the latter more valuable and would forfeit his *fief-rente*. If the choice was between two *fiefs-rentes,* he would generally keep the one giving him the greater income and benefits. Undoubtedly his choice was also governed by an evaluation of the lords' power and chances of success in hostilities. From 1200 to 1214 when John of England and Philip Augustus of France bribed hundreds of men in the Low Countries and southwestern France with *fiefs-rentes,* the *status quo* of feudal relations was upset. Men shifted their loyalty back and forth so rapidly that their feudal relations became a tangled skein. Because Dept has traced in great detail the fortunes of many of the Flemish lords who held of both John and Philip, we shall cite here only a few examples.[23] Around 1202 Geoffrey de Sottegem received a *fief-rente* from John; in 1208 he acquired one of 80 *l.* from Philip and had to forfeit his other fief. In 1212 John sent envoys with letters close to various Flemish lords promising to restore their *fiefs-rentes* if they would serve him and break with Philip. Geoffrey was one of the men approached. The Mise Roll of 1213 shows that Geoffrey and others accepted John's offer, for it records the payment of their *fiefs-rentes* in September of that year. Philip immediately confiscated their fiefs held of him.[24] Adam de Wallencourt and William, *châtelain* of Saint-Omer, also forfeited their *fiefs-rentes* held from Philip upon doing homage for ones granted by John.[25] The same feudal fluctuations occurred in southwestern France, though on a lesser scale. In 1200 Savaric de Mauléon received from John a fief of 200 *l.* of Anjou, forfeited it when he joined Philip Augustus, and later re-

---

12). Sczaniecki gives a list of lords holding *fiefs-rentes* not only of French lords but also of the French and English kings (*Essai,* pp. 99–100).

[23] Dept, *Influences,* pp. 74–96, 107–15; Pièces justificatives, no. 3; Appendices, no. 1.

[24] Lyon, *E.H.R.,* LXVI, 166.

[25] *Ibid.,* p. 166.

ceived it back from John and continued to hold it until 1233. In 1226 William l'Archevêque regained the fief of 100 m. forfeited during John's reign when he went over to Philip Augustus.[26]

When the bitter quarrel between Count Guy of Flanders and Philip IV of France resulted in war, many men had to decide which of their liege lords they should support. In the following period of flux men continually lost their land or *fiefs-rentes* because at a particular moment they happened to be on the losing side. These cases are typical of many about 1297. In a letter of 14 June 1297 John, lord of Harecourt, notified Guy that he was renouncing his rights to the fief of 300 *l.* held of Guy and that he had withdrawn from his homage. He stated that his first loyalty was to Philip IV and that his support must go to the king of France in the war against Guy; furthermore, that as proof of what he had said he was sending back to Guy the letters containing the grant of the *fief-rente*. On 21 June 1297 Baldwin, lord of Fontaine, renounced all his rights to a fief of 60 *l.* held of Guy for the past three years and declared that he was the loyal ally of the king of France and the enemy of Guy.[27]

Such decisions and shifts became common in the years leading up to and during the Hundred Years' War. In 1304 Philip IV of France granted Duke John II of Brabant a fief of 2,500 *l.*; in 1332 Philip VI confirmed it while concluding an alliance with Duke John III. But in 1333 John concluded an alliance with Edward III of England and forfeited his fief held of Philip. In 1339, however, Edward gave him one of 1,500 *l.*[28] From 1297 the counts of Hainaut had held a fief of 6,000 *l.* from the French kings; it was scrupulously paid down almost until the middle of the fifteenth century. Only at one period did the counts of Hainaut fail to receive their yearly installments; in

---

[26] Mauléon: *Rot. Norm.*, p. 28; *Pat. R. 1225–32*, pp. 229, 234; *C.L.R. 1226–40*, pp. 91, 108, 127; *Cl.R. 1231–34*, p. 199. Archevêque: *Pat. R. 1225 –32*, pp. 102, 396; W. W. Shirley, *Royal and Other Historical Letters Illustrative of the Reign of Henry III* (London, 1862), I, no. 248.

[27] Lyon, *R.B.P.H.*, XXXII, 430–31. For other such cases see Funck-Brentano, *Philippe le Bel*, pp. 215–22; J. F. Verbruggen, *De Slag der Gulden Sporen* (Antwerpen, 1952), pp. 213–37. See also H. Nowé, *La bataille des éperons d'or* (Bruxelles, 1945), pp. 47–50. See Appendix, no. 18.

[28] *Foedera*, II, ii, 749, 799, 928, 974, 981, 985, 989, 1103, 1244; Jean de Klerk, *Les gestes des ducs de Brabant*, ed. J. F. Willems (Bruxelles, 1839), Codex Diplomaticus, I, nos. 174, 176, 179. See also De Sturler, *Relations politiques*, pp. 321–48. See Appendix, no. 23.

the years following 1328 when Count William I was a partisan of
Edward III of England there is no record of payment of the fief. Not
until 1343, when William II deserted Edward, is there evidence that
this fief was restored to the counts of Hainaut.[29] John of Hainaut,
lord of Beaumont and brother of Count William I, was granted a fief
of 1,000 *l.* by Edward III in 1327 and received it yearly until 1346
when he switched his support to Philip VI who gave him a fief of
3,000 *l.* ; Edward immediately pronounced forfeiture.[30] A similar fate
befell the *fiefs-rentes* of the dukes of Guelders and counts of Juliers
when they left Philip for Edward.[31]

Homage could be done for *fiefs-rentes* in person or by proxy. In
the eleventh and twelfth centuries, when few were granted, homage
was generally done in person regardless of where the grantor and
grantee lived. For instance, in 1103, 1110, and 1163 the Flemish
counts went to Dover and did homage to the English kings in the
presence of English and Flemish witnesses. Also in 1163 the vassals
of the Flemish count did homage to Henry II for *fiefs-rentes* held of
him. In 1172 Count Baldwin V of Hainaut and six of his vassals
went to Henry II in Normandy to do homage for *fiefs-rentes*.[32] If
both grantor and grantee were men of the Continent, it was easier
to arrange for doing homage in person.[33] But even among the lords

---

[29] Lyon, *R.B.P.H.*, XXXII, 431.

[30] *C.P.R. 1327–30*, p. 10 ; *C.Cl.R. 1341–43*, p. 437 ; *C.Cl.R. 1343–46*, p.
175 ; L. Devillers, *Cartulaire des comtes de Hainaut* (Bruxelles, 1881), I,
nos. 153–54, 170, 186. See also Zeper, *Jan van Henegouwen*, pp. 95 ff., 283 ff.

[31] For example, in 1338 Philip ordered that Count William of Juliers
should not be paid the arrears of his *fief-rente* "quia est inimicus Regis, et
reddidit ei homagium suum ut dicitur" (Viard, *Journaux du trésor Philippe
VI*, no. 5295). In 1370 Robert of Namur received from Edward III of England a fief of "600 florins with the shield [for] homage and fealty done by
him to the king and in compensation of an annual rent which he had for life
of Charles, the king's adversary of France, with the king's license, which rent
he has surrendered on account of such homage done to the king" (*C.P.R.
1367–70*, p. 389). See also *C.P.R. 1377–81*, pp. 184, 187 ; *Foedera*, III, ii,
1050.

[32] Vercauteren, *Actes de Flandre*, nos. 30, 41 ; Delisle, *Recueil des actes
Henri II*, I, no. 152.

[33] Brunel, *Actes de Pontieu*, nos. 139, 180 ; Chantereau le Febvre, *Traité
des fiefs*, Preuves, pp. 17, 125, 207 ; *Layettes*, I, nos. 1355–56, II, nos. 2020,
2053, 2926, 2986 ; Viard, *Revue des Questions Historiques*, LIX, 352–55. See
also Butkens, *Trophées*, Preuves, pp. 96–97, 103 ; L. A. J. W. Sloet, *Oorkondenboek der Graafschappen Gelre en Zutfen* ('s-Gravenhage, 1872), no.

of the Continent the practice of receiving or doing homage by proxy became common. In 1298, for example, Ralph of Clermont, constable of France, received in the name of Philip IV the homage of John de Hangest for a fief of 520 l.; the next year he received the homage of Baldwin de Hazebrouck. In 1260 the seneschal of Saintonge received in the name of Alphonse of Poitiers the homage of a certain Henry Orenous de Marcillé for a fief of 20 l.[34] In 1299 Count Guy of Flanders gave to Albert, lord of Clingberg, a fief of 100 l.; Guy's eldest son John I, count of Namur, received the homage for this fief.[35]

At the outset of the thirteenth century the English kings began to rely heavily on the proxy method. Like their contemporaries, they became ever more burdened with the growing tasks of governing and had less time for such functions as receiving homage. Moreover, almost all the fiefs granted by the kings were to men on the Continent and after John's loss of Normandy and Anjou, when they visited the Continent less frequently, the receiving of homage in person became more arduous. Homage was still done to them in person when they went to the Continent and men continued to go to England to do homage, but henceforth most homage for *fiefs-rentes* was done by proxy. John empowered such men as William Longespée, Hugh Boves the mercenary captain, Reginald de Dammartin of Boulogne, and the Flemish lords Adam Keret and William Cresec to secure vassals by means of the *fief-rente*, to receive the homage for the fiefs, and to give the recipients letters patent as official record of the transactions.[36] Henry III empowered his lieutenants in Gascony to grant fiefs to the men of that region and to receive their homage.[37]

535; De Saint-Genois, *Monuments*, II, 675–76, 680–81; Brouwers, *Chartes et règ.*, II, nos. 345, 361–62, 364, 366; Doenniges, *Acta Henrici VII*, p. 185; V. F. de Gudenus, *Codex Diplomaticus* (Frankfurt, 1768), pp. 626–27; W. Sauer, *Nassauisches Urkundenbuch* (Wiesbaden, 1885), I, i, no. 484; J. M. Lappenberg, *Hamburgisches Urkundenbuch* (Hamburg, 1842), I, no. 119; Ilgen, *Quellen Rheinischen Territorien*, I, ii, no. 13.

[34] Sczaniecki, *Essai*, p. 107.

[35] A. Kluit, *Historia Critica Comitatus Hollandiae et Zeelandiae* (Leiden, 1777), I, i, no. 380; A.D.N., B. 1266/4138; De Saint-Genois, *Monuments*, II, 880.

[36] *Rot. Pat.*, pp. 10, 11 b–12, 93; *Rot. Claus.*, I, 119; *Foedera*, I, i, 86.

[37] The Gascon Rolls contain numerous letters empowering such royal officials as the seneschals to receive homage in the royal name.

The resumption of active military and diplomatic participation in continental affairs by Edward I and Edward III compelled them to accomplish much of their business through envoys who were given *carte blanche* to act in the royal name. Royal embassies constantly traveled up and down the Rhine, and between the courts and towns of the Low Countries, granting *fiefs-rentes* and receiving homage. Richard II and the three Henrys received homage almost exclusively by proxy. It was thus that feudal relations were established with the dukes of Bavaria, the counts of La Mark, and the archbishops of Cologne.[38] Just as the English kings conducted business through royal agents, so some of the German princes sent officially accredited ambassadors to England in the fifteenth century to bargain for *fiefs-rentes* and, if successful, to do homage in their name. In 1438 Henry, bishop of Münster, sent three men to England with powers to negotiate with Henry VI. They were, if possible, to obtain a *fief-rente* and then to use their power of attorney "ad faciendum, et prestandum, pro nobis Henrico episcopo prefato et nomine nostro, prefato domino regi homagium."[39] Besides facilitating homage for a single fief, the system of proxy enabled a lord to do homage for his own *fief-rente* and also for those held by his vassals from his lord.[40] Simplifying some of the routine work, as it did, homage by proxy was used by all lords and vassals when it suited their purposes. In all cases, however, the lords insisted that the homage and fealty be done

[38] The following letters patent of Edward III dated 1341 show how these envoys functioned: "Rex etc. Sciatis quod nos, de fidelitate et circumspectione dilectorum et fidelium nostrorum, Johannis Darcy, Reginaldi de Cobham, et Walteri de Manny confidentes, ad tractandum et concordandum, pro nobis et nostro nomine, cum dilecto nobis Amadeo domino Aule Nove milite de mora sua nobiscum contra nobis adversantes, facienda, ac feodum, vadia et remunerationem congruam sibi constituendum; et ea, que sic per eos facta fuerint, sufficienti securitate firmandum, prefatis [envoys] ... plenam, tenore presentium, concedimus et committimus potestatem" (*Foedera*, II, ii, 1176). See also *Foedera*, II, ii, 1191 ; III, i, 312 ; *Foedera* (1704–35), IX, 660 ; X, 161–63. For the dukes of Bavaria see *Foedera* (1704–35), VIII, 854, 858, 859 ; IX, 715 ; "Calendar of Diplomatic Documents," in *D.K.R.*, I, i, 312 ; P.R.O., Diplomatic Documents of the Exchequer, E. 30/1375, 1508. Mark: *Foedera* (1704–35), X, 700, 745 ; "Calendar of French Rolls," in *D.K.R.*, XLVIII, app., 332. Cologne: *Foedera* (1704–35), VIII, 2–3 ; IX, 346 ; X, 161–63, 626, 834.

[39] *Foedera* (1704–35), X, 698–70 ; "Dip. Doc. Exch.," in *L.I.*, no. 49, p. 46.

[40] *Rot. Pat.*, pp. 11 b–12 ; *Pat. R. 1225–32*, pp. 99–100.

to and by accredited men, and that there be an official record of the transactions.

It was common everywhere for the more important lords to compile records of all the fiefs held of them; these feudal registers, together with various enactments, litigation, and legal pronouncements bear witness that homage was regarded as essential for the *fief-rente* as for the ordinary fief.[41] In 1213 when Simon de Montfort assigned a fief of 500 *l.* to Adam Cheverel, it was granted under the obligation of homage; so, too, was another *fief-rente* granted by Simon in 1218 to Bertrand de Gourdon. In 1286 John de Harecourt withheld payment of a fief of 200 *l.* to the countess of Dreux because she had not done homage upon coming into possession of it; he agreed to make payment once the countess had performed the homage.[42] In 1293 John of Avesnes, count of Hainaut, granted the knight John de Bar a fief of 200 *l.* with the penalty that if "lidis cuens de Bar, qui adont seroit, ne voloit faire homage au conte de Haynnau et à ses oirs, si com dit est, lidis fiés revenroit au conte de Haynnau et à ses hoirs, contes de Haynnau."[43] In a judgment handed down by the *parlement* of Paris in 1280 it was ruled that the fief of 80 *l.* taken on the royal coffers by William de la Mure would not be paid because he had failed to do homage. In litigation of 1313 between John Teisson and Henry d'Avangour over payment of a fief "de

---

[41] See, for example, Poncelet, *Livre des fiefs*; C. de Borman, *Le livre des fiefs du comté de Looz sous Jean d'Arckel* (Bruxelles, 1875); L. Galesloot, *Le livre des feudataires de Jean III, duc de Brabant* (Bruxelles, 1865); A.G.R., Galesloot, *Inventaire des archives de la cour féodale de Brabant* (Bruxelles, 1870–84), I, no. 4; S. Bormans, *Les fiefs du comté de Namur* (Namur, 1882); C. J. Kremer, *Akademische Beiträge zur Gülch- und Bergischen Geschichte* (Mannheim, 1769), I, nos. 27, 37; H. Beyer, L. Eltester, A. Goerz, *Urkundenbuch der mittelrheinischen Territorien* (Coblenz, 1865), II, 467–73; L. F. C. von der Brügghen, *Die Lehensregister der Propsteilichen Mannkammer des Aachener Marienstifts 1394–1794* (Bonn, 1952), pp. 178, 247, 298–99, 430–31; G. Hertel, *Die ältesten Lehnbücher der Magdeburgischen Erzbischöfe* (Halle, 1883). See Plate V.

[42] A. Molinier, "Catalogue des actes de Simon et d'Amauri de Montfort," *Biblio. de l'École des Chartes,* XXXIV (1873), nos. 74, 154; G. A. de la Roque, *Histoire généalogique de la maison de Harcourt* (Paris, 1662), III, 215–17.

[43] De Reiffenberg, *Monuments,* I, no. 76, p. 429. For other examples from the Low Countries see H. Laurent and F. Quicke, "Documents pour servir à l'histoire de la maison de Bourgogne en Brabant et en Limbourg (fin du XIVe siècle)," *B.C.R.H.,* XCVII (1933), nos. 1, 4, 6.

ducentis minis frumenti," Henry argued that the fief should revert to him because of John's failure to do homage. Henry's argument was based on the feudal custom of Brittany that entailed homage to be done for a fief when coming into possession of it. But, strangely enough, the court ruled that "secundum consuetudinem ducatus Normannie" no performance of homage was required.[44]

Although no evidence of a time limit set on the performance of homage can be found in England and Germany, there are cases in France and the Low Countries where homage had to be done within a certain period. In 1230, for example, Count Theobald IV of Champagne, conceding a fief of 30 *l.* to Guy, lord of Arcis, stipulated that Guy had to do homage within a year or payment of the fief would be stopped. In 1405 Charles VI of France insisted that the heirs of Reginald, duke of Guelders, must do homage within three months for their *fief-rente*. In 1296 when Count Guy of Flanders granted Henry, lord of Blamont, a fief of 100 *l.* homage was to be done also within three months.[45]

As with the ordinary fief, homage had to be done for a *fief-rente* whenever there was a change in the lord or the vassal through death or through alienation. A certain John de Boissière, holding a fief of 55 *l.* from the bishop of Paris, sold 15 *l.* of it in 1225 to William Barbete who then did homage to the bishop. In 1239 Hugh d'Antigny, lord of Pagny, did homage to Count Theobald IV of Champagne for a fief of 140 *l.* on the fairs of Bar formerly belonging to the late lord, Gerard de Vienne.[46] To supplement the *livres des fiefs* of the Low Countries there are also concessions showing that when a

[44] Boutaric, *Actes du parlement de Paris* (Paris, 1863), I, no. 2274; Beugnot, *Les olim ou registres des arrêts* (Paris, 1848), II, 608. Philip VI of France withheld payment of fiefs on numerous occasions because he had not received homage. In 1338–39 the heirs of a certain John of Brabant failed to do homage for a *fief-rente* with the following result: "Tamen, nichil ei solvatur, donec constet de homagio, quia interim dictus redditus est Regis." In one instance the count of Geneva, having finally done the required homage, was permitted to receive the arrears due him (Viard, *Journaux du trésor Philippe VI*, nos. 5220, 5376, 5498).

[45] Chantereau le Febvre, *Traité des fiefs*, Preuves, p. 207; Lacomblet, *Urkundenbuch*, IV, no. 35; De Saint-Genois, *Monuments*, II, 859–60.

[46] Guérard, *Cartulaire de l'église Notre-Dame de Paris* (Paris, 1840), I, no. 48; M. H. d'Arbois de Jubainville, *Histoire des ducs et des comtes de Champagne* (Paris, 1863), V, no. 2512; Chantereau le Febvre, *Traité des fiefs*, Preuves, p. 241. See also *Layettes*, II, no. 2810; V, nos. 408, 411.

man came into possession of a fief his homage was required.[47] In 1273 when Countess Margaret of Flanders granted Jakemon Louchard, citizen of Arras, a fief of 200 *l.*, she promised that if Jakemon ever desired to give this fief to any of his children she would receive them as her liege men. In 1286 her successor, Count Guy of Flanders, received the homage of Jeanne, daughter of Jakemon, for the fief recently given to her by Jakemon.[48] In England we find Hugh de Courtenay, son of Countess Isabelle d'Albe Marle, informing the exchequer in 1297–98 that the sheriff of Devonshire had always paid the countess "de annuo feodo suo" 18 *l.* 6 *s.* 18 *d.* and that as her legal heir he should also receive the fief. The officers of the exchequer, having determined that Hugh had done homage to the king for the fief, ordered that henceforth the sheriff of Devon should pay the installments out of the issues of his county.[49]

Following customary feudal practice, the guardian did homage for the *fief-rente* when the legal heir was a minor. In 1269 Jeanne, the widow of Peter Preton, did homage to Alphonse of Poitiers for a fief of 20 *l.* with the stipulation that when the heirs of Peter became of legal age they would do homage for the fief. In 1250, while yet a minor, Matilda, the daughter of Conrad of Mulenark, inherited his fief of 100 *l.* held from the duke of Brabant. As her guardian, Count Walerand of Juliers did homage for the fief.[50]

Concerning the investiture of a man with a *fief-rente* we have only such evidence as follows. In 1270 the lord John de Los alienated to Peter de la Brosse a fief of 30 *l.* : "me de predicto redditu desesivi in manu ballivi Vernolii, et eumdem ballivum loco et nomine dicti Petri de predicto redditu investivi et sesivi."[51] We know that investiture by

---

[47] The following entry in Bormans, *Les fiefs du comté de Namur,* is typical : "Li sires de Blans Mons tient en fief do conte de Namur CC lievrees de terres, à tournois petis . . . sor les rentes de Namur. . . . Desqueiles CC lievrees de terres li dis sires de Blans mons est en la feialteit et hommage dou conte de Namur" (p. 22). See Plate V.

[48] De Saint-Genois, *Monuments,* II, 639, 733, 738; A.E.G., De Saint Genois, *Inv. Fl.,* no. 175. See Appendix, no. 1.

[49] P.R.O., L.T.R. Memoranda Rolls, E. 368/69.

[50] Sczaniecki, *Essai,* p. 106; Butkens, *Trophées,* Preuves, p. 91; Lacomblet, *Urkundenbuch,* III, 830.

[51] *Layettes,* IV, no. 5686. See also no. 5606. In 1211 Ralph Goujon surrendered his rights to a fief of 40 *l.* held from Philip Augustus. Later the son of Ralph was permitted to come into possession of it: "Ad preces et peticionem ejusdem Radulfi, filium ejus, Radulfum, de predictis quadraginta libris

proxy was normal procedure.[52] But as for evidence describing the ceremony, unfortunately there is none; one can only assume that it resembled the ceremony customary for the ordinary fief except that the vassal would more likely receive an advance payment or a regular installment for his fief to signify formal possession instead of some symbolic object like a stick or a piece of turf. Generally as soon as the vassal had received investiture, he was given all or part of the annual installment; if not, he was given written evidence that certain revenues would be paid on a designated date. The Mise and Prest Rolls for John's reign show that knights often came from the Continent to England, were invested with *fiefs-rentes,* and then received an advance payment.[53]

Whatever form of tenure may have applied to the ordinary fief during the formative period of feudalism, by the thirteenth century the principle of heritability had been firmly established throughout western Europe. Be the source a feudal register of the Low Countries, the German *Sachenspiegel,* the English lawyer Bracton, or the French Beaumanoir, all are agreed that the word *feudum* implied heritability. Was it not natural, then, that this form of tenure should also be applied to the *fief-rente* whose development lay in the period when heritability was establishing itself as the principal tenure? The records of France and the Low Countries in particular emphasize that *feudum* conveyed the idea of heritability. In 1206–7 Philip Augustus granted a fief of 20 *l.* "Guillelmo Havart et heredi ejus masculo de uxore sua desponsata, ... ad usus et consuetudines Normannie."[54] In the *livres des fiefs* of Brabant are such entries as the following. Godfrey, the son of a certain Baldwin, received from Duke

---

... ad vitam suam investivimus" (Delisle, *Cart. normand,* no. 1108). For other examples see Doenniges, *Acta Henrici VII,* I, 24; Gudenus, *Codex Diplomaticus,* V, 864–65, 979–80.

[52] In 1299 Count Guy of Flanders granted a fief of 100 *l.* to Albert, lord of Clingberg. Albert received investiture from Guy's son John I, count of Namur (Kluit, *Historia Critica,* I, i, no. 380; De Saint-Genois, *Monuments,* II, 880). The English kings granted their representatives power to grant *fiefs-rentes* and receive the homage, and also to invest the vassals with the fiefs.

[53] *Rot. Mis. (1209–10),* p. 166; *Rot. Praest.,* pp. 186, 208, 241.

[54] Delisle, *Cart. normand,* no. 1084; L. A. Léchaudé-d'Anisy, *Scaccarium Normannie sub Regibus Francie* (Mémoires de la Société des Antiquaires de Normandie, Sér. 2, vol. V, Paris, 1846), p. 157. For other examples see *Layettes,* I, no. 441; II, nos. 1653, 2035, 2053; III, no. 4109; Brunel, *Actes de Pontieu,* nos. 139, 187, 288; D'Arbois de Jubainville, *Histoire de Cham-*

John III "XX libras in feodum hereditarie tendendas de eodum jure feodali brabantino." Gomprecht de Gherstorp held 65 *écus* "a duce et suis heredibus per eum et suos heredes imperpetuum jure brabantino in feodo."[55] In Germany heritable *fiefs-rentes* were granted by the emperors as well as by the lesser lords and princes. In 1219 Frederick II granted a fief of 300 *l.* to Godfrey, count of Blandrata and his heirs. In 1293 King Adolf conceded to Godfrey von Eppenstein and to "heredibus suis legitimis" a fief of 25 *m.* In 1279 Bishop Frederick of Speyer granted a fief of 5 *l.* to Raymond von Offenbach stating that upon Raymond's death his son, if of legal estate, should inherit the fief. All the records of the princes along the Rhine afford like examples.[56] Every *fief-rente* granted by the English kings in the eleventh and twelfth centuries was heritable; in the following three centuries, even though *fiefs-rentes* came to be governed more and more by other types of tenure, heritable fiefs can still be found. The fief of the counts of Flanders was heritable; so too was that of the counts of Hainaut. John gave heritable *fiefs-rentes* to Count Robert of Dreux, Counts Theobald and Henry of Bar, Count William I of

pagne, V, 220; *Recueil historiens France,* XXI, 263, 518–19; A. Du Chesne, *Histoire généalogique de la maison de Béthune* (Paris, 1639), p. 185.

[55] Galesloot, *Feudataires de Jean III,* pp. 62, 75. A.G.R., Galesloot, *Cour féodale,* I, no. 4, Spechtboek: "Willem van Saijne hout achthondert gulden siaers rijnssche ... ende houden tot enen erfleen vanden hertoge van Brabant" (fol. 15r); "Peter van Magrey ende Marie van Lobbewairt houden 11 *l.* ouder grote siaers erfleliker renten" (fol. 28r); "Jan van Oppem heren Jans soen ... hout ... XL swaer gulden siaers erffelic ..." (fol. 31r). For other examples see Butkens, *Trophées,* Preuves, pp. 150, 162, 164, 183, 187; Verkooren, *Inv. Brab.,* nos. 117, 150, 371, 640; Quicke, "Une enquête sur les droits et revenus du duc de Limbourg, seigneur de Dalhem et des Pays d'Outremeuse (1389–1393)," *B.C.R.H.,* XCVI (1932), 370, 380. For Flanders see De Saint-Genois, *Monuments,* II, 639, 675–76, 680, 692. There are dozens of cases in A.G.R., *Trés. Fl.,* Sér. I; A.E.G., collections of De Saint Genois, Gaillard, and Diegerick; A.D.N., Sér. B. For Namur see Brouwers, *Chartes et règ.,* II, 364–67, 488, 507; A.E.N., Piot, *Inv. Namur,* nos. 591, 597, 604 ff. There is also evidence for Hainaut, Luxemburg, Liège, Holland, and Guelders.

[56] E. Winkelmann, *Acta Imperii Inedita* (Innsbruck, 1885), I, no. 158; Böhmer, *Acta Imperii Selecta,* no. 455; Böhmer, *Urkundenbuch der Reichsstadt Frankfurt,* I, 280; A. Hilgard, *Urkunden zur Geschichte der Stadt Speyer* (Strassburg, 1885), no. 396. See also J. W. C. Roth, *Die Geschichtsquellen des Niederrheingau's* (Wiesbaden, 1880), I, ii, no. 60; P. Hasse, *Schleswig-Holstein-Lauenburgische Regesten und Urkunden* (Hamburg, 1886), II, no. 862. See Appendix, nos. 1, 2, 5, 13, 15, 23, 24, 25.

Holland, and numerous others. In the fourteenth and fifteenth centuries heritable fiefs were conceded to the dukes of Guelders and the counts of Namur, La Mark, and Juliers.[57]

Upon the death of a man holding a *fief-rente,* the principle of primogeniture was customarily applied, the fief descending intact to the eldest son. We have previously seen that the grant of Philip Augustus to William Havart in 1206–7 stipulated that the fief would descend to a legitimate male heir. In 1211 a fief of 40 *l.* held of Philip Augustus by Ralph Goujon passed to his eldest son. In a grant of either 1200 or 1207 the count of Pontieu stipulated that if the heirs of a certain grantee were to receive the fief there must be a male heir.[58] Other French evidence shows that the concessions specified heirs of a direct line or at times of a collateral line.[59] Primogeniture was the rule in every principality of the Low Countries; it prevailed in Rhenish Germany; it is found wherever the English kings granted *fiefs-rentes.*[60] Why it was deemed advisable to apply primo-

---

[57] Besides these important princes numerous minor lords held heritable fiefs. In 1242 Ebulus de Rocheford was granted a fief of 100 *l.* "pro se et heredibus suis" (*R.G.,* I, no. 311). In 1337 William van Duvenvoorde was given 500 *l.* sterling "a tenir en fee et en homage de nostre dit seignur ... par sire William, et par ses heirs, desusditz, perpetuelment a touz jours" (*Foedera,* II, ii, 973).

[58] Delisle, *Cart. normand,* nos. 1084, 1108; Brunel, *Actes de Pontieu,* no. 180. See also Funck-Brentano, "Philippe le Bel et la noblesse Franc-Comtoise," *Biblio. de l'École des Chartes,* XLIX (1888), no. X.

[59] Count Theobald IV of Champagne granted to Hugh, lord of Ulrin, a fief of 80 *l.* in 1224; Hugh did homage and recognized "quod si forsitan contingeret me quod absit, decedere sine haerede de corpore meo procreato, dictae octoginta lib. ad praedictum Comitem, vel haeredes suos libere deuenirent" (Chantereau le Febvre, *Traité des fiefs,* Preuves, p. 162). A fief of 50 *l.* granted by Louis IX in 1248 to Jacques de Levant of Genoa had by 1256 been inherited by his brother Simon (Sczaniecki, *Essai,* p. 147).

[60] Low Countries: A.G.R., *Trés. Fl.,* Sér. I, no. 2075; A.E.G., De Saint Genois, *Inv. Fl.,* no. 101; Butkens, *Trophées,* Preuves, p. 100; A.G.R., Galesloot, *Cour féodale,* I, no. 123, fol. 143ᵛ; no. 572, fol. 54ᵛ; Galesloot, *Feudataires de Jean III*; De Borman, *Le livre des fiefs*; A.E.N., Piot, *Inv. Namur,* nos. 709, 759, 760; Bormans, *Fiefs de Namur,* pp. 90, 92 ff. Germany: Sauer, *Nassauisches Urkundenbuch,* I, ii, no. 906; F. X. Remling, *Urkundenbuch zur Geschichte der Bischöfe zu Speyer* (Mainz, 1852), I, no. 396; Lacomblet, *Urkundenbuch,* II, no. 864; III, no. 26. England: R. G., I, nos. 321, 3897; *C.L.R. 1226–40,* pp. 78, 134, 167, 188, 219, 349, 503; *Cl.R. 1227–31,* p. 431; *Cl.R. 1251–53,* p. 144; *C.P.R. 1350–54,* p. 344; *Rot. Claus.,* I, 603. See Appendix, nos. 11, 23.

geniture will be discussed later when we come to study the functions of the *fief-rente*. For the present it is sufficient to point out that it was easier for the lord to pay all the money to one man and make him solely responsible for whatever service might be required; with the ordinary fief this concentration of responsibility in one man had always proved most efficient. Although some grants stipulated that if a man should leave no male heirs the fief should revert back to the lord,[61] wherever one looks he can find numerous cases where women inherited *fiefs-rentes,* received them as the original recipient, and did homage for them.[62] Again, this was a practice which had become common with the ordinary fief. For France, Sczaniecki has shown that if the widow of a vassal holding a *fief-rente* did not inherit the fief *in toto,* according to feudal custom she usually received half of it as her dowry; she could also act as guardian if the heir was a minor.[63] Indivisibility of *fiefs-rentes,* though common to all the regions, was strictly applied only by the English kings.[64] There is nothing to suggest that they permitted the *fief-rente* to be held in parage or partitioned in any manner. On the Continent both parage

---

[61] In 1230, for example, the count of Provence granted a fief of 50 *l.* to John Ebriac and his male heirs (F. Benoit, *Recueil des actes des comtes de Provence,* Paris, 1925, II, no. 414). See also Sczaniecki, *Essai,* p. 148; Langlois, *Philippe le Hardi,* p. 432.

[62] France: Fawtier, *Comptes du trésor,* no. 1529: "Domina Johanna, soror Regis Navarre, pro pensione sibi ordinata super redditu defuncti Philippi de Navarra, videlicet pro medietate de 1564 *l.* 17 *s.* par., quas idem dominus Philippus percipere solebat in Thesauro." The fief held of the French kings by the counts of Hainaut occasionally was inherited by their wives or female heirs. In 1352 Countess Margaret did homage to King John for the fief of 4,000 *l.* Jacqueline of Bavaria, countess of Hainaut, was still in receipt of the fief of 4,000 *l.* in 1429 (Devillers, *Cart. de Hainaut,* I, no. 218; V, nos. 1659, 1827). Germany: In 1278 Elizabeth, the widow of Count Henry of Saarwerden, came into possession of a fief of 100 *m.* formerly held by Henry of the archbishop of Trier (Goerz, *Regesten der Erzbischöfe zu Trier von Hetti bis Johann II. 814–1503,* Trier, 1861, p. 54). In 1352 the daughters of a certain Hans Apetey received from Volkmar von Vorsfelde a fief of 4 *m.* formerly possessed by their father (Bode, *Urkundenbuch der Stadt Goslar,* IV, no. 469). England: Two countesses of Flanders, Jeanne (1202–44) and Margaret (1244–78), did homage to Henry III and Edward I for *fiefs-rentes.* In 1242 Henry III granted Juliana, the wife of William of Kingcsham a fief of 10 *m.* (*R.G.,* I, no. 1088).

[63] *Essai,* p. 148.

[64] In 1229, for example, having received a fief of 140 *l.* from Count Theobald IV of Champagne, the count of Chaalons recognized that "neque ego,

and partitioning can be found,[65] but by the last quarter of the four-teenth century fiefs could not be held in parage from the French kings.[66]

However much the tenure of heritability governed the *fief-rente,* it was not always the dominant form in all the regions. It prevailed in Germany throughout the Middle Ages almost to the exclusion of other tenures.[67] It prevailed six to one over other forms of tenure in all the states of the Low Countries except Hainaut where Didier found more life *fiefs-rentes* than heritable ones.[68] In France it pre-vailed into the thirteenth century and then yielded to life tenure which was to predominate in the following two centuries.[69] The same transition occurred under the English kings; by the thirteenth and fourteenth centuries they favored life concessions over heritable con-cessions two to one.[70] Easy to terminate, the *fief-rente* was logically

neque ille qui tenebit Comitatum Cabilonen. poterimus ponere extra manum nostram" (Chantereau le Febvre, *Traité des fiefs,* Preuves, p. 193).

[65] France: *Layettes,* II, no. 2055; III, nos. 4266, 4384; Boutaric, *Actes du parlement,* I, no. 2198; Fawtier, *Comptes du trésor,* nos. 325–26. Ger-many: Lacomblet, *Urkundenbuch,* III, no. 107. Low Countries: Butkens, *Trophées,* Preuves, p. 164; A.G.R., Verkooren, *Inv. Brab.,* unpublished, under the dates 24 November 1384 and 1407; A.E.N., Piot, *Inv. Namur,* no. 709.

[66] Sczaniecki, *Essai,* pp. 150–51.

[67] I have found only a few instances of life tenure in the German records. In 1092 when Gerhard von Stumpenhusen received a fief of 8 *l.* it was re-cognized that "hanc pactionem seruari debere sibi soli dum uixerit" (Lappen-berg, *Hamburgisches Urkundenbuch,* I, no. 119). See also Böhmer, *Acta Imperii,* no. 1143.

[68] Didier, *Revue du Nord,* XVII, 278. There were, however, a considerable number of life *fiefs-rentes* donated throughout all the Low Countries. See, for example, De Saint-Genois, *Monuments,* II, 675–76, 734, 860, 877, 881; A.G.R., *Trés. Fl.,* Sér. I, nos. 2073, 2086; A.D.N., Sér. B. 1199/7844, 499/7597, 4056/145.401; Brouwers, *Chartes et règ.,* II, nos. 378, 396; Galesloot, *Feudataires de Jean III,* pp. 58, 224; Quicke, *B.C.R.H.,* XCVI, 372, 380; Bormans, *Les seigneuries féodales du pays de Liège. Table des reliefs* (Liège, 1871), p. 270; Van Mieris, *Groot Charterboek,* II, 437; III, 576. See Appendix, no. 19, and Plate VI.

[69] Sczaniecki, *Essai,* pp. 142 ff. For examples of life tenure see *Layettes,* I, no. 1653; IV, nos. 5606, 5665, 5725; V, nos. 289, 694; Kern, *Acta Imperii,* nos. 114, 148, 152, 157, 307, 309; A.N., J. 620–626; Chantereau le Febvre, *Traité des fiefs,* Preuves, pp. 102, 111.

[70] In 1253 Henry III granted a fief of 20 *l.* to Reginald de Sancto Lomano "quod vixerit" (*R.G.,* I, no. 2252). Edward I granted Bernard VI, count of Armagnac and Fezensac, "100 *l. morlanorum* so long as he shall live" (*R.G.,*

suited to life tenure—a tenure tailored to the demands of the lord and the capabilities of the vassal. When in need of the particular services of a certain well-qualified man, a lord could grant him a *fief-rente* for life and thus insure himself against having to pay the fief to a successor who might not be able, or who might no longer be needed, to perform the services. But in actual practice life tenure was little different from heritable tenure. *Fiefs-rentes* granted for life, rather than disappearing at the death of the grantee as one would expect, often continued to exist; the grantee's heir was permitted to do homage for the fief if he could perform the required services.[71]

More than other types of fiefs, the *fief-rente* accommodated itself to all sorts of provisional and conditional tenures. In all western Europe *fiefs-rentes* were granted with the provision that they should be paid until lands of equal value could be provided. More specifically, the English kings stated that certain *fiefs-rentes* would exist until lands could be provided through marriage, wardship, or escheat. Sometimes the English kings donated fiefs until the recipients could be provided for otherwise, that is, by any means that would provide an equivalent income. In France, the Low Countries, and England, *fiefs-rentes* were assigned to men until they could be provided with lands marked out for conquest. In the same areas *fiefs-rentes* were to

---

III, no. 1269). In 1440 Henry VI granted Diedrich, archbishop of Cologne, a fief of 600 m. "dum ipsi rex et archiepiscopus vixerint in humanis" (*Foedera*, 1704–35, VIII, 22).

[71] In 1246 Count Theobald IV of Champagne granted to John de Hangest a fief of 30 l. for life unless Theobald should decide to give it to John's heirs (Chantereau le Febvre, *Traité des fiefs*, Preuves, p. 238). Stephen de Sancerre held a life fief of 100 l. from Alphonse of Poitiers; upon his death, however, it was regranted to his son Stephen (*Layettes*, III, no. 4076). See also Delisle, *Cart. normand*, no. 223; Sczaniecki, *Essai*, pp. 146–47. Edward III of England granted William de Grandison a *fief-rente* for life; yet it was regranted to his son Otto III by Richard II (*C.P.R. 1348–50*, p. 370; *Foedera*, 1704–35, VII, 761). The *fief-rente* granted for life to the duke of Bavaria by Richard II was still being paid to the succeeding dukes in the middle of the fifteenth century (*C.P.R. 1396–99*, pp. 25, 247; "Cal. Dip. Doc." in *D.K.R.*, XLV, app. i, 327; P.R.O., Dip. Doc. Exch., E. 30/1246(1 –2), E. 30/1247, E. 30/1372, E. 30/480–481). On rare occasions heritable fiefs were converted into life fiefs. For example, in 1364 Charles V of France converted a life fief of 1,500 l. belonging to Emenion and John de Pommiers into a heritable one (Delisle, *Mandements et actes divers de Charles V (1364 –1380)*, Paris, 1874, no. 22).

serve as remuneration to men who, because of their loyalty and service during hostilities, had seen their fiefs of land confiscated by the enemy; it was generally provided that the *fiefs-rentes* would be paid until the lands could be recovered. In the Low Countries and England fiefs were frequently granted during the lord's will, during his pleasure, and so long as it was pleasing to him. In France they were granted until the assignment of revenues, or a piece of land conveniently located near the grantee. The English kings often granted fiefs with the provision that they would be paid as long as the vassal faithfully served his lord. A clause of redemption, where the lords stipulated that whenever they so desired the *fief-rente* could be repurchased for a lump sum, accompanied concessions in all the regions. Though seldom found in France and England, this clause accompanied at least half of the *fiefs-rentes* granted in Germany and the Low Countries regardless of what tenure governed them. Provisional and conditional tenures were common in all the regions but were the most prominent in England and then in France. From the thirteenth century on the English kings used these tenures as frequently as the life tenure; in the same period they were used extensively in France and the Low Countries; in Germany they were rarely used.

Some actual cases will serve to illustrate the various tenures outlined above. In 1237 Simon, count of Pontieu, granted Geoffrey de la Capelle a fief of 30 *l.* to be held "quousque predictas triginta libras turonensium annui redditus dicto Galfrido et heredibus suis assignaverimus in terris nostris, vel redditibus aliis vel in alio loco competenti." In 1245 the emperor Frederick II granted a fief of 100 *m.* to Imbert, lord of Beaujeu, until he would be provided with an equivalent fief of land.[72] In 1254 Henry III of England granted to Robert de Cantilupo 40 *m.* "nomine feodi, donec ei providerit in 40 marcatis terre de wardis, vel eschaetis regis." In 1203 King John of England granted a fief of 50 *l.* to John Malerbe until he could provide land of that value "in maritagium aut alibi."[73] In an agreement

[72] Brunel, *Actes de Pontieu,* no. 309; *Layettes,* III, no. 4076; Winkelmann, *Acta Imperii,* I, no. 383. See also Delisle, *Cart. normand,* no. 67; *Layettes,* II, no. 2053; III, no. 4089; IV, no. 2053; Wauters, *Table chronologique,* VII, 524; Sczaniecki, *Essai,* pp. 122–23.

[73] *R.G.,* I, no. 3937; *Rot. Pat.,* p. 23. See also *Rot. Chart.,* pp. 64, 70; *Pat. R. 1225–32,* pp. 405–6; *R.G.,* I, nos. 296, 2372, 2378, 2409.

of 1229 Louis IX of France promised to assign to Centulle, count of Astarac, 1,000 *l.* of land in Agen "si idem dominus rex conquireret terram illam"; meanwhile, Centullo was to receive a fief of 100 *l.*[74] In 1226 Hugh, viscount of Thouars, was promised the castle of Lodun and its appurtenances when the region in Poitou where it was located should be conquered by the English. He was to receive a fief of 500 *m.* from Henry III until acquiring the castle; when he got possession of the castle the fief would be discontinued.[75] In 1296 Count Guy of Flanders granted to John d'Assenghien a fief of 50 *l.* to compensate for the seizure of his lands in Artois by the count of Artois during hostilities with Philip IV of France; the fief was to be enjoyed until the lands could be recovered. Two years later Guy granted John de Gavre, lord of Scornay, 200 *l.* of Flanders yearly because his loyal service to Guy had resulted in the forfeiture of lands worth 200 *l.* to the king of France.[76] Evidence of fiefs granted because of lands lost is most abundant in the English records. In 1299 Edward I granted *fiefs-rentes* to about 350 Gascon lords and knights who had lost their lands during the war in Gascony between Edward and Philip the Fair. The letters of concession appearing in the Gascon Rolls[77] are confirmed by the Issue and Liberate Rolls of 28 Edward I (1299) which contain entries relating to the payment of the first installments of these fiefs.[78] An account rendered by

[74] *Layettes,* II, no. 1999. See also nos. 2986, 3471, 2061 ; Sczaniecki, *Essai,* pp. 144–45.

[75] *Pat. R. 1225–32,* pp. 99–100. See Appendix, no. 20.

[76] De Saint-Genois, *Monuments,* II, 857; A.D.N., B. 4058/145.447. See also A.E.G., De Saint Genois, *Inv. Fl.,* nos. 996, 1337 ; B. 4058/145.448.

[77] The following grant is typical : "Sciatis quod concessimus dilecto nobis Reymundo de Campanha, militi, ... 125 *l.* chipotensium, annis singulis duobus terminis, ad scaccarium nostrum ... percipiendas ... quousque terre et tenementa dicti Reymundi, que occasione dicte guerre capta sunt in manum dicti regis Francie, sibi fuerint restituta, vel nos ei aliter duxerimus providendum" (*R.G.,* III, no. 4528). For the other grants see *R.G.,* III, nos. 4530 ff.

[78] P.R.O., E. 403/105, mm. 4–6 ; P.R.O., C. 62/75, mm. 1–2, 5. In the Issue Roll there first appears the rubric "Liberationes facte diversis Vasconiis de prestito super brevia sua de liberate currentes." Then follows the first entry : "Domino Johanni Russel' militi super brevem suum de liberate currens et continens D libras chipotensium que valent in sterlingis C libras quinque chipotenses computatur pro uno sterlingo. Quas rex sibi concessit singulis annis percipiendas ad duos terminos ad scaccarium suum de exitibus terrarum et tenementorum alienigenarum tam religiosorum quam aliorum in regno Anglie existencium que occasione guerre inter dictum regem et regem Francie

the royal officers John de Sandale and Thomas of Cambridge in the year 1301 again records the payment of these fiefs.[79] In the account rendered for 1391 by the receiver general of Limburg, Jean Sack de Wijck, is an entry stating that a certain Gosuin de Heer will receive payment on a fief of 100 florins held from the duke of Burgundy "tant qui lui plaira."[80] Henry III of England granted a fief of 20 *l.* to Walter de Godarville for sustaining himself in the royal service "quamdiu regi placuerit."[81] In 1213 Adam Cheverel received from Simon de Montfort a fief of 500 *l.* to be paid until it could be assigned in lands located near Adam. In 1302 Philip IV granted a fief of 1,000 *l.* to John de Chalon-Arlay until he could be provided for "alibi in locis competentibus."[82] John of England granted Hugh de

nuper mote capi fecit idem rex in manum suam quousque terre et tenementa dicti Johannis que occasione dicte guerre capta sunt in manum dicti regis Francie sibi fuerint restituta vel donec dictus dominus rex Anglie sibi aliter duxerit providendum. De quibus D libris chipotensium medietas est CCL librae chipotensium que valent in sterlingis L libras quinque chipotenses computatur ut prius unde tercia pars est IIII*xx* III libras dimidiam marcam chipotensium que valent in sterlingis XVI libras I marcam quas recepit XXVIII° die novembris pro tercia parte dicte medietatis de primo termino dicti brevis scilicet de presenti termino Sancti Michaelis. Et debet eidem L marcas de eodem termino." Then follow the names of the other men and the payments made to them. In the Liberate Roll appear the writs which give the authority for the issues made out of the exchequer. Beside the marginal notation "Pro diversis hominibus de Vasconie" appears the first writ of *liberate*: "Rex thesaurario et camerariis suis salutem. Liberate de thesauro nostro Seynhorono de Mauriet et fratri eius vel eorum attornato quinquaginta libras chipotensium vel valorem eorundem in moneta currente in regno nostro unam videlicet medietatem in termino Sancti Michaelis proximo futuro et aliam medietatem in termino Pasche proximo sequenti et sic de anno in annum ad eosdem terminos quinquaginta libras chipotensium vel valorem eorundem in moneta predicta de illis quinquaginta libris chipotensium quas ei concessimus singulis annis percipiendas ad terminos predictos ad scaccarium nostrum quousque terre et tenementa predictorum Seinhoroni et fratris eius que occasione guerre inter nos et regem Francie nuper mote in manum ipsius regis capta fuerunt sibi fuerint restituta vel donec sibi aliter duxerimus providendum. Teste rege apud Waverle XXV die augusti anno etc. vicesimo septimo. Consimiles litteras de diversis pecuniarum summis habent subscripti videlicet." Then follow the names and sums. See Plates I–II.

[79] P.R.O., E. 101/157/5.

[80] A.G.R., *C.C.*, no. 2436, fol. 50v.

[81] *Cl.R. 1227–31*, p. 521; *C.L.R. 1226–40*, p. 160–81. See also *R.G.*, I, no. 558; III, nos. 1143, 1232; IV, no. 1913.

[82] Molinier, *Biblio. de l'École des Chartes*, XXXIV, no. 74; Funck-Brentano, *Biblio. de l'École des Chartes*, XLIX, no. 10.

Lacy "60 m. de feodo per annum, quod ei concessimus quamdiu ipse nobis fideliter serviet." [83] In 1267 Duke John I of Brabant granted to Thierry, lord of Heinsberg, "redditum centum lib. Lovan. in feodum, apud Lovanium ... quem redditum Dux et ejus haeredes redimere possunt pro mille lib. Lovan." In 1302 William, lord of Petersheim, became the man of Count John I of Namur for a heritable fief of 80 l. and agreed that the counts of Namur were entitled "rachater les quatre vins livres par an desus dites de mi ou de mes hoirs pour wit cens livres paiement de Namur." [84] In 1280 the archbishop of Mainz granted a fief of 6 m. to a man for castle-guard with the proviso that he could redeem it whenever he desired for a sum of 60 m. [85]

The prominence of these provisional tenures stems from their advantages to the lord. In the first place they gave the grantor almost absolute control over the duration of a *fief-rente*; prompted by certain reasons, he could usually terminate the fief at once, an act impossible under hereditary or even life tenures. Because the lord could thus so easily control the *fief-rente*, it naturally was more useful to him for many purposes than the ordinary fief. Even if it were possible to attach provisional tenures to fiefs of land the lord would encounter great difficulty in carrying out their provisions, for he did not have the control over a piece of land that he did over the source of money which paid the *fief-rente*. In case of differences between lord and vassal the lord could terminate a *fief-rente* in the time it took to transmit the order to the proper financial officer; with land he might be compelled to take it by force. Moreover, the provisional tenures attached to the *fief-rente* could almost be made to order for the services desired by a lord. When a man's service was needed, the *fief-rente* would provide the basis of obligation; when the need was gone, relations could be severed and the lord would not

---

[83] *Rot. Pat.,* p. 45 b; *R.G.,* I, no. 433. See also *R.G.,* I, nos. 282, 342, 3769. See Plate VI.

[84] Butkens, *Trophées,* Preuves, I, 103; Brouwers, *Chart. et règ.,* II, no. 366. Such grants are contained in A.G.R., *Trés. Fl.,* Sér. I, nos. 949, 1050, 1230, 2070–71, 2082–83; E. Gachet, "Un cartulaire de Guillaume Ier, comte de Hainaut," *B.C.R.H.,* IV (1852), no. 76; Wampach, *Urkunden,* IV, no. 213; V, no. 227; VII, no. 1090. See Appendix, nos. 24–25.

[85] Sauer, *Nassauisches Urkundenbuch,* I, ii, no. 967; Böhmer, *Acta Imperii,* no. 455. See also Gudenus, *Codex Diplomaticus,* II, 984, 1052; Kremer, *Gülch- und Bergischen Geschichte,* I, no. 20; Lappenberg, *Hamburgisches Urkundenbuch,* I, no. 403; Lacomblet, *Urkundenbuch,* III, no. 218.

find himself paying for something no longer advantageous as sometimes happened with a life or heritable *fief-rente*. Under these tenures the feudal contract could be legally severed. With a life or heritable *fief-rente* it was possible and just as easy for the lord to sever the feudal ties if for some reason he felt it was necessary, but it would have had to be done illegally. In this case the vassal did not have the leverage he would have had with a fief of land. Probably two courses were open to him, but he stood to profit little from either; he might have recourse to the standard feudal justice open to a vassal who had been wronged by his lord or he could stage a feudal revolt. In either case the lord would appear a likely victor. Nevertheless a lord seldom terminated life or heritable fiefs, not from fear of the immediate consequences of such illegal action, but because frequent indulgence in such arbitrary action would demonstrate that he could not be depended upon to fulfil his feudal obligations. His chances of acquiring other vassals by means of *fiefs-rentes* would thus be impaired and men would soon realize that feudal contracts with him were worthless. It was much wiser for him to insure his legal right of ceasing payment of the fief by tacking on one of these provisional clauses.

A second advantage provided by these tenures was their flexibility in case of emergencies which affected the lord's resources. Needing a vassal immediately but having no land at his disposal, the lord could grant a *fief-rente* until lands could be provided; in the mind of the lord this was probably a stopgap measure until nature or feudal perquisites brought back into his possession sufficient lands. Without doubt some lords would never have granted as many *fiefs-rentes* as they did if they had not envisaged the substitution of land which would reduce the drain on their financial resources. A *fief-rente* granted until lands could be provided was certainly regarded with favor by the vassal for he then could hope to secure in the future a piece of land which would bring him more social, economic, and political prestige than a *fief-rente*. Sometimes his expectations were fulfilled and the *fief-rente* ceased its existence,[86] but, interestingly

---

[86] In 1402 Duke Philip the Bold of Burgundy granted to Robert Tenke the land of Bois in exchange for a fief of 200 *l.* held by Robert since the time of Louis de Male, count of Flanders (A.E.G., L. Gachard, *Notice historique et descriptive des archives de la ville de Gand*, Bruxelles, 1854, May, 1402; *Verzameling Diegerick*, nos. 11, 77). For many good examples in France and

enough, there is much evidence showing that the terms of these provisional tenures were not implemented. Fiefs granted "during pleasure" and under other provisional tenures frequently continued to be paid until the death of the grantee; sometimes even his heirs were granted the fief. That often lands were never substituted is particularly evident in England. In 1216 John granted William de Casingham a fief of 30 m. until land of that value could be provided; William never received land. He was paid 30 m. yearly until 1229 when the tenure was made heritable and the yearly installment reduced to 10 l.; this fief was still being paid to William in 1253. A *fief-rente* governed by the same tenure was granted to Hugh de Vivona in 1230; he was still in possession of this fief when he died in 1259.[87] Such instances are also numerous on the Continent.[88] In effect, then, many grants with provisional tenures were tantamount to life *fiefs-rentes*, but the insertion of a provisional clause assured the lord of being able to withdraw legally from the contract if circumstances so dictated.

Despite acknowledging evidence in France that often lands were never substituted for *fiefs-rentes*, Sczaniecki concurs with Mitteis in regarding the provisional phraseology connected with many grants as proof that the *fief-rente* was but a transitory feudal institution— an expedient developed to meet demands no longer fulfilled by the conventional fief and destined for a limited existence: "Leur conversion en terres ou leur rachat devaient être normalement envisagés au moment de leur concession."[89] However well such a view may fit

---

Germany see Sczaniecki, *Essai*, pp. 127–28. In 1244 Henry III of England "concessit Petro de Jeneve manerium de Dalun' cum pertinenciis tenendum quamdiu regi placuerit pro 40 l. quas percipit ad scaccarium de feodo suo, ita quod quamdiu illud tenuerit rex quietus erit de feodo predicto" (*Cl.R. 1242–47*, p. 281). See also *C.P.R. 1247–58*, p. 194; *C.P.R. 1258–66*, pp. 201, 302; *C.L.R. 1240–45*, p. 4; *Cl.R. 1227–31*, p. 378.

[87] *Rot. Pat.*, p. 185; *Pat. R. 1225–32*, p. 276; *Cl.R. 1251–53*, pp. 311, 364; *C.L.R. 1226–40*, p. 168; *C.P.R. 1258–66*, p. 42. See also *Rot. Chart.*, p. 187b; *Cl.R. 1256–59*, p. 422; *R.G.*, I, no. 4226.

[88] In 1259 Louis IX of France granted Julien de Péronne a fief of 40 l. payable by the Temple until land could be assigned; in 1338 the treasury was still paying the fief to Julien's heirs. In 1254 Alphonse of Poitiers granted to Jean des Maisons a fief payable by the treasury until assignment of land; in 1338 the treasury was still paying the fief (*Essai*, pp. 124–26). For cases in the Low Countries see *R.B.P.H.*, XXXII, 432–33.

[89] *Essai*, p. 129; Mitteis, *Lehnrecht*, pp. 476 ff.

legalistic reasoning and the phraseology of the documents, it is not always in accord with what occurred. Though in the Low Countries and Germany a very large number of *fiefs-rentes* granted heritably could be redeemed by the lord at any time, the evidence indicates that they seldom were. Within France Sczaniecki has shown that heritable *fiefs-rentes* predominated down into the thirteenth century and then were supplanted by fiefs granted for life only. There is nothing to indicate that the English kings considered *fiefs-rentes* any more transitory than ordinary fiefs. What alone seems certain is that the *fief-rente* appeared when money made it possible and that it was used by the lords until it no longer served their purposes. That estates of land called fiefs still remained at the end of the fifteenth century when *fiefs-rentes* had disappeared, does not affirm the permanent quality of the former. They were by then true fiefs in name only; the feudalism of land had long been dead. To see in the various conditions tacked to concessions of *fiefs-rentes* proof of its transitory character, as did Mitteis and Sczaniecki, is to overlook, it seems to me, the real purpose of these conditions. That the lords often did not act upon the provisional clauses seems to suggest that they regarded them not as terms demanding fulfillment in the near future, but as escape valves enabling them upon necessity to surmount a tight financial situation or to withdraw legally from a feudal relation no longer profitable. They were actually terms of insurance for the lord made possible by the maneuverability of the *fief-rente*; they could never have accompanied such a fixed thing as a fief of land.

There is not sufficient documentary evidence to say with certainty that *fiefs-rentes* granted in place of lands lost during hostilities or until lands could be provided by conquest were regularly replaced. The few occasions when the provisions were met by the lords and the *fiefs-rentes* terminated are scarcely basis for generalization.[90] Obvi-

---

[90] The evidence is chiefly English. In 1242 Guy de Rocheford and his heirs were granted a fief of 150 *m.* "donec terram suam, quam propter servicium nostrum amiserunt, recuperaverint" (*R.G.*, I, no. 309). In 1251 Guy was granted the "manor of Naileston, with wards, escheats, advowson of the church and all that can fall in" (*C.P.R. 1247–58*, p. 86). It is not known whether Guy's lands in Gascony were ever restored to him. In 1245 Henry III promised Bozo de Mastac, count of Bigorre, "to assign to him land to the value of 250 *l.* a year of the lands late of W. de Percy during the minority of the heir for the fee he is accustomed to receive at the exchequer and for

ously if a projected conquest failed, lands could not be provided; nor could lands be returned to a man having lost them when they could not be retaken from the enemy. Surely many Gascon lords never got back their lands, so little successful were English military operations in that theater between 1294 and 1304. Likewise, in spite of Courtrai, Count Guy and his successors retook little of the land lost previously to Philip IV of France and consequently continued to pay the fiefs envisaged at the outset as temporary grants. Naturally payment of the fief depended upon the recipient's loyalty; should he by contrivance retrieve his land, the *fief-rente* would be forfeited.

That some fiefs were redeemable has been stated, but on what terms and by what sort of transaction? The purchase price was invariably set at ten times the annual value of the fief. But it is significant that the transaction of repurchase did not normally end feudal relations between lord and vassal; the lords usually stipulated that the purchase price was to be used by the recipient to acquire land or some income equal in annual value to the *fief-rente*. This land or income, when acquired, would be held in fief of the lord.[91] By providing the lord with an escape from the yearly burden of paying the fief, this procedure generally worked to his financial profit

the land which he lost beyond seas by reason of his service" (*Pat. R. 1232–47*, p. 459).

[91] In 1314 Robert, count of Wernemburg, did liege homage to William I, count of Hainaut and Holland, for the sum of 1,000 *l.* and designated 100 *l.* secured yearly from his own goods and allods as the annual income to be held in fief (Devillers, *Monuments*, III, no. 145, p. 50). In 1304 Godfrey, a knight of Luxemburg and son of Godfrey of Neumagen, did homage to Count Henry VII of Luxemburg "pro triginta libris treverensis denariorum pro quibus ego Go. antedictus assignam dicto domino H. tres libratas in bonis meis allodialibus quas quidem tres libratas antedicto domino meo H. assignavi in domo mea et aliis bonis que habeo apud Numagin" (A.G.R., Verkooren, *Inv. Lux.*, no. 440). Examples of this type of transaction are abundant in Luxemburg (Verkooren, *Inv. Lux.*, nos. 508, 513, 517–19, 525, 528; Wampach, *Urkunden*, vols. I–VII). In 1280 Sifrid von Rheinberg received from the archbishop of Mainz a fief of 5 *m.* He promised: "Si ipse [the archbishop], successores sui aut ecclesia Maguntina predictos quinque marcarum redditus voluerint redimere aut etiam rehabere, ego illos pro quinquaginta marcis denariorum Aquensium eis restituere teneor omni occasione cessante eosdem denarios conversurus in quinque marcarum redditus, qui pro castro predicto situm habeant congruentem, aut de bonis meis, que proprietatis titulo possideo, tantos redditus debeo demonstrare habendos perpetuo nomine castrensis feodi a prefato domino archiepiscopo" (Sauer, *Nassauisches Urkundenbuch*, I, ii, no. 968). See Appendix, nos. 24–25.

and, in addition, transferred the burden of finding a yearly income to the vassal. Strangely enough this technique was prevalent in Germany and the Low Countries but not in France and England. This cannot be satisfactorily explained, it seems to me, by a lack of financial resources at least on the part of the Low Country princes. Perhaps the German and Low Country lords chose to use the technique of repurchase rather than the provisional clauses so favored by the English and French kings which, in general, made no provision for future feudal relations. The repurchase clause invariably provided that another fief would supplant the *fief-rente* and furnish the basis for a continuing feudal relation; unless he so desired, a German and Low Country lord never lost a vassal. It might also be suggested that the German and Low Country lords got the idea of repurchase from another feudal transaction extremely common in these areas. A lord would initially grant a lump sum to a man with the proviso that it be used to acquire some land or income equal to one-tenth of the value of the lump sum. A man could either buy an annual cash income from some source of revenue to be held in fief from the grantor of the lump sum,[92] or he could buy some land or set aside a piece of his own land worth yearly a tenth of the lump sum to be held in fief.[93] It seems likely that there may have been some connection between these two types of feudal transaction.

The practice of granting a lump sum to obtain an annual income or a piece of land in fief leads us into one of the most controversial problems connected with the *fief-rente*. Could a lump sum of money, as some scholars have contended, be granted as a fief and could such a sum be considered a *fief-rente*? Kienast and Clason would answer yes. Kienast, however, would call this type of grant a *Geldlehen* be-

---

[92] In 1296 Walter, lord of Waës, received from Count Guy of Flanders 500 *l.* with which to purchase 50 "livrées de terre au tournois" to be held in fief from Guy (De Reiffenberg, *Monuments*, I, no. 107, p. 290). In 1314 John the Blind, count of Luxemburg, granted to Frederick of Blankenheim a sum of 5,000 *l.* for purchasing various revenues to be held in fief from John (Verkooren, *Inv. Lux.*, no. 521). See also Wauters, *Table chronologique*, V, 100; VI, 508, 517, 646; De Saint-Genois, *Monuments*, I, 354, 356.

[93] This statement refers just to Germany and the Low Countries; in France and England few fiefs were redeemable. See, however, E. Petit, *Histoire des ducs de Bourgogne* (Dijon, 1885), V, no. 3522; VI, no. 4883; D'Arbois de Jubainville, *Histoire de Champagne*, IV, 849 ff.; Du Chesne, *Histoire généalogique de Béthune*, Preuves, p. 185; *Pat. R. 1234–37*, p. 192; *Pat. R. 1268 –72*, p. 337; *C.P.R. 1272–79*, p. 152.

cause the element of an annual income is absent and it could not therefore accurately be termed a *Rentlehen*. Both argue that there were cases where lords granted vassals lump sums for homage and fealty, as well as for the promise of feudal service.[94] Sczaniecki, on the other hand, has argued quite cogently that a lump sum could not be a *fief-rente*.[95] This view, it seems to me, is more correct.

When *fiefs-rentes* were redeemed with a lump sum which was to be employed in securing another fief quite obviously the lump sum was not the fief. To show this more clearly let us suppose the recipient failed to secure another fief with the lump sum. In this case the vassal would hold nothing in fief from the lord and feudal relations between lord and vassal would come to an end. But if the recipient did buy an annual income such as a right to a sum taken upon tolls, duties, or other like revenues, the annual income acquired could be considered a *fief-rente*. It should be noted, however, that this method of securing a *fief-rente* was rarely used. Instead, the recipients customarily designated a part of the income arising from their own lands, whether feudal or allodial, and took it in fief from the donor.[96] Coming upon this type of feudal transaction, Didier thought it was a sort of fiction but nevertheless believed that a *fief-rente* was created.[97] An annual income was indeed taken in fief but it cannot be considered a *fief-rente*. Actually the annual income was a fief of land or, as it is generally styled, a *fief de reprise*. The vassal has not gone outside his fief and secured an additional income; he has only

[94] Kienast, *H.Z.*, CLVIII, 26: "Es wurden nicht nur Renten als Lehen gegeben, sondern auch einzelne Geldsummen, ohne dass der Beliehene das Kapital in eine Rente umwandelte. Es empfiehlt sich deshalb, die ganze Gruppe nicht als Rentenlehen, sondern als Geldlehen zu bezeichnen." See also Clason, *Pensionsverhältnisse*, p. 22. In a review of Sczaniecki's book, Ganshof favors the view of Kienast (*R.B.P.H.*, XXVII, 241).

[95] *Essai*, pp. 162–66.

[96] For Germany see Böhmer, *Acta Imperii*, no. 1025; Gudenus, *Codex Diplomaticus*, V, 626; Goerz, *Mittelrheinische Regesten* (Coblenz, 1881), III, nos. 2236, 2376, 2691, 2834 ff. For the Low Countries see Bondam, *Charterboek van Gelderland*, III, 2, 6, 77, 121, 146; De Saint-Genois, *Monuments*, II, 680, 708, 808, 961, 993; A.G.R., *Trés. Fl.*, Sér. I, nos. 2076–77; A.D.N., B. 4058/145.436; Lyon, *Revue du Nord*, XXXV, 221–32. For France see Sczaniecki, *Essai*, pp. 84–85.

[97] *Le droit des fiefs*, p. 54. Sczaniecki disagrees (*Essai*, p. 7). Cf. Petot, *Constitution de rente aux XIIᵉ et XIIIᵉ siècles*, pp. 60–61; Lyon, *Revue du Nord*, XXV, 221–32.

taken a part of his own possessions in fief. A *fief-rente* would have augmented his income. There is no doubt that only his own land was involved because, should he die without heirs, or should he fail to honor his feudal obligations, the land producing the annual income would escheat or be forfeited to the lord. What the vassal has done is merely to pretend that the portion of income set aside from his own land was paid yearly to him by his lord but, whether or not he believed this, he was in reality only juggling his annual income and in no way adding to it. A lump sum of money obtained for the lord a vassal along with part or all of his lands, but neither lump sum nor income from land can be considered a *fief-rente*. By securing vassals and lands in this manner, the lord increased his feudal power and prestige and, most important, constructed a larger and more unified feudal holding by chipping away at salients of allodial land. The benefits for the grantee are not obvious. For a lump sum of money, usually quite modest, he entered into a feudal relation which imposed upon him certain obligations and seemingly gave him slight advantage. We can only suggest that either he desperately needed money or he desired the protection and patronage of a powerful lord.

A similar but somewhat more complicated transaction was common in Germany. A lord would grant a man an annual income in fief with the stipulation that it continue to be paid until a certain agreed sum had been reached; then the annual installments would cease. With the money received, the recipient would be obliged to acquire a yearly income equal to a tenth of the total sum. Invariably the recipients either took part of their own land in fief or bought some additional land.[98] Sometimes the lords admitted that they did not have the ready money at their disposal to pay a lump sum outright and that it would have to be paid by yearly installments.[99] Such

---

[98] In 1275 King Rudolf granted to Peter von Bertholfesheim and his son an annual income of 6 m. payable "tamdiu quousque sexaginta marcas, quas supradicti Petrus et eius filius in emptiones prediorum convertent, et a nobis et imperio recipient in feodum" (Böhmer, *Urkundenbuch Frankfurt,* I, 173). See also pp. 180–82, 192–93, 224–25; Goerz, *Mittelrheinische Regesten,* IV, nos. 2096, 2308; W. Mummenhoff, *Regesten der Reichsstadt Aachen 1301–1350* (Köln, 1937), nos. 291, 293, 408; Lünig, *Corpus Juris Feudalis,* III, 43 ff.; Van Mieris, *Groot Charterboek,* II, 301.

[99] In 1294, for example, King Adolf granted to Werner I von Falkenstein-Minzenberg a *Burglehen* of 100 m. and stated that "quia paratam pecuniam non habemus" Werner or his heirs were entitled to draw upon certain royal

donations might seem to be *fiefs-rentes,* but in reality they were only lump sums.

Lump sums appear frequently in the records in the form of subsidies granted along with *fiefs-rentes.* In 1208 Hugh, lord of Fauche, recognized that he had taken his castle of Fauche in fief from Blanche of Navarre, regent of Champagne, and Theobald her son; he did liege homage and not only received a fief of 20 *l.* but also an additional sum of 200 *l.* In 1219 Guy, lord of Tyle-Châtel, became the liege man of Blanche and Theobald in return for a fief of 50 *l.* and a lump sum of 100 *m.*[100] In 1245 Henry III of England granted Amadeus, count of Savoy, a fief of 200 *m.* and a sum of 1,000 *l.* as compensation for his homage.[101] We have here lump sums added to *fiefs-rentes* as inducements for securing the desired service or vassalage. Lump sums also induced men to take their castles or lands in fief from the donors. In 1397 Duke Philip the Bold of Burgundy granted to Regnier, lord of Schoonvoorst, a sum of 12,000 *l.*; in return Regnier became the vassal of Philip and took his castle of Kerpen in fief. In 1402 Conrad, lord of Schleiden, became the vassal of Duke Philip with the promise to hold his castle of Schönberg in fief and make it available to Philip in time of war.[102] Another transaction involved giving a sum of money to acquire a man's homage. Thus in 1337 Edward III of England granted Eustace Piscair, a Flemish knight, 100 *l.* "quas ei concessimus ratione homagii et fidelitatis."[103] In 1339 Duke John III of Brabant granted 200 *l.* to Her-

incomes "quousque nos vel successores nostri in imperio eis satisfaciant de pecunia prelibata." This arrangement was to last until the 100 *m.* was paid; the money was then to be employed to secure some land in fief (Sauer, *Nassauisches Urkundenbuch,* I, ii, no. 1174). In 1266 Diethard, count of Catsenellenbogen, granted Henry, son of a certain Wolfram, a sum of 30 *m.*: "Verum si dicto Henrico XXX marcas ad terminum predictum non persolverimus, sibi III marcas in reditibus annuatim assignabimus tamdiu tenendas, donec sibi predicti denarii fuerint a nobis persoluti" (Böhmer, *Urkundenbuch Frankfurt,* I, 139). See also Böhmer, *Acta Imperii,* nos. 512, 522.

[100] Chantereau le Febvre, *Traité des fiefs,* Preuves, pp. 33, 106. See also Sczaniecki, *Essai,* p. 162.

[101] *Pat. R. 1232–47,* p. 469; *C.P.R. 1247–58,* p. 9; *C.L.R. 1245–51,* pp. 20, 40, 115, 168.

[102] A.G.R., Verkooren, *Inv. Brab.,* unpublished, 18 March 1397; 2 February 1402. See also Wampach, *Urkunden,* II, nos. 246, 254, 414, 432; *Pat. R. 1232–47,* p. 192; Sczaniecki, *Essai,* p. 165.

[103] *Foedera,* II, ii, 997. For other examples see *C.P.R. 1345–48,* p. 514; F. Devon, *Issues of the Exchequer* (London, 1837), pp. 270–71.

man de Pentling for his homage. In 1394 the duke of Burgundy granted John de Looz of Heinsberg, 2,000 francs for his homage.[104] At times lords added subsidies to *fiefs-rentes* granted to men for military service. Count Guy of Flanders, holding a fief of 300 *m.* from Edward I of England, received a subsidy of 300,000 *l.* to help in the war against Philip IV of France.[105] Subsidies of 10,000 *l.*, 60,000 *l.*, and 100,000 florins were granted by Edward III to Duke John III of Brabant between 1337 and 1339 in return for John's military assistance against Philip VI of France. Also in 1339 John received from Edward a fief of 1,500 *l.*[106] The French kings in particular seem to have favored this practice. In 1294 Philip IV granted Count Henry VII of Luxemburg a fief of 500 *l.* plus a subsidy of 6,000 *l.* The same year Philip gave to the dauphin of Vienne a fief of 500 *l.* plus a subsidy of 10,000 *l.* Of the many *fiefs-rentes* granted by Philip VI at the onset of the Hundred Years' War almost all were accompanied by subsidies.[107] The same practice existed in the Low Countries. In 1296, for example, Count Guy of Flanders granted William, lord of Hornes, a fief of 100 *l.* and added to it a military subsidy of 2,000 *l.*[108] It was equally common, especially in the last part of the thirteenth century, to grant subsidies for military assistance without any

[104] A.G.R., Verkooren, *Inv. Brab.*, no. 625 ; *Inv. Brab.*, unpublished, 2 June 1394. There are also like cases under the dates 2 December 1387 and 18 February 1397. See also Devillers, *Cart. de Hainaut*, I, no. 383.

[105] *C.P.R. 1272–81*, p. 2 ; *C.Cl.R. 1279–88*, p. 9 ; "Cal. Dip. Doc.," in *D.K.R.*, XLV, app. ii, 288. Numerous documents refer to the various subsidies granted to Guy which may have been included in the sum of 300,000 *l.* On 6 January 1297 Edward promised Guy 60,000 *l.* yearly as long as the war with France should last (P.R.O., Dip. Doc. Exch., E. 30/38). Receipts for payments on a sum of 10,000 *l.* are contained in E. 30/42, 45. In the Treaty Roll of 22 Edward I (P.R.O., C. 76/8) is an agreement dated 6 April 1295 whereby Edward promises Guy a sum of 200,000 *l.* if his son should marry Guy's daughter (this entry will be no. 256 in the edition soon to be published by Mr. Pierre Chaplais for the P.R.O.).

[106] *Foedera*, II, ii, 749, 799, 928, 974, 981, 985, 989, 1103, 1244 ; Jean de Klerk, *Les gestes des ducs de Brabant*, Codex Diplomaticus, I, nos. 174, 176, 179 ; A.G.R., Verkooren, *Inv. Brab.*, no. 619. See also De Sturler, *Relations politiques*, pp. 321–48. See Appendix, nos. 14, 16.

[107] Kern, *Acta Imperii*, nos. 90–92, 307 ; A.N., J. 624/20. In 1296 Philip IV granted Count Floris V of Holland a fief of 4,000 *l.* plus a subsidy of 25,000 *l.* (Kern, *Acta Imperii*, no. 309). See also Viard, *Revue des Questions Historiques*, LIX, 352–54.

[108] De Saint-Genois, *Monuments*, II, 860. See Appendix, no. 17.

fief-rente being involved; these were of course nothing but non-feudal military subsidy treaties. In 1298, for example, Adolf, king of Germany, granted Engelbert de la Mark 400 *m.* "in subsidium" for his military assistance.[109] In 1398 when John, lord of Heinsberg, promised the military service of 200 men to Albert of Bavaria, count of Hainaut and Holland, he received a subsidy of "vier duysent Rynsche gulden."[110] The kings of France and England, having the advantage of substantial financial resources, granted hundreds of such subsidies from the thirteenth through the fifteenth century.[111]

In addition to the forms of lump sums dealt with so far, which were clearly non-feudal, there were other grants of lump sums so worded or so lacking in information that confusion arises as to whether they were feudal. Many such cases are found in the Low Countries, Lorraine, Franche-Comté, and Germany where lump sums alone were granted and homage received for them. Though they might appear to be fiefs, my investigations confirm the opinion of Sczaniecki that they probably were not; the sums were certainly intended to be converted into a fief to be held from the donor but the clause providing for conversion was merely omitted.[112] There were other grants of lump sums which to all appearances were given

---

[109] Lacomblet, *Urkundenbuch,* II, no. 981.

[110] Van Mieris, *Groot Charterboek,* III, 679.

[111] In 1231 Henry d'Avaugour promised, among other things, military assistance to Louis IX of France and received in return the guarantee of a 2,000 *l.* subsidy should hostilities break out. In 1337 Adolf II, bishop of Liège, promised the military service of 500 men-at-arms for use against England in return for a subsidy of 15,000 *l.* (*Layettes,* II, no. 2135–36; A.N., J. 527/13; Viard, *Revue des Questions Historiques,* LIX, 386; Sczaniecki, *Essai,* p. 164). It should be noted, however, that the bishops did hold a *fief-rente* of 2,000 *l.* in 1354 from the French kings (A.N., J. 527/17–18). In England, as early as the reign of John, subsidies were given to Low Country princes and thereafter the practice became increasingly common. In 1297–98 Edward I promised 20,000 *l.* in subsidies to Burgundian lords. In 1337 Thierry, lord of Heinsberg, promised Edward III the service of 200 men-at-arms for a subsidy of 30,000 florins (Dept, *Influences,* pp. 126–27; *Foedera,* I, ii, 871, 888; II, ii, 992, 979, 991). In 1295 Duke John II of Brabant received a subsidy of 4,000 *l.* (P.R.O., E. 30/38, 1376). Writs concerning this payment are in the *Liberate Roll of 1295* (P.R.O., C. 62/73, m. 7). See also P.R.O., Various Accounts, E. 101/619/10.

[112] *Essai,* pp. 164–65. Gislebert de Mons obviously was referring to such a transaction when he related that in 1184 Count Baldwin V of Hainaut granted Baldwin Caron "600 libras in feodo ligio" (*Chronicon,* p. 115).

for a man's homage and service; further investigation reveals, however, that they were actually given in order to secure the man's land in fief. What is misleading is that the text bearing upon the donation has no reference to the land; indication that the lump sum was actually awarded to a man for taking his land in fief from the donor almost always appears in another document. We have, therefore, what might seem to be a fief when in 1263 Hugh, count palatine of Burgundy, gave Humbert, lord of Montluel, a sum of 200 *l.* and received his homage. But from another document of 1263 we learn that Humbert agreed to hold his lands in fief from the count of Burgundy.[113] In 1233 Henry III of England and Geoffrey Ridel II, lord of Blavia, came to an agreement whereby Henry was to pay a lump sum of 600 *m.* to Geoffrey and so acquit himself henceforth of paying a fief of 100 *m.* It was stipulated, however, that Geoffrey was to hold his lands in fief from Henry and that he and his heirs should remain "faithful in the service of the king and heirs"; if they did not fulfil these promises they were to be excommunicated by the archbishop of Bordeaux.[114]

The single example cited by Kienast to bolster his contention that a lump sum could be a fief was a donation of 50 *l.* in 1228 by the countess of Luxemburg to the knight Diethard von Pfaffendorf "pro hominio."[115] In view of what has just been said, the 50 *l.* could have been intended to secure land or an income in fief, or it could have been remuneration for Diethard's taking his land in fief. Could it not also have been merely remuneration for his homage? It is not easy, however, to explain away the following cases, all involving a lump sum granted for homage and the promise of military service on the part of the vassal and his heirs. In 1401 Louis of Orléans, acting for Charles VI of France, granted Duke William of Juliers and Guelders

---

[113] *Essai*, p. 165.

[114] *Pat. R. 1232–47*, p. 192.

[115] Kienast merely refers to the donation (*H.Z.*, CLVIII, 22). The complete text follows: "Ego Dithardus miles de Paffendorf omnibus, ad quos presens scriptum perveniret, notum facio, quod domina mea E. comitissa Luccelburgensis et Rupensis et march. Arlunensis pro hominio, quod ei feci, quinquaginta libras Treverensium mihi persolvit sub testimonio scabinorum Luccelburgensium" (Goerz, *Urkundenbuch mittelrheinischen Territorien*, III, no. 351). Mitteis expresses the view that this is not a *fief-rente*: "Von einer eigentlichen Belehnung ist nicht die Rede, es liegt ein reiner Pensionsvertrag vor" (*Lehnrecht*, p. 520, n. 226).

a sum of 50,000 *écus* of gold in return for William's homage and military service.[116] The same year John, lord of Reifferscheid, did homage to the king of France and promised to serve him against the king of England for a sum of 4,000 *écus* of gold.[117] In 1402 Count Adolf of Cleve and La Mark received a sum of 40,000 gold florins from Charles VI for his liege homage and faithful service.[118] Reginald, duke of Juliers and Guelders, received a sum of 40,000 crowns from Charles; he too did liege homage and promised military service for the defense of France.[119] Sczaniecki would argue that in spite of what the texts say these donations are not *fiefs-rentes*; they are, in reality, non-feudal grants camouflaged by the façade of feudal phraseology which, by the fifteenth century, was meaningless. He would equate these grants with the ordinary non-feudal subsidies previously noted.[120] Such may very well have been true if we are prepared to admit that feudalism was completely dead at the outset of the fifteenth century. But how then can one explain why such grants should so carefully employ feudal terminology when dozens of contemporary grants emanating from the French kings, as well as from other princes, did not? There must have been a difference in the minds of the grantors between the two varieties of subsidies. For these four grants of Charles VI, it seems to me there is an explanation provided by the records more reasonable than Sczaniecki's which, however suggestive, is supported by no evidence. The dukes of Juliers and Guelders, the counts of Cleve and La Mark, and the lords of Reifferscheid had been in receipt of sizable *fiefs-rentes* from the French kings long before they received these lump sums. As far back as 1281 the dukes of Guelders were the vassals of the kings for a *fief-rente*. In 1328 Count William of Juliers had become the man of Philip VI for a fief of 600 *l.* Later when Juliers and Guelders were united, their dukes still received a *fief-rente*. A document of 1388 states that Charles VI had granted a fief of 4,000 gold francs to William of Juliers and Guelders; there is no reason

---

[116] Lacomblet, *Urkundenbuch,* IV, no. 3; A.N., J. 522/26–27.

[117] A.N., J. 522/29.

[118] Lacomblet, *Urkundenbuch,* IV, no. 8.

[119] *Ibid.,* no. 35; A.N., J. 522/30–31. On 3 April 1405 John, lord of Heinsberg, did liege homage to Charles VI and promised military service at the royal wages. He received a subsidy of 2,000 francs (A.N., J. 522/32).

[120] *Essai,* pp. 163–64.

to suppose that the dukes were not receiving the fief in 1401.[121] The lords of Reifferscheid had received a fief of 400 *l.* in 1353.[122] In 1378 before Cleve and La Mark were united Engelbert, count of La Mark, did liege homage for a fief of 2,000 *l.* and Rudolf, count of Cleve, became the liege man of Charles V for a fief of 1,000 old francs.[123] These fiefs continued to be paid down to the end of the fourteenth century. [124] It seems certain, therefore, that in spite of the feudal terminology describing these transactions the lump sums were not *fiefs-rentes*; they were really subsidies granted in addition to the *fiefs-rentes,* and the *fief-rente* was the nexus responsible for the homage and service. So long had these men been the recipients of yearly installments for their fiefs that any concession, whatever its nature, was regarded as being feudal and so described. The *fief-rente* was the feudal foundation upon which the lump sum was super-imposed; the latter in no way was a fief or established a feudal relation.

If all the evidence just reviewed is not sufficient to raise strong doubt as to whether a lump sum could be a *fief-rente,* there is still a more convincing argument. With the concession of any type of fief went the basic assumption that it was able annually to provide an income for the vassal. The lump sum obviously did not fulfil this requirement; it eventually was consumed, leaving nothing in exist-ence that can be considered a fief. We may conclude that a real *fief-rente,* like the ordinary fief of land or enfeoffed office or right to a revenue, had to supply its holder with a yearly income whose source could reasonably be expected to yield it in perpetuity.[125]

In so far as evidence permits us to say, the ceremony for granting *fiefs-rentes* was similar to that for ordinary fiefs. Although there are cases where the relatives of the donor gave their permission to a donation,[126] most often they were granted solely upon the authority

---

[121] Kern, *Acta Imperii,* nos. 21, 80; A.N., J. 522/4, 19. See also J. 522/10ter, 11, 12, 13, 16.

[122] A.N., J. 622 B/69.

[123] A.N., J. 623/82, 83.

[124] A.N., J. 623/93; J. 626/128.

[125] Lyon, *E.H.R.,* LXVI, 169.

[126] In 1344, for example, Herman von der Gowische with the consent of his mother and brother granted Hans von Levede and Arnd Zabel a fief of 3 *m.* payable on the tithe of Rammelsberge to which his mother had the right as her dowry (Bode, *Urkundenbuch Goslar,* IV, no. 240/41). In 1425 Humph-

of the donor who would frequently be the only witness, if indeed there was one. Numerous donations of the English kings simply carried the phrase "teste me ipso" or "teste rege." Commonly there were witnesses of the donor and at times of both parties. A confirmation or *vidimus* was often carried out in the presence of a notary who drew up the document and attached to it his seal along with those of the interested parties and their witnesses.[127] Usually such actions or precautions were considered sufficient guarantee by the vassals, but occasionally we find that the donors offered certain collateral as proof of their good faith or secured certain men to stand bail.

Generally a vassal could not alienate a *fief-rente* except with the approval of the lord. At times the transaction was carried out by the parties concerned in the presence of the lord's representatives who frequently were joined by witnesses of the alienor and new recipient of the fief. Sometimes the relatives of the alienor gave their consent to the alienation. In France, at least, lords were quite insistent upon approving alienations to religious institutions, probably because such occasions gave them opportunity to collect the *droit d'amortissement*. In most cases the whole fief was alienated. The alienor thus lost all rights over the fief and a new feudal relation was opened up between grantor and the new possessor of the fief.[128] All could be done in a single ceremony. In 1273 John de Ghistelles, lord of Maison, sold with the consent of his eldest son John to Chrétien le Grand, bourgeois of Bruges, a fief of 100 *l.* for the sum of 1,200 *l.* Margaret, countess of Flanders, approved the transaction and was represented not only by her bailiff of Bruges but also by some witnesses, the *échevins* of Bruges. The fief was first handed over to the bailiff in the presence of the witnesses and then he invested Chrétien with it who henceforth held it from Margaret.[129]

rey, duke of Gloucester and husband of Jacqueline of Bavaria, countess of Hainaut and Holland, approved her grant of 1,000 *écus* of gold in fief to the duke of Berg (A.G.R., Verkooren, *Inv. Brab.*, unpublished, 13 March 1425).

[127] There are examples in the A.N., J. 620/32; J. 623/88bis; J. 624/34; J. 625/82; J. 626/108, 114. On 30 May 1397 a notarial certificate was drawn up as evidence of the homage done by Rupert the Elder, count palatine of the Rhine and duke of Bavaria, to representatives of Richard II of England for a fief of 1,000 *l.* (P.R.O., Dip. Doc. Exch., E. 30/335). See Appendix, no. 22.

[128] Sczaniecki, *Essai*, pp. 152–59.

[129] De Saint-Genois, *Monuments*, II, 637. See also pp. 697, 737, 829; *Inv.*

For France Sczaniecki has shown that alienation of *fiefs-rentes* whether to other members of the feudal class, to bourgeois, or to the church was extremely common. The frequency of such alienations in the fourteenth century led him to comment that "fiefs-rentes sont devenus eux aussi objets de commerce." Where the fief was alienated *in toto* the lord customarily received as the price of his approval a tenth of the purchase price; where the fief was alienated gratuitously to the church, he collected the amortization tax. There could be partial as well as total alienation of the fief.[130] In general, Sczaniecki's conclusions for France are likewise valid for the Low Countries. Alienation of *fiefs-rentes* was practiced in every principality. As in France, alienations became numerous in the fourteenth century, and indeed it can be said, especially for Flanders and Brabant, that there was a virtual commerce in alienation throughout the fourteenth and fifteenth centuries. With the few cases of partial alienation in the Low Countries, no evidence has been found to indicate that the lords received either the amortization tax or the ten per cent tax on the sale.[131] Alienations of *fiefs-rentes* occurred also in Germany, but to a

des archives de Lille, I, no. 378; Brouwers, *Chart. et règ.,* II, no. 525; A.E.N., Piot, *Inv. Namur,* no. 919. In 1244 Count Matthew of Pontieu confirmed and approved the sale made by Aleaume de Fontaine, lord of Long, to Gilles Langlois, bourgeois of Abbeville, of a fief of 10 *l.* Henceforth Gilles was responsible for the service owed for the fief (Brunel, *Actes de Pontieu,* no. 356). In 1257–58 Louis IX approved the alienation of a fief of 36 *l.* by John and Philip de Nemours to the convent of Sainte-Porte; the transaction was conducted in the presence of royal officials at Paris (*Layettes,* III, nos. 4393–94). See also L. de La Trémoille, *Livre de comptes 1395–1406. Guy de La Trémoille et Marie de Sully* (Nantes, 1887), no. 5; J. Tardif, *Monuments historiques* (Paris, 1866), no. 825. In 1274 *Wildgrave* Godfrey sold a fief of 50 *m.* with the consent of his son Conrad, other members of his family, and his feudal lord, Duke Louis of Bavaria (Goerz, *Mittelrheinische Regesten,* IV, no. 37). See also no. 529; III, no. 1355.

[130] In 1225 John de Boissière sold to William Barbete 15 *l.* from a fief of 55 *l.* held from the bishop of Paris; William did homage to the bishop for the 15 *l.* (*Essai,* p. 153). See also pp. 151 ff. for examples of alienation, as well as *Layettes,* II, no. 2778; III, no. 4394; IV, nos. 408, 5134, 5665; Viard, *Journaux du trésor Philippe IV,* nos. 3700, 5250, 5367; *Journaux du trésor Charles IV,* nos. 5017, 9049, 9053, 9909, 9911.

[131] In 1295 Count Guy of Flanders confirmed the sale of a fief of 100 *l.* by Walter de Bourbourg to Beatrice, the widow of Michel de Cassel, a bourgeois of Ypres. This 100 *l.* was alienated from a fief of 140 *l.* held from Guy; Walter remained in possession of a fief of 40 *l.* whereas Beatrice came to hold the fief of 100 *l.* from Guy (De Saint-Genois, *Monuments,* II, 141–42). See also

much less degree than in France and the Low Countries.[132] Apparently the English kings permitted no alienation of *fiefs-rentes*.

Although as a rule lords on the Continent permitted their vassals to alienate *fiefs-rentes,* some donations in France and the Low Countries specifically forbade the vassals to alienate them outside of the immediate family. Generally this restriction was imposed upon those fiefs which were the most valuable and demanded the most important services. A fief of 1,300 *l.* granted in 1281 by Philip III of France to Count Reginald of Guelders could not be transferred to another person. When Philip IV granted a fief of 500 *l.* to Count Henry VII of Luxemburg in 1294 it was with the limitation that neither Henry nor his heirs were able to alienate it. In 1347 Philip VI gave Count William I of Namur a fief of 1,000 *l.* with the restriction "que nostre dit cousin, ne ses diz hoirs, ou successeurs, contes de Namur, puissent la dicte rente baillier, transporter, traire ou aliener, hors de leurs mains, en quelque maniere que ce soit, fors tant seulement de hoir en hoir, qui contes de Namur seront." [133]

Besides freedom of alienation vassals holding *fiefs-rentes* were entitled to certain other rights. Whenever disputes arose between claimants over *fiefs-rentes* or when differences occurred between lord and vassal, the litigation was carried on in the lord's court before the feudal peers. Litigation connected with fiefs held of kings or great princes was frequently taken to the royal or princely courts for decision. Thus the holder of a *fief-rente* seemed to have the same rights to feudal justice as did the holder of an ordinary fief. In a case decided before the *parlement* of Louis IX of France, William, the son of Hugh d'Arcis, claimed that a fief of 150 *l.* held from the king by his father was heritable and that he should be permitted to succeed to it. The *parlement* declared that the fief had been granted

---

A.E.G., De Saint Genois, *Inv. Fl.*, nos. 1653–54; *Inv. de Termonde,* 14 July 1478 and 30 December 1479; *Verzameling Diegerick,* no. 2; A.D.N., B. 1256/7812, 1292/398, 1332/1351; Bormans, *Fiefs de Namur,* pp. 123, 160, 185, 190, 199, 248, 251, 294 ff.; Gachet, *B.C.R.H.,* IV (1852), nos. 47–50, 90–91; A.G.R., Verkooren, *Inv. Brab.,* no. 257; Van Mieris, *Groot Charterboek,* III, 552; Poncelet, *Actes des princes-évêques de Liège,* nos. 136, 158.

[132] See n. 129.

[133] Kern, *Acta Imperii,* nos. 21, 80, 90; Bovesse, *B.C.R.H.,* XIV (1949), no. 18. See also Devillers, *Monuments,* III, no. 426, p. 585; Viard, *Journaux du trésor Charles IV,* no. 1669; Chantereau le Febvre, *Traité des fiefs,* Preuves, p. 193; Sczaniecki, *Essai,* p. 149.

only for life and should not descend to William; nevertheless, Louis IX decided to grant William a fief of 100 *l.* In 1280 the *parlement* decided that William de la Mure had forfeited a fief of 80 *l.* because he had failed to render homage for it. In another case the *parlement* ordered the count of Dammartin to reinstate the knight John de Fayel in possession of a fief of 30 *l.* of which he had been dispossessed by the count without any judgment.[134] In disputes between lord and vassal over the obligation of the former to pay a *fief-rente,* a board of arbitration would sometimes be appointed to investigate the claims and render a decision. In 1276, for example, the lord of Morbecque, the lord of Kienville, and Baldwin, canon of Morbecque, were constituted a board to arbitrate differences between William, *châtelain* of Saint-Omer, and Boisard de Renenghes. The arbitrators decided that Boisard's claim to a fief of 60 *razières* of wheat was valid and that William was obliged to pay it annually.[135] A dispute between Walerand "dit Duchine" and Gillart du Vivier over rights to a fief of 40 *l.* from the count of Flanders and marquis of Namur was judged by the bailiff and the men of the feudal court of the marquis of Namur; the court rendered a decision in favor of Gillart.[136] In disputes involving the English kings inquests made by royal officers often resulted in ascertaining whether the claims of the vassal were just. In 1238, for example, an inquest determined that the claims of Walter Maylard to a fief of 4 *l.* were just in that Henry II had granted Walter's father a heritable fief of that sum.[137]

Although in England the kings were the only lords to grant *fiefs-rentes,* it is of interest to point out that had other English lords done so and had they then failed to pay the installments, their vassals could undoubtedly have obtained justice in the royal courts by securing a writ of annuity *ex camera.*[138] This writ was developed by the lawyers some time late in the reign of Henry III to meet the needs of those

---

[134] Boutaric, *Actes du parlement,* I, nos. 943, 1650, 2274. See also nos. 396, 475, 945, 1116, 1164; Beugnot, *Les olim,* II, 608–9.

[135] A.D.N., B. 964/1898. See Appendix, no. 4.

[136] De Saint-Genois, *Monuments,* II, 994. In 1340 seven men of the count of Namur settled a dispute between the count and Simon de Kelle concerning payment of a fief of 40 *l.* (A.E.N., Piot, *Inv. Namur,* no. 614).

[137] *Cl.R. 1237–42,* p. 75.

[138] See particularly Maitland, *History of English Law,* II, 133–34; G. J. Turner, *Brevia Placitata* (Selden Society, London, 1947), LXVI, cxxxi–cxxxiii.

7*

who had been granted non-feudal annuities but who had recourse to no royal writ should their annual installments not be paid. These annuities were really personal obligations of the grantors but, in developing this writ, the lawyers had recourse to the fiction that the payments issued out of the grantors' chambers because they could not conceive of an annuity as issuing from an incorporeal source; the annuities, like the customary rents, had to issue out of something corporeal. Rights to the ordinary rents could be obtained by securing the assize of novel disseisin, a legal action used for recovering land; it was likewise considered valid for rents which were conceived as thinglike because they issued from and were paid by the land. But the annuities paid personally by the grantors had no such thinglike attributes; thus the need for a new writ. In so far as we can determine these annuities were used to pay lawyers, clerks, and various officials. Is it not likely that had *fiefs-rentes* been involved the writ of annuity would have been applicable?[139]

Cases of subinfeudation, though never numerous, can be found throughout all four areas. In 1296 Godfrey, lord of Merenberg, granted Henry, governor of Frankfurt, 4 *m.* "titulo feodali" from the 20 *m.* that he held "in feodo a serenissimo domino nostro Adolfo Romanorum rege."[140] In 1262 Philip, lord of Houels, received in fief from the duchess of Brabant and her son Henry "sex caratas vini," part of a fief of "sexaginta caratas vini" held by the dukes of Brabant from the emperors of Germany.[141] In 1285 Edward I of

---

[139] *Brevia Placitata* (p. 31): "Le Rey etc. Nous vous comandoms ke vous iusticez W. de C. ke adreyt e sanz delay rende a G. de E. X mars ke luy sunt arere de un annuel rente de III mars par an [kyl luy deit de sa chambre] si com il dist e si com renablement mustrer purra ke rendre luy deiue ke mes ne etc." See also pp. 109–12; *Year Book 21–22 Edward I*, pp. 129, 541. It is interesting to note that Bracton was aware of these annuities and distinguished them from the ordinary rents: "Si autem sit redditus qui detur alicui ex tenemento ... aut datur cum districtione vel sine ... Si autem redditus sit proveniens ex camera ..." (Henry de Bracton, *De Legibus et Consuetudinibus Angliae,* ed. G. E. Woodbine, New Haven, 1940, III, 117).

[140] Böhmer, *Urkundenbuch Frankfurt,* I, 296. See Lacomblet, *Urkundenbuch,* II, no. 906.

[141] Butkens, *Trophées,* Preuves, I, 100. In 1342 John de Leefdael did homage to the count of Namur for a fief of 30 *l.*: "Et les quelz trente livrees de tiere il a assigne a nous, nos hoirs et successeurs, a prendre et a rechevoir chascun an sur les quatre cens librees de terre au tournois ... que treshaut et tresnobles mon treschiers sires, li dux de Brabant, li doit en la ville de Lou-

England recognized that Gaston de Béarn of Gascony had granted
to Garsion de Lamarque a fief of 50 *l.* out of a fief of 2,000 *l.* held
of the English kings.[142]

Vassals sometimes used *fiefs-rentes* to pay their debts. The vassal
would ask his lord to make payment of his *fief-rente* directly to the
creditor and to continue to do so until the debt was paid in full. In
France, however, Sczaniecki discovered that often four years was the
maximum time that a fief could be so used.[143] In 1296 Count Guy
of Flanders recognized that Count Reginald of Guelders had promised to him for the payment of certain debts the money normally
received from the king of France for a fief of 1,300 *l.* Reginald
notified Philip IV that the money should go to Guy and promised
meanwhile not to demand from Philip the installment for that year.
In 1371 letters of Count Louis de Nevers of Flanders were reproduced in which he recognized that Duke John III of Brabant had
assigned to the merchant Andrien Royer "une somme de chinq mille
et quatre cens livres parisis monnoie de Flandres, la quelle il a assignet de recevoir sur sa rente heritable quil tient de nous en fief
sur nostre thonlieu dou Dam. C'est assavoir diiswiit cens livres parisis
a deus termes cescun an." Louis promised to pay Andrien Royer the
yearly amount of the fief until the debt was paid, and ordered the
collector of the tolls at Damme to pay the money to Andrien "ou
au porteur."[144] Occasionally the recipient of a *fief-rente* would borrow money from his lord and assign over to the lord the annual

---

vain" (A.E.N., Piot, *Inv. Namur,* no. 665). See also De Saint-Genois, *Monuments,* II, 697, 708, 959; A.G.R., *Trés. Fl.,* Sér. I, nos. 2070–71; A.E.G.,
De Saint Genois, *Inv. Fl.,* no. 681; Bormans, *Fiefs de Namur,* p. 100; Brouwers, *Chart. et règ.,* II, no. 444; Van Mieris, *Groot Charterboek,* II, 51. See
Appendix, no. 25.

[142] *R.G.,* III, no. 954. See also IV, no. 1880. For France see Sczaniecki,
Essai, p. 151.

[143] *Essai,* pp. 158–59. In 1238, for example, Hugh de Vallery pledged the
installments of his fief of 30 *l.* held from Count Theobald IV of Champagne
for certain of his debts. During the four years, however, Hugh still owed
feudal service to Theobald. At the end of four years the fief was to be free
of any obligation (D'Arbois de Jubainville, *Hist. de Champagne,* V, no.
2494).

[144] A.D.N., B. 4053/145.393; B. 4053/145.408; De Saint-Genois, *Monuments,* II, 850, 854; A.G.R., *Trés. Fl.,* Sér. I, no. 1270. See also A.G.R.,
Verkooren, *Inv. Brab.,* pt. 2, pp. 176, 191, 211; Wampach, *Urkunden,* V,
nos. 63, 279, 326.

installment of the fief until the loan had been repaid. In 1286 Walerand of Luxemburg, lord of Ligny, received a loan of 2,000 *l.* from Count Guy of Flanders. In turn Walerand pledged his land of Donze and his "fiefs de bourse" held of Guy until the loan should be paid in full.[145] There is some evidence that if a vassal wanted to terminate a feudal relation resting upon a *fief-rente,* he could purchase himself out of it. For example, attached to the fief of 100 *l.* granted in 1296 to Henry, lord of Blamont, by Count Guy of Flanders was the right of Henry or his heirs to purchase their freedom from the feudal relation by paying to the counts of Flanders within three months of doing homage a sum of 1,000 *l.* Having paid the sum, they were to be free and quit of all feudal services.[146]

As for the obligations and rights of the donor of a *fief-rente,* they were similar to those traditionally imposed upon the donor of an ordinary fief. The lord was required faithfully to fulfil the feudal contract and in so far as payment of the fief was concerned he generally did. Scrupulous payment on the part of the donor is testified to not only by the monotonous orders for payment and by the receipts which bulk large in all the archives,[147] but also by records pertaining to the concessions and legal actions. All the concessions had the usual phrase dealing with faithful payment and many stated in addition that tardiness of payment or non-payment of the annual installments would bring various penalties to the lord. In France the kings and lords promised to pay so much in amends for each day or each week the installment was in arrears; the penalties varied from 2 *s.* to 10 *s.* per day or 10 *s.* to 20 *s.* per week. In 1259, for example, Count Theobald V of Champagne granted a fief of 60 *l.* to

---

[145] De Saint-Genois, *Monuments,* II, 738. In 1250 Hugh d'Antigny received a loan of 480 *l.* from the count of Champagne "pro quibus obligavit feodum in quo idem rex ipsi Hugoni annuatim tenetur" (Sczaniecki, *Essai,* p. 159, n. 234).

[146] De Saint-Genois, *Monuments,* II, 859–60.

[147] For England the Liberate, Close, and Patent Rolls are filled with writs directing payments on yearly installments. Many receipts are found in the *Diplomatic Documents of the Exchequer.* Such financial records as the Issue Rolls and Wardrobe Books help to emphasize the regularity with which the installments were paid. For France there is similar evidence in the *Journaux du trésor,* the *Layettes,* and the accounts of the *baillis* and *prévôts.* In the Low Countries we have abundant financial records for all the principalities, as well as numerous receipts found in the charters of the dukes of Brabant. For Germany there is no evidence. See Appendix, nos. 16, 28.

Baldwin de Aourgiis with the promise that he would pay him 20 *s.* for every week the installments were overdue.[148] In 1275 Count Guy of Flanders granted John de Cornus a fief of 99 *hoeuds* of wheat, 381 *hoeuds* of oats, and 80 *l.* Guy added that if the payments fell short, he would add a third of the total sum for damages. In 1285 John de Lannoit sold to Warnier le Pourchiel of Lille a fief of 20 *l.* To insure prompt payment John promised that if the fief was not paid within forty days after Warnier received possession, he could seize another fief of John's held of the count of Flanders.[149]

With the same care that the lords fulfilled their own commitments so they also honored those of their predecessors or those of other lords when for some reason—conquest, inheritance, or escheat—they contracted the obligations of the latter. Sczaniecki has referred to numerous documents showing the French kings honoring grants of *fiefs-rentes* by the counts of Boulogne, Mâcon, and Flanders, as well as by Alphonse of Poitiers.[150] After acquiring Normandy, Philip Augustus confirmed upon occasion concessions made previously by the English kings. In 1200 John had given a fief of 400 *l.* to Count Robert of Dreux; in 1204 Philip Augustus not only confirmed this grant but increased it by 100 *l.*[151] Turning to the Low Countries, we find John, lord of Wildenburg, reminding Duke Philip the Bold of Burgundy in 1386 that Count Louis de Male of Flanders had granted him a fief of 40 francs. Philip confirmed the fief and John did homage for it.[152] Sometimes when a fief had been partitioned among co-heirs, question arose over payment of *fiefs-rentes* granted previously by the former lord of the fief. Naturally none of the co-heirs wanted to assume the entire obligation for paying in full the fiefs

---

[148] *Layettes,* III, no. 4557. See also II, no. 4162; IV, no. 4703; Fawtier, *Comptes du trésor,* no. 1418; Delaborde, *Actes Philippe-Auguste,* I, no. 403; Sczaniecki, *Essai,* pp. 140–41.

[149] De Saint-Genois, *Monuments,* II, 654, 728. See Appendix, no. 3.

[150] A. Molinier, *Correspondance administrative d'Alphonse de Poitiers* (Paris, 1900), II, no. 1714; Viard, *Journaux du trésor Philippe IV,* no. 3270. See also Beugnot, *Les olim,* II, no. 9; *Layettes,* II, no. 1990; III, nos. 3592, 3866, 3973; *Essai,* pp. 134–35.

[151] *Rot. Chart.,* p. 58; Delisle, *Cart. normand,* no. 89. See also *Essai,* p. 135. See Appendix, no. 20.

[152] Quicke and Laurent, *B.C.R.H.,* XCVII (1933), no. 6. In 1424 John, count palatine of the Rhine, confirmed a donation of a fief of 80 florins by his nephew John IV to Elbert van Alphen (A.G.R., Verkooren, *Inv. Brab.,* unpublished, anno 1424).

which, prior to partition, were paid from the resources of a unified and richer block of feudal possessions. The evidence suggests that a compromise was effected whereby the co-heirs would each pay a share of the fiefs.[153]

Yet, however careful most lords were to pay *fiefs-rentes,* there is evidence showing that at times some were in arrears on payments or had failed completely to honor their obligations.[154] According to Gislebert de Mons, none of the ten German and French princes granted *fiefs-rentes* by Richard I of England in 1194 received payment of their fiefs. Such scholars as Kienast, Cartellieri, and Sczaniecki have concurred with Gislebert, pointing out that only Boniface of Montferrat actually received any installments.[155] But more recently A. L. Poole has done much to restore the reputation of Richard by uncovering evidence which suggests that Richard honored his grants to at least half of these men. The fact remains, however, that the other half never received any money and that most of the others did not receive their annual installments for any extended period of time. Almost all of them dropped out of the English alliance and later had to be wooed back by John.[156] Often vassals contrived to

---

[153] See Sczaniecki, *Essai,* p. 135.

[154] Receiving a request from Reginald of Fauquemont in 1394 for the arrears of his fief, Duke Philip the Bold of Burgundy ordered his officers of the *chambre des comptes* at Lille to determine the arrears due in order that they could be paid. Attached to the order was a memorandum on which was jotted down various sums owed to Reginald (Quicke and Laurent, *B.C.R.H.,* XCVII, 1933, no. 11). See also A.G.R., Verkooren, *Inv. Brab.,* unpublished, 16 November 1392, 6 April 1401; Wolters, *Codex Diplomaticus Lossensis,* no. 490. Upon investigating the rolls of the English chancery in 1270 the royal officers found that a sum of 546 *l.* was in arrears to William Arnold de Cadylak on his fief of 25 *l.* Henry III promised to pay this amount as quickly as possible, providing the exchequer records tallied with those of the chancery (*C.P.R. 1266–72,* p. 492). See also J. Stevenson, *Letters and Papers during the Reign of Henry VI* (London, 1861), I, 383; G. Williams, *Official Correspondence of Thomas Bekynton, Secretary to King Henry VI* (London, 1872), I, nos. 133–35.

[155] Gislebert de Mons, *Chronicon,* p. 285: "Conventiones tamen eorum in nulla parte fuerunt observate; nec mirum, cum rex Anglie nemini umquam vel fidem vel pactum servasset, nec omnes illi nominati, cum quibus fedus firmaverat, conventiones suas observare consuevissent." Cf. Kienast, *Deutschen Fürsten,* I, 136–42; Sczaniecki, *Essai,* pp. 133–34; A. Cartellieri, *Philipp II. August, König von Frankreich* (Leipzig, 1910), III, 72, 147 ff., 174.

[156] A. L. Poole, "Richard the First's Alliances with the German Princes in 1194," *Studies in Medieval History, Powicke,* pp. 90–99.

reach an agreement with the lord whereby all or a part of the arrears would be paid. If, however, the lord refused to respond to the complaints of the vassal, then the latter could and did refuse his feudal service.[157] Of course the vassal could resort to renouncement of his fief, but this was not at all satisfactory because he thereby gained nothing and the lord always stood to be the winner financially. Not holding anything tangible belonging to the lord, the vassal had little leverage. If, however, he felt the fief important enough to hold his lord to the terms of the feudal contract, he could resort to force. A good account of such action has come down to us from a collection of documents out of late fourteenth-century Limburg. On 19 September 1393 Arnold de Hoeman, *châtelain* of Odenkirchen, renounced his feudal tie with Philip the Bold, duke of Burgundy, because a *fief-rente* granted to him by Count Louis de Male of Flanders had not been paid either before or after Philip had acquired the Flemish and Brabançon possessions. At the same time Arnold sent letters of defiance to Philip. We next learn from a letter of 25 July 1394 addressed by Margaret of Flanders to her husband Philip that Arnold has refused an offer of payment of the arrears and has announced his intention of continuing hostilities. Later on 15 September 1394 Margaret notified Philip that the financial possibilities of paying the arrears due to Arnold were being investigated. In another letter of the same date we find that Arnold has again refused payment of the *fief-rente* under certain conditions offered to him. Finally, a document of March 1396 informs us that Arnold is in full revolt against the duke.[158]

---

[157] Cf. Sczaniecki, *Essai*, pp. 141–42.

[158] Quicke and Laurent, *B.C.R.H.*, XCVII (1933), nos. 9–10, 18, 28–29, 43. The letters of defiance are quite to the point (no. 10) : "Sachiez que je, Arnoul de Hoemen, chevalier, chastelain de Oedenkerken, vostre ennemi vueil estre et tous voz soubzmanans et tous voz officiers et tous ceulz que je sur vous et sur voz soubzmanans et officiers puisse guerroier, et vueil mon honneur parmi ce avoir gardée." In 1312 Florent Berthout, lord of Malines, declaring that he had never received any payments on a fief held from the count of Namur, stated that he would not be able to render homage for it (Brouwers, *Chart. et règ.*, II, no. 419). In 1417 Conrad, lord of Schleiden, notified Elizabeth, duchess of Brabant, Luxemburg, and Limburg, that a fief of 90 florins held of her was three years in arrears and that unless she responded with prompt payment he would resort to force to collect the money (F.-X. Wurth-Paquet, *Table chronologique des chartes et diplômes relatif à l'histoire de Luxembourg*, Luxembourg, 1870, no. 803). Vassals of the English

While discussing the matter of multiple lordship we saw how hostilities could lead to the forfeiture of *fiefs-rentes*. Forfeiture was carried out more easily with a *fief-rente* than with any other type of fief; all that had to be done was to cease paying the fief. The lord could, if he desired to stop short of pronouncing forfeiture, merely hold up the installments with the hope that this form of pressure would induce the vassal to fulfil his feudal obligations. More often, however, the lord resorted to forfeiture. The French and English kings were continually confiscating *fiefs-rentes* of vassals who had shifted their loyalties. In 1259 Geoffrey de Bosc-Guillaume, the heir of Avise d'Equetot, put in a claim to a fief of 34 s. held by Avise of Philip Augustus which had been confiscated because she had gone to England without the royal permission; Geoffrey did not get the fief. In 1317 William Pizdoe received from the king a fief of 33 l. forfeited by Martin Poncins because of a crime committed.[159] When the dukes of Limburg, who had received a *fief-rente* from Richard I of England, and the counts of Bar, who had received one of 250 l. from John in 1199, shifted their military support to Philip Augustus during the course of the struggle between the French and English kings, their fiefs were immediately confiscated.[160] In an inquest held around 1389 by the officers of Duke Philip the Bold of Burgundy to ascertain his rights in Limburg, a region he had recently acquired from Countess Jeanne of Brabant, it was specified that the receiver of Limburg should not pay any *fiefs-rentes* to men who had become

kings also occasionally had their difficulties in securing payment. In 1341 Edward III told Gerlac, count of Nassau, that because of financial difficulties he would not be able to pay Gerlac's fief until midsummer. Should he fail to do so, Gerlac could withdraw his homage (*C.Cl.R. 1341–43*, p. 132). See also *Cl.R. 1254–56*, p. 305 ; Shirley, *Royal Letters of Henry III*, I, no. 1055 ; II, no. 896 ; P.R.O., Dip. Doc. Chanc., C. 47/28/6(13). See Appendix, nos. 15, 18.

[159] Boutaric, *Actes du parlement*, I, no. 396. See also no. 2274 ; Sczaniecki, *Essai*, pp. 132–33. Sczaniecki interprets the phrases used by the English kings —"quamdiu nobis fideliter servierit" and "quamdiu fuerit ad fidem et servitium nostrum"—as not expressing precarious tenure but rather as expressing the right of the lord to confiscate a fief should the vassal not fulfil his obligations. In some cases Sczaniecki may be correct, but many times these phrases only meant that if the vassal no longer desired to serve the king or if the king no longer needed the vassal's service, the fief could be terminated ; in these cases it was not a matter of forfeiture but a form of provisional tenure.

[160] *Foedera*, I, ii, 106 ; Wampach, *Urkunden*, I, no. 550. See also Kienast, *Deutschen Fürsten*, I, 155–56.

and were at present the enemies of Jeanne or Philip.[161] We have already cited cases where during hostilities vassals renounced their fiefs because they had decided to go over to the enemy; such declarations of renouncement and defiance were really formalities because in any event the fiefs would have been forfeited. Whether the traditional feudal aids were applied to the *fief-rente* is uncertain. Nowhere is there any reference to the practice; the records permit only speculation. Lords known to be in possession of *fiefs-rentes* can be found paying the aids but they also held lands which could have imposed the obligation. There would seem to be no reason to deny their applicability, but unfortunately it cannot be positively affirmed. With the incidents, however, the situation is different. We have already seen that the lords exercised their right of forfeiture. On the Continent there is abundant proof that they also claimed their rights to relief, escheat, and wardship. For Germany and particularly the Low Countries the feudal registers afford the best evidence that we have on relief.[162] In the bishopric of Liège Herbert de Rosa, citizen of Liège, "relevavit V solidos bone monete supra redditus domini episcopi de theolonio in Leodio." [163] In Flanders John de Wernez held "en fief VII^{xx} libr. par an dont il est requerez en un hommage de plain relief." [164] The evidence in France,

---

[161] Quicke, *B.C.R.H.*, XCVI (1932), 381–82. In 1350 Count Louis de Male of Flanders granted to Louis of Namur a fief of 500 *l.* The fief was assigned "sur le thonlieu de Tenremonde, et lesquelles furent jadis au seigneur Dainghien a nous confisqués, acquises et forfaites par le meffait du dit seigneur Dainghien, perpetré et machiné sur et encontre nostre propre personne" (T. de Limburg-Stirum, *Cartulaire de Louis de Male,* Bruges, 1901, II, no. 691). See Appendix, no. 15.

[162] For Germany there are examples in such registers as Von der Brügghen, *Lehensregister Aachener Marienstifts*; Hertel, *Die ältesten Lehnbücher der Magdeburgischen Erzbischöfe*; W. Lippert and H. Beschorner, *Das Lehnbuch Friedrich's des Strengen Markgrafen von Meissen und Landgrafen von Thüringen 1349/1350* (Leipzig, 1903); P. Wagner, *Die Eppsteinschen Lehensverzeichnisse und Zinsregister des XIII. Jahrhunderts* (Wiesbaden, 1927).

[163] Poncelet, *Livre des fiefs,* p. 9. See also pp. 13, 16–18, 31, 37 ff.; Bormans, *Les seigneuries féodales de Liège,* pp. 9, 75, 143, 386.

[164] E. de Coussemaker, *Fiefs et feudataires de la Flandre maritime,* in *Annales du Comité Flamand de France,* XIII (1875), 33. See also pp. 28–32. Among the *Comptes en rouleaux* are the so-called *Reliefs des fiefs* for the town of Bruges, for Ghent and the *châtellenie,* for Courtrai and the *châtellenie,* and for Alost and Grammont; on many of the rolls are entries noting payment for *fiefs-rentes,* as well as for ordinary fiefs. The following examples

though less plentiful than in the Low Countries, shows nevertheless that French lords collected relief when a fief changed hands. In 1228 Hugh de Mareuil did homage and paid relief for a fief of 100 s. to the bishop of Paris. In 1244 Gilles Langlois bought a *fief-rente* whose donor was the count of Pontieu; Gilles was obliged to pay relief to the count.[165] There is no evidence showing that the English kings collected relief on *fiefs-rentes*.

In France, Flanders, and Namur there are cases where provision was made for escheat. We find, for example, that some time about 1200 the count of Pontieu granted to Count Ralph of Eu in augmentation of a fief recently inherited from Count Henry of Eu a fief of 40 *l.* John stipulated that if Ralph had heirs from his marriage with the daughter of Henry then the fief should go to them. But if "autem de ipsa heredem non habuerit, predicte XL libre in manum meam libere et quiete redibunt."[166] Granting a fief of 45 *l.* to Conon de Béthune, Gerard de Saint-Aubert provided that if Conon should die without heirs the fief would escheat back to him. In 1293 Count Guy of Flanders granted John de Bar, brother of the count of Bar, a fief of 200 *l.* If John should die without legal heirs, the fief would go to the count of Bar; if the count was unwilling to do homage for the fief, it would then escheat to Guy.[167]

are typical. A.G.R., Nélis, *Inv.*, Reliefs des fiefs de la ville de Gand et de la châtellenie du Vieux-Bourg de Gand, no. 1917: "De Victor de la Faucille pour le relief dun fief quil a achate a Vincent de la Faucille son frere contenans cinq livrez groz de rente heritable par an . . .X *l.*" Reliefs des fiefs du comté d'Alost et de Grammont, no. 1762: "Premiers de demselle Clare de Vremde fille de Henry le Vremde bourgoise d'Alost qui achetta de Ghiselbrecht de Brerleghem XLVIII livres parisis de rente heritable par an a prendre et rechevoir pour chascun an heritablement sur le tierche part de la grande disme d'Alost appartiens audit Ghiselbrecht quil tient en fief et hommage de monsigneur. . . . Receu pour le relief X *l.* parisis." See also De Schoutheete de Tervarent, *Livre des feudataires des comtes de Flandre au pays de Waes* (Saint-Nicolas, 1873), p. 47. For Namur see Bormans, *Fiefs de Namur*, pp. 22, 69, 81, 104, 107; A.G.R., *C.C.*, no. 3221, Recettes générales de Namur, fol. 78ᵛ; A.G.R., *Manuscrits divers*, no. 15, Cartulaire du comté de Namur, fols. 173ʳ–174ʳ. For Brabant see Galesloot, *Feudataires de Jean III*, pp. 3, 6, 13, 14, 17, 19, 73 ff.; A.G.R., Galesloot, *Cour féodale*, *Eda-Boek* (no. 11), *Hooft-leenboek* (no. 18), *Leenboeck van Overmaeze* (no. 522), and also nos. 33, 119–23. See Plate V, and Appendix, no. 2.

[165] Guérard, *Cartulaire Notre-Dame de Paris*, I, no. 174; Brunel, *Actes de Pontieu*, no. 356.

[166] Brunel, *Actes de Pontieu*, no. 180. See also *Layettes*, II, no. 2926.

[167] *Inv. des archives à Lille*, no. 1197; De Saint-Genois, *Monuments*, II,

The incident of wardship was common to all the continental areas. The guardian was chosen according to local feudal custom. Sometimes the lord himself exercised the incident, sometimes he permitted others to pay for the right to enjoy it, and at still other times the nearest relative of the minor would receive investiture of the fief, enjoy its income, and look after the minor until he reached majority. In 1319 the duchess of Brittany received from the revenues of the *bailliage* of Troyes 2,000 *l.* "pour le fié de ses enfants qu'elle tient en bail."[168] In 1397 Countess Jeanne of Brabant recognized that Margaret van Schoonhoven and her husband Everard Boet had transported to Thierry van den Heetvelde, minor son of Thierry senior, a fief of 10 *l.* As guardian, the father did homage to Jeanne on behalf of his son.[169] In 1368 Warnier de Daules, guardian of the minor heir of John de Hemetines, relieved "30 livrées de terre" held from the count of Namur.[170]

We are not certain what happened when the holder of a *fief-rente* had only a daughter. Probably the institution of marriage applied, with the lord giving his consent to marriage during the lifetime of the girl's father or, as guardian after the father's death, awarding the girl to a desirable suitor. The records do tell us, however, that after a woman inheriting a *fief-rente* had been married, henceforth the husband acted for her. In 1410, for example, Ernekin de Saint Géry, the husband and guardian of Marie, eldest daughter of Collart Chetfalieze, reached an agreement with Count William II of Namur. Ernekin sold back to William a fief which Marie had inherited "en le valeur de noef muis de moulture, qui gisoient sur le molin de Bovingne." In 1444 John de Crouble, husband of Jeanne, daughter

---

817. For Namur see De Reiffenberg, *Monuments,* I, no. 115, p. 299. See Appendix, no. 22.

[168] Longnon, *Documents de Champagne,* III, 167. See also p. 283 and Sczaniecki, *Essai,* pp. 149–50.

[169] A.G.R., Verkooren, *Inv. Brab.,* unpublished, 4 January 1397. See also *Inv. Brab.,* no. 5826.

[170] Bormans, *Fiefs de Namur,* p. 90. For a case in Luxemburg see Verkooren, *Inv. Lux.,* no. 1724. In 1279 Frederick, bishop of Speyer, made known that Raymond of Offenbach held in fief 5 *l.* It was stipulated that, upon the death of Raymond, his sons would receive the fief when they had attained their majority. Apparently Frederick intended to act as guardian should Raymond die before his sons had attained the legal age of heirs (Remling, *Urkundenbuch Bischöfe Speyer,* no. 396).

of Lyonne de Goignies, relieved a *fief-rente* in the county of Namur which his wife had inherited upon the death of her father.[171]

Though some *fiefs-rentes* were granted in serjeanty, in general few were granted to men performing the various services less than knight service. For France, Sczaniecki has convincingly shown that most of the crossbowmen, men-at-arms, and numerous functionaries were remunerated by other means. Down almost to the thirteenth century the court functionaries were maintained and nourished by the lord in his household or given small *rentes* in nature, some of which were feudal. But increasingly in the thirteenth century the functionaries, as well as the military serjeants, came to be paid wages or modest non-feudal *rentes*, usually ranging in value from ten to thirty pounds.[172] After noting as ingenious, but completely unsupported by evidence, the attempt of some scholars to find a body of crossbowmen in the entourage of the count of Champagne (1222-29) remunerated by *fiefs-rentes*, Sczaniecki points out some concessions in serjeanty.[173] Such concessions, however, were rare; most serjeants were remunerated with wages or non-feudal *rentes*.[174] A similar picture emerges from the English records. When not in receipt of a fief of land, the serjeants of the English kings received daily wages or, more customarily, yearly non-feudal payments called fees. The Pipe Rolls of the twelfth and thirteenth centuries show that such functionaries as the approver, moneyer, engineer, clerks, and goldsmith were so paid.[175] To these can be added the forester, hounds-

---

[171] Borgnet, *Cartulaire de la commune de Bouvignes* (Namur, 1862), II, no. 168; Piot, *Inv. Namur*, no. 1329; Bormans, *Fiefs de Namur*, p. 291. See also p. 88.

[172] *Essai*, pp. 44-48.

[173] *Essai*, p. 45. The entry referred to is in the "Feoda Campanie" of D'Arbois de Jubainville, *Histoire de Champagne*, II, nos. 529-32. It merely lists four names under the rubric "Isti sunt balistarii." In 1226 Louis VIII granted his chamberlain a fief of 40 l. in exchange for a fief of two *muids* of wheat; in 1220 Baldwin, the huntsman of Philip Augustus, was given a fief of 20 l.; and in 1224 Louis granted Geoffrey, his falconer, a fief of 24 l. (*Essai*, p. 46; R. Davidsohn, *Philipp II. August von Frankreich und Ingeborg*, Stuttgart, 1888, p. 323).

[174] Sczaniecki cites numerous examples (pp. 46-48). See also Petit-Dutaillis, *Étude sur la vie et le règne de Louis VIII* (Paris, 1894), nos. 277, 376-77, 444, 456; Delisle, *Actes de Philippe-Auguste*, nos. 1667, 1670, 1700, 1854 ff.

[175] For payments to these men see *P.R. 2 Hen. II*, pp. 4, 113; *P.R. 5 Hen. II*, p. 2; *P.R. 4-10 Hen. II*, pp. 113, 13, 18, 67, 71, 20; *P.R. 2-7 Ric. I*,

men, and bailiffs of Normandy,[176] and such serjeants as the royal valet, the buyer of the royal wine, the serjeant-at-arms, falconers, yeomen, controllers of customs, helmet-makers, tellers, and the under-chamberlain.[177] In the few instances where *fiefs-rentes* were conceded to serjeants, all were crossbowmen.[178]

The pattern for the Low Countries differs from that of England and France only in that *fiefs-rentes* awarded to serjeants were more prevalent. Although the financial records indicate that most functionaries were awarded non-feudal *rentes*, not to be overlooked in these records is a sprinkling of *fiefs-rentes*. We learn, for instance, from the *Compte du domaine* of Namur for 1355–56 that Jacques de Bossinnes "pannetier de nostre dit singneur" received from the count 13 *l.* 12 *d.* "pour son fief heritable ... pour cause de le pannetrie du castiel de Namur." William de Peynes, chamberlain of the castle of Namur, received a fief of 30 *l.*[179] One item in an account rendered for 1393–94 by Jean Sack de Wijck, receiver of Limburg, was a fief of "30 viez escuz" to John de Weert, butler of the duchess of Brabant.[180] In an account rendered by the receiver of the county of Guelders for the years 1294–95 under the rubric "Idem feodatis castri Montfort et alibi" appear payments for *fiefs-rentes* to "magistro Johanni et filio suo balistariis ... duobus portariis ... duobus custodibus" and four other serjeants.[181]

It cannot be said from the evidence at hand whether the *ministeriales* who performed court and administrative tasks—the closest

pp. 156, 136, 301, 158, 175, 113; *P.R. 5–10 Ric. I*, pp. 158, 175, 113, 290, 160, 167; *P.R. 9–15 Hen. II*, pp. 20, 30, 130, 2, 2, 170; *P.R. 1–5 John*, pp. 129, 149, 258, 284, 7.

[176] T. Stapleton, *Magni Rotuli Scaccarii Normanniae sub Regibus Angliae* (London, 1840–44), I, 50, 127, 154, 156, 209; II, 304.

[177] *R.G.*, I, nos. 2262, 3164; *Cl.R. 1256–59*, p. 250; *Cl.R. 1261–64*, p. 164; *Cl.R. 1268–72*, p. 186; *C.P.R. 1358–61*, p. 257.

[178] In 1203 Consiliatus "balistarius regis" was granted a fief of 40 *l.*, and in 1232 Henry III granted his crossbowman Halingrat a fief of 50 *l.* of Bordeaux (*Rot. Chart.*, p. 113 b; *Pat. R. 1225–32*, p. 487). See also *Rot. Claus.*, I, 146; *C.L.R. 1240–45*, pp. 231, 272, 299, 304; *C.L.R. 1245–51*, p. 145.

[179] A.E.N., *Comptes du domaine*, no. I, fols. 61v, 62r. On fols. 68r ff. and 90v are entries relating to the wages of the *châtelain*, his functionaries, and some serjeants.

[180] A.G.R., *C.C.*, no. 5725, fols. 14r–14v. Master Peter van Aken, carpenter, held a fief of 20 gold *royaux* from Duke Wenceslas of Brabant (Verkooren, *Inv. Brab.*, no. 5154).

[181] Meihuizen, *Rekening Betreffende Gelre*, p. 15.

German equivalent to serjeants of other areas—received *fiefs-rentes*. We do know from numerous records, however, that a considerable number of *fiefs-rentes* were granted to those *ministeriales* rendering castle-guard. Particularly good examples of this are found in the Goslar document of 1244 referred to previously and in a document of 1311 which records the "bona pheodalia ecclesie et episcopi Halberstadensis" : "Johannes de Quenstede ministerialis—item ii talenta Halb. . . . Wernerus de domo i talentum in moneta Halb., i talentum in theloneo ibidem." [182]

There is abundant evidence that *fiefs-rentes* were granted to bourgeois throughout France, Germany, the Low Countries, and England. But because to deal at length with this custom could not be otherwise than repetitious, it will suffice merely to point out that the feudal law governing *fiefs-rentes* held by aristocrats was no less binding upon the bourgeois.[183] Because homage was never performed for land, money, kind, or any object given in free alms, there is no reason to confuse annual incomes granted in fief with those granted as alms. Grants of annual incomes as alms appear as early as *fiefs-rentes* and are plentiful by the later Middle Ages. In all the financial records the payments of alms are placed beside those of *fiefs-rentes* and non-feudal *rentes*. Too often the payments are not separated but

---

[182] See above pp. 28–29, and Bode, *Urkundenbuch der Stadt Goslar*, I, no. 606; III, no. 475; G. Schmidt, *Urkundenbuch der Stadt Halberstadt* (Halle, 1878), no. 332. See also Goerz, *Urkundenbuch mittelrheinischen Territorien*, II, 467–73. For the *ministeriales* see H. Niese, *Die Verwaltung des Reichsgutes im 13. Jahrhundert* (Innsbruck, 1905), pp. 222 ff.; Ganshof, *Étude sur les ministeriales en Flandre et en Lotharingie* (Bruxelles, 1926); K. Bosl, *Die Reichsministerialität der Salier und Staufer* (Stuttgart, 1950), I, 188–89; II, 575.

[183] France: *Recueil historiens France*, XXIII, 657; Sczaniecki, *Essai*, p. 107. Germany: In 1297 King Adolf granted Eberlin, citizen of Speyer, a fief of 10 m. (Hilgard, *Urkunden Stadt Speyer*, no. 192). See also Böhmer, *Acta Imperii*, no. 61, for a *fief-rente* granted by Henry VII in 1309 to another bourgeois of Speyer. Low Countries: De Limburg-Stirum, *Cartulaire de Louis de Male*, I, no. 487; De Saint-Genois, *Monuments*, II, 639, 728, 841, 880; Bormans, *Fiefs de Namur*, pp. 97, 123, 250–51; Brouwers, *Chart. et règ.*, II, no. 378; Van Den Bergh, *Oorkondenboek van Holland*, II, no. 359. England: In 1290 Edward I granted to Aicard Forton, bourgeois of Bourg-sur-Mer, a fief of 30 *l.* of Bordeaux "pro feodo suo" (*R.G.*, I, no. 1792). Henry III granted in 1242 to "Bartholomeo de Fujer, civi Lugdunensi" a fief of 20 *l.* (*R.G.*, I, no. 1087). See also *R.G.*, I, no. 2409; IV, no. 1913. See Appendix, no. 1.

are included under one rubric such as "Feoda et elemosine."[184] It is then difficult to distinguish the real *fiefs-rentes* without the help of additional records. When holders of *fiefs-rentes* alienated them to religious institutions, they were obviously turned into alms.[185] These alienations attained such proportions on the Continent by the fourteenth century that the financial records eventually came to contain more alms than *fiefs-rentes*; lack of supplementary evidence makes it impossible to determine how many of these alms had originally been *fiefs-rentes*.[186] In England a document will sometimes state that an annual income has been granted in fief to a religious institution. For example, in 1213 John directed payment "fratribus de Chartuse . . . de feodo 50 *m*." We can be certain that here the word *feudum* had no feudal connotation because other writs of payment in the Liberate Rolls state that the brothers of the Charter House are to be paid 50 *m*. yearly "of established alms."[187] In cases of this kind *feudum* means nothing but a non-feudal income or fee; for the English kings never alienated *fiefs-rentes* to the church nor did they permit it to be done by their vassals.

For years a feud has been in progress between the school of Pirenne and that of Giry and Luchaire over the nature of the commune. Pirenne and his followers have argued that during its period of development the commune, basically the product of social and economic forces, was not a part of the feudal hierarchy and was not what Luchaire called a *seigneurie collective*. They furthermore denied that the commune had been called into being by military necessity, that is, by the need of the lord or prince for fortified points with strong

---

[184] Sczaniecki, *Essai*, pp. 136–38, 155–57; Fawtier, *Comptes du trésor*, p. xlv; *Recueil historiens France*, XXI, 263, 267, 277, 279; XXII, 640; Longnon, *Documents de Champagne*, III, 82–84; A.G.R., Nélis, *Comptes en rouleaux*, no. 1. See also R. Monier, *Les institutions financières du comté de Flandre du XIe siècle à 1384* (Paris, 1948), pp. 31 ff. References to alms are numerous in the financial records of France, England, and the Low Countries. In Germany the evidence comes principally from the concessions.

[185] Sczaniecki, *Essai*, pp. 155–57.

[186] *Ibid.*, pp. 155–56.

[187] *Rot. Claus.*, I, 153 b; *C.L.R. 1226–40*, pp. 24, 75, 104, 127. In 1274 the seneschal of Gascony was ordered to pay the abbess "Fontis Ebrordi" the arrears "de feodo suo quod de nobis apud Burdegalam similiter percipere debet per annum" (*R.G.*, III, no. 23). For free alms in English law see Maitland, *History of English Law*, I, 240–41.

garrisons.[188] Despite a recent defense of the Giry–Luchaire theory by Petit-Dutaillis, Pirenne and his followers seem to have the better of the argument in so far as concerns the early period of urban growth in the eleventh and twelfth centuries.[189] It was admitted by both sides that later all self-governing towns, whether or not communes, came to acquire a corporate character and as such came to be considered a fictitious person and so a *seigneurie*.[190] By the thirteenth century it can be said that the self-governing town had not only assumed the role of lord and vassal but had also adopted the behavior of the feudal aristocrat. This development explains why one finds German towns of the Rhine area granting *fiefs-rentes* to feudal lords in return for their homage, fealty, and the promise of a stipulated amount of military assistance whenever necessary for the defense of the town. Usually the vassal was also received as a citizen of the town. All the evidence comes from the Rhine area and pertains in great part to Cologne. Between 1263, the year of the first concession, and 1467, the year of the last, Cologne granted *fiefs-rentes* to thirty-four different feudal families.[191] Because all the concessions are alike, the citation of one will suffice to explain their nature. On 7 May 1263 Walerand, brother of Count William of Juliers, became a *Bürger* of Cologne and promised whenever necessary to come to the aid of the town with nine knights and fifteen squires; Cologne granted him a fief of 100 *m.* for which he did homage and fealty.[192] Later we shall have occasion to comment more fully upon this form of feudal transaction; it is

---

[188] For the views of Giry see his *Histoire de la ville de Saint-Omer*, and his *Les établissements de Rouen* (Paris, 1883), I, 439. For Luchaire see his *Institutions monarchiques* (2d éd., Paris, 1892), and his *Les communes françaises* (Paris, 1890). For an excellent summary of these views, as well as those of the Pirenne school, see C. Stephenson, *Borough and Town* (Cambridge, Mass., 1933), pp. 6–15, 215–19. For other arguments against the Giry–Luchaire theory see S. R. Packard, "The Norman Communes under Richard and John, 1189–1204," *Haskins Anniversary Essays in Mediaeval History*, ed. C. H. Taylor (Cambridge, Mass., 1929), pp. 231–54.

[189] Petit-Dutaillis, *Les communes françaises* (Paris, 1947), pp. 82–123.

[190] Stephenson, *Borough and Town*, p. 217, n. 4.

[191] These grants are found in Ennen and Eckertz, *Quellen Stadt Köln*, vols. II–V. Many are duplicated in Lacomblet, *Urkundenbuch*, vols. II–IV.

[192] Ennen and Eckertz, *Quellen Stadt Köln*, II, no. 450. For other examples see II, nos. 449, 452–54, 457; III, nos. 485, 521, 527; IV, nos. 11, 217, 488; V, nos. 14, 73, 76, 403, 405.

enough for now to have called attention to its prominence in Germany.

One problem yet remains for consideration—the difference between what the English lawyers call a tenurial rent (rent service) and a non-tenurial rent (a rent constituted by lord) and between what the French lawyers call a *rente foncière* and a *rente constituée*. To which type of rent, or *rente*, did the *fief-rente* belong?[193] The tenurial or *foncière* type was created whenever an individual, called the creditor, transferred to another individual, called the debtor, the proprietorship of an immobile piece of property, be it land or a house, and reserved the right over this property of receiving from the debtor a determined yearly sum called a rent. This transaction thus put into being a landlord and a tenant whose proprietorship over some form of property resulted in his owing a yearly rent. Such an annual income was created only as a result of certain economic benefits envisaged by landlord and tenant; feudal considerations were not a part of such a transaction which involved neither fief holding, nor vassalage, nor mutual feudal obligations. And indeed the annual income was paid by tenant to landlord rather than the reverse as was the case with *fiefs-rentes*. Obviously, then, *fiefs-rentes* cannot be placed in the category of tenurial rents or *rentes foncières*.

On the other hand, the non-tenurial rent or *rente constituée* was born out of an operation whereby the lord of a piece of land or other property sold or gratuitously gave to another individual the right of receiving on his property a stipulated annual income. This operation also has traditionally been associated with transactions evolving out of economic considerations. A landlord might have a sudden need for a sum of money and so would sell for a stipulated price an annual income to be paid by his property or to be assigned upon a rent or rents received from his tenants. In the latter case he still reserved all his other rights over the land from which he received the rent but merely made arrangements for the annual income to be paid by what is called a tenurial rent. It might also happen that an individual,

---

[193] For this subject see C. Lefebvre, *Observations sur les rentes perpétuelles* (Paris, 1914), pp. 72 ff.; Petot, *Constitution de rente aux XIIe et XIIIe siècles*, pp. 59–81; Olivier Martin, *Histoire de la coutume de la prévôté et vicomté de Paris* (Paris, 1922), I, 441–98; Didier, *Revue du Nord*, XVII, 265–67; Sczaniecki, *Essai*, pp. 108–12; G. Waitz, *Deutsche Verfassungsgeschichte*, VI, 27; Maitland, *History of English Law*, II, 130–34.

8*

desiring to invest some money in order to provide himself with the security of an annual income, would buy an annual income from some person who would assign its payment on his property. The constitution of an annual income could also be gratuitous and the income could be assigned for life or heritably and be paid in money or kind. Such transactions, as Petot has remarked, were prompted by motives which gave birth to a variety of juridical acts such as providing legacies, gifts, dowries, and fiefs. Because non-tenurial rents or *rentes constituées,* like the tenurial rents or *rentes foncières,* have been explained and sharply distinguished by lawyers on the basis of private law and economic incentive, and because feudal thinking did not loom large in the definition or the division of the two categories, it is not wholly accurate to place the *fief-rente* in either category. It is nevertheless the constituted income that the *fief-rente* most resembles and consequently with which it should be associated.

It is evident that in general the *fief-rente* fell within the framework of traditional feudal custom. But when such custom was not adequate for the characteristics peculiar to this new fief, it was amended. From a juridical study of the *fief-rente* one is convinced that feudal custom had to become more flexible to meet the new demands of a changing feudal age—a conclusion that becomes more apparent from a study of the finance of the *fief-rente*.

III

The Finance of the Fief-Rente

A study of the finance of the *fief-rente* is more than an investigation of the techniques used for payment; it is actually an inquiry into the financial history of medieval western Europe. While tracking down the sources utilized to pay *fiefs-rentes*, one learns about the great number of monetary resources made available to the medieval prince by the economic revolution in progress. The type of financial resources relied upon to pay *fiefs-rentes* shows the stage attained in the development of the money economy and indicates the leading forms of economic specialization in the different regions. It is not strange that the revenues of towns, tolls, and duties bore the brunt of financing the *fief-rente* in the Low Countries and the Rhineland. Nor is it surprising to discover *fiefs-rentes* assigned on the incomes of the Champagne fairs, or to learn that duties on wine in Luxemburg and southern France, wool customs in England, societies of bankers and the Templars in England and France, and incomes in kind throughout the areas more backward economically, were significant in the payment of *fiefs-rentes*. But even more enlightening is the glimpse into the mechanics of finance in each medieval state. The complete financial apparatus of every ruler is bared, from the most insignificant of his revenues and officers on up to the central treasury and its administration. Thus it is possible to compare the techniques and efficiency of the financial systems and so to conclude that those of England, France, and such Low Country states as Flanders and Brabant, were the most efficiently and highly organized, and to admit that the organization developed by the English kings had attained the highest degree of perfection permitted by the age. To one who has worked with the unprinted as well as the printed financial records of England, France, and the Low Countries, their tremendous bulk serves as an impressive reminder that much of the Middle Ages in western Europe was characterized not by economic hibernation but by a dynamic economic movement leading rapidly to the modern world.

Contrary to what might be expected, the earliest concessions of *fiefs-rentes* were not predominantly in kind. It is quite possible that some of the fiefs expressed in values of money may have been paid in kind, but there is no evidence to verify this suggestion. Only in France, and then only in the eleventh and early twelfth century, did fiefs in kind prevail; thereafter fiefs of money dominated,[1] although fiefs in kind never disappeared. In Germany almost all the earliest fiefs were of money.[2] In the Low Countries the eleventh and twelfth centuries saw *fiefs-rentes* about evenly divided between kind and money; thereafter, at least four-fifths were of money.[3] The English kings never granted more than a handful of fiefs in kind; all their early concessions were in money.[4] The early evidence is too spotty and too often inadequate to say definitely what arrangements were first made to provide payment. For France, England, and the Low Countries, however, the evidence seems to show the grantors assigning the fiefs principally on the administrative districts such as the *prévôtés, châtellenies, domaines,* and counties, as well as upon duties and tolls, fairs, and seignorial incomes.[5] Apparently in none of the

---

[1] See Ch. I, pp. 25–26; Sczaniecki, *Essai,* pp. 159 ff.

[2] See Ch. I, pp. 28–29.

[3] See Ch. I, pp. 29–31.

[4] See Ch. I, pp. 33–39. It should be emphasized that the fiefs in kind were **extremely few and occurred only in Normandy.** Reference was made previously to the "duas quadrigatas vini" held by Richard de Hugleville of Normandy from William I (Ch. I, p. 25). The only other fiefs in kind are found in the Norman Pipe Rolls toward the end of the twelfth century. In 1180 there is a payment to the "militibus de Pormort 28 *s.* pro 2,000 harengorum de feodo"; in 1195 a payment to "Willielmo de Amiens 6 *s.* pro 1 sextario grossi bladi de feodo" (Stapleton, *Mag. Rot. Scacc. Norm.,* I, 59, 127).

[5] Some time between 1151 and 1182 the count of Soissons held from Count Henry I of Champagne a fief of 30 *l.* "in theloneo et pedagio Castri Theodorici" (D'Arbois de Jubainville, *Histoire de Champagne,* II, Documents, V). In 1200 Count Theobald III of Champagne assigned a fief of 60 *l.* "in nundinis Barri" (Chantereau le Febvre, *Traité des fiefs,* Preuves, p. 17). A fief granted in 1195 by the count of Pontieu was assigned on the revenues of the *vicomté* of Abbeville (Brunel, *Actes de Pontieu,* no. 139). Fiefs granted by Philip Augustus in 1185, 1191, and 1192 were assigned, respectively, on the *prévôté* of Poissi, the *prévôté* of Paris, and the royal granaries of Lorris (Delisle, *Cat. des actes Philippe-Auguste,* nos. 136, 334, 358; Delaborde, *Actes de Philippe-Auguste,* I, no. 403). A fief of 300 *m.* was granted in 1182

regions except England and Normandy were the financial systems sufficiently organized to encourage assignment upon a central treasury. Certainly some fiefs were paid by the treasuries, such as they were, but there is little evidence of this practice.[6] It was common only in Germany for concessions to stipulate the *camera* as the source of payment; and this *camera,* it should be understood, was not that of a large feudal state but simply the treasury of an abbey, bishop, or ordinary feudal lord.[7] Not until the thirteenth century are the records adequate for a detailed investigation of the finance of the *fief-rente.*

No matter by what name the treasuries of the different feudal states were known, all were paying *fiefs-rentes* by the thirteenth century. From then until the end of the fifteenth century the role of the treasury is significant, particularly in England and France where fully eighty-five per cent of all *fiefs-rentes* granted by the kings were assigned on their treasuries. Although the number of *fiefs-rentes* paid by the treasuries of the French lords, the Low Country princes, and the German emperors and princes is comparatively much less, still it is not insignificant. But to comprehend fully the value of the treasury as the disbursing agent for *fiefs-rentes* and to gain a basis for comparison, it is essential to study the relation between treasury and *fief-rente* in each region.

In France the kings and likewise some lords assigned their fiefs *in bursa,* the equivalent of their treasury. In 1229 Athon Arnaud de Castel-Verdun received from Louis IX 50 *l.* "annuatim de bursa."[8] Some time around 1260 the count of Boulogne granted a

by Frederick I of Germany on the tolls of Nimwegen (Bondam, *Charterboek van Gelderland,* II, no. 64). In 1185 the count of Hainaut assigned a fief of 200 *l.* "in winagio de Roia" (Gislebert de Mons, *Chronicon,* p. 182). The Pipe Rolls for the reigns of Henry II and Richard I have numerous entries showing that the revenues of counties paid the fiefs of the counts of Flanders, the archbishop of Cologne, and many anonymous Flemish knights. There is also evidence in the Great Rolls of the Norman Exchequer. For example, in 1198 Henry de Gray, bailiff of Verneuil, rendered account of 700 *l.* for the farm of this *praepositura.* Among the payments accounted for was "20 *l.* de feodo" of William Lestanc (Stapleton, *Mag. Rot. Scacc. Norm.,* II, 311). See also I, 68, 132, 138, 157.

[6] See below p. 106.
[7] In 1048, for example, the abbot of Fulda granted a fief of 8 talents "a camera abbatis" (Dronke, *Codex Fuldensis,* no. 749). See also Ch. I, p. 28.
[8] *Layettes,* II, no. 2020. See also Sczaniecki, *Essai,* pp. 4, 114.

fief of 10 *l.* "in bursa" to a certain William de Ruella. In 1261 a certain Marc de Voigny held a fief "in bursa" from Count Theobald V of Champagne.[9] The equivalence of *bourse* and *trésor* is well shown by a grant of Louis IX: in 1257 the brothers John and Philip de Nemours swore in the presence of royal officials at Paris that they had received their fief of 36 *l.* of Paris "in bursa domini regis, ad domum milicie Templi Parisiensis."[10] Occasionally fiefs were assigned "in coffris domini regis."[11] In accordance with the evolution of the royal treasury, *fiefs-rentes* were, for the most part, assigned on the Temple up to 1295, on the *trésor* of the Louvre from 1295 to 1303, and simply on the *trésor* in the fourteenth and fifteenth centuries.[12] Thus in 1259 John de Mont-Saint-Jean received from Louis IX a fief of 300 *l.* "apud Templum."[13] The *fiefs-rentes* granted late in the century by Philip IV to the counts of Guelders and Luxemburg, the dukes of Lorraine, and the dauphins of Vienne, were all assigned on the Temple at Paris.[14] A series of Temple accounts from 1286 to 1295 indicate that it paid out large sums yearly for the royal *fiefs-rentes*.[15] Other lords also used the Temple. In 1253 Charles of

[9] Sczaniecki, *Essai*, p. 115. The counts of Nevers and the dukes of Burgundy also granted fiefs on their *bourse* (*Essai*, p. 115).

[10] *Layettes*, III, nos. 4393–94. See also no. 4266; Sczaniecki, *Essai*, p. 115.

[11] For example, in 1229 Louis IX granted Jocelin de Champchevrier a fief of 50 *l.* "in coffris domini regis," and in 1254 Alphonse of Poitiers granted a fief of 15 *l.* "in coffris nostris" to Raymond de Saint-Martin (*Layettes*, II, no. 2035; III, no. 4109).

[12] See Viard, *Journaux du trésor de Philippe IV*, pp. i–lxii; *Journaux du trésor de Charles IV*, pp. i–cix; *Journaux du trésor de Philippe VI*, pp. i–lxxiv; Lot and Fawtier, *Le premier budget de la monarchie française* (Paris, 1932); Fawtier, *Comptes du trésor*, pp. v–lxxi. Borrelli de Serres gives a detailed account of the reorganization of the treasury under Philip IV (*Divers services publics*, III, 5–45).

[13] *Layettes*, III, no. 4550. For the role of the Templars in the royal finances see Delisle, *Mémoire sur les opérations financières des Templiers.*

[14] Kern, *Acta Imperii*, nos. 21, 80, 90, 303, 307. See also Langlois, *Registres perdus des archives de la chambre des comptes de Paris* (Paris, 1916), nos. 16–17, 35, 54, 65; Delisle, *Opérations des Templiers*, nos. 16, 26, pp. 47–49, 59, 92, 146, 148–49. See Appendix, no. 12.

[15] Delisle, *Opérations des Templiers*, pp. 118–31. Frequently when fiefs are combined under one rubric "Feoda, dona et hernesia" it is impossible to ascertain the amount paid just for fiefs. At other times the sums paid for fiefs are listed separately as, for example, in an account of 1289—*Feoda ad parisienses*: 5,547 *l.* 6 *d.* In an account for 1292 we find *Feoda ad hereditatem*: 406 *l.* 8 *s.* 2 *d.*, and *Feoda ad vitam*: 693 *l.* 11 *s.* 6 *d.*

Anjou granted to the knight Arnulph de Cison a fief of 60 *l.* on the Temple. In 1266 Agnes of Bourbon gave Count Robert of Dreux a fief of 200 *l.* payable by the Temple.[16] The growing breach between the Templars and Philip IV resulted in Philip's locating the treasury at the Louvre in 1295 where it remained until 1303. During this period numerous fiefs were assigned on the Louvre.[17] In one of the earliest accounts for the *trésor du Louvre,* that of 1296, are many examples of *fiefs-rentes.*[18]

Meanwhile the treasury was being reorganized under the direction of royal functionaries, and in 1303 when it was moved back to its old quarters at the Temple it was completely administered by royal servants; the Templars were no longer connected with the royal finances. Henceforth, regardless of location, we hear simply of the *thesaurus* or *trésor* upon which the majority of *fiefs-rentes* came to be assigned.[19] During the early phases of the Hundred Years' War hundreds were so granted by Philip VI; seldom in fact were any granted on other sources.[20] In spite of the difficulty mentioned previously in distinguishing *fiefs-rentes* from alms and non-feudal *rentes,* a reasonably accurate estimate of the volume of *fiefs-rentes* paid by the treasury can be obtained from such records as the *Journaux du trésor* of Philip IV, Charles IV, and Philip VI; the *Ordinarium Thesauri* of 1337–38; and the various other *Comptes du trésor.*[21]

[16] *Layettes,* III, no. 4089; Huillard-Bréholles, *Titres de la maison ducale de Bourbon* (Paris, 1867), I, no. 444; Delisle, *Opérations des Templiers,* p. 47.

[17] In 1296 Philip granted Bouchard, bishop of Metz, a fief of 2,000 *l.* on the "Lou[v]re de Paris"; in 1297 Robert, count of Boulogne, received a fief of 1,000 *l.* "sur le Trésor du Louvre"; and the same year Béraud de Mercœur received a fief of 200 *l.* on the Louvre (Kern, *Acta Imperii,* no. 114; Langlois, *Registres perdus,* nos. 3–4, 12, 30 ff.).

[18] J. Havet, "Compte du trésor du Louvre (Toussaint 1296)," *Biblio. de l'École des Chartes,* XLV (1884), 249–50; Fawtier, *Comptes du trésor,* pp. 1–24.

[19] For examples of the early fourteenth century see Langlois, *Registres perdus,* nos. 9, 22, 23, 26, 27, 28, 68, 69, 73; Funck-Brentano, "Philippe le Bel et la noblesse, Franc-Comtoise," *Biblio. de l'École des Chartes,* XLIX (1888), 238–53, no. 10; Kern, *Acta Imperii,* no. 157; L. Ménard, *Histoire civile, ecclésiastique et littéraire de la ville de Nîmes* (Nîmes, 1873), I, 367, 370; Du Chesne, *Maison de Béthune,* Preuves, p. 185.

[20] The following references represent only a few of the examples in the *hommages* of *Série J.,* A.N.: J. 620/24, 30, 32, 34, 37, 39, 45–46, 48; J. 621/51–52, 59–60, 62, 83, 86. See Appendix, no. 23, and Plate IV.

[21] See Viard, *Journaux du trésor de Philippe VI,* nos. 5179–5396.

The *feoda* for *Noël* 1298 total 3,242 *l.* of Paris; for the terms of *Saint-Jean* and *Noël* 1299, 6,709 *l.* of Paris; and for *Noël* 1301, 3,104 *l.* of Paris. The arrears of fiefs granted heritably, for life, or during pleasure total 27,055 *l.* 10 *s.* 2 *d.* of Paris for the term *Toussaint* 1327. For *Noël* 1349 the *Redditus ad hereditatem* total 19,338 *l.* 16 *s.*; the *Redditus ad vitam,* 9,837 *l.* 3 *s.* 7 *d.*[22] An *ordonnance* establishing the royal budget for 1314 allocated approximately 60,000 *l.* for payment of fiefs and alms.[23] The sums so decrease in the fifteenth century that by *Noël* 1477 we find only 160 *l.* paid for *fiefs-rentes* granted for life or during pleasure; 410 *l.* 8 *s.* were paid for *pensiones ad voluntatem,* which obviously were not *fiefs-rentes.*[24]

In England, though we lack evidence specifically stating the financial source, it seems reasonable to suggest that the few *fiefs-rentes* granted by the kings before 1118—a time when the definite existence of the exchequer can be established—were paid either out of the royal chamber or out of its more highly developed successor, the treasury.[25] Or perhaps they were paid directly from the issues of the counties; we cannot, however, affirm this for no Pipe Rolls are extant until 1130. When the chancery enrollments begin in 1199 we have official evidence for the payment of *fiefs-rentes* by the exchequer; prior to this there is but one reference to payment of a *fief-rente* by the exchequer. Describing a meeting of Henry II and Count Philip of Flanders in 1175 at Caen, Benedict of Peterborough states that they concluded a treaty and that Henry granted to Philip "1,000 *m.* esterlingorum recipiendas ad scaccarium."[26] The chancery enrollments, the Issue Rolls of the exchequer, and the numerous receipts for payments prove that the exchequer paid the bulk of *fiefs-rentes* during the next three centuries.[27]

---

[22] Fawtier, *Comptes du trésor,* pp. lvi–lviii, lxi, lxiv.

[23] Boutaric, *Notices et extraits de documents inédits relatifs à l'histoire de France sous Philippe le Bel* (Paris, 1865), no. 40.

[24] Fawtier, *Comptes du trésor,* p. lxxi.

[25] For the early development of the royal treasury and exchequer see R. L. Poole, *The Exchequer in the Twelfth Century* (Oxford, 1912), pp. 21–41; T. Madox, *The History and Antiquities of the Exchequer of the Kings of England* (2d ed., London, 1769), I, 154–96; *Dialogus de Scaccario,* ed. A. Hughes, C. G. Crump, and C. Johnson (Oxford, 1902), pp. 13–28; Tout, *Chapters,* I, 74–99. See also J. H. Round's chapter, "The Origin of the Exchequer," in *The Commune of London and Other Studies* (Westminster, 1899).

[26] Benedict of Peterborough, I, 246–47.

[27] In 1199 John granted Geoffrey de Cella a fief of "100 *l.* sterlingorum

During the reigns of John and Henry III some *fiefs-rentes* were assigned on the royal chamber. Under Henry III some were also granted on the wardrobe which by then had superseded the chamber in most of the royal financial operations not handled by the exchequer.[28] It comes as a surprise to learn from the chancery enrollments and the Wardrobe Books that even though relatively few *fiefs-rentes* were originally granted on the chamber or wardrobe prior to the reign of Edward III, both, and in particular the wardobe, were important in the finance of the *fief-rente*. Commonly one finds the wardrobe paying fiefs assigned on the exchequer. To understand this somewhat peculiar arrangement it must be realized that already with Henry II the chamber and its subsidiary, the wardrobe, were not only paid sums by the exchequer but were receiving and paying large sums of money independently of the exchequer.[29] When the

---

annuatim recipiendas ad scaccarium nostrum"; in 1242 Henry III conceded to "Reimundo, vicecomiti de Frunzak, 100 *l.* sterlingorum, singulis annis percipiendas ad scaccarium nostrum Londonie"; and in 1370 Edward III granted Herman de Bosco a fief of 50 *m.* at the exchequer (*Rot. Chart.*, p. 11; *R.G.*, I, no. 372; *C.P.R. 1367–70*, p. 375). There are other grants and writs ordering payment in *Rot. Claus.*, I, 91 b, 95; II, 142 b; *Foedera*, II, ii, 971, 992, 997, 1098, 1101, 1104; *Rot. Lib.*, p. 17. For payments see F. Devon, *Issue Roll of Thomas de Brantingham, A.D. 1370* (London, 1835), pp. 90, 118, 126, 128, 131, 439, 441, 462–63, and *Issues of the Exchequer* (London, 1837), pp. 32–33, 37, 100, 233; P.R.O., E. 403/61 (anno 1290), mm. 1–2; E. 403/105 (anno 1299), mm. 4–6. For receipts see Palgrave, *The Antient Kalendars and Inventories of the Treasury* (London, 1836), I, 47, 49, 85–87, 147; "Cal. Dip. Doc.," in *D.K.R.*, XLV, app. i, 287, 325–26; XLVIII, app., 763; P.R.O., E. 30/46, 1228, 1320, 1415, 1432. See Appendix, nos. 14, 16, 30, and Plates I–II.

[28] In 1216 John granted Richard Lucet a fief of 15 *m.* "de camera nostra." In 1254 Archenbald, count of Périgord, was granted a fief of 300 *l.* of Bordeaux payable by the chamber (*Rot. Pat.*, p. 185; *R.G.*, I, no. 3769). See also *R.G.*, I, nos. 2073–74, 2094, 3894; *Rot. Norm.*, p. 29; *Rot. Chart.*, p. 218 b. For payment of fiefs by the chamber and its castle treasuries during the reign of John see Jolliffe, *Studies in Medieval History, Powicke*, pp. 117 –42. In 1242 Henry III conceded to Guy de la Palu 40 *m.* payable "de garderoba nostra" (*R.G.*, I, no. 931). See also *R.G.*, I, nos. 264, 301; *Pat. R. 1232 –47*, p. 309; *C.L.R. 1226–40*, p. 257. There is also evidence in the Wardrobe Debentures (P.R.O., E. 404/500/252, 305; E. 404/501/47, 53, 91; E. 404/ 502/111, 139, 142; E. 404/503/123).

[29] For the chamber and wardrobe see Tout, *Chapters*, I, 158–69, 188–205; C. Johnson, "The System of Account in the Wardrobe of Edward I," *Transactions of the Royal Historical Society*, 4th ser., VI (1923), 50–72; J. H. Johnson, "The System of Account in the Wardrobe of Edward II," *Trans.*

wardrobe separated itself from the chamber and became the paramount private financial department of Henry III, it continued the
same practice on a much expanded level. This private royal treasury
constantly had to be nourished in order to fulfil its financial obligations. Not only did it provide for all the royal necessities and whims,
and pay a considerable household staff, but it took over the functions of a war treasury, particularly in the reigns of Henry III,
Edward I, and Edward III. Being mobile and migrating about with
the king as it did, it was much more suited for paying many of the
royal obligations than was the stationary exchequer located at Westminster.[30] Especially did it facilitate payments to royal creditors on
the Continent when the kings were there. A creditor who normally
received money from the exchequer would then receive it from the
wardrobe, thus obviating the need for the creditor to go or send
messengers to England, or for the exchequer to make arrangements
on the Continent to pay the money or to send it by messengers. The
evidence for this practice is most plentiful when Henry II was conducting the Poitevin campaigns, when Edward I was in Flanders in
1297, and when Edward III was in the Low Countries at different
times between 1338 and 1340. It was the wardrobe that did the
on-the-spot financing of these expeditions. The exchequer was not
concerned where the money went as long as it had the authority to
issue the money. The exchequer and its accounting officials received
this authority to pay large sums to the wardrobe from the royal writs,
in particular the writs of *liberate*; in return it required the wardrobe
officials to account yearly for all the money they handled. Frequently,
as Tout has pointed out, the sums accounted for in the Wardrobe
Books closely tally with the sums received from the exchequer. What
must be remembered, however, is that although the wardrobe paid a
great number of *fiefs-rentes,* in the last analysis it was the exchequer
that supplied the money.

Roy. Hist. Soc., 4th ser., XII (1929), 75–104, and *English Government at
Work,* I, 206–49; Jolliffe, "The *Camera Regis* under Henry II," *E.H.R.,*
LXVIII (1953), 1–21, 337–62; S. B. Chrimes, *An Introduction to the
Administrative History of Mediaeval England* (Oxford, 1952), pp. 77 ff. Entries
such as the following become common during the reign of John : "Joscelinus
de Walpol r.c. de 700 m. pro habenda benevolentia R. In thes. Nil. Et ipsi
R. in camera sua 200 m. per breve R. Et debet 500 m. Idem r.c. de eodem
debito ... Et ipsi R. in camera sua 200 m." (*P.R. 10 John,* p. 15).
   [30] Tout, *Chapters,* I, 195.

A few entries may help to clarify the foregoing discussion. In the summer of 1230 the wardrobe, recently supplied with sums of 20,000 *m.* and 2,000 *l.* from the exchequer, was daily paying *fiefs-rentes,* salaries, and other war expenses to the English army in Poitou. It paid 200 *m.* to "Willelmo de Rupe domino de Jovenzyaco, et ... 12 *l.* 10 *s.* ei liberandis de annuo feodo 25 *l.* quas percipit ad scaccarium domini regis." On 17 July 1230 Geoffrey de Ponte, a Poitevin baron, was granted a fief of 100 *m.* "ad scaccarium nostrum in Anglia." On 27 August 1230 the wardrobe clerks, Kirkham and Crowcombe, were ordered to pay from the wardrobe 700 *m.* to Reginald de Ponte and 100 *m.* to his son Geoffrey.[31] On 23 September 1230 letters patent confirmed the previous grant of 17 July and ordered the fief to be paid at the exchequer; it was also ordered to be so paid by writs of *liberate* for the years 1232–33 and 1238–41.[32] It may therefore be assumed that in time of peace *fiefs-rentes* were paid by the exchequer when so ordered by writs of *liberate,* but that if hostilities were in progress in Poitou, the wardrobe, being there, would pay the fiefs.

In Germany comparatively few *fiefs-rentes* were assigned on the treasuries which were always called chambers. Such grants usually came from the emperors, although in 1092 the archbishop of Bremen granted a fief of 8 *l.* "de camera nostra" to a certain Gerhard von Stumpenhusen, and in 1239 the archbishop of Trier granted a fief of 4 *l.* on his chamber to the countess of Luxemburg and her son.[33] It is significant to note that the two emperors most often granting fiefs on their treasuries were Frederick II and Henry VII, both of

---

[31] *Cl.R. 1227–31,* p. 431; *C.L.R. 1226–40,* p. 150; *Pat. R. 1225–32,* pp. 386, 397–99; *Cl.R. 1227–31,* p. 430.

[32] *C.L.R. 1226–40,* pp. 187, 211, 236, 308, 317, 378, 430, 473, 502; *C.L.R. 1240–45,* pp. 44, 77. Both Count Guy of Flanders and John de Bar customarily received fiefs from the exchequer during the reign of Edward I, but when the wardrobe accompanied Edward to Flanders in 1297 it paid the fiefs as well as military subsidies and wages (*Wardrobe Book 25 Edward I,* British Museum, Add. MS. 7965, fols. 155v–156v, 158r). Likewise when Edward III was in the Low Countries in 1338 the wardrobe paid fiefs. Baldwin, archbishop of Trier, received 506 *l.* 5 *s.* for his fief and wages. William de Vord' received 195 *l.* for his fief of 20 *l.* and war wages. Count Robert of Varneburg received 172 *l.* 10 *s.* "super feodo suo ... pro retentia sua" (*Wardrobe Book 12–16 Edward III,* P.R.O., E. 36/203, fols. 328, 334).

[33] Lappenberg, *Hamburgisches Urkundenbuch,* I, no. 119; Goerz, *Regesten der Erzbischöfe zu Trier,* p. 42.

whom spent much of their reigns in Italy and Sicily where there was
a highly developed money economy. A grant of a fief of 300 ounces
of gold in 1248 by Frederick II to Guy, dauphin of Vienne, was
payable "de camera nostra." Conceding a fief of 200 m. in 1312 to
Manfred de Claromonte, Henry VII ordered it to be paid "a camera
dicti domini imperatoris." [34]

The treasuries of the Low Country princes, called *bursa* or *bourse*,
took a more active part in the finance of the *fief-rente*. The princes
who relied most heavily on the *bourse* were the counts of Flanders,
the dukes of Brabant, and the bishops of Liège. Typical of the
numerous examples is one of 1295. In that year Louis de Beaujeu,
lord of Breucq, declared that Count Guy of Flanders had recognized
to owe "cescun an hiretablement a mi et men hoir cent livres de
Paresis de fief en bourse." [35] In addition to such concessions on the
bourse there is other evidence that Low Country treasuries paid *fiefs-
rentes*. Some of the states had developed central financial organizations long before the fourteenth century but by that time almost all
had a treasurer called a *receveur général* or *Rentmeester* who administered a central treasury. To this treasurer were rendered yearly
the accounts of all the administrative and financial officers and to
him also were paid the varied incomes of the prince; he was then
responsible for making payments from the receipts to princely creditors. [36] When fiefs are found, therefore, to be paid by the *receveur*

---

[34] Huillard-Bréholles, *Historia Diplomatica Friderici Secundi*, VI, ii, 665–
66; Doenniges, *Acta Henrici VII*, p. 185. In 1245 Frederick II granted Imbert de Beaujeu 100 m. "in feodum de camera nostra" (Winkelmann, *Acta Imperii*, I, no. 383). The German chamber was different from the English chamber
and wardrobe; it can be more accurately compared to the exchequer in that
it did not have the household character which typified the English chamber.

[35] A.E.G., De Saint Genois, *Inv. Fl.*, no. 766. In 1256 Count Theobald of
Bar received "quatre cens livreez en bourse" (A.G.R., *Trés. Fl.*, Sér. I, no.
2065). See also De Saint-Genois, *Monuments*, II, 675, 808, 880; De Saint
Genois, *Inv. Fl.*, nos. 136, 144, 393, 673, 996; Gaillard, *B.C.R.H.*, 2d sér.,
VI, no. 315. For Brabant there are examples of fiefs paid by the *bourse* in
the *Livre des feudataires de Jean III* edited by Galesloot: "Arnoldus de Haycrusse, X libras parisiensis in bursa annuatim" (p. 10); "Egidius de Hertsberge, L libras annuatim in bursa" (p. 37). See also pp. 117, 120–21, 217–18,
264. Reyner, son of Reyner Wieris, received 8 m. "annuatim in camera de
Balen" (p. 233). For Liège see Poncelet, *Livre des fiefs*, pp. 17, 263, 324–25,
328, 330, and *Les feudataires de la principauté de Liège*. See Appendix, no.
6, and Plate III.

[36] For the financial institutions of the Low Countries see P. Monier, *Les*

général or out of the *recette générale*, it is as though they were actually paid by the *bourse*. Good evidence for this financial procedure is provided by the concessions and receipts for payment, but even better evidence comes from the so-called accounts of the *recettes générales*. In an account of receipts and issues rendered by Thomas Fin, receiver general of Flanders, for 1308–9 there are four payments for "fieveis en bourse." An account for 1335–36 contains five entries relating to annual installments of *fiefs-rentes*.[37] Fiefs assigned on the *renenghes de Flandre* are found both in the accounts of the *recettes générales* and in the *Comptes des renenghes*. The word *renenghe* literally means account and refers to the annual accounting of all the receivers of incomes in kind and money (*receveurs des briefs et espiers*) before a high financial court of auditing officers representing the count. At this session the receivers accounted for their receipts, for their disbursements, and for the balance remaining. Such an accounting was like that in England where the barons of the exchequer twice yearly reviewed the accounts of the responsible financial officers such as the sheriffs.[38] When a *fief-rente* was said to be paid on the *renenghes de Flandre*, it meant that the installments were paid from the money or kind accounted for by the receivers to the treasury officials. In reality, then, the *fiefs-rentes* were paid by the *bourse*. In the *Compte de renenghe* of 1381 six fiefs are so paid.[39] Indicative of the many *fiefs-rentes* paid by the

institutions financières du comté de Flandre du XIe siècle à 1384 (Paris, 1948), and *Les institutions centrales du comté de Flandre de la fin du IXe siècle à 1384* (Paris, 1944), pp. 69–71 ; P. Thomas, "La renenghelle de Flandre aux XIIIe et XIVe s.," *Bul. de la Com. Hist. du Dépt. du Nord*, XXXIII (1930), 168–70 ; Ganshof and De Sturler, in *Geschiedenis van Vlaanderen*, II, 109–88 ; J. Buntinx, in *Algemene Geschiedenis der Nederlanden*, II, 367–69.

[37] A.G.R., Nélis, *Inv.*, nos. 1, 5. See also De Saint-Genois, *Monuments*, II, 822, 860, 877, 880 ; A.D.N., B. 1412/3739 ; B. 4060/145.474 ; B. 498/3919 ; B. 4058/145.447. See Appendix, nos. 13, 15, 17, and Plate III.

[38] Monier, *Institutions financières*, pp. 58–61.

[39] The following entry is typical: "Item a messire Renaud de Berghes, chevalier, de le rente que monsigneur li a donnee a sa vie et les tient de lui en hommage a paiier au Noël paiiet a lui pour le terme dou Noël lan iiiixx. C *l*." In an account rendered by the receiver general for 1444, Jacques de Horne, lord of Montigny, received "la somme de XL *l*. tournois quel tient en fief de monseigneur et prent par an sur les renenghes de Flandres" (A.G.R., C.C., no. 7802, fols. 6r, 15r–16r ; no. 2705, fol. 72v). See also no. 7800, fols. 5r–5v, 14v ; no. 2708, fol. 25r ; A.D.N., B. 4055/145.395 ; B. 1843/50.164 ;

recettes générales of Brabant, Limburg, Namur, Hainaut, and Guelders, is an account rendered for 1390–91 by the receiver of Limburg, Jean Sack de Wijck, recording payment of dozens of fiefs. One cluster of entries under the rubric "Assignacions et rendages des fiefs heritables par an" concerns payment of eight *fiefs-rentes,* their sum total coming to 964 *m.* 4 *s.*[40]

Except for the dukes of Guelders, the Low Country princes apparently paid few *fiefs-rentes* out of their household treasuries, as did the English kings out of their chamber and wardrobe. All the evidence we have is a fragment of a *compte d'hôtel* of the dukes of Guelders for 1308 recording the payment of twelve fiefs,[41] and a similar document of Count Guy of Flanders for the years 1270–75 in which appears one entry referring to a *fief-rente.*[42] Lack of evidence for this practice is explained partly by the fact that the administrative machinery of the Low Country princes never became as highly specialized or organized as that of the English kings; there was no need for great specialization because the states were so small. And it should be noted that none of the rulers of the Continent developed their household or private treasuries in any way comparable to that of their English counterparts; the exchequer-wardrobe relation was peculiarly English.

The English and French kings whose financial organizations were large enough to warrant subsidiary treasuries located at strategic points about their realms occasionally assigned fiefs on these sources. The exchequer of Caen, similar in almost every respect to that in

A.G.R., *Trés. Fl.,* Sér. I, no. 2073; De Saint-Genois, *Monuments,* II, 675, 680, 733–34, 850. See Appendix, nos. 5, 7.

[40] A.G.R., *C.C.,* no. 2436, fols. 17ᵛ–18ʳ. For Brabant see A.G.R., *C.C.,* nos. 2350–60. For Namur see De Saint-Genois, *Monuments,* II, 842, 961, 994; Brouwers, *Chart. et règ.,* I, nos. 198, 242; II, nos. 361, 363, 377, 396; A.E.N., Piot, *Inv. Namur,* nos. 416, 694, 699, 724, 811, 820, 1045. For Guelders see Meihuizen, *Rekening Betreffende Gelre,* pp. 7–8, 19, 23–25, 30–31 ff. For Holland see A.D.N., B. 1179/7844; Van Mieris, *Groot Charterboek,* II, 300; III, 82. See Plate II.

[41] A.G.R., Nélis, *Inv.,* no. 2824: "Item dedimus Hermanno de Lindenberg racione feodi sui IIIIᵒʳ marcas. ... Item domino Franconi de Berke racione feodi sui quatuor marcas ..."

[42] Buntinx, *Het Memoriaal van Jehan Makiel Klerk en Ontvanger van Gwijde van Dampierre (1270–1275),* Bruxelles, 1944, p. 95: "Encore a Ph[ellipe] encovent a rendre au conte de Bar [sen] fief et pour le fief monsigneur Renaut de Bar 500 lb. a [le] feste de Bar." See also p. 88.

England, was so used by the English kings until John lost Normandy;[43] it was then taken over by the French kings who used it as had their predecessors.[44] Sometimes the records state that fiefs were paid by the exchequer at Rouen but in reality the Caen exchequer made the payments; during the thirteenth century the Norman exchequer met alternately at Caen and Rouen, but there were not two exchequers.[45] The English kings pressed into service for paying fiefs an exchequer at Dublin and Bordeaux, as well as a chamber at Bordeaux.[46]

But there were methods other than the treasury for financing the *fief-rente*. Everywhere we find *fiefs-rentes* assigned directly upon the revenues of administrative districts; this had the advantage of making payment of the installments more certain. When *fiefs-rentes* were assigned on a central treasury, there were many people competing for funds often inadequate; when they were assigned on a local revenue, the holders were almost sure of getting the money before it was sent to the treasury. The recipient would be paid by the accountable officer, who would be credited with the amount expended when rendering account of his receipts and issues at the treasury. The French kings, at least through the thirteenth and early fourteenth

[43] In 1200 John granted Nicholas Lechat a fief of 50 l. "pro homagio et servicio suo recipiendas ad scaccarium Cadomi" (*Rot. Norm.*, p. 32). See also *Rot. Pat.,* pp. 6 b, 12 b, 22 b, 23; *Rot. Chart.,* p. 58; *Rot. Norm.,* pp. 50, 96. For the Caen exchequer see Palgrave's classic introduction to his edition of the Great Rolls of the Norman Exchequer.

[44] Count Robert of Dreux who had received a fief of 400 l. of Anjou from John on the Caen exchequer had this fief confirmed and increased to 500 l. of Anjou by Philip Augustus in 1204. It continued to be paid by the Caen exchequer (*Rot. Chart.,* p. 58; Delisle, *Cart. normand,* no. 89). See also nos. 59, 111–12, 116, 1207; Léchaudé-d'Anisy, *Scaccarium Normannie sub Regibus Francie,* p. 155.

[45] In 1295 John de Harecourt received a fief of 1,000 l. on the exchequer at Rouen (Langlois, *Registres perdus,* no. 381). See also Léchaudé-d'Anisy, *Scaccarium Normannie sub Regibus Francie,* p. 157. For Norman finances in the thirteenth century see J. R. Strayer, *The Administration of Normandy under Saint Louis* (Cambridge, Mass., 1932), pp. 32–55.

[46] In 1279 Adam de Norf, constable of Bordeaux, was ordered to pay 9 m. to Oliver de la Bard "in partem solucionis annui feodi sui quod percipit ad scaccarium nostrum Burdegale" (*R.G.,* II, no. 355). In 1305 Fergand de Estissaco notified Edward I's officials at Bordeaux that they owed him "30 l. de camera nostra Burdegale in festo Pasche annis singulis percipiendas" (*R.G.,* IV, no. 4711). For Dublin see *Cl.R. 1231–34,* pp. 335, 526; *Pat. R. 1232–47,* p. 489.

century, granted fiefs upon the *prévôtés, vicomtés, bailliages,* and *sénéchaussées.* This was also done by such other lords as Alphonse of Poitiers and the counts of Anjou and Pontieu.[47] The English kings of the twelfth century paid some fiefs out of the farm of the English counties, as well as out of the Norman *vicomtés.*[48] While ruling over Anjou, they paid fiefs from the issues of that county.[49] During the reigns of John, Henry III, and Edward I, fiefs were paid out of the issues of Poitou, the Limousin, and the *prévôté* of Bordeaux.[50] But the administrative districts of the English kings never figured largely in the finance of the *fief-rente;* the Pipe Rolls of the thirteenth and fourteenth centuries record few *fiefs-rentes* paid by the counties. In Germany only occasionally were fiefs assigned upon a *Vogtei.*[51] But

---

[47] In 1297 Philip IV granted a fief of 500 *l.* to Simon de Melun, marshal of France, payable by the *prévôté* of Orléans (Tardif, *Monuments historiques,* no. 992). In 1298 John de Saint Germain received a fief of 60 *s.* on the *prévôté* of Paris (Langlois, *Registres perdus,* no. 44). See also *Recueil historiens France,* XXI, 261, 263, 265, 267, 270, 279; XXII, 576, 633–34, 640; Fawtier, *Comptes royaux,* I, 1–2, 29–30, 47–49, 169–71, 341, 345, 366, 381, 390, 612–13. In a financial evaluation of the *châtellenie* of Pontoise in 1332 are fiefs both in money and kind (A. M. de Boislisle, *Le budget et la population de la France sous Philippe de Valois,* Paris, 1875, pp. 14–15). For Pontieu see Brunel, *Actes de Pontieu,* nos. 139, 180, 238, 252, 258, 411, etc. For Anjou see *Layettes,* III, no. 4589. For Poitiers see Tardiff, *Monuments historiques,* nos. 825, 855, 872; Sczaniecki, *Essai,* pp. 116–17; *Layettes,* III, nos. 3592, 4162.

[48] In the twelfth century the counts of Flanders received their fief from the revenues of the counties (*P.R. 2–3–4 Hen. II,* pp. 36–37, 39–40, 82–83, 89, 91, 136, 149, 152). See also *P.R. 5 Hen. II,* pp. 8, 34, 51, 64; *P.R. 6 Hen. II,* pp. 1, 8, 43, 45; *P.R. 10 Ric. I,* pp. 59–60. In 1180 Robert de Stoteville rendered account of 750 *l.* "de firma Lillebone de 5 annis scilicet de 150 *l.* per annum. . . . camerario Tancarville 300 *l.* scilicet 60 *l.* per annum de feodo" (Stapleton, *Mag. Rot. Scacc. Norm.,* I, 68, 132, 138, 157). See also S. R. Packard, *Miscellaneous Records of the Norman Exchequer, 1199–1204* (Northampton, Mass., 1926), p. 10.

[49] In 1202 John ordered the seneschal of Anjou to pay Geoffrey of Tours "50 *l.* Andegavensis de feodo suo" (*Rot. Norm.,* p. 52). The same year the seneschal paid the fief of Savaric de Antenois (*Ibid.*).

[50] In 1200 the seneschal of Poitou was ordered to pay the fiefs of William Teberd and William Genemunt (*Rot. Norm.,* p. 34). In 1264 the seneschal of the Limousin paid 50 *l.* to Raymond, viscount of Turenne, for his fief (*C.P.R. 1258–66,* p. 380). In 1337 Thomas de le Bret was granted a fief of 40 *l.* upon the issues of the *prévôté* of Bordeaux (P.R.O., Gascon Roll, C. 61/49, m. 4ᵛ).

[51] In 1365 Conrad "greve von Werningherode" granted a fief "in der vog-

for the Low Countries the administrative districts were in general relied upon more than the treasuries. The *domaines* of the dukes of Brabant bore the brunt of the financial load. After Duke John I acquired Limburg as a result of his victory at Woeringen in 1288 and thus came into possession of the rich revenues provided by the strategically located Pays d'Outre-Meuse, the *domaines* of Maastricht, Rolduc, Fauquemont, and Dalhem paid a large share of the fiefs throughout the fourteenth and fifteenth centuries. Though somewhat less important, the *domaines* of Tirlemont, Bois-le-Duc, Assche, Bruxelles, Terveuren, and Vilvorde also paid *fiefs-rentes*.[52] Sometimes the Flemish counts paid fiefs from the revenues of their administrative units. From the accounts of the *baillis* and of the *briefs* and *espiers* we know that fiefs were paid by the officers accountable for the revenues of the *châtellenies, bailliages,* and *prévôtés*.[53] That Lille seemed to pay more fiefs than the other *bailliages* may be explained by the preservation there of a larger number of

---

hedie to Gosler" (Bode, *Urkundenbuch Goslar*, IV, no. 846). In 1351 Volkmar von Vorsfelde enfeoffed the brothers Hans, Ebeling, and Tile Apetey with a fief of 4 *m.* payable on the *Vogtei* of Goslar (*Ibid.,* no. 442). See also IV, no. 469.

[52] Statistics from the accounts of Maastricht are strong evidence for the importance of its revenues. For the year 1358–59 Maastricht paid 6 fiefs; for 1359–60, 22; for 1360–61, 26; for 1366–67, 28. Although the number of fiefs paid declines in the fifteenth century, in 1499 the "Here van Witham" received a fief of 96 *l.* which his predecessors had received from the issues of Maastricht as early as 1358 (A.G.R., Nélis, *Inv.,* nos. 2436–56; *C.C.,* nos. 5463, 5485–86). In 1363 Rolduc paid 18 fiefs and Dalhem, 6. In 1370 Rolduc paid 14 and Fauquemont, 5 (A.G.R., Verkooren, *Inv. Brab.,* nos. 2003–2125, 2725–2812). For 1370–71 the domain of Tirlemont paid 16 fiefs and continued to do so until 1385. Thereafter it paid considerably less (A.G.R., Nélis, *Inv.,* nos. 2468–79). In the fifteenth century the domain of Bois-le-Duc paid on the average of 17 to 18 fiefs yearly between 1405 and 1410 (A.G.R., *C.C.,* nos. 5234–39). See also Quicke, *B.C.R.H.,* XCVI (1932), 347–416. See Appendix, no. 28.

[53] In the account of the *espier* of Lille for 1187 are three payments of fiefs (Monier, *Institutions financières,* p. 82). We learn from the account of the *espier* and *briefs* of Flanders for 1255–56 that the *bailliage* of Bruges paid nine fiefs; Alost, five; Ypres, eight; Lille, two; Courtrai, six; Douai, two. For other *bailliages* see A.E.G., Gaillard, "Inv. de Flandre," *B.C.R.H.,* VI (1853), no. 72bis. For fiefs assigned on the *briefs* and *espier* see A.D.N., B. 1332/1351; B. 1492/1868; B. 4064/145.557; B. 4324; A.E.G., De Saint Genois, *Inv. Fl.,* no. 1408; Gachard, *Notice historique,* 9 April 1326. See Appendix, no. 3.

9*

records. But many fiefs were paid by the *bailliage* of Menin and the *châtellenies* of Bourbourg, Cassel, Alost, Dendermonde, Douai, and Orchics.[54] As H. Nowé has well shown in his study on the *baillis* of Flanders, *châtellenie* and *bailliage* were synonymous terms for administrative districts when speaking of the fifteen large *bailliages* such as Ghent and Bruges. This means that for *fiefs-rentes* assigned on the revenues of the fifteen large districts it is immaterial whether the records use the word *bailliage* or *châtellenie*. But there were sub-*bailliages* comprising the large *bailliages,* as in the case of Menin, and these sub-*bailliages* should not be confused with the larger unit called also *bailliage* or *châtellenie*.[55] There is good evidence that the administrative districts of Namur and Guelders also paid *fiefs-rentes* and undoubtedly this was true in the other Low Country states.[56]

Considering now the actual revenues from which the medieval ruler received his support, we find that the typical seignorial incomes were marked out to pay *fiefs-rentes*. The kings of France and England, the counts of Flanders, Namur, and Hainaut, and the dukes of Brabant assigned fiefs upon tallages.[57] Even the special tallage

---

[54] The *châtellenie* of Lille paid eleven fiefs in 1332–33 (A.D.N., B. 4324, fols. 8v, 9r, 10v). In an account of the *châtellenies* of Douai and Orchies for 1372–73 under the rubric "Aumosnes et fiefs a heritage assignes sur le gavene de Douay" appears this entry: "A monsigneur Ricard Pourcel pour sen fief quil tient de monsigneur de Flandres a heritage ... X *l.*" (B. 4626, fol. 4v). The accounts of Dendermonde for 1364–65 and 1371–72 show payments for three and four fiefs (A.G.R., Nélis, *Inv.*, nos. 212, 219). In 1388 William of Juliers recognized to hold a fief of 1,500 *l.* on the lands of Dendermonde and Beveren from Duke Philip the Bold of Burgundy (A.G.R., *Trés. Fl.*, Sér. I, no. 2086). See Appendix, nos. 20, 22.

[55] H. Nowé, *Les baillis comtaux de Flandre* (Bruxelles, 1929), pp. 72–77.

[56] An account for the *domaine* of the town and district of Guelders for 1348–49 lists seven fiefs as being paid (A.G.R., *C.C.*, no. 6675, fols. 8v, 10r). The account of the *domaine* of Namur for 1355–56 contains at least fifteen *fiefs-rentes*. Probably many more *rentes* were also fiefs but the evidence is lacking to so classify them (A.E.N., *Domaines*, no. 1, fols. 60r–64r). There are also examples in the account of 1409–10 (*Domaines*, no. 2, fols. 124r–128r) and for 1438–39 (A.G.R., *C.C.*, no. 10929). See also Balon, *An. Soc. Arch. de Namur*, XL, nos. 8–9.

[57] France: In 1271 Peter d'Alençon granted a fief of 100 *l.* to Erard, lord of Valery, "in tallia Carnot" (Du Chesne, *Histoire de la maison de Chastillon sur Marne*, Paris, 1621, Preuves, p. 70). The dukes of Burgundy assigned fiefs on their *tailles* of Pommart (Petit, *Histoire des ducs de Bourgogne*, VI, no. 5303). In a document from the reign of Philip Augustus, the *Scripta de Feodis,* a certain Gerard de Esquaiencort is shown holding "X libras ad tal-

levied upon Jews under English rule was used.[58] Incomes derived from grain mills frequently figure in the payment of fiefs in the Low Countries, particularly in Flanders, Brabant, Namur, and Hainaut. Revenues from wind and watermills were used by the counts of Holland.[59] Incomes from forests were used in Flanders and Hainaut.[60] Also used were the cellars of the bishops of Liège and the dukes of Luxemburg,[61] the profits of justice in England and Germany,[62]

liam de Moileins ... et XII libras in tallia de Monciaco" (*Recueil historiens France*, XXIII, 647). England: In 1202 a royal official in Normandy received an order from John to pay Hugh de Montfort "200 *l.* andegavensis quas recepistis de taillagio hominum suorum de Ponte Episcopi in solucione feodi sui" (*Rot. Norm.*, p. 63). For the Low Countries see De Saint-Genois, *Monuments*, I, 226; II, 764; Bormans, *Fiefs de Namur*, p. 110; Piot, *Inv. Namur*, no. 676; Galesloot, *Feudataires de Jean III*, p. 58; A.G.R., *Trés. Fl.*, Sér. I, no. 65; *C.C.*, no. 3221.

[58] In 1203 it was provided that William de Bueles should receive "100 *l.* andegavensis de taillagio Judiorum de feodo suo" (*Rot. Norm.*, p. 79). See also p. 99.

[59] William, lord of Dendermonde, owed in the year 1308 a fief of 500 *l.* to Walter d'Enghien on the receipts of the toll and mill of Dendermonde (A.E.G., *Inv. analytique du pays de Termonde*, 26 December 1308). In 1278 John, lord of Audenarde, held a fief of 100 *l.* from Duke John I of Brabant "as molins de Brays à Brusielle" (Butkens, *Trophées*, Preuves, I, 111). In 1339 Godfrey, lord of Waës, held a fief of 68 *l.* from Count William I of Namur "sur le molin Faullerech, sur le tonlieu de le mercherie, et sur les botages et amages de la ville de Namur" (A.E.N., Piot, *Inv. Namur*, no. 604). In 1438–39 the account for the domain of Namur shows a fief paid "sur le grant molin de Sambre" (A.G.R., *C.C.*, no. 10929). The counts of Hainaut assigned fiefs on the mills of Avesnes (De Saint-Genois, *Monuments*, I, 2 ff.). In 1350 Albert, count of Holland and Hainaut, granted to Walter van der Maalsteden a fief of 50 *l.* "te nemen van den renten van den wintmolen ende watermolen toet Reymerswale" (Van Mieris, *Groot Charterboek*, III, 110).

[60] In 1293 John of Avesnes, count of Hainaut, granted to John de Bar, brother of the count of Bar, a fief of 200 *l.* on the woods of Mormal (De Reiffenberg, *Monuments*, I, no. 76, p. 429). In 1296 Count Guy of Flanders granted to John d'Assenghien a fief of 50 *l.* "sur le bois de Nieppe" (De Saint-Genois, *Monuments*, II, 857).

[61] In 1336 "Dominus Henricus li Biaus de Leodio miles, scabinus Leodiensis, relevavit in palatio quatuor marcas bone monete sitas supra cellerariam Leodiensem" (Poncelet, *Livre des fiefs de Liège*, p. 345). In an account of the *cellerier* of Luxemburg for 1380–81 are recorded the payments of three fiefs (Vannérus, *Les comptes luxembourgeois du XIVème siècle. Compte rendu par le cellerier de Luxembourg du 1er août 1380 au 1er octobre 1381*, Luxembourg, 1899, pp. 5–6, 13, 28).

[62] In 1257 Henry III of England promised to pay 224 *l.* to Guy de Lusignan for his fief "out of the first issues of the present eyre of justices in the

pannage and fisheries in Liège, Brabant, and Luxemburg,[63] the *Bede* in Germany and Holland,[64] the *cens* in France and Germany,[65] church revenues in England and Holland,[66] scutage in England,[67] the profits of coinage in Brabant,[68] the *gabelle* in France,[69] escheats in

county of Norfolk" (*C.P.R. 1247–58*, p. 552). See also *Cl.R. 1268–72*, p. 17. In 1286 King Rudolf I granted to Count Adolf of Nassau a fief of 20 m. "a iudicibus nostris in Frankenvort" (Böhmer, *Acta Imperii*, no. 455).

[63] In 1288 Henry VI, count of Luxemburg, granted to the knight "Werri dit Troussien" a fief of 10 l. "a prendre et a recevoir a no pescherie de Thionville" (Wampach, *Urkunden*, V, no. 227). In 1315 Thierry de Oise relieved a fief of 20 s. "supra piscaturam de le Naÿe" (Poncelet, *Livre des fiefs de Liège*, p. 20). In the same year John de Perweis relieved a fief of 20 s. plus "iiii capones supra tentoria pannorum" (*Ibid.*, p. 20). For Brabant see Butkens, *Trophées*, Preuves, I, 104.

[64] In 1290 Count Diedrich of Cleve granted to Gerlach, lord of Isenburg, a fief of 10 m. out of the *Bede* of his land of Wesel (Goerz, *Mittelrheinische Regesten*, IV, no. 1756). In 1308 Archbishop Henry II of Cologne granted to Simon, lord of Lippe, a fief of 50 m. out of the *Bede* of Gesecke and Rüden (Lacomblet, *Urkundenbuch*, III, no. 70). In 1235 Nicholas, lord of Putten, granted 8 l. "annuatim in feodum de petitione mea Pittis" to William Hugenzoon (Van Den Bergh, *Oorkondenboek van Holland*, I, no. 356). See also II, no. 385.

[65] In 1192 Philip Augustus granted to John le Noir in fief "XX libras Parisiensium de redditibus singulis annis capiendas in censu nostro Lorriaci" (Delaborde, *Actes de Philippe-Auguste*, no. 403 ; Delisle, *Actes de Philippe-Auguste*, no. 358). In 1267 William de Lamberville "tenet de Rege tres sol. et xi denarios de censu, unde est homo regis ligius" (Léchaudé-d'Anisy, *Scaccarium Normannie sub Regibus Francie*, p. 179). See also *Recueil historiens France*, XXIII, 624. In a document of 1311 listing the fiefs held of the bishop of Halberstadt appears the following entry : "filius Alberti militis de Veltem curiam Halb., item XV solidos de censu arearum" (Schmidt, *Urkundenbuch der Stadt Halberstadt*, I, no. 332).

[66] In 1257 Amauvin de Varesio was paid 631 l. 13 s. 2 d. from the issues of the archbishopric of Dublin and void bishoprics of Ireland for the arrears of his fief, wages, and horses lost in time of war in Gascony (*C.P.R. 1247–58*, p. 562). In 1244 Peter of Geneva received his fief of 50 l. from the issues of the bishopric of Chichester (*C.L.R. 1240–45*, p. 255). In 1316 William I, count of Holland and Hainaut, granted a fief of 25 l. to William van Duvenvoorde "op onse tiende van Haesardwoude" (Van Mieris, *Groot Charterboek*, II, 168). Arnold, lord of Steene, received in 1317 a fief of 300 l. "op die tiende tusschen der poerte van Leyde ende Doedins lane" (*Ibid.*, II, 182).

[67] Bernard de Bailleul received 16 m. in part payment of his fief of 20 m. from a scutage granted to John (*P.R. 10 John*, p. 31).

[68] In 1296 Henry of Luxemburg, lord of Ligny, received from the duke of Brabant a fief of 400 l. "païement coursable en Brabant, sur sa monnoie de Brabant" (Butkens, *Trophées*, Preuves, I, 135).

England,[70] and the *aides* of Ghent and Bruges.[71] None of these revenues figured prominently but all had a part in the finance of the *fief-rente*.

Another source of payment was the revenues of towns. They were a favorite source of assignment for German lords as well as for the dukes of Brabant and the counts of Namur, Flanders, and Guelders.[72] We have seen that all the fiefs granted by the town of Cologne were assigned on its revenues. The French and English kings seldom used the town revenues.[73] The new incomes in the form of indirect taxes made possible by the revived economic activity of western Europe

[69] In 1230 the count of Provence granted a fief "in redditibus gabelle et portus civitatis Nicie" (Benoit, *Actes des comtes de Provence*, I, no. 132).

[70] In 1249 Henry III ordered the fief of Eustace de Bailleul to be paid "from first moneys arising from the king's escheats in one of his bailiwicks" (*C.L.R. 1245–51*, p. 258). See also *Cl.R. 1254–56*, p. 246.

[71] In 1320 Count Robert de Béthune of Flanders granted a fief of 1,800 *l.* to Guy de Châtillon, count of Blois, on the *aides* of Ghent and Bruges (A.G.R,. *Trés. Fl.*, Sér. I, no. 2027).

[72] In 1212 the Emperor Otto IV granted William Pusterla and his heirs a fief of 25 *m.* "de redditibus nostris quos in civitate Astensi habemus (et) annuatim nobis debet commune Astense" (Böhmer, *Acta Imperii*, no. 256). See also nos. 522, 525 ; Gudenus, *Codex Diplomaticus*, V, 713. In 1343 Duke John III of Brabant granted to the count of Catsenellenbogen a fief of 200 *l.* on the tolls and receipts of Brussels. In the same year he granted the count of La Mark a fief of 200 *l.* on receipts of the village of Liere (Butkens, *Trophées*, Preuves, I, 179, 181). In 1383 Duke Wenceslas and Duchess Jeanne granted Godfrey of Looz, his wife, and son a fief of "ses hondert gulden peters ... op hoir renten van Loven" (Quicke, *B.C.R.H.*, XCIII, no. 16). In 1281 the knight Philip de Gomeignies acknowledged receipt of his fief of 12 *l.* which he received yearly on the revenues of the town of Namur (Borgnet, *Cartulaire de la commune de Namur*, I, no. 55). In 1298 Guy de Dampierre, marquis of Namur, granted Gilles, lord of Berlaimont, a fief of 120 *l.* "sour toutes les rentes de nos bourgesies de Namur que on nous doit au Noël et à le saint Jehan-Baptiste" (De Reiffenberg, *Monuments*, I, no. 115, p. 299). In 1280 Count Guy of Flanders granted Ralph d'Estrées a fief of 100 *l.* on the incomes of Lille (De Saint-Genois, *Monuments*, II, 680). In 1364 the duke of Guelders granted John de Kok van Opynen a fief of 289 *l.* "vyt onser gruyten van Arnhem" (Nijhoff, *Gedenkwaardigheden uit de Geschiedenis van Gelderland*, II, no. 133). See Appendix, no. 2.

[73] The fief of 10 *l.* received in 1243 by Reginald de Drumare from Henry III of England was paid out of the farms of Bristol, Andover, or Southampton (*R.G.*, I, no. 1494; *C.L.R. 1240–45*, pp. 275, 291 ; *C.L.R. 1245–51*, pp. 200, 294). See also *C.L.R. 1240–45*, p. 39 ; *C.L.R. 1245–51*, pp. 14, 201–2, 219, 255 ; *Cl.R. 1242–47*, p. 284. For France see Sczaniecki, *Essai*, p. 118.

presented unlimited opportunity for the payment of fiefs. The counts of Champagne paid most of their fiefs from the revenues of their famous fairs. In the documents edited by Chantereau le Febvre are thirty-seven fiefs assigned on the fair revenues between 1150 and 1275.[74] One has only to consult the registers of fiefs edited by A. Longnon and D'Arbois de Jubainville, and to check quickly the financial records, to see that the large number of *fiefs-rentes* granted by the counts of Champagne was possible solely because of the fairs of Lagny-sur-Marne, Bar, Provins, and Troyes.[75] A few fiefs were granted on fairs by the kings and other lords of France and occasionally by the kings of England.[76] Market revenues helped the counts of Holland pay their fiefs;[77] hallage and stallage served the French kings, the bishops of Liège, and the Flemish counts.[78] But the revenues that paid the most *fiefs-rentes* were the tolls, duties, and

[74] In 1208, for example, Blanche of Navarre, regent of Champagne, and her son Theobald granted to Hugh, lord of La Fauche, a fief of 20 *l*. "in nundinis Barri" (Chantereau le Febvre, *Traité des fiefs*, Preuves, p. 33). For other grants see pp. 57, 61, 102, 105–7; *Layettes*, I, nos. 1208, 1355–56; II, nos. 1653, 2044.

[75] A brief register of fiefs (1249–52) indicates that John de Tullo held a fief of 20 *l*. "in nundinis Sancti Aygulfi." A document listing fiefs held of the counts of Champagne in 1274–75 notes: "C'est ce que Guillaumes de Saint-Croiz tient de ma dame la roïne de Navarre: c'est à savoir XIˣˣ lb. de tournois à paier, les cent et X lb. en la foire de Bar sur Aube, et les autres C et X lb. en la foire de la Saint Jean à Troies." In 1316 "Messire Heude, sire de Mont-Ferrant, fist I homage pour reson de XXX livrées de terre que il prent en deniers sur la foire de Bar, le lundi après Pasques" (Longnon, *Documents de Champagne*, I, nos. 5293, 6451, 7432). Under the issues of the *bailliage* of Troyes, Meaux, and Provins for 1288 is the rubric "Fiez et aumones de la foire Seint Jehan de Troies." Then follows a long list of payments (Longnon, *Documents de Champagne*, III, 81 ff.).

[76] In 1205 Philip Augustus granted Robert de Bommiers a fief of 50 *l*. on the fair of Saumur (Delisle, *Actes de Philippe-Auguste*, no. 939). In 1341 the duke of Burgundy granted to Peter de la Pallu a fief of 60 *l*. on the fairs of Chalon (Sczaniecki, *Essai*, p. 117). In 1242 Henry III of England granted to Albert del Guarait a fief of 25 *l*. on the exchequer "donec idem Albertus vel heredes sui recuperaverint redditum illum in feria de Luches, quem Albertus, pater suus, habuit de dono Ricardi regis, avunculi nostri" (*R.G.*, I, no. 282). See also *C.P.R. 1247–58*, p. 2. See Appendix, no. 8.

[77] Van Mieris, *Groot Charterboek*, II, 437.

[78] Delisle, *Cart. normand*, no. 1105; Poncelet, *Livre des fiefs de Liège*, p. 98. In 1341 the count of Flanders granted to John de Neuville a fief of 30 *l*. "sur les halages et stelages de la ville du Chesne" (A.E.G., De Saint Genois, *Inv. Fl.*, no. 1699).

customs. In Germany, Flanders, and Holland various sorts of tolls paid more fiefs than any other financial source. Their part in payment of fiefs was hardly less prominent in Brabant, Liège, Namur, and Guelders. The customs of England, particularly those on wool, were essential for financing the *fief-rente* in the fourteenth century. All sorts of duties and tolls were pressed into service by the French kings and, on a smaller scale, by the rulers of Hainaut and Luxemburg. So essential were these revenues and so diverse their nature that they merit closer examination.

The grants of the German emperors were assigned upon tolls spread all over the Empire.[79] The counts of Schleswig-Holstein granted their fiefs on the tolls of Hamburg.[80] In 1257 Count Diedrich of Cleve assigned a fief of 300 *m.* "de theloneo scilicet nostro Novinagiensi."[81] The archbishops of Mainz often assigned fiefs on the tolls of Bopard; the archbishop of Cologne paid a fief of 1,000 *m.* to Duke Henry II of Brabant in 1235 on the tolls of Nuys.[82] Some lords assigned fiefs upon the *Kornrente* and the revenues from duties on wine.[83] The counts of Flanders assigned at least half of their fiefs on the tolls of Damme;[84] also important were the tolls of Dendermonde, Rupelmonde, Bruges, Cassel, Gravelines, Bergues, and Me-

---

[79] In 1182 Frederick I granted to Count Otto II of Guelders a fief of 300 *m.* on the tolls of Nimwegen. In 1219 Frederick II granted Godfrey, count of Blandrata, a fief of 5 *d.* "in pedagio Taurinensi." King Rudolf conceded a fief of 6 *m.* to Peter von Bertholfesheim "de thelonio navium apud Frankenvort" (Bondam, *Charterboek van Gelderland*, II, no. 64; Winkelmann, *Acta Imperii*, I, no. 158; Böhmer, *Urkundenbuch Frankfurt*, I, 173).

[80] For example, in 1292 a fief of 60 *m.* was given "in nostro theloneo et ungeldo in Hammenburch" (Lappenberg, *Hamburgisches Urkundenbuch*, I, no. 862). See also P. Hasse, *Schleswig-Holstein-Lauenburgische Regesten und Urkunden* (Hamburg, 1886), II, no. 862.

[81] Ilgen, *Quellen Rheinischen Territorien*, II, i, no. 12.

[82] Goerz, *Mittelrheinische Regesten*, III, no. 1000; Butkens, *Trophées, Preuves*, I, 79.

[83] Günther, *Codex-Diplomaticus Rheno-Mosellanus*, III, no. 159; Sauer, *Nassauisches Urkundenbuch*, I, ii, no. 967.

[84] In 1273, for example, Guy and Margaret of Flanders granted Jakemon Louchard, citizen of Arras, a fief of 200 *l.* "a nostre tonlieu dou Dam a prendre et a rechevoir a deus termines en lan" (A.E.G., De Saint Genois, *Inv. Fl.*, no. 175). In 1282 Guy granted Gerard of Luxemburg, lord of Durbui, a fief of 200 *l.* on the tolls of Damme (A.G.R., *Trés. Fl.*, Sér. I, no. 2068). See also A.G.R., *Trés. Fl.*, Sér. I, nos. 1270, 1279, 2027, 2071, 2073, 2083, 2085; A.D.N., B. 4058/145.440. See Appendix, nos. 1, 7.

nin.[85] Although the concessions provide the best evidence for this
practice, some extant accounts of the tolls of Damme, Rupelmonde,
and Dendermonde help to complete the picture.[86] The original concession gave authority to the officer of the toll concerned to pay the
fief out of his toll receipts without further order. The payment of
fiefs authorized would then appear yearly when he rendered account
of his receipts and issues to the receiver general and he would be
credited with these amounts. The tolls and duties utilized by the
dukes of Brabant were even more varied; those from the Pays
d'Outre-Meuse were the most prominent. Most fiefs were assigned
upon the tolls of Maastricht. A document containing an account of
the fiefs paid by Maastricht for the years 1379, 1380, and 1381
shows, respectively, twenty-one, seventeen, and fourteen *fiefs-rentes*
paid.[87] Scarcely less important were the tolls of Rolduc, Dalhem,
and others in the lands beyond the Meuse.[88] The book of fiefs of
John III compiled around 1350 shows fourteen different tolls and
duties used to pay *fiefs-rentes*.[89] In the thirteenth and fourteenth

[85] See De Saint-Genois, *Monuments*, II, 637, 707, 841, 881; A.D.N., B.
4065/145.576; A.E.G., *Inv. des chartes du Pays de Termonde*, 26 December
1308, 7 February 1363, 29 March 1383. See Appendix, no. 24.

[86] A.G.R., Nélis, *Inv.*, Comptes des censiers du tonlieu de Damme, nos.
622–85; Tonlieu de Rupelmonde, nos. 692–705; Tonlieu de Termonde, nos.
714–31. There are also grants by the counts and other lords upon the *vinage*
(C. Duvivier, *La querelle des d'Avesnes et des Dampierre jusqu'à la mort
de Jean d'Avesnes (1257)*, Bruxelles, 1894, Preuves, II, no. 54; A.D.N., B.
499/7597; B. 1256/7812).

[87] A.G.R., Nélis, *Inv.*, no. 2498.

[88] There are numerous receipts for payments on these tolls in Verkooren,
Inv. Brab. See also Butkens, *Trophées*, Preuves, I, 96, 103, 179, 183; Quicke,
B.C.R.H., XCVI, 372 ff.; A.G.R., Galesloot, *Cour féodale*, no. 33, fols. 88r–
94v. The following is typical of the references in Galesloot to fiefs paid by the
toll of Rolduc: "Her Arnoert van Moelnarken hout V marc tsiaers anden 'tol
Rode." Other examples are in the *Leenboeck van Overmaeze* (no. 572).

[89] The following entries are typical: "III marcas lovaniensis annui reditus
supra telonium de Thiele ... VIII marchas annuatim in thelonio rodensi ...
X libres turonenses apud Slocwachte supra flumen apud Antwerpiam ... CC
libras lovaniensis terre supra winagium de Thiele ... V marchas argenti annuatim ad viam publicam de Lurke ... III libras ad pontem trajectensem ...
X libras parisienses supra molendinum ducis in Merchtinis ... de redditibus
suis supra hallam geldoniensem ... X libras annuatim ex piscaria de Wyc."
Sometimes the cloth hall of Brussels paid the *fiefs-rentes* of the dukes; for
example, in 1340 Duke John III granted Count William I of Namur a fief
of 400 *l*. on the *halle aux draps* (A.G.R., Verkooren, *Inv. Brab.*, no. 640).

centuries the counts of Holland assigned *fiefs-rentes* on the tolls of Niemandsvriend, Ammers, and Dordrecht.[90]

The evidence for the English kings assigning *fiefs-rentes* on tolls, customs, and duties is abundant. The practice of assigning fiefs on customs began prior to the fourteenth century but was only fully developed with the reign of Edward III. In 1327 John of Hainaut, lord of Beaumont, was granted a fief of 1,000 *m.* "out of the customs in the port of London."[91] Twice yearly, thereafter, the collectors of the customs of wool import of London were ordered by letters close to pay 500 *m.* to John. These orders which regularly appear until 1346 when John went over to the French kings are supplemented by others that add more detail to the transactions.[92] In 1330 the exchequer was directed to credit the collectors of the London customs with the 1,000 *m.* paid to John for that year. The following year the collectors were directed to disregard an order to pay John 500 *m.* since "it has been ascertained by looking at various rolls that John has been satisfied with this amount." In 1340 the collectors were ordered to pay 500 *m.* to John or to the "merchants of the society of Bardi, John's attorneys."[93] Sometimes the customs of London were insufficient and John had to be provided for elsewhere. In 1341 the collectors of the port of Ipswich were directed to permit John to take 100 sacks of wool in part payment of debts owed to him. In the same year William de Bohun, earl of Northampton, received orders to pay "1,050 *m.* of old sterling of England to John when he has brought 100 sacks of wool to Flanders." In

---

For the use of similar revenues in Namur, Guelders, Hainaut, and Luxemburg see Brouwers, *Chart. et règ.*, II, no. 345 ; De Saint-Genois, *Monuments,* II, 848 ; A.E.N., Piot, *Inv. Namur,* nos. 597, 604, and *Domaines,* no. I, fol. 61ᵛ ; Bormans, *Fiefs de Namur,* p. 97 ; Sloet, *Oorkondenboek Gelre en Zutfen,* nos. 535, 799, 810 ; De Saint-Genois, *Monuments,* I, 2 ff. ; Wampach, *Urkunden,* VII, no. 1090 ; A.G.R., Verkooren, *Inv. Lux.,* nos. 1250, 1260. See Appendix, no. 29, and Plate V.

[90] Van Mieris, *Groot Charterboek,* II, 5, 24, 182, 191, 283, 538, 747 ; III, 50–51, 515, 576 ; Van Den Bergh, *Oorkondenboek van Holland,* I, no. 357 ; II, no. 359.

[91] *C.P.R. 1327–30,* p. 10.

[92] *C.Cl.R. 1327–30,* pp. 247, 352 ; *C.Cl.R. 1330–33,* pp. 3, 72, 231, 244, 386, 459, 499 ; *C.Cl.R. 1333–37,* pp. 37–38, 77, 220, 425, 573, 611 ; *C.Cl.R. 1339–41,* pp. 2, 49, 317 ; *C.Cl.R. 1341–43,* pp. 437, 601 ; *C.Cl.R. 1343–46,* pp. 161, 163, 210, 273, 289, 309, 421, 518.

[93] *C.Cl.R. 1330–33,* pp. 72, 349 ; *C.Cl.R. 1339–41,* p. 566.

1345 John de Wesenham, receiver of customs on wool for the realm, paid 550 m. to John.[94] Edward III, regarding John of Hainaut as an extremely powerful and useful ally, made every attempt to pay the fief promptly. Thus in 1342 the collectors of London were ordered so to "ordain the payments from the customs that John will be one of the first ones to receive his payment of 1,000 m. yearly." Apparently John was not satisfied, for in the next year Edward again reminded the collectors to give more prompt attention to John's payments than to those of the other royal allies, and to make sure that certain arrears owed to him were paid.[95] It would only be tedious to cite other cases where fiefs were assigned on the wool customs of various ports, but it should be pointed out that the customs of Bordeaux were frequently used to pay fiefs to men in Gascony.[96]

Sczaniecki has drawn attention to some of the duties, tolls, and customs used by the French kings. He has noted that they assigned numerous fiefs upon the customs of Nemours, Péronne, and Mâcon, and a few upon those of Paris and Chinon. The bishops of Paris granted fiefs on the crossing of Conflans; the counts of Mâcon, on that of Mâcon.[97] To these can be added many others including Roye en Vermandois, Cormeilles en Paris, Gien, Marmande, Choisy, Montargis, Mansiaco, and the bridge of Corbeil.[98] *Fiefs-rentes* were also assigned on the duties received from the *salin* of Carcassonne and the halls of Rouen.[99]

---

[94] *C.Cl.R. 1341–43,* pp. 46, 70; *C.Cl.R. 1343–46,* pp. 210, 622.

[95] *C.Cl.R. 1341–43,* p. 437; *C.Cl.R. 1343–46,* p. 175. In 1349 Robert of Namur received his fief of 1,200 florins from the customs of London (*C.Cl.R. 1349–54,* p. 32). In 1346 Thierry, lord of Montjoie and Fauquemont, received his fief out of the customs of London and Boston (*C.P.R. 1345–48,* p. 61). See also P.R.O., Foreign Accounts, Enrolled, E. 364/3.

[96] In 1247 Henry III ordered that the fief of 20 l. belonging to Gerard de Burgo be paid "de consuetudinibus civitatis regis Burdegale." In 1255 "Aldebertus, miles de Brigeriaco" received a fief of 10 m. "de Magna custuma nostra Burdegale." And in 1337 "Guccardus de Lebret, vicecomes Tartasii" received payment from the customs of Bordeaux "pro feodo suo" (*Cl.R. 1247–51,* p. 6; *R.G.,* I, Supplement, no. 4436; P.R.O., Gascon Rolls, C. 61/49, m. 40r).

[97] Sczaniecki, *Essai,* pp. 117–18.

[98] Langlois, *Registres perdus,* nos. 42, 50–51, 66, 100, 111, 179, 235, 390, 478, 686, 811.

[99] *Ibid.,* nos. 537, 539.

The Templars, as we have seen, served the French kings in the role of royal treasurers down into the fourteenth century. In another capacity, that of private bankers, they served also the English kings. In his monograph on the financial operations of the Templars, Delisle has shown that John and Henry III arranged to have many *fiefs-rentes* paid by the treasuries of that order.[100] He also pointed out that John granted numerous fiefs to lords in southwestern France and that some were paid by the treasury of the Templars at La Rochelle. In order to prove his good faith and solvency to the grantees, John frequently deposited in the treasury at La Rochelle sums adequate to pay annual installments for a certain number of years.[101] For a man of John's unsavory reputation such a guarantee was considered necessary by many of the men who entered into feudal relations with him. In 1214 when John granted Alice, countess of Angoulême, a fief of 500 *l.* he deposited 2,500 *l.* in the treasury of the Templars at La Rochelle and ordered its commander to pay 500 *l.* annually to Alice.[102] In the same year and in the same place John deposited 30,000 *l.*, a sum representing five yearly installments to be paid to Ralph, count of Eu, for his fief.[103] In 1248 Hugh le Bigod made a fine of 700 *m.* with Henry III for certain wardships. Henry ordered 500 *m.* of the 700 *m.* to be deposited in the New Temple and then paid by the Templars to Thomas of Savoy, count of Flanders, for his fief of 500 *m.* In 1253 Henry ordered the exchequer to deposit 500 *m.* yearly in the New Temple for the fief of Thomas.[104] In 1224 the commander of the Templars in England was ordered to pay 200 *m.* at the feast of Saint Michael and 300 *m.* at Easter to Hugh de Lusignan X, viscount of La Marche and Angoulême, for his fief of 500 *m.* customarily received at the exchequer. The money was to be paid to Hugh or his representative at Paris.[105] These and many other

---

[100] Delisle, *Mémoire sur les opérations financières des Templiers.* See also A. Sandys, "The Financial and Administrative Importance of the London Temple in the Thirteenth Century," *Essays in Medieval History Presented to Thomas F. Tout* (Manchester, 1925), pp. 147–62.

[101] *Ibid.*, pp. 11–12.

[102] *Ibid.*

[103] *Ibid.*

[104] *C.P.R. 1247–58*, pp. 9, 195. See also *Pat. R. 1225–32*, p. 322 ; *C.L.R. 1226–40*, p. 433.

[105] *Pat. R. 1225–32*, p. 436. See also *C.P.R. 1247–58*, p. 100. With the exception of Flanders the Templars apparently played no part in the finance

entries show that the Templars loaned large sums to John and Henry III for paying *fiefs-rentes* and financing their military operations. The greatest service of the financial system of the Templars, however, was that it enabled the English kings to deposit lump sums in the treasuries and to use this money as collateral in their financial relations with the holders of *fiefs-rentes*.

The numerous merchant-bankers and the societies of merchants and banking houses of western Europe that developed rapidly in the thirteenth century and expanded their services in the fourteenth were constantly used by the English kings to facilitate the payment of *fiefs-rentes*. The transactions between the kings and merchants were generally of three kinds: the merchants loaned the money to the kings so that they could promptly pay the yearly installments, the merchants paid the recipients directly and collected their money later from the exchequer or such royal revenues as the wool customs, or the merchants merely acted as intermediaries, either paying the money for the kings to the recipients or going to the kings and receiving the money in the name of the recipients. In the case of the large banking societies such as the Italian, their international organization greatly facilitated these transactions. In 1248 Henry III licensed his step-brother, Guy de Lusignan, "to accept a loan of 1,000 *l.* from merchants and others upon his yearly fee of 200 *l.* at the exchequer of London granted him by charter: and the king will pay the amounts to the said merchants, at the terms stated in their contracts, and any loss they incur through non-payment of the money at the appointed terms." The next year Lothering Conradi, citizen and merchant of Siena, was reimbursed from the exchequer for the 1,000 *l.* which he had loaned to Guy for his fief.[106]

---

of the *fief-rente* in other areas. In 1288 Peter du Sak, commander of the Templars in Flanders, acknowledged receipt of 80 *l.* from the receiver of Flanders, a sum apparently paid by the Templars to a man for his *fief-rente* (De Saint-Genois, *Monuments*, II, 760).

[106] *C.P.R. 1247–58*, pp. 5, 243. See also p. 257. In 1273 a writ of *liberate* from Edward I was made out to "Aldebrandino mercatori de Luka, et sociis suis, 200 *l.*, pro illis 200 *l.* quas mutuarunt karissimo avunculo nostro Guydoni de Leziniaco, et in quibus dominus H. rex, pater noster, eidem Guidoni tenebatur, de residuo finis 1,000 *m.* quem idem pater noster fecit cum ipso pro remissione feodi 500 *m.*" (E. A. Bond, "Extracts from the Liberate Rolls, Relative to Loans Supplied by Italian Merchants to the Kings of England in the Thirteenth and Fourteenth Centuries," *Archaeologia*, XXVIII, 1840, 273–74). See also pp. 207–326; *Pat. R. 1232–47*, p. 356; *C.P.R. 1247–58*,

In 1292 Brache Gerard of the banking society of the Peruzzi received from the exchequer 100 *l.* in behalf of Count Guy of Flanders for "feodo suo de termino Sancti Michaelis." The following year John Musard, merchant of Douai, received 100 *l.* for the fief of Guy.[107]

The "Diplomatic Documents of the Exchequer" are filled with acquittances by holders of *fiefs-rentes* for payments received from merchants and bankers. In 1304, for example, the exchequer received an "acquittance by John, lord of Cuyk, for 250 *l.* received in part payment of the sum of 1,000 *l.* due to him ... and for an obligation for 500 *l.* in full of the said sum to be paid by the merchants of the societies of the Frescobaldi and Ballardi."[108] That Edward III's campaigns were financed by merchants and bankers of the Low Countries and Italy is well known.[109] This is confirmed by numerous entries for the reign of Edward concerning the payment of *fiefs-rentes*, wages, subsidies, and other war expenses.[110] The

pp. 9, 37; *C.P.R. 1266–72*, appendix, p. 736; *C.P.R. 1272–81*, p. 274; *C.L.R. 1245–51*, p. 90.

[107] P.R.O., Dip. Docs. Exch., E. 30/46. A financial account of the Frescobaldi for the regnal years 23–28 Edward I contains entries concerning payments to the count of Bar, the lord of Cuyk, John de Châlons, and Otto de Grandison, all of whom held *fiefs-rentes* from Edward (P.R.O., E. 101/126/13). See also *C.P.R. 1258–66*, p. 380; *C.P.R. 1266–72*, p. 322; *Foedera*, I, ii, 435.

[108] "Cal. Dip. Doc.," in *D.K.R.*, XLVIII, app., 575. See also *C.Cl.R. 1339–41*, p. 581.

[109] S. Terry, *The Financing of the Hundred Years' War, 1337–1350* (London, 1914); Lucas, *The Low Countries and the Hundred Years' War*; E. B. Fryde, "Edward III's Wool Monopoly of 1337: A Fourteenth-Century Royal Trading Venture," *History*, XXXVII (1952), 8–24. Certain notes on this subject kindly put at my disposal by Dr. Fryde clearly show the role of the Italian bankers in the finance of the Hundred Years' War. Much of the money loaned by them helped to pay the *fiefs-rentes* granted by the kings.

[110] The following are typical entries: 14 April 1339—"Sir William de Duneloerd, lord of Osterhout, acknowledges he has received from Gerard Bonsegne and his companions, merchants of the company of the Bardi, in name of John de Haynaud, lord of Biaumont, 2,000 florins of Florence in part of a greater sum which the said merchants promised to pay to the said John for the king of England; for which sum he promises the merchants shall have the acquittance of John de Heynaud. Antwerp." 18 June 1348—"Acquittance by (Hamo de Mirabello) for 800 florins 'd'or de l'escu' received from the king of England by the hands of Walter de Chiriton and Gilbert de Wendlingburgh, merchants of London, in part payment of 750 *l.* due to him

Wardrobe Debentures are filled with receipts made out by royal envoys to Italian bankers for sums loaned to them for the purpose of financing their military and diplomatic activities in the Low Countries in the years just before 1340. Much of the money was used to pay the large *fiefs-rentes* received by the Low Country princes. At Dordrecht on 2 July 1337 the royal envoys, William de Monte Acuto, William de Clynton, and Henry, bishop of Lincoln, received 2,500 florins of gold from the Peruzzi. On 4 July they received 1,600 florins, and on 28 July two payments of 4,800 florins and 7,233 florins of gold. Earlier on 18 April Edward III had ordered the Bardi to pay 2,000 *l.* to these men to further the arduous negotiations "ad partes transmarinas."[111] While in Brabant and Hainaut the same men received more money from the Bardi.[112] Countless examples of such transactions are recorded in the unpublished accounts preserved in the Public Record Office.[113]

Certain records indicate that the improved banking techniques developing in the thirteenth and fourteenth centuries were sometimes used to facilitate payment of *fiefs-rentes*. There is no better example of a letter of credit than the following. In 1254 Henry III empowered Lupus, bishop of Mauritania, and his archdeacon, Peter Garcias, to draw "a quocumque mercatore seu mercatoribus voluerint, usque ad summam centum marcarum sterlingorum, in quibus Rex eis tenetur de annuo feodo quod eis concessit, et viginti marcas ultra, de dono Regis." Henry agreed to reimburse the merchant later upon a specified date.[114] In 1406 Henry IV transmitted an order by letters close to "John Orlandyn of Florence living in London to make a letter of exchange to his fellows dwelling in foreign parts for 2,000 *m.* payable to the king's son Lewis duke

---

for arrears of his fees for 2½ years ending Michaelmas next. Bruges in Flanders" ("Cal. Dip. Doc.," in *D.K.R.*, XLVIII, app., 580–81).

[111] P.R.O., E. 404/500/121–27.

[112] P.R.O., E. 404/500/128, 138, 147. See also E. 404/500/158, 305; E. 404/501/365–67; E. 404/502/167; E. 404/503/64, 148, 259.

[113] In an account of 11–17 Edward III concerning the transactions of the Bardi and Peruzzi with Edward, one finds the Bardi paying William, count of Juliers, 12,000 florins of Florence in 1339. They paid Henry of Flanders 3,300 florins of Florence for war expenses and "pro redditu suo de termino Sancti Johannis Baptiste anno xiii°" (P.R.O., E. 101/127/32). See also E. 101/634/28.

[114] *R.G.*, I, no. 4071. See also no. 35.

of Bavaria and count palatine of the Rhine." This sum was in payment for the fief Louis held of Henry.[115]

It was quite natural that the English kings involved the Jews in the payment of *fiefs-rentes*. At times, apparently short of money, the kings would cancel certain debts owed by recipients of *fiefs-rentes* to Jewish creditors and in turn relieve the Jews of financial obligations to the royal exchequer. In 1251, for example, Henry III in order to pay 10 *l.* to John le Gras for his fief relieved him from paying 10 *l.* "de debito quod debet Bonenfant' de Exonia, Judeo."[116] In 1261 Philip Marmion was relieved of paying a debt of 34 *l.* and 1 *m.* to a Jew of London called Hagin; this sum was to be considered payment for Philip's fief of 40 *m.*[117] In Germany the Jews also helped to pay *fiefs-rentes* but in a different way; the special taxes levied upon them were often reserved for payment of *fiefs-rentes* by the emperors and a few other princes. In 1277 King Rudolf granted a fief of 10 *m.* to Sifrid von Runkel payable on the taxes coming from the community of Jews at Wetflar.[118] In 1283 Werner, the archbishop of Mainz, granted a fief of 20 *m.* to Boppo, count of Henneberg; it was to be paid from the tax received from the Jews living in Erfurt.[119]

One is impressed by the conciseness and accuracy of the information on *fiefs-rentes* in the records of the more efficiently organized states. Without doubt the essential records were those containing the concessions, confirmations, and *vidimus* in that they provided the ultimate authority for the existence of a fief. The varied financial records nevertheless provided the surest means of maintaining an up-to-date check over every *fief-rente*. In general one feels that every penny paid out for a fief was strictly accounted for. Of all the princes, the kings of England seemed the most concerned with maintaining a rigid system of account for all the money issued for *fiefs-*

---

[115] *C.Cl.R. 1405–09*, p. 34. See also p. 442.

[116] *Cl.R. 1247–51*, p. 434.

[117] *Cl.R. 1259–61*, p. 400; *R.G.*, I, no. 2354. See also *Cl.R. 1259–61*, p. 400; *R.G.*, I, no. 3115; *C.P.R. 1247–58*, p. 216; *C.Cl.R. 1272–79*, p. 302.

[118] Goerz, *Mittelrheinische Regesten*, IV, no. 433. In 1293 King Adolf conceded a fief of 25 *m.* to Godfrey von Eppenstein "de precariis Judeorum nostrorum frankenvordensium" (Böhmer, *Urkundenbuch Frankfurt*, I, 280–81). See also Hilgard, *Urkunden zur Geschichte der Stadt Speyer*, no. 192; Böhmer, *Urkundenbuch Frankfurt*, I, 296, and *Acta Imperii*, no. 601.

[119] Beyer, *Urkundenbuch Stadt Erfurt*, I, no. 348.

rentes.[120] Evidence also points to an efficient system of account in Flanders, Brabant, and France.[121] Gradually realizing that their own records were not adequate, all the princes, no matter how insignificant their political sway, began to require formal receipts from the holders of *fiefs-rentes* each time a payment was made. By the late thirteenth century this was a regular practice everywhere. For England this type of transaction seems to comprise the bulk of the "Diplomatic Documents of the Exchequer" in the fourteenth and early fifteenth centuries, and there are also many receipts in the "Kalendars and Inventories of the Exchequer."[122] In France, Flan-

---

[120] In 1248 Henry III promised to pay 50 *l*. at Michaelmas next to Bernard de Ventadour, archdeacon of Limoges, for his *fief-rente*. The letters patent stated: "It is not certain that so much is due to him [Bernard], so he shall bring with him at the same term his letters patent" (*C.P.R. 1247–58*, p. 19). In 1270 "upon scrutiny of the rolls of the chancery the king has found that from the time when he first granted to William [Arnaldi de Cadylak] a yearly fee of 25 *l*. because of his having been disinherited in the parts of Pergorz, there are in arrear to him 546 *l*., in the whole of which the king will satisfy him as soon as he can, on condition that if it can be found at the exchequer or elsewhere that the king is not bound to him in so much, the king will cause him to be satisfied in the form aforesaid of what is due him" (*C.P.R. 1367–70*, p. 492). See also *R.G.*, I, nos. 1444, 3143, 3391; *Rot. Lib.*, pp. 15, 17, 57; *Rot. Claus.*, I, 180 b, 602 a–b; *Cl.R. 1334–37*, p. 386.

[121] In 1291, for example, Theobald, count of Bar, acknowledged receipt of all the arrears owed to him for his fief of 400 *l*. held from Count Guy of Flanders; he declared that he had been paid by the knight Colart Willikant. Attached to Theobald's letter is an account of the arrears from 1286 to 1290. It stated that for 1286 Theobald had been paid by a comital officer, Sohier de Bailleul, but that four years were in arrears not only for his fief of 400 *l*. but also for one of 50 *l*. owed to Reginald of Bar. Guy acknowledged that he owed a total of 1,800 *l*. to Theobald and Reginald (*A.E.G., De Saint Genois, Inv. Fl.*, no. 547). See also Appendix, no. 10. When the duke of Burgundy acquired Limburg in 1389 he had an inquest made to determine his rights and obligations. Those making the inquest discovered that the revenues of Limburg and Rolduc were paying more money for *fiefs-rentes* than should be paid and as a result ordered that no more fiefs be paid until the pertinent records could be checked for verification (Quicke, *B.C.R.H.*, XCVI, 1932, 370–73). See Plate VI. See also A.D.N., B. 1186/12458, 14496[bis]; B. 4062/145.518.

[122] The following examples are typical: "Acquietancia de 400 *m*. annui feodi comiti Sabaudie per regem Anglie debeti pro duobus annis videlicet de annis domini 1277 et 1278. Datum anno domini 1281. ... Littera acquietancie comitis Sabaudie de 400 *m*. receptis a domino Edwardo rege Anglie pro arreragiis feodi primi suo ad scaccarium ipsius domini regis in Anglia debiti sub dato anno domini 1286." In 1397 Rupert junior, count palatine

ders, and Brabant the receipts are no less numerous.[123] Records of receipt are scanty for Germany;[124] there are more records even for such tiny states as Namur, Hainaut, and Holland.[125]

Just as homage could be done and received by proxy, so this procedure could be applied to expedite the payment of *fiefs-rentes*. The practice, common already in the early thirteenth century, attained its height in the fourteenth. Because of their location across the Channel, the English kings paid numerous fiefs by proxy, especially during the Hundred Years' War.[126] Many were the grantees who sent proctors empowered to secure their installments from the English exchequer.[127] On the Continent agents of the recipients were

of the Rhine and duke of Bavaria, acquitted Richard II for the sum of 500 *m*. received "racione feodi" (Palgrave, *Antient Kalendars*, I, 85–86; "Cal. Dip. Doc.," in *D.K.R.*, XLVIII, app., 600). In 1422 Diedrich, archbishop of Cologne, made out a receipt for "mille nobilia aurea ... ratione feodi quod praedictus praecarissimus dominus noster rex nobis de sua gratia ... constituit" (P.R.O., E. 30/428). See also G. P. Cuttino, *The Gascon Calendar of 1322* (Camden Society, London, 1949), 3d ser., LXX, nos. 935, 937, 939, 978, 984, 988, 989, 1076, 1123–24. See Appendix, no. 30.

[123] For France the following is a typical receipt: "Nous Jehans, sires de Haveskerke chevaliers, faisons savoir a tous que nous quitons nostre tres haut et tres puissant singneur Philippe, par le grace de Diu, roi de Franche de toutes choses que nous li pousiens demander par quelcomque maniere que ce fust iusques au jourdui parmi sis cens livrees de terre au parisis que il nous a donnees si comme il apert par ses lettres que nous en avons. En tesmoing de la quel chose nous avons seelees ces lettres de nostre seel donnees le joesdi apries le feste Saint Mahiu lapostre, lan de grace mil trois cens et un" (A.N., J. 544/14). For Brabant Verkooren's inventory shows receipts to be the most prominent type of document in the acts of the dukes. See examples under nos. 2003, 2009, 2013, 2053, 2098–99, 2130, 2149, 2878, 5808, 5921, etc. See Appendix, nos. 8, 11, 28, and Plate VI. For receipts in Flanders see De Saint-Genois, *Monuments*, II, 680, 692, 697, 700, 737, 760, 785, 799, 877; A.G.R., *Trés. Fl.*, Sér. I, nos. 2062, 2069, 2073, 2075, 2085; Gaillard, *B.C.R.H.*, VI (1853), nos. 172–74, 176, 178, 185, 187–88, etc.

[124] Gudenus, *Codex Diplomaticus*, V, 713, 751.

[125] Namur: Brouwers, *Chart. et règ.*, I, nos. 198, 214, 242; II, no. 338; Piot, *Inv. Namur*, no. 1027. Hainaut: De Saint-Genois, *Monuments*, I, 303–5, 307. Holland: Van Mieris, *Groot Charterboek*, III, 110; Van Den Bergh, *Oorkondenboek van Holland*, II, no. 1074.

[126] In 1205 John ordered Geoffrey Fitz-Peter to pay from the treasury to Frank Columby, "nuncio comitis Flandrie 850 *m*. de feodo eius comitis de uno annuo" (*Rot. Claus.*, I, 22). See also *Foedera*, I, i, 259; *Rot. Lib.*, pp. 9–10; *C.P.R. 1264–68*, p. 41; "Cal. Dip. Doc.," in *D.K.R.*, XLVIII, app., 587; P.R.O., E. 30/428a, 1230, 1421.

[127] On 14 January 1426 Louis, count palatine of the Rhine, appointed Fre-

often empowered to obtain the money. Frequently the original concessions stated that the installments would be paid to the grantee or to his legally designated and empowered attorneys. This practice prevailed in France, Flanders, and Namur.[128]

The peculiarities and arrangements of each state for financing *fiefs-rentes* are almost endless; it would be tedious to enumerate them all. A few, however, should be pointed out. The English kings commonly advanced sums on the yearly installments.[129] Men setting out on pilgrimages were often paid in advance the installments for

derick de Mitra as his procurator to receive from the king of England the sum of 2,000 m. in payment of the fief of 1,000 m. due for the years 1424 and 1425. On 25 June 1426 Frederick de Mitra gave acquittance to Walter de Hungerford, treasurer of England, for the 2,000 m. On 29 August Louis made out a receipt to Henry VI for the money received by his procurator. Louis usually sent his procurators to England every three or four years to collect the yearly installments. Thus on 1 September 1440 he appointed Nicholas de Wachenheim and two others as his procurators to collect four sums of 1,200 m. each, due at Easter 1437, 1438, 1439, and 1440. These sums were for the *fief-rente* of Louis and the portion of the dowry still owed to his father who had married the daughter of Henry IV. At London on 5 December 1440 the three procurators gave the treasury a receipt for these sums ("Cal. Dip. Doc.," in *D.K.R.*, XLV, app. i, 325–26; XLVIII, app., 763). Most of the Low Country princes sent envoys to England to collect the annual installments. The following entry is typical: "Noverit universi me Borzewey de Swyner militem recepisse per manus Johannis Pisto de Ludeco, attornati mei et procuratoris generalis, de excellentissimo principe et domino, domino Ricardo secundo, Dei gratia rege Anglie et Francie, per manus thesaurarii et camerarorum eiusdem domini regis de scaccario suo centum marcas monete Anglie in partem solucionis cuiusdam annui feodi quingentorum florenorum ... [28 October 1391]" (P.R.O., E. 30/1228).

[128] In 1192 when Philip Augustus granted a fief of 20 l. to John le Noir he stipulated that it could be paid to John or to "ejus certo nuncio" (Delaborde, *Actes de Philippe-Auguste,* I, no. 403). On 8 January 1291 John, the brother of Count Henry of Bar, empowered Geoffrey de Ransières to receive payment on a *fief-rente* held from the count of Flanders (De Saint-Genois, *Monuments,* II, 799). See also pp. 692, 721; A.D.N., B. 4056/145.411; Piot, *Inv. Namur,* no. 701; A.G.R., *C.C.,* Cartulaire de Namur, fol. 156ᵛ; Verkooren, *Inv. Brab.,* unpublished, 2 November 1386. See Appendix, no. 10.

[129] In 1206 an advance payment was made to Philip de Albiniaco: "Die Lunae in Ebdomoda Pentecost' apud Portesmouth Philippo de Albiniaco de prestito per senecallum 10 m. scilicet dicere que est de feodo suo" (*Rot. Praest.,* p. 271). There are dozens of such entries in the Prest Rolls. Many, too, are in the unpublished Prest Roll of 14–17 John (P.R.O., Various Accounts, E. 101/325/2, mm. 1–4).

the years they expected to be absent.[130] Sometimes the French records designated *fiefs-rentes* by a particular name such as "feodum Locharum," "fié de Herbignies," and "feodum Feritatis Alesiae." These names, appearing for generations in the royal financial records, mean that these fiefs had been originally granted to a recipient in return for his surrendering certain lands, castles, or rights to the grantor. The "feodum Locharum," for example, referred to a fief of 600 *l.* granted in 1249 by Louis IX to Dreu de Mello in return for ceding over the castles of Loches and Châtillon-sur-Indre.[131] In both France and Flanders the counts and kings arranged to assign *fiefs-rentes* upon revenues located near the recipients.[132] In France, Champagne, Germany, and Brabant it was sometimes the practice to refuse payment of the fief because it had not been requested or because the recipient had failed to appear personally for the installment.[133]

We must now grapple with a question which, although of a juridical nature, cannot be solved apart from the finance of the *fief-rente*. Sczaniecki denied, as we have seen, that a *fief-rente* could be assigned on an estate of land ("sur un fonds de terre").[134] He insisted that it could be assigned only upon a treasury or upon the revenues of the donor, never directly upon a source of revenue. Previously Petot and Didier had arrived at similar conclusions.[135]

---

[130] In 1239 Henry III by writ of *liberate* ordered to be paid to "Robert de Sabloil 200 *m.* in advance for the 23rd year of his yearly fee of that amount, and another 200 *m.* of his fee for the 24th year, in order that he may make his pilgrimage to the Holy Land" (*C.L.R. 1226–40*, p. 378). See also *C.L.R. 1240–45*, p. 29; *C.L.R. 1226–40*, p. 81.

[131] Sczaniecki, *Essai*, pp. 111–12.

[132] A.G.R., *Trés. Fl.*, Sér. I, no. 2065.

[133] Sczaniecki, *Essai*, p. 139. Under the "Despens en la baillie de Chaumont" in the *Compte de la terre de Champagne (1340–1341)* one finds the following entries: "A ma dame Marguerite, mere dou dit mon seigneur Guillaume, de XX lb. neant, que nulz ne les a demandées. ... A mon seigneur Pierre de Chambleix, de XL lb. neant, qu'il ne les a pas demandées" (Longnon, *Documents de Champagne*, III, 353). In the account of receipts and expenses of Limburg for 1391–92 the following entry appears after a list of fiefs paid: "Item est assavoir que encore sont plusieurs qui doivent avoir fiefs de jour en jour escheaus comme dessus est dit lesquelx nont point este requis ne demandez au receveur" (A.G.R., *C.C.*, no. 2436, fol. 76ᵛ).

[134] See Ch. I, p. 16.

[135] Petot, *Constitution de rente aux XIIᵉ et XIIIᵉ siècles*, pp. 59–81; Didier, *Revue du Nord*, XVII, 78–82.

Now if this is to say that a fief of land, a mill, a toll, a duty, or an office could not be granted to a man in order to provide a stipulated yearly income, it is unqualifiedly correct. When land, offices, or sources of revenues were assigned, there was no suggestion of a *fief-rente*; simply a fief of land or an enfeoffed office or revenue had come into existence. Thus far the relation of the *fief-rente* to land causes no difficulty. Problems immediately arise, however, when one asks whether a *fief-rente* could be assigned on an estate of land. When Sczaniecki employs *sur* it means to me "on" and not "in". An annual income assigned *in* lands is a fief of land, but an annual income assigned *on* lands is a *fief-rente*. When Sczaniecki so phrases his views seemingly to rule out *fiefs-rentes* from being paid directly by income-producing land, then an objection must be raised. If my interpretation is correct, Sczaniecki would seem to limit *fiefs-rentes* to those granted on treasuries or on revenues having no immediate connection with land. This view is far too narrow and even contradictory to what the records actually tell us. To accept it would be to exclude a considerable proportion of the *fiefs-rentes* granted. The problem, it seems to me, can be resolved upon the basis of possession of the land. If a vassal received possession of land producing his annual income he became responsible for getting out of it what it was supposedly worth and so came to hold an ordinary fief. When a lord, however, assigned an annual income on his own lands without handing over possession to the vassal, then a *fief-rente* had come into being. The lord retained possession of the land and remained responsible for its producing the amount to pay the fief. The vassal had no need to concern himself with the land and probably never even saw it; he cared little whether the money came directly from land, a treasury, or a revenue as long as he received payment every year. But we must now turn to the records if we would anchor this argument on more than just hypothetical assertion.

As far as can be ascertained the *fief-rente* held by the counts of Flanders from the English kings was paid during the course of the twelfth century from the issues of the various counties. Throughout the reign of Henry II, for example, the Pipe Rolls contain entries such as the following: "Et in terris datis Comiti Flandrie Chirchetun' pro 200 *l*. blancorum." "Et in terris datis Comiti Flandrie 76 *l*. blancorum in Bentun'." "Et in terris datis Comiti Flandrie in Duneham 60 *l.*"[136] Yearly these same lands appear in the Pipe Rolls as paying the *fief-rente* of the Flemish counts.[137] What occurred was that certain lands of the king were designated to pay the fief and, though they appear to have been given to the counts, they were not. They were administered by the responsible sheriffs who yearly paid the annual issues to the counts; the counts probably never saw the lands that paid their fief. During the same century *fiefs-rentes* assigned to the count of Boulogne, to Flemish knights, and to other Low Country lords were similarly paid.[138] To illustrate the difference between assigning an annual income *in* land and assigning it *on* land let us examine some concessions in France. In 1206 Philip Augustus granted to Peter de Tilli "in feodum et homagium, septuaginta libras reddituum in terra, et propter hoc assignamus eidem terram et manerium quod fuit Roberti de Frieboiz cum omnibus pertinenciis."[139] Here we have an annual income assigned *in* land; it is not a *fief-rente*. But in the following examples the annual income is assigned *on* land and we are thus dealing with *fiefs-rentes*. In 1216 Simon de Montfort assigned "200 livrées de terre" to Nègre de la Redorte "sur les lieux de la Redorte, Trausse, Tours et Palairac."[140] In 1245–46 Alphonse of Poitiers granted to Henry de Bernaize "quater viginti libratas annui redditus sitas super terram Helye Geberti, in feodis de allodio, ab ipso Helya Geberti ratione guerre forisfactam."[141] Scanning the Low Country evidence we find Count Robert de Béthune of Flanders granting in 1316 to Henry of Flanders a fief of 1,000 *l.*, half assigned on the land of Assebrouck and its appurtenances and half on the woods of Nieppe.[142] In 1302 Count John I of Namur gave Baldwin de Poperode a fief of "trois cens

---

[136] *P.R. 2 Hen. II*, pp. 24, 36, 39.

[137] *P.R. 3 Hen. II*, pp. 82, 83, 89; *P.R. 5 Hen. II*, pp. 8, 34, 51; *P.R. 28 Hen. II*, pp. 14, 50, 123.

[138] *P.R. 10 Ric. I*, p. 121: "Et Flandrensibus 110 s. de feodis suis in Anglia per breve G. f. Petri quod attulit de computandis sibi 60 l. quas predictis Flandr' liberavit de predictis feodis." See also pp. 115, 153, 154, 190; Kienast, *Deutschen Fürsten*, I, 75.

[139] Delisle, *Actes de Philippe-Auguste*, II, no. 927; *Cat. des actes de Philippe-Auguste*, no. 972; Léchaudé d'Anisy, *Scaccarium Normannie sub Regibus Francie*, p. 156.

[140] Molinier, *Biblio. de l'École des Chartes*, XXXIV, no. 130. See also nos. 74 and 154.

[141] *Layettes*, II, no. 3471.

[142] A.E.G., De Saint Genois, *Inv. Fl.*, no. 1314.

livrees de terre par an" on the seigniory of Ninove.[143] Such grants were perhaps most numerous in Hainaut. In 1341, for example, Count William II granted Mul de Binsuelt a fief of "LX livrées de revenue" and listed the annual incomes of certain lands, places, and woods that would pay the fief.[144] Going into Germany we find King Richard granting a fief of 100 m. in 1260 to the count of Catsenellenbogen; 50 m. were to be paid from imperial possessions in Tribur.[145] Were we to add to these examples the many others dispersed throughout the records, they would but confirm that it was accepted practice for lords to use the income from their lands to pay *fiefs-rentes*.

Frequently lands upon which *fiefs-rentes* were assigned were evaluated to determine if they were capable of producing the required income. For example, Mather, lord of Montmorency, received from Philip III of France a fief of 500 l. Damville and its appurtenances were designated to pay the fief and it was ordered "quod fiat appreciatio per gentes nostras."[146] In 1333 the count of Hainaut granted Louis de Nevers, count of Flanders, 1,000 "livrées de terre" to be paid from the lands of Blaton and Feignies. Louis immediately ordered two of his men to make a survey of these lands to see whether they contained the value of 1,000 *livrées de terre*.[147]

---

[143] A.G.R., *Trés. Fl.*, Sér. I, no. 1050. See Appendix, nos. 22, 24.

[144] Devillers, *Cart. de Hainaut*, I, no. 82. In 1328 the knight Robert de Manchicourt sold to Count William I of Hainaut a fief of "quarante livrées de tierre au blanc, que li dis mesires Robiers avoit à hiretage, sur le tierre de Blaton" (Devillers, *Monuments*, III, no. 226, p. 211). In another document of the fourteenth century entitled "Che sont li hommaige ke mesire de Behaygne avoit en le contet de Haynnau" appears the following entry: "Item, Bauduins, castellains de Biaumont, pour cent livrées de terre u environ, pour le quarte partie de le ville de Sorre-le-Castiel, des bos, des terres, en prés, en yauwes, en rentes et en justices lieges" (no. 293, p. 348). In 1347, William I, count of Namur, appeared before the bailiff and men of the fief of Hainaut "et dist que sour no ditte chière dame le contesse il avoit siis sens livrées de tière au tournois par an, lesquelz on li devoit assir, faire et assener en le conté de Haynnau en aucun ciertain lieu, et qu'il les tenoit en fief et en hommage" (Devillers, *Cart. de Hainaut*, I, no. 180, p. 303). See also Didier, *Revue du Nord*, XVII, 280–81; Duvivier, *La querelle des d'Avesnes et des Dampierre*, II, 448.

[145] Goerz, *Mittelrheinische Regesten*, III, no. 1647.

[146] Du Chesne, *Histoire généalogique de la maison de Montmorency et de Laval* (Paris, 1624), Preuves, p. 127.

[147] A.G.R., *Trés. Fl.*, Sér. I, no. 257. See Appendix, no. 22.

The expression *livrées de terre* or *libratae terrae* requires explanation. Along with Mitteis, Sczaniecki is certain that at the moment of conceding a *fief-rente* all grantors envisaged its eventual replacement by a fief of land producing an annual income of equal value.[148] As we have noted, *fiefs-rentes* were granted throughout western Europe with the provision that they would be paid only until land of equal value could be provided. And, as both Sczaniecki and Didier have remarked, often with such grants the fiefs were designated in *libratae terrae* or *livrées de terre*. This expression, undoubtedly adopted from its use when conceding fiefs of land, obviously suggested the idea of a piece of land able to provide annually a certain income. Throughout western Europe it had become common when granting land to evaluate it in terms of annual income rather than in area or in revenue-producing resources.[149] The latter method could produce no accurate estimate of the fief's value nor was it essential for the recipient to know the material details of his fief. Basic only was the knowledge that he was coming into possession of land capable of producing so much in cash income yearly. It was natural that this expression should find its way into use with a *fief-rente* assigned until land could be provided. And knowing, as we do, the traditional medieval conception of fiefs as thinglike, or at least as ultimately coming out of the land, it is not difficult to understand why *fiefs-rentes* were linked to land. The vassal desired more collateral behind the *fief-rente* than the good faith of the donor and frequently got the guarantee that should the installments cease there would be land that could be taken over and that would provide a comparable income.

On the other hand, it should be remembered that with these fiefs granted until lands could be provided, the evidence indicates that often land was never substituted and that the recipient received payment on the fief until his death. It should also be recalled that many heritable and life fiefs were granted and, so far as we can

[148] Mitteis, *Lehnrecht und Staatsgewalt*, p. 476: "Die ersten Rentenlehen, die wir kennen, hatten wohl nur vorläufigen Charakter; sie sollten sobald als möglich in Landlehen umgewandelt werden." Sczaniecki, *Essai*, pp. 122–29.
[149] Stenton, *The First Century of English Feudalism* (p. 164, n. 1): "The description of an estate as so many *libratae terrae* represents an estimate of the amount of money which it ought to bring in, yearly, to its lord under normal conditions." For examples of such grants see pp. 164–68. See also Didier, *Revue du Nord*, XVII, 79.

discover, were never replaced with land. It would be difficult indeed to support the contention of Sczaniecki and Mitteis that land generally supplanted *fiefs-rentes*; that, consequently, the *fief-rente* was but a transitory feudal institution; and that only the fief of land had a permanent quality, the *fief-rente* being but temporarily superimposed upon the traditional feudalism.[150] However vigorously the medieval German lawyer and feudal custom might deny that incorporeal objects could be enfeoffed, and however often the same view might find expression in legal treatises of the seventeenth and eighteenth centuries, money was constantly enfeoffed in medieval Germany as elsewhere and showed no signs of being any more transitory, so far as feudalism was concerned, than land itself.[151]

Even if lands were never substituted for a *fief-rente*, which meanwhile was paid from the income arising from land, the use of the expression *livrées de terre* in the records is nevertheless understandable; land was actually underwriting the payment of the fief. But if the fief with a clause of intended conversion into land was granted upon and continued to be paid by a treasury, the use of *livrées de terre* seems strange. And it is stranger still to find *livrées de terre* used when a fief is granted upon a treasury or other revenues without any mention of conversion into land, as happened, for example, with dozens of fiefs granted by the counts of Namur.[152] For this unliteral

---

[150] Sczaniecki, *Essai*, p. 129; Mitteis, *Lehnrecht und Staatsgewalt*, p. 476.

[151] For such expressions see the section "De Feudis de Camera et Caneva" by Roeschius in Jenichen, *Thesaurus Juris Feudalis*, vol. II; Mitteis, *Lehnrecht und Staatsgewalt*, pp. 475 ff.; Mitteis, *Der Staat des hohen Mittelalters*, pp. 385 ff.; Kienast, *H.Z.*, CLVIII, 25 ff.; Bloch, *Société féodale*, I, 269. Bloch points out that the same opinion concerning fiefs of money prevailed in Italy.

[152] In 1296, for example, Guy, marquis of Namur, granted to Henry, lord of Berlaimont, a fief of "cent livrées de terre au tournois en deniers par an ... à noz recheveurs de le terre de Namur" (De Reiffenberg, *Monuments*, I, no. 37, p. 47). In the same year Guy granted to Henry, lord of Ligny, a fief of 200 *livrées de terre* to be paid by the receiver general of Namur (no. 39, p. 51). In 1270 a certain Yde de Lambres held from Countess Margaret of Flanders "100 soldées de terre de fief à bourse" payable on the treasury at Bruges (A.E.G., De Saint Genois, *Inv. Fl.*, no. 144). In 1285 John de Harecourt, marshal of France, held from Count Guy of Flanders "cent livrées de terre au tournois que ledit Gui lui avoit données en fief de bourse" (De Saint-Genois, *Monuments*, II, 733). In 1399 the count of Réthel granted John, count of Linang and Richecourt, a fief of 60 *livrées de terre* to be paid from the *vinage* of Réthel (A.G.R., Verkooren, *Inv. Brab.*, unpublished, 8 January 1399). See Appendix, no. 13.

use of *livrées de terre* when actually *livres* or *librae* should have been used, I can only suggest that because the source of payment mattered so little and because the use of *livrées de terre* had become such a habit, the distinction between it and *livres* came to be lost.

Reference to the source of payment raises yet another question—was the *fief-rente* considered a personal obligation of the donor? Sczaniecki, after reviewing the evidence presented by Petot and supplementing it with more of his own, has concluded that it was.[153] By tracing with the help of Petot the evolution of the *constitution de rente*, we can see that Sczaniecki's conclusion is valid. We find at first that an actual source of income was alienated by a lord to provide a *rente*. Then the *rente* was assigned on a source of revenue which remained in the lord's patrimony; occasionally the lord came to insert a clause that if the land failed to provide the income he would make good the deficit. The next step was to designate a subsidiary source to guarantee payment. But prevalent almost down to the end of the twelfth century was the idea that the source and it alone was responsible for paying the *rente*. If it failed to do so, that was merely unfortunate for the grantee; as yet personal obligation of the grantor was foreign to feudal logic and the *rentier* had no claim on the rest of the patrimony should the designated source dry up. But in the thirteenth century a radical change occurred. Donors rapidly came to assign the *rentes* simply upon the revenues of their domains without specifying the source. The *rentier* also came to be accorded the right to seize lands or goods to the value of the *rente* if unpaid. Thus all the domain became liable for the grantor's debts and, if it was unable to pay the obligations, the debtor himself was considered personally liable. Petot well expresses this transition: "L'évolution était donc complète. Pour satisfaire aux conditions diverses des milieux où le contrat avait été successivement employé, la pratique coutumière avait conçu d'abord la rente constituée comme une sorte d'usufruit; puis, en passant par le système mixte de l'*obligatio propter rem,* elle tendait à la fin du XIIIe siècle, à en faire une dette personnelle."[154] According to Sczaniecki, the *fief-rente* was obviously a personal debt because it actually needed no one source of assignment, and often had none. A fief, perhaps

---

[153] *Essai,* pp. 112–22. Medieval German opinion was that annual incomes granted under personal obligation were not fiefs. See above n. 151.

[154] Petot, in *Publications de l'Université de Dijon,* I, 59–81.

originally assigned on the revenue of a toll, could be transferred to
land, and later transferred to a treasury. The source of payment was
not a matter of concern because ultimately it was the grantor who
was personally responsible for the fief. When the source was changed
it was only to relieve the financial strain put upon a particular revenue or to place the source of payment closer to the recipient.
Sczaniecki has cited many good examples of such transference in
France,[155] but it is in the Low Countries and England that the fortunes of a fief can best be traced and the personal liability of the
donors best illustrated. By piecing together scattered records one can
construct the financial history of the *fief-rente* held by the counts
of Hainaut from the kings of France. In 1297 Philip the Fair granted
to John of Avesnes, count of Hainaut, a fief of 6,000 *l*. Of this sum
4,000 *l*. were to be assigned on Flemish conquests and 2,000 *l*. were
to be paid by the treasury at Paris. Until the conquests had been
made, however, the 4,000 *l*. were to be paid by the treasury. Although
in 1309 the entire 6,000 *l*. were still being paid by the treasury, by
1315 we find Count William I complaining that the 4,000 *l*. assigned on the *châtellenie* of Lille had not been paid. Immediately
(24 October) the king ordered two of his representatives to verify
this charge and by December we find letters of the king whereby
he assigned the 4,000 *l*. on the homages of Hugh de Maude, Gerard
de Pottes, Matthew du Val, and Robert de Maude with the promise
that should these sources be insufficient he would assign the deficit
on other lands. The source of payment for the 4,000 *l*. fluctuated
back and forth in the years that followed and meanwhile 300 *l*. of
it was alienated by the counts of Hainaut. In 1353 we find the
countess of Hainaut receiving 3,700 *l*. at the treasury. Then in 1365
Charles V assigned the *rente*, now 4,000 *l*. again, on the emoluments
of the passage tolls and issues of the *bailliage* of Vermandois. The
bailiff and receiver of Vermandois was ordered henceforth to pay
the sum yearly and account for it at the *chambre des comptes*. In
1389 Charles VI ordered his treasurers to pay the arrears of the fief
owed to Albert of Bavaria—the count of Hainaut at that time—from
the revenues of Vermandois. If these were insufficient, they were
authorized to pay the difference from the treasury or other sources.
In 1392 the receiver general of the *aides* of France paid 9,000 francs
on the fief and in the same year orders were given to the receivers of

---

[155] *Essai*, pp. 119–22.

the *aides* of Noyon and Rheims to pay respectively 4,500 florins. In 1406 Charles VI confirmed the fief of 4,000 *l.* and stipulated that the *aides* of Vermandois should pay it. Later in the same year, however, Charles granted to Count William IV a pension of 6,000 *l.* to pay the arrears of the 4,000 *l.* The pension was to be paid yearly by the town of Tournai until a total of 19,000 *l.* was paid, the amount of the arrears owed on the fief of 4,000 *l.* A few days later Charles changed the source of payment from Tournai to the *aides* of France. In 1408 the collectors of the *aides* of Paris were ordered to pay the arrears of the fief of 4,000 *l.* Apparently in 1412 the 19,000 *l.* had not yet been paid up because the king again ordered it to be paid in the form of a pension of 6,000 *l.* out of the revenues of Tournai. That year the *aides* of Amiens were supposed to pay the current installments on the fief of 4,000 *l.* From 1418 onward the revenues of Vermandois again paid the fief and in 1435 the duchess of Burgundy, who had come into possession of the fief, continued to receive it from Vermandois.[156]

The fief held of the English kings by the counts of Juliers is particularly interesting to trace. On 15 March 1329 Edward III of England made the original concession of the fief to Count William of Juliers; it consisted of 600 *l.* paid yearly out of the exchequer.[157] On 3 September 1329 the fief was transferred to the customs in the port of Boston; accompanying this order of transfer was a mandate to the collectors of customs authorizing the annual payment.[158] On 1 June 1330 the collectors were notified that they should pay William 600 *l.* notwithstanding "any assignments made elsewhere upon the customs."[159] The following year Edward, with the assent of parliament, assigned to the merchants of the society of the Bardi the issues from all the old and new customs of England for that year

---

[156] This reconstruction has been principally based upon the following sources: De Saint-Genois, *Monuments,* I, 400–3; Devillers, *Monuments,* III, nos. 406–7, 426; Devillers, *Cart. de Hainaut,* I, nos. 231, 282; II, nos. 463, 673, 691, 695, 700, 701, 713; III, nos. 883–84, 911, 913, 919, 921, 955, 1055; V, no. 1827; A.D.N., B. 1187–1190; B. 1180–81; B. 1183–84; B. 1186; B. 1191. See Appendix, nos. 21–22.

[157] *C.P.R. 1327–30,* p. 438.

[158] *Foedera,* II, ii, 771, 793.

[159] *C.Cl.R. 1330–33,* p. 38. On 4 November William's attorneys, the merchants of the society of the Bardi, received 450 *m.* from the collectors for the Michaelmas term (p. 73).

except those previously assigned to certain men. One of these previous assignments was the fief of Count William.[160] Until the summer of 1333 the collectors of the customs in Boston paid the fief of William.[161] On 20 July 1333 the collectors of the customs in Lincoln were ordered to pay the fief because the staples of wool, hides, and wool-fells had been established at Lincoln.[162] In 1334, however, the port of Boston was again paying the fief and continued to do so until the fall of 1340.[163] On 2 October 1340 the collectors of Boston were notified that effective that year William's fief had been increased to 1,000 l.; Boston would continue to pay 600 l. yearly and the remaining 400 l. would be paid by the exchequer.[164] On 12 March 1354 a tripartite agreement was concluded between Edward III, Count William, and Henry de Bruseleye, the king's merchant. It was agreed that Henry, instead of William, should receive the 1,000 l. yearly "in satisfaction of certain sums of money due to him [Henry] from the marquis [William] which are said to amount to 4,633 l. 6 s. 8 d." This contract was to remain in force until the sum had been paid.[165] From this period until some time in the reign of Henry VI when record of the fief ends, all the writs of *liberate* and the receipts show that the exchequer paid all the yearly installments.[166] This constant fluctuation of the source of payment for *fiefs-rentes* should leave no doubt as to the personal obligation of the grantors.

The dominance of the *fief-rente* in money should not lead us to neglect those granted in kind. With the exception of the English kings, all the princes granted a significant number of fiefs in kind: of wheat, oats, rye, cheese, chickens, fish, beer, wine, coal, or cloth.

---

[160] *C.Cl.R. 1330–33*, p. 280.
[161] *Ibid.*, pp. 265, 357, 462, 512.
[162] *C.Cl.R. 1333–37*, pp. 58–59. See also p. 159.
[163] *Ibid.*, p. 271. See also pp. 228, 399, 441–42.
[164] *C.Cl.R. 1339–41*, p. 541.
[165] *C.Cl.R. 1354–60*, p 2.
[166] *Foedera* (1704–35), VI, 596; "Cal. Dip. Doc.," in *D.K.R.*, XLV, app. i, 587, 594–95; *C.P.R. 1396–99*, p. 566; *Foedera* (1704–35), VIII, 80; P.R.O., E. 30/1324(2); E. 30/1233. Transfers of source of payment were numerous also in Flanders. In 1300, for example, Philip IV of France confirmed a fief of 200 l. granted by Count Guy of Flanders to John, lord of Dampierre. It had been assigned on the toll of Damme but now Philip transferred payment to the *renenghe* of Flanders (De Saint-Genois, *Monuments*, II, 894).

For France Sczaniecki has indicated that fiefs in kind appeared at the same time as those in money, but not before; nor were they more numerous in the early period than those in money. Their greatest prominence came before the early thirteenth century—a time when they began to melt away before the pressure of the expanding money economy. In the thirteenth and fourteenth centuries fiefs of money were commonly substituted for those in kind, but in spite of this some fiefs in kind persisted to the end of the Middle Ages. There were some occasions, in fact, when a fief in kind was substituted for one in money, and sometimes fiefs were paid either in money or kind. Fiefs in kind, generally quite modest in value, never had the importance of those in money. The counts of Champagne and the kings of France sometimes rewarded minor functionaries with fiefs in kind. More frequently, ecclesiastical establishments used them to secure the performance of minor services. Juridically, according to Sczaniecki, the fief in kind was like that in money.[167]

As for Germany and the Low Countries, the evidence points to conclusions similar in many respects to those of Sczaniecki for France. In Germany the fief in kind sprang up in the eleventh century and can be found even in the fourteenth century, although after the middle of the thirteenth century it no longer had any prominence. The emperors seemed to grant as many fiefs in kind as did the secular and ecclesiastical princes.[168] In the Low Countries the fief in kind followed the same chronological pattern of growth but

---

[167] *Essai,* pp. 159–62.

[168] In 1204 the Emperor Philip of Suabia granted to Duke Henry I of Brabant "in rectum foeudum . . . annuatim sexaginta carratas vini" (Butkens, *Trophées,* Preuves, I, 55). In 1294 King Adolf granted to "strenuo viro Cunrado dicto undern Juden militi, . . . duas carratas vini boni percipiendas annis singulis de vino nostro in Bopardia" (Böhmer, *Acta Imperii,* no. 512). In 1190 the archbishop of Mainz granted to Duke Godfrey III of Brabant "quinquaginta carratas vini, quas a nobis in feodo habuit" (Butkens, *Trophées,* Preuves, I, 44). In a document of 1370 listing the vassals of Count Henry von Spanheim appears the following entry: "Item Rudolf von Blafelden hat von uns zu lehen IIII malder korns von dem obersten hofe zu Meruldes und V malder korns von dem nidersten hofe zu Meroldes und VII gense" (Reimer, *Urkundenbuch von Hanau,* II, iii, no. 603). See also Goerz, *Mittelrheinische Regesten,* II, no. 1862; IV, no. 2300; Gudenus, *Codex Diplomaticus,* II, 984–85. For remarks on the fief in kind in Germany see W. Endemann, *Studien in der Romanisch-Kanonistischen Wirtschafts- und Rechtslehre bis gegen ende des sieben-zehnten Jahrhunderts* (Berlin, 1883), II, 106.

differed in that its decline, if indeed there was one, is not perceptible in the thirteenth and fourteenth centuries. Fiefs in kind can be found down to the end of the fifteenth century and it is possible to trace such fiefs from their concession to their disappearance without encountering any variation in their source of payment.[169] Money was substituted for kind and vice versa but there was no trend either way.[170] Fiefs in kind seemed to be most prominent in Namur and other such regions which lagged behind the economic development of Flanders and Brabant, but even in these latter regions there were many.[171] Always nominal in value, they never secured anything

---

[169] In 1370, for example, John Hartsceve de Dormale of Brabant received "de feodo suo XXV capones." His successors were still being paid this fief in 1496 (A.G.R., Nélis, *Inv.*, nos. 2468–92; *C.C.*, no. 4028). See Appendix, nos. 4, 11.

[170] In 1356 Wenceslas, duke of Brabant, promised to indemnify Arnold, lord of Stein, for a fief of "216 muids d'épautre" which Arnold had forfeited to the count of Namur for serving Wenceslas. In 1357 Arnold received this same fief in kind from Wenceslas and made out a receipt. But in the next reference to Arnold we discover that his *fief-rente* is "50 royaux d'or" and henceforth he received payment in money (A.G.R., Verkooren, *Inv. Brab.*, nos. 952, 1608, 2030, 2176). In 1253 Duke Henry III of Brabant granted the lord of Ligny a fief of "deux tonneaux de vin du Rhin" in place of a fief of 20 *l.* of Flanders (A.G.R., Verkooren, *Inv. Brab.*, no. 56). In 1275 Count Guy of Flanders declared that Michael, lord of Auchy, had ceded to him the fief of oats and money received annually "sur le Gaule de Cambresis" which had the value of 120 *l.* per year. Guy gave in exchange a fief of "12 muids et 3 hoeuds de froment, 381 hoeuds d'avoine, et 40 liv. monnoie de Flandre ... sur l'espier et les rentes de Cassel" (De Saint-Genois, *Monuments*, II, 649). See Appendix, no. 3.

[171] See Piot, *Inv. Namur*, nos. 636, 918, 925, 1329; Brouwers, *Chart. et règ.*, II, nos. 507, 525, 538; Borgnet, *Cartulaire de la commune de Bouvignes* (Namur, 1862), II, no. 168; Bormans, *Fiefs de Namur*, pp. 34–35. For Flanders see De Saint-Genois, *Monuments*, II, 654, 675–76, 810, 932, 995; A.D.N., B. 1179/7844; B. 1292/398; B. 1332/1351; B. 1492/1868; B. 1543/460. In Brabant one finds such fiefs as "36 muids d'avoine, 60 muids de charbon, 200 monceaux de bois, 20 muids de froment, 30 maldres de seigle, and 40 maldres de blé" (A.G.R., Verkooren, *Inv. Brab.*, nos. 5430, 5448; pt. 2, typescript copy, pp. 142, 228, 234, 501). See also Butkens, *Trophées*, Preuves, I, 111, 118, 121, 136, 187. For Luxemburg see Wurth-Paquet, *Table chronologique des chartes*, nos. 261, 297, 323. For Guelders see Sloet, *Oorkondenboek*, no. 505. For Liège see Bormans, *Seigneuries féodales du pays de Liège*, pp. 9, 16, 51; Poncelet, *Livre des fiefs de Liège*, pp. 20, 393; Bormans and Schoolmeesters, *Cartulaire de l'église Saint-Lambert*, II, no. 777.

but the most petty of services. In Flanders the abbeys of Saint-Bavon and Saint-Pierre granted fiefs in kind.[172] Didier has drawn attention to the practice in Hainaut of monasteries conceding fiefs of chickens in order to secure sufficient attendance at their courts; not able to be considered as remuneration because of their small value, such fiefs merely set up the feudal obligation of suit to court. Men in receipt of these fiefs were known as *hommes de chapons* or *hommes de fief sur plume*.[173] Evidence of fiefs in kind granted by the English kings is limited to a few instances from the Great Rolls of the Norman Exchequer and to an English text from the year 1224.[174] With the treasury practically empty at the death of John, the problem of paying the installments of numerous *fiefs-rentes* in arrears fell to the regent William Marshal. According to the account of William's executors he paid twenty-nine knights by giving them garments of silk that had been stored in the royal castle of Corfe. Several other knights received their installments partly in silk and partly in money. But such an act, obviously a stopgap measure, was never reverted to again.[175]

It is hoped that from this study of the finance of the *fief-rente* has emerged an understanding of how each feudal state managed to pay the yearly installments, as well as a realization of the many

---

[172] In 1347, for example, Zegher Parys sold to the abbey of Saint-Pierre a fief of "huit muids de froment" which his father had held from the abbey and which he had inherited (Van Lokeren, *Chartes et documents de l'abbaye de Saint-Pierre,* Gand, 1871, II, no. 1178). See also no. 313. In 1344 the men of the feudal court of Saint-Bavon recognized that John Rynvisch had sold to the abbey a fief consisting of "la livraison journalière de deux pains de seigle, du poids de 20 l., et en une redevance annuelle de 18 hulsters de seigle" in exchange for a fief of 30 l. (Van Lokeren, *Histoire de l'abbaye de Saint-Bavon,* Gand, 1855, II, 64). A certain knight Simon de Coquina "tenet in feodum ab ecclesia Sancti Bavonis . . . unum modium et dimidium siliginis" (A.E.G., *Libri Censi, Bisdom Gent,* no. 31).

[173] Didier, *Revue du Nord,* XVII, 277–78.

[174] See Stapleton, *Mag. Rot. Scacc. Norm.,* I, 127. See Ch. I, p. 25.

[175] *Rot. Claus.,* I, 602 b–603: "Rex baronibus suis de scaccario salutem. Computate David abbati Sancti Augustini Bristoll', Henrico filio Geroldi, et Johanni de Erlegh' executoribus testamenti Comitis Willielmi Marescalli octo pannos sericos quos idem comes recepit de thesauro nostro apud Corfe, et quos liberavit per praeceptum nostrum Henrico de Maluy pro viginti marcis, de medietate annui feodi quadraginta marcarum quas recipere consuevit de domino J. Rege patre nostro etc." See also Painter, *William Marshal,* pp. 202–3.

elements common to the administrative organizations of the various feudal states. But these observations, however enlightening, can become meaningful only when it is known why such effort was expended upon the finance of the *fief-rente*. The answer lies in the use made of it by the feudal princes.

IV

The Political and Diplomatic Role of the Fief-Rente

In a milieu characterized by a growing money economy coupled with an increasing lack of land the feudal lord sought to supplement the ordinary fief of land with something that would fulfil his purposes equally well. He found this in the *fief-rente*; it helped him, on the one hand, to accomplish certain political and diplomatic objectives and, on the other, to meet increased military demands. Sczaniecki, expanding upon views previously expressed by Clason, Kienast, and Mitteis, strongly urged that the *fief-rente* was foremost a political and diplomatic instrument; he considered its military aspect unimportant. On the other hand, Low Country historians, those of the Latin States of the Crusaders, and such scholars as Brussel, Boutaric, and Delbrück firmly believed that the military uses of the *fief-rente* supplied the only reasonable explanation for its pre-eminence in the twelfth, thirteenth, and fourteenth centuries. It will be our task in this and the following chapter to describe the uses of the *fief-rente* so as to determine with surety its ultimate place in the feudalism of western Europe.

1. THE POLITICAL USES OF THE FIEF-RENTE

Too often the concessions of *fiefs-rentes* are worded so vaguely that the reason for which they were granted is obscure. Thus when there is no evidence available to supplement a concession which merely states that a fief has been granted, one can never know the purpose for the grant.[1] Slightly more informative are grants such as that of 1296 when John of Avesnes, count of Holland and Hainaut, granted

---

[1] In 1205 John of England granted Thomas de Fesnes 20 m. "in feodum per annum" and received his homage (*Rot. Claus.*, I, 56 b). In 1254 Henry III granted Aymo de Chanteney 25 m. "nomine feodi" (*R.G.*, I, no. 3739).

John, lord of Arcle, 80 *l.* "en fief et en homaghe as us et as custumes de Hollande," or that of 1349 when Count John of Seyne recognized that he held a fief of 100 *l.* from Duke John III of Brabant according to the feudal custom of Brabant.[2] But all that can be concluded from such evidence is that the recipients had to fulfil whatever obligations were dictated by the feudal custom of Holland and Brabant. In France the kings and lords commonly granted *fiefs-rentes* "ad usus et consuetudines Normandiae" and "ad usus et consuetudines Pontivi." At times fiefs were granted to reward men for the past performance of loyal but unspecified service or to secure faithful service in the future, but we remain uninformed as to the type of service rendered. In 1284, for example, Guy de Dampierre, marquis of Namur, granted a fief of 100 *l.* to John, lord of Picquegny, "pour le bon service qu'il nous a fait et pour ce qu'il soit plus tenus a nous."[3]

We may be certain when fiefs were granted simply for a man's homage that there was a reason for the grantor to open up a new feudal relation even though we cannot know what it was.[4] One has more basis for conjecture, however, when the concessions state that

---

[2] Van Den Bergh, *Oorkondenboek van Holland,* II, no. 967; Butkens, *Trophées,* Preuves, I, 183. For such evidence in France see Sczaniecki, *Essai,* p. 34.

[3] A.G.R., *C.C.,* no. 56, Cartulaire de Namur, fol. 150r. In 1293 King Adolf of Germany granted a fief of 25 *m.* to Godfrey von Eppenstein for his meritorious work (Böhmer, *Urkundenbuch Frankfurt,* I, 280–81). See also Goerz, *Mittelrheinische Regesten,* III, no. 575; IV, no. 1756; Brunel, *Actes de Pontieu,* no. 139; Delisle, *Cart. normand,* no. 67; *Rot. Claus.,* I, 91 b; *Pat. R. 1225–32,* p. 385; A.G.R., *Trés. Fl.,* Sér. I, nos. 1026, 1050; Van Mieris, *Groot Charterboek,* II, 319; Wurth-Paquet, *Table chronologique de Luxembourg,* no. 495; A.D.N., B. 4058/145.440.

[4] For example, in 1230 Otto, count of Guelders, granted the lord Gerard de Zinseke a fief of 8 *m.* for his homage and fealty (Sloet, *Oorkondenboek Gelre en Zutfen,* no. 535). In 1302 the squire Daniel de Blise received in fief 40 *l.* from the count of Namur and stated: "J'en sui devenus ses homs et luy en ay fait hommage" (Brouwers, *Chart. et règ.,* II, no. 364). See also nos. 810 and 1078 in Sloet; nos. 366–67, 396, and 488 in Brouwers; Butkens, *Trophées,* Preuves, I, 133; Wampach, *Urkunden,* II, no. 235; Van Den Bergh, *Oorkondenboek van Holland,* II, nos. 967, 1017–18; A.G.R., *Trés. Fl.,* Sér. I, no. 2069. Many examples of *fiefs-rentes* granted for homage by Philip VI of France are found in J. J. Guiffrey, *Histoire de la réunion du Dauphiné à la France* (Paris, 1868), Table chronologique, nos. 8, 10, 22–24 ff., and pp. 16 ff.

the fief has been granted to secure the recipient's liege homage. Before all homage became liege, this was an easy way to convert simple to liege homage or to acquire a man's liege homage for the first time. Employed most frequently by the great lords, it enabled them to construct more intimate feudal relations. Thus if a *fief-rente* secured the liege homage of a sub-vassal, the tie with that vassal's immediate lord was definitely weakened. This occurred principally when a lord such as the king of France would grant a *fief-rente* to a man heretofore only the vassal of the count of Flanders or of the king of England. Even after the concept of liegancy came to dominate all homage, *fiefs-rentes* were used to gain a man's paramount feudal loyalty. Sczaniecki has noted that the French kings and counts of Champagne granted many fiefs to tighten feudal bonds and expand their feudal lordship.[5] For the kings it was a means of expanding their power not only in the royal domain but in the lands outside. Alphonse of Poitiers, Charles of Anjou, and many of the Low Country princes used the *fief-rente* for the same purpose;[6] apparently the German lords and English kings did not.

Let us turn now from the cases where the records are silent on the service obtained by the *fief-rente* to those which show beyond doubt its political value. All lords, and in particular the kings and princes, attempted in one way or another to obtain lordship over as much land as possible. *Fiefs-rentes* therefore proved valuable as remuneration to men for taking their lands in fief. Some of the land over which feudal rights were thus secured was already held in fief of another lord. In 1215, for example, Thomas de Cousi, lord of Veruins and already the vassal of his brother Ingram and Philip Augustus, received from Count Theobald IV of Champagne a fief of 30 *l.* In return he took "in feodo et homagio ligio, quicquid habeo apud Triam le Bardol, et apud Charmentre, et in partibus illis, cum

---

[5] *Essai*, pp. 80–82.
[6] In 1230, for example, Geoffrey, lord of Argenton in Poitou, did "hominagium ligium" to Louis IX "contra omnem creaturam que possit vivere et mori, salva fidelitate vicecomitis Thoartii, pro ducentis et quinquaginta libris Turonensium" (*Layettes*, II, no. 2053). In 1229 Theobald IV, count of Champagne, granted to Everard de Chervey a fief of 100 *s.* "et per hoc devenit homo meus ligius salva ligeitate domini de Chacenaio et sciendum quod quicunque post decessum dicti Evrardi, dictum feodum tenebit, erit homo meus ligius contra omnes homines" (Chantereau le Febvre, *Traité des fiefs*, Preuves, p. 200). See also *Layettes*, II, no. 2035; III, no. 4109.

pertinentiis earumdem villarum."[7] There are similar cases in Germany. In 1346, for example, Count Diedrich of Loen and Chiny took the house and village at Gruitrode in fief from the archbishop of Cologne in return for a fief of 25 large measures of wine and a sum of 3,500 m.[8] Though much more abundant, the Low Country evidence usually deals with *fiefs-rentes* acquiring allodial land in fief. In this connection, however, the *fief-rente* should not be confused with those numerous instances where a lord would grant to a holder of allodial land a lump sum of money for which the holder would take all or part of his land in fief. This of course was nothing other than a *fief de reprise*.[9] There are hundreds of examples of this type of transaction especially for Luxemburg, Brabant, the Pays d'Outre-Meuse, Guelders, Holland, and Namur; obviously it was cheaper for the lord to transfer allodial land into fiefs by means of the lump sum rather than the *fief-rente*. But cases where the *fief-rente* was used to achieve this end are nevertheless numerous. In 1257, for example, Diedrich, son of Count Diedrich V of Cleve, received from Duke Henry III of Brabant a fief of 50 m. and took in fief from Henry his allod located in the territory "Heshuizerweerd bij Lobid." In 1300 Duke John II of Brabant granted Thierry de Walcourt, lord of Rochefort, and his heirs a fief of 12 *ames* of Rhenish wine for which Thierry took in fief a certain allod and mill evaluated at an annual income of 60 l. of small Louvain; Thierry agreed to hold this allod in fief in addition to the fief of wine.[10] Around 1343 the lord of Blankenheim recognized to hold in fief of the count of Namur "Adensgawes, Honesmolem et Bodeme, qui astoient frans alues," as well as 40 l.[11] Besides the Low Country

---

[7] Chantereau le Febvre, *Traité des fiefs*, Preuves, p. 57. In 1229–30 John de Seignelay received a fief of 40 l. from Count Theobald IV of Champagne. In turn John did liege homage to Theobald reserving, however, his first liegancy to his brother Stephen. He furthermore promised "quod heres ille meus qui tenebit Bellummontem habebit feodum illud et exinde erit homo ligius dicti comitis, salva tamen ligeitate domini Stephani fratris mei" (*Layettes*, II, no. 2044). See also I, no. 1356.

[8] Lacomblet, *Urkundenbuch*, III, no. 428.

[9] Ch. II, p. 72. See Appendix, no. 9.

[10] Sloet, *Oorkondenboek Gelre en Zutfen*, no. 799; Butkens, *Trophées*, Preuves, I, 136–37. See also pp. 162, 187.

[11] Bormans, *Fiefs de Namur*, pp. 22–23; Van Den Bergh, *Oorkondenboek van Holland*, II, no. 653. See also De Reiffenberg, *Monuments*, I, no. 57,

princes only the counts of Champagne and dukes of Burgundy frequently used *fiefs-rentes* to convert allodial land into fiefs; seldom did the French kings and other French lords secure allodial land by this method.[12]

When lords desired to obtain possession of various lands or sources of income held by other men, they often did so by substituting *fiefs-rentes*. The recipients would turn over the land or whatever it might be, along with all their rights to it, and receive a *fief-rente*. In this way lords were able to get direct control of strategic pieces of land politically or economically valuable. For lords intent upon expanding their domain, as for example the French kings, the *fief-rente* was a costly but eminently swift expedient for realizing their objectives.[13] In 1249 we find Preu de Mello handing over possession of the castle and the *châtellenies* of Loches and Châtillon-sur-Indre with all the appurtenances to Louis IX of France in return for a fief of 600 *l.*[14] In 1281 Philip III made known that Reginald, count of Guelders, had surrendered his lordship over the lands of Harefleu and all the rights and revenues belonging to the seigniory. As compensation, Philip granted Reginald a fief of 1,300 *l.* payable by the Temple of Paris; this agreement was confirmed by Philip IV in 1293.[15] Viard has well described how, in the early years of his reign, Philip VI acquired Dauphiné and numerous other lands by substituting *fiefs-rentes*.[16] Like the kings, many French lords also substituted *fiefs-*

p. 200; Piot, *Inv. Namur*, no. 878; De Saint-Genois, *Monuments*, II, 772–73, 995; A.D.N., B. 276/10.552; B. 1208/2944.

[12] For a discussion of the problem and some examples see Sczaniecki, *Essai*, pp. 83–89. Unfortunately many of the examples selected by Sczaniecki to show the conversion of allodial lands into fiefs were ill chosen. In reality these lands were already held in fief of other lords and the *fiefs-rentes* granted merely persuaded the recipients to hold their lands in fief from an additional lord. See particularly p. 85. In this same category are the cases selected from pp. 57, 115, and 143 of Chantereau le Febvre, *Traité des fiefs*, Preuves. Apparently the English and German rulers never acquired allodial land in fief by this technique.

[13] Sczaniecki, *Essai*, pp. 82–83.

[14] *Layettes*, III, no. 3834.

[15] Kern, *Acta Imperii*, nos. 21, 80.

[16] Viard, *Revue des Questions Historiques*, LIX, 345–48. See also Guiffrey, *Histoire du Dauphiné*, Pièces justificatives, nos. 2, 20. Many of the homages for *fiefs-rentes* found in the *Table chronologique* of Guiffrey were undoubtedly done by lords of the Dauphiné whom Philip VI was drawing into his orbit of influence. In 1394 John le Maingre, marshal of France, granted to

rentes to gain coveted land. In 1217, for example, the abbey of Saint-Riquer transferred to the count of Pontieu the woods of Titre and Cahaule for a fief of 40 *s.*, and other lands along with the marsh of Garde for a fief of 1 *muid* of oats.[17]

Abundant evidence shows this practice to have been common also in the Low Countries. In 1269 Reginald, lord of "Hans sor Lesche," accompanied Count Henry V of Luxemburg throughout all the lands held by him in fief of the count, and renounced all his rights over them. He stated that the count had granted him and his heirs "en eschainge de ces chozes" a fief of 15 *l.*[18] In 1288 the count of Hainaut gave Rasse de Winthi a fief of 180 *livrées de terre* in exchange for lands surrendered to the count.[19] In 1232 Robert, count of Dreux, exchanged his lands held of Countess Jeanne and Count Ferrand of Flanders for a fief of 80 *l.*[20] In Germany cases of substitution of *fiefs-rentes* for lands appear quite early and are numerous on into the thirteenth and fourteenth centuries. We have already seen that as early as 1048 a certain Wernhard handed over to the abbey of Fulda lands around "XXX hubae" in area for a fief of 8 talents, and that in 1092 Gerhard von Stumpenhusen handed over certain lands to the archbishop of Bremen for a fief of 8 *l.* In 1246 Count Friedrich von Hostaden received a fief of 60 *m.* for granting his county of Hostaden and the castles of Are, Hart, and Hostaden to the archbishop of Cologne.[21] There is evidence of only a few such grants by the English kings.[22]

Guy VI of La Trémoille fiefs of 2,000 *l.* and 600 *l.* in exchange for the county of Beaufort-en-Vallée (De La Trémoille, *Guy de La Trémoille*, no. 27).

[17] Brunel, *Actes de Pontieu*, no. 252. See also no. 258. In 1254 the knight John de Maison granted certain designated houses to Alphonse of Poitiers: "Pro hac autem donatione et concessione, dicto comiti, uxori et heredibus suis a me factis, dictus comes dedit michi et concessit quinquaginta libras Turonensium, in perpetuum quolibet anno percipiendas in coffris suis" (*Layettes*, III, no. 4106). See also C. P. Cooper, *Report of Foedera* (London, 1869), appendices B–D, Inventaire du trésor des chartes, p. 303.

[18] Wampach, *Urkunden*, IV, no. 116.

[19] A.D.N., B. 1259/2901.

[20] A.D.N., B. 1260/551. See also De Saint-Genois, *Monuments*, II, 707, 762, 877, 998; A.D.N., B. 1492/1868; Borgnet and Bormans, *Cartulaire de la commune de Namur*, no. 60; De Saint-Genois, *Monuments*, I, 269, 331, 357; Van Den Bergh, *Oorkondenboek van Holland*, II, no. 125; Wauters, *Table chronologique*, V, 163.

[21] Lappenberg, *Hamburgisches Urkundenbuch*, I, no. 119; Dronke, *Codex*

At times *fiefs-rentes* were granted to resolve pretensions and rights to lands. In France and the Low Countries the kings and powerful lords commonly used the *fief-rente* to win from men with claims to certain fiefs renunciation of all their rights. Receiving a fief of 300 *l.* in 1259 from Louis IX, Stephen de Mont-Saint-Jean surrendered all pretensions to the castle of Ferté-Alais.[23] In 1254 the count of Champagne granted John of Brittany and his wife Blanche a fief of 3,000 *l.* in return for renouncing all claims to the kingdom of Navarre.[24] In 1283 Gilles, lord of Berlaimont, ceded his rights to the usage of forest in Namur, to the river below the bridge at Floies, to the mill at Flum, and to some fields at Sausoy to Count Guy of Flanders who in turn donated a fief of 20 *l.* to Gilles.[25] In 1327 Count John I of Namur renounced all pretensions to Zeeland and received from Count William I of Hainaut a fief of 600 *l.* plus a sum of 4,000 *l.*[26]

Occasionally the *fief-rente* facilitated inheritance settlements, especially when some of the heirs were unprovided for with land due to a lack of it or to other considerations. Thus in 1247 Ralph de Mauléon, male heir of Savaric de Mauléon, divided his inheritance and granted to his sister Alice a fief of 1,000 *l.* in perpetuity.[27] Upon

---

Diplomaticus Fuldensis, no. 749 ; Goerz, *Mittelrheinische Regesten,* III, no. 473. See also Goerz, II, nos. 20, 254, 637 ; III, no. 291.

[22] In 1264 Henry III granted a fief of 50 *l.* to Peter de Montfort. Peter "quit-claimed to the king all his right and claim to the woods pertaining to his manor of Ridelington, which he holds of the fee of the earl of Warwick, which woods are in the king's forest of Rutland" (*C.Ch.R. 1257–1300,* p. 51). See also p. 266.

[23] *Layettes,* III, no. 4550.

[24] Sczaniecki, *Essai,* p. 83. In 1268 Count Robert of Dreux renounced certain claims to the inheritance of his mother in favor of Agnes, dame of Bourbon ; he received a fief of 200 *l.* (Huillard-Bréholles, *Maison de Bourbon,* I, no. 444). In 1269 Hervé de Beaujeu surrendered his claim to Beaujeu in favor of Reginald de Forez, lord of Beaujeu, for a fief of 100 *l.* (De Charpin-Geugerolles, *Cartulaire des francs-fiefs du Forez 1090–1292,* Lyon, 1882, no. 77).

[25] De Saint-Genois, *Monuments,* II, 710. See also p. 995.

[26] De Saint-Genois, *Monuments,* I, 278. See also Devillers, *Cart. de Hainaut,* V, no. 1819 ; Wurth-Paquet, *Table chronologique de Luxembourg,* no. 536 ; Wauters, *Table chronologique,* IV, 304 ; V, 296 ; VI, 223, 625 ; IX, 562–63. For Germany see Reimer, *Urkundenbuch von Hanau,* I, i, 555.

[27] *Layettes,* III, no. 3607. In 1218 Count William II of Pontieu recognized that his father John had granted his brother Guy a fief of 40 *l.* (Brunel, *Actes de Pontieu,* no. 258).

the death of Bouchard de Metz in 1244, the inheritance was so arranged by his sons John and Baldwin of Avesnes that John received a fief of 700 *l*. and the lordship of Elroeungt.[28] In 1236 Duke Henry II of Brabant and his brother Godfrey of Louvain reached a settlement as to Godfrey's share of their father's inheritance; Duke Henry provided Godfrey with a fief worth annually 1,000 *l*. of Louvain of which 600 *l*. was a *fief-rente* and the remaining 400 *l*. a fief of land.[29] Not unlike such inheritance arrangements was the practice of creating appanages. Having succeeded to the fief, the eldest son would frequently provide for his younger brothers by creating for them out of his fief appanages of land and also of money. Thus in 1241 Louis IX of France granted his brother Alphonse of Poitiers a fief of 6,000 *l.*, and in 1247 gave his other brother Charles of Anjou a fief of 5,000 *l*.[30] Though found more often in France, appanage arrangements appear too in Flanders and Namur.[31]

Lords sometimes granted *fiefs-rentes* to all sorts of relatives seemingly for no reason other than nepotism. Most guilty of this were the English kings, in particular Henry III, who made lavish grants to the numerous relatives he accrued during the course of his long reign. Only his desire to provide well for all members of the royal family and his complete lack of sense in financial matters can explain this liberality; he realized almost nothing in the way of services for, in reality, the *fiefs-rentes* were granted to a pack of parasites. The Savoyard uncles of Eleanor, queen of England, were rich beneficiaries of her marriage to Henry. Amadeus IV, count of Savoy, received 1,000 *l*. for his homage and a fief of 200 *m*.; Boniface,

---

[28] Duvivier, *La querelle des d'Avesnes et des Dampierre*, I, 135 ff. In 1297 John of Namur, son of Count Guy of Flanders and Namur, was granted the administration and government of Namur. He stated that he was obliged to pay his younger brother Guy a fief of 1,000 *l*. yearly (De Saint Genois, *Inv. Fl.*, no. 940).

[29] Butkens, *Trophées*, Preuves, I, 212. See also Wolters, *Codex Diplomaticus Lossensis*, nos. 496–97.

[30] *Layettes*, II, no. 2926; Sczaniecki, *Essai*, p. 90.

[31] In 1306, for example, Count Robert de Béthune of Flanders granted his brother Philip of Flanders a fief of 3,000 *l*. to be paid by various revenues of Flanders (A.E.G., De Saint Genois, *Inv. Fl.*, no. 1128; A.G.R., *Trés. Fl.*, Sér. I, no. 65). In 1314 Count John I of Namur granted his brother, Henry of Flanders, count of Lode, a heritable fief of 2,500 *l*. of Paris to be paid from diverse revenues of the county of Namur (Brouwers, *Chart. et règ.*, II, no. 428).

archbishop of Canterbury, received a fief of 200 m.; Philip, bishop-elect of Lyon and later count of Savoy, a fief of 200 m.;[32] William bishop-elect of Valence and Henry's chief councilor, a fief of 600 m.;[33] and Thomas of Savoy, count of Flanders by his marriage with Countess Jeanne, a fief of 500 m.[34] By virtue of the marriage of his mother Isabella to Hugh X of Lusignan, count of La Marche, Henry was also burdened with the support of the Lusignan family. In 1224 Hugh X received a fief of 500 m.; in 1242 his son Hugh XI, a fief, of 400 m., and two other brothers, Geoffrey and Guy, fiefs of 300 m.[35] In the Low Countries, the other area in which such grants were prominent, we find Count William I of Holland and Hainaut granting in 1310 to his brother John of Beaumont 300 l. of Holland "te houden ten rechten leene."[36] In 1428 Jacqueline of Bavaria, countess of Hainaut and Holland, granted out of "pure

---

[32] Amadeus: *Pat. R. 1232–47*, p. 469; *C.L.R. 1245–51*, pp. 20, 40, 115, 227, 308, 379. Boniface: *C.P.R. 1247–58*, p. 386. Philip: *C.P.R. 1258–68*, pp. 197, 304, 335, 735.

[33] *C.L.R. 1245–51*, pp. 142, 175, 208–9, 227, 253, 256, 283, 307, 347, 378; *R.G.*, I, no. 2699. Edward I continued to pay William's fief until his death in 1297; then Aymer, his son and heir, received the fief (P.R.O., Issue Rolls, E. 403/61, m. 1; E. 403/84, m. 1; E. 403/85, m. 1; E. 403/88, m. 1; E. 403/89, m. 1; E. 403/94, m. 1; E. 403/101, m. 1; Liberate Rolls, C. 62/70, m. 2; C. 62/71, m. 3; C. 62/72, m. 3; C. 62/73, m. 7). See also Matthew Paris, *Chronica Majora* (R.S., London, 1872), III, 240–41; IV, 85, 205, 359; V, 316, 674–75; Florence of Worcester, *Chronicon ex Chronicis* (English Historical Society, London, 1849), II, 188; *Flores Historiarum* (R.S., London, 1890), II, 237–38, 244; William Rishanger, *Chronica et Annales* (R.S., London, 1865), p. 2.

[34] *Foedera*, I, i, 259, 268; *C.L.R. 1226–40*, p. 496; *C.L.R. 1240–45*, p. 78; *C.L.R. 1245–51*, pp. 224, 349; *C.P.R. 1247–58*, pp. 195, 387, 553; *C.P.R. 1258–66*, p. 509; *Pat. R. 1232–47*, p. 489.

[35] Hugh X: *Pat. R. 1216–25*, p. 436. Hugh XI: *R.G.*, I, nos. 321, 3897; *C.P.R. 1247–58*, p. 35. Geoffrey: *R.G.*, I, no. 301; *Pat. R. 1232–47*, p. 309; *C.P.R. 1247–58*, pp. 3, 40, 98, 100. Guy: *R.G.*, I, no. 301; *Pat. R. 1232–47*, pp. 309, 502; *C.P.R. 1247–58*, pp. 5, 83. See also Matthew Paris, *Chronica Majora*, IV, 650; *Annales de Theokesberia* (R.S., London, 1864), I, 165; *Flores Historiarum*, II, 252, 418. For *fiefs-rentes* granted to Earl Richard and to Simon and Peter de Montfort see *C.L.R. 1240–45*, pp. 231, 273, 299; *C.L.R. 1245–51*, pp. 42, 84, 144, 171, 195, 325, 380; *C.P.R. 1247–58*, pp. 23, 458, 472, 628; *Cl. R. 1254–56*, p. 245; *R.G.*, I, nos. 2154, 2157, 2402. Henry's sisters, Isabella and Margaret, also had *fiefs-rentes* (*R.G.*, I, no. 3082; *C.P.R. 1247–58*, pp. 101, 313–14, 415, 532).

[36] Van Mieris, *Groot Charterboek*, II, 104. See also Van Den Bergh, *Oorkondenboek van Holland*, I, no. 356.

et libérale vollentet" to her mother Duchess Margaret a heritable fief of 800 *l.* of Tours "en pur don." [37]

Desiring for some reason to augment a man's fief, whether of land or money, and lacking lands or other sources of income with which to do so, lords commonly resorted to the granting of *fiefs-rentes.* In 1216–17, recognizing that Count Theobald III of Champagne had previously granted him a fief of 30 *l.*, Albert, lord of Darniaco, stated that Theobald IV's mother, Blanche of Navarre, had granted him "in augmentum" of his fief a second fief of 15 *l.* payable by the fairs of Bar.[38] In 1299 the knight Sifrid von Lindawe recognized that Wernhard Ringrave had granted him and his heirs 25 *m.* "in augmentum feodi mei."[39] In 1337 William I, count of Hainaut, granted Mul de Binchuelt a fief of 60 *l.* and stated that "en acroissant le dit fief" he had added another fief of 20 *l.* of Tours.[40]

In the marriage pacts so vital in the feudal world we find a more

---

[37] Devillers, *Cart. de Hainaut,* V, no. 1643. See also Devillers, *Monuments,* III, nos. 414–15 ; De Saint-Genois, *Monuments,* I, 351 ; Sczaniecki, *Essai,* pp. 89–90.

[38] *Layettes,* I, no. 1208 ; Delisle, *Cart. normand,* no. 89. In 1287 Philip IV augmented by 200 *l.* the fief of 300 *l.* previously granted by Philip III to Ferri, duke of Lorraine (Delisle, *Opérations des Templiers,* p. 49). See also Brunel, *Actes de Pontieu,* no. 180; Luchaire, *Études sur les actes de Louis VII,* no. 353 ; *Layettes,* II, no. 1990; Petit, *Histoire des ducs de Bourgogne,* VI, no. 4118.

[39] J. W. C. Roth, *Die Geschichtsquellen des Niederrheingau's. Geschichtsquellen aus Nassau* (Wiesbaden, 1880), I, ii, no. 60. See also Günther, *Codex-Diplomaticus Rheno-Mosellanus,* no. 159 ; Goerz, *Mittelrheinische Regesten,* II, no. 1862.

[40] Devillers, *Cart. de Hainaut,* I, no. 6. See also Butkens, *Trophées,* Preuves, I, 104, 179, 181 ; Galesloot, *Cour féodale,* I, no. 33 ; Verkooren, *Inv. Brab.,* nos. 105, 117, 371. In 1347 to reward the good service rendered by John de Neuville, Count Louis de Male of Flanders granted him "en acroissement dou don du don de XXX librees de terre au parisis ... le somme de XX parisis ... chascun an" (A.D.N., B. 499/7597). See also B. 4064/145.557 ; B. 1260, fol. 56ᵛ ; A.E.G., De Saint Genois, *Inv. Fl.,* nos. 1408, 1699. In 1325 Count John I of Namur granted to Sohier de Courtrai "pour le boin service quil a fait et sera encore quarante livres de parisis cescun an ... outre les sissante livres parisis que nous lui aviens doune ... a tenir en fief" (A.E.N., Piot, *Inv. Namur,* no. 460). See also no. 724 and Van Mieris, *Groot Charterboek,* I, 605. The English evidence is also plentiful. For example, in 1242 Henry III granted to Robert de Rancon 50 *l.* yearly "in augmentum feodi sui centum marcarum" (*R.G.,* I, no. 799). See also *C.L.R. 1226–40,* p. 145 ; *R.G.,* I, no. 3787 ; *C.P.R. 1266–72,* p. 121.

specific political use of the *fief-rente*; it was granted as a dowry or as the marriage gift brought by the man to his bride. This use was well established in France, Germany, and England, but was especially prevalent in the Low Countries.[41] In 1286 at the request of Reginald, count of Guelders and duke of Limburg, Sifrid, archbishop of Cologne, promised that he would give Margaret, daughter of the count of Flanders, an annual income of 4,000 *l.* as her dowry upon consummation of her marriage with Reginald; the money was to be held in fief by Reginald. In 1320 Robert de Béthune, count of Flanders, granted to Guy de Châtillon, count of Blois, a fief of 1,800 *l.* on the tolls of Damme and the aids of Ghent and Bruges; this was to be the dowry of Beatrice, the sister of Robert.[42] In 1286 Count Guy of Flanders assigned to his son William a *rente* of 8,000 *livrées de terre* upon the occasion of his marriage with Aélis, daughter of Ralph de Clermont, lord of Nesle and constable of France.[43]

In the previous chapter it was pointed out that some monasteries of Hainaut granted nominal *fiefs-rentes* in kind to insure adequate attendance at their court sessions.[44] Evidently this practice was not widespread because only one other case has been found, and that for Flanders.[45] It was doubtless unnecessary to grant many *fiefs-*

---

[41] For France see Brunel, *Actes de Pontieu,* nos. 195, 317; Delisle, *Cat. des actes de Philippe-Auguste,* no. 1438; Fawtier, *Comptes du trésor,* no. 1390; Sczaniecki, *Essai,* p. 90. For Germany see Ilgen, *Quellen Rheinischen Territorien,* II, i, no. 12; Mummenhoff, *Regesten der Reichsstadt Aachen,* no. 773; Remling, *Urkundenbuch Bischöfe Speyer,* no. 534; Goerz, *Mittelrheinische Regesten,* IV, no. 2363; Lacomblet, *Urkundenbuch,* II, no. 906; III, nos. 36, 431. For England see *C.Cl.R. 1405–1409,* p. 34; *Foedera* (1704–35), X, 40; "Cal. Dip. Doc.," in *D.K.R.,* XLV, 325–27.

[42] A.E.G., De Saint Genois, *Inv. Fl.,* no. 406; A.G.R., *Trés. Fl.,* Sér. I, no. 2027. See also Van Mieris, *Groot Charterboek,* II, 437. See Appendix, no. 22.

[43] A.E.G., De Saint Genois, *Inv. Fl.,* no. 414. When Henry de la Hulpe, bastard brother of Duke John III of Brabant, was married in 1355, he received a fief of 200 *l.* from John (Verkooren, *Inv. Brab.,* unpublished, pt. 2, p. 366). In a letter of 1402 Philip the Bold, duke of Burgundy, recognized that Louis de Male, count of Flanders, had granted to Robert Tenke, knight and chamberlain of the count, upon his marriage with Trise, natural daughter of Louis, a fief of 200 *l.* (A.E.G., *Verzameling Diegerick,* no. 11). See also De Saint Genois, *Inv. Fl.,* nos. 189, 766; Butkens, *Trophées,* Preuves, I, 59, 88, 133; Devillers, *Cart. de Hainaut,* I, nos. 97, 172, 268, 328; II, no. 450; Bormans, *Fiefs de Namur,* pp. 69, 88; Wampach, *Urkunden,* V, no. 279.

[44] Ch. III, p. 145.

[45] In 1273 Countess Margaret and her son Guy granted a fief of 200 *l.* to

rentes specifically to obtain suit to court; according to feudal custom this service had to be performed by the holder of any fief. In Germany Archbishop Wicbold granted in 1299 a fief of 400 *m.* on the toll of Neusz to Diedrich, son of the count of Cleve, who promised Wicbold never again to collect tolls at Rheinberg.[46] In 1297 when King Adolf granted a fief of 10 *m.* to Eberlin, citizen of Speyer, he stipulated that Eberlin and his heirs were to receive him and his heirs in hospitality whenever they were in Speyer.[47] In France a fief of 1,100 *l.* granted in 1247 by Ralph de Mauléon to his sister Alice was to be held for the nominal service of "un besant de plaid et à une paire d'éperons dorés de service."[48] Occasionally upon the *adoubement* of a knight or the ennoblement of a man, the lord would grant him a *fief-rente*. The fief of 100 *l.* given in 1259 to John de Heinnibal of Rome by Count Theobald V of Champagne was done so "quando decoravit eum cingulo militari." The fief of 500 *l.* conceded by King Philip V in 1317 to Peter Dueza, brother of Pope John XXII, was to enable Peter to maintain honorably the noble estate to which he had just been elevated.[49] Similar grants were made by the English kings but the information is so scanty that it would be rash to conclude that they were *fiefs-rentes*; they are not designated as feudal and most occurred in the fourteenth and fifteenth centuries, a time when normally non-feudal incomes were granted for such purposes.[50]

Jakemon Louchard, citizen of Arras, "a tel service ki chi apres est devises. Chest asavoir kil doit estre trois fois en lan a nos plais a Douay." If Jakemon failed to attend a session, he had to pay a fine of 5 *s.* (A.E.G., De Saint Genois, *Inv. Fl.,* no. 175). See also nos. 416, 482; A.D.N., B. 1561, fol. 36ᵛ. This document is analyzed in De Saint-Genois, *Monuments,* II, 639–40. See Appendix, no. 1.

[46] Lacomblet, *Urkundenbuch,* II, no. 1026.

[47] Hilgard, *Urkunden zur Geschichte der Stadt Speyer,* no. 192. In 1309 the emperor Henry VII increased the amount of the fief to reward the faithful service of Eberlin (Böhmer, *Acta Imperii,* no. 601).

[48] *Layettes,* III, no. 3607. In 1244 Count Matthew of Pontieu confirmed the grant of a fief of 10 *l.* by Aleaume de Fontaine to Gilles Langlois. The new vassal was required every year to furnish Matthew with a pair of white gloves (Brunel, *Actes de Pontieu,* no. 356). For other examples of such nominal service see Sczaniecki, *Essai,* p. 33. See Appendix, no. 2.

[49] Longnon, *Documents de Champagne,* I, no. 6442; Sczaniecki, *Essai,* p. 78.

[50] The following case is but one of hundreds out of the fourteenth and fifteenth centuries; it cannot safely be considered a *fief-rente*. In 1346 Edward

Some princes granted *fiefs-rentes* to intimate friends, companions, and councilors as reward for their loyal service. To note but two of those so favored by the French kings, we find that Peter de la Brosse, chamberlain of Philip III, held fiefs of 20 *l.* and 30 *l.*[51] In 1303 William de Nogaret was granted a fief of 300 *l.* by Philip IV and in the following year another of 500 *l.*[52] In the Low Countries Count William I of Hainaut and Holland granted a fief of 25 *l.* in 1316 to his trusted councilor and chamberlain, William van Duvenvoorde; later William received a second fief of 200 *l.* on the toll of Malines.[53] Upon coming into possession of the hereditary chamberlainship of Namur in 1284 William de Laminne received a fief consisting of four *muids* of *mouture* paid by the mill of Renise, forty chickens to be taken on the revenues of the county of Namur, and the "droiture de l'hôtel" when the count and countess were in residence; later in the year Guy, count of Flanders and marquis of Namur, exchanged this fief for one of 15 *l.* of Louvain to be paid from the revenues of the town of Namur. The marshal of Namur, who was bound to accompany the count "en ost ou en chevauchie," received a *fief-rente* called a "fief de la mariscalchie." There is evidence out of the thirteenth and fourteenth centuries that the counts granted fiefs of robes or clothing to such intimates as the chamberlain and butler.[54] With a lower echelon of princely servants such as officers administering lands, *châtelains*, and functionaries performing more menial tasks, evidence of their receiving *fiefs-*

III granted to John Darcy " 'le filz,' that he may the better support the estate of a banneret which he has received from the king, of an annuity of 200 *l.* at the exchequer" (*C.P.R. 1345–48*, p. 142).

[51] *Layettes*, IV, nos. 5650, 5686–88 ; Langlois, *Règne de Philippe le Hardi*, p. 38.

[52] L. Ménard, *Histoire de Nîmes*, I, 367, 370. For grants by Louis IX see Sczaniecki, *Essai*, p. 78. In his introduction to *Les journaux du trésor de Charles IV*, Viard noted fourteen "principaux seigneurs de l'entourage du roi" who received *fiefs-rentes*. To these can be added the names of many distinguished bourgeois who held important positions of trust and were close to the king (pp. lxxx–lxxxi). In 1289 Philip IV granted a fief of 128 *l.* to Pellerin, chamberlain of Charles of Valois ; in 1297 he granted a fief of 500 *l.* to Simon de Melun, marshal of France (Tardif, *Monuments historiques*, nos. 855, 948, 992).

[53] Van Mieris, *Groot Charterboek*, II, 168, 232.

[54] Bormans, *Fiefs de Namur*, Intro., pp. 105–9 ; De Reiffenberg, *Monuments*, I, no. 19, p. 23. For more of these *fiefs de dignité* see pp. 29, 107, 193 in Bormans, and Didier, *Revue du Nord*, XVII, 274–75.

rentes is limited to a few references out of France and the Low Countries.[55]

Why there is so little evidence of *fiefs-rentes* granted to functionaries is readily understood when one realizes that in the twelfth century feudal lords began to pay them with non-feudal incomes in kind or money rather than with fiefs of land, and that this method of payment continued until eventually they came to be paid wages. For France Sczaniecki has shown that the royal functionaries came to be paid non-feudal *rentes* in the early thirteenth century and that gradually toward the end of Louis IX's reign these *rentes* were replaced by wages. There was much the same development in such large feudal states as Champagne.[56] In England the Pipe Rolls show many royal officials in receipt of fixed yearly payments from the counties during the twelfth and thirteenth centuries.[57] In Normandy such officials as foresters, bailiffs, *châtelains,* and seneschals received yearly incomes.[58] Throughout the thirteenth, fourteenth, and fifteenth centuries men of this type were normally granted yearly salaries or retaining fees and frequently supplied with items of maintenance such as robes. In 1258, for example, the barons of the exchequer were ordered to pay Ralph de Gorges, king's valet, his fee of 20 *l.* In 1270 Robert del Estre, buyer of the royal wine, was granted a yearly fee of 40 *s.* "ad sustentacionem suam in servicio

---

[55] In 1217 Louis, son of Philip Augustus, confirmed to his *châtelain* of Arras that office and gave him a fief of 10 *m.* (Wauters, *Table chronologique,* VII, 515). In 1279 Count Reginald of Guelders granted a fief of 30 *m.* of Cologne to Godfrey Berch, *châtelain* of the castle of Kessel. In 1330 Count John I of Namur conceded to his valet, Jean Semale, a fief of 40 *muids* of spelt. In 1427 Duke Philip the Good of Burgundy received in fealty and homage Colard de la Gliseule, his "escuyer d'escuyerie," for a ficf of 100 *écus* of gold (Wauters, *Table chronologique,* V, 662; A.G.R., *Trés. Fl.,* Sér. I, no. 66; Devillers, *Cart. de Hainaut,* V, no. 1926). See also Devillers, III, no. 293; Wauters, VI, 299; Delisle, *Actes de Philippe-Auguste,* no. 334.

[56] *Essai,* pp. 78–79.

[57] *Probator: P.R. 2 Hen. II,* pp. 4, 113. *Monetarius: P.R. 5 Hen. II,* p. 2. *Ingeniator: P.R. 4–10 Hen. II,* pp. 113, 13, 18, 67, 71, 20. *Clericus: P.R. 2–7 Ric. I,* pp. 156, 136, 301, 158, 175, 113. *Presbyter: P.R. 9–15 Hen. II,* pp. 20, 30, 130, 2, 2, 170. *Capellanus: P.R. 5–10 Ric. I,* pp. 158, 175, 113, 290, 160, 167. *Aurifaber: P.R. 1–5 John,* pp. 129, 149, 258, 284, 7.

[58] Stapleton, *Mag. Rot. Scacc. Norm.,* I, 50, 127, 154, 156, 209; II, 304. See the remarks of C. H. Haskins, *Norman Institutions* (Cambridge, Mass., 1918), pp. 44–45, 59, 105, 110, 115; F. M. Powicke, *The Loss of Normandy* (Manchester, 1913), pp. 281, 332, 366.

nostro." In 1279 Raymond Sanche of Toulouse, king's clerk and professor of law, was granted a *feodum* "pro stipendiis sui salarii per annum, quamdiu erit in nostro servicio." [59] It would be repetitious to cite similar evidence for the Low Countries but it should be emphasized that in this region the financial records generally distinguished between the *rentes* paid out as fiefs and those paid out simply as yearly salaries.[60]

2. THE DIPLOMATIC ROLE OF THE FIEF-RENTE

The more ordinary uses of the *fief-rente* which helped the feudal lord to increase his power and prestige and to fulfil various feudal and political obligations have so far been our principal concern. Now we should consider the diplomatic functions of the *fief-rente*. Here, however, one encounters difficulty. When a fief is granted to make a man act as a diplomatic agent, there is no question that this use is diplomatic. But when a fief is granted to establish the good relations which would insure military support in time of war, the line between diplomatic and military is almost non-existent. Such use cannot be called either purely diplomatic or purely military; it is some of each. I therefore take issue with those scholars who see in this use only the diplomatic value and stop short of re-

---

[59] *Cl.R. 1256–59*, p. 250; *Cl.R. 1261–64*, p. 164; *Cl.R. 1268–72*, p. 186; *R.G.*, III, no. 329. See also *C.P.R. 1358–61*, p. 257. All types of servants and officials were paid by yearly fees : yeomen, controllers of customs, king's confessor, falconers, under-chamberlain, helmet-makers, tellers, barons of the exchequer, escheators, and justices of the common pleas and king's bench.

[60] In the account of the receiver of Flanders for the year 1308–09 the annual issues in money are listed under "Aumosnes," "Fieveis en bourse," and "Pensions" (A.G.R., Nélis, *Inv.*, no. 1). In the account for 1335–36 they are listed under "Fiefs et rentes heritaules" and "Rentes et pensions a vie." A similar distinction can be found in A.D.N., B. 4240, Compte du domaine ; A.G.R., Nélis, *Inv.*, no. 2436, Recettes générale of Limburg for 1390–91. Similar breakdowns can be made in the French financial records. See, for example, Fawtier, *Comptes du trésor*, p. xlvii, and nos. 753, 1061, 1877, 1879, 1905, 2223. In the *Compte de la terre de Champagne* (1340–41) the annual payments are separated under the following rubrics : "Fiez a heritage," "Fiez et aumosnes," "Fiez et aumosnes hors foires," and "Pensions, dons et gaiges à vie" (Longnon, *Documents de Champagne*, III, 282–87).

cognizing the ultimate aim—military assistance. And when these scholars go on to base the pre-eminence of the *fief-rente* on its political and diplomatic usefulness, completely subordinating the military, they are seeing only part of the total picture. But let us stop here for the moment and turn to those *fiefs-rentes* granted solely for diplomatic purposes. This task is best approached by studying each region individually.

It has become increasingly evident in the course of this study that in Germany the *fief-rente* was not as flexible as in other parts of western Europe. Nowhere is this more apparent than in the evidence relative to its diplomatic functions which shows it granted only to men in a position to supply reports of significant political developments or to those negotiating in the grantor's interest. In 1223 the podesta of Asti, Girard Manaria, promised in the name of the commune to pay 300 *l.* to Master Opizoni, subdeacon and papal notary. This sum was a fief which the emperor Frederick II had given "eidem magistro in utilitates suas, quamdiu ipse magister vixerit." [61] When granting a fief of 300 ounces of gold to the dauphin of Vienne in 1248, Frederick II also awarded one of 15 ounces of gold to the dauphin's chamberlain.[62] And in 1350 Baldwin, archbishop of Trier, granted a fief of 20 florins to Diethard, *Kemmerer de Wormatia.*[63] Some evidence may have been overlooked but these cases represent almost all of a diplomatic nature to be found in the German records.

In the Low Countries, though the princes never used the *fief-rente* to contract alliances or to develop spheres of influence in other states as was done by the French and English kings, the records do reveal that they used it for persuading men to act as envoys and to further their interests. Often the specific purpose for a grant is not stated but the position of the recipient is so well known that his role as an agent or source of information cannot be doubted. In 1280 Count Guy of Flanders granted John de Blanor, lord of Loy and *avocat* at the French court, a fief of 40 *l.* to be held during his life.

[61] Böhmer, *Acta Imperii,* no. 1143.

[62] Huillard-Bréholles, *Historia Diplomatica Friderici Secundi,* VI, ii, 665–66. See also Chevalier, *Inventaire des archives des Dauphins* (Paris, 1869), I, 13.

[63] Gudenus, *Codex Diplomaticus,* V, 626–27. See also Doenniges, *Acta Henrici VII,* p. 185.

In the same year Guy gave Ralph de Nesle, chamberlain of France, a heritable fief of 200 *l.* in liege homage. Guy ordered that Ralph should receive upon the death of his father Simon de Clermont, lord of Nesle, the latter's *fief de bourse* of 220 *l.* and should henceforth hold both fiefs as a single homage. We have receipts of both Ralph and Simon until 1287 when Ralph came into possession of his father's fief of 220 *l.* and also the office of constable; thereafter Ralph gave receipt for both fiefs until hostilities broke out between Guy and Philip IV.[64]

Men of similar status received *fiefs-rentes* from the dukes of Brabant and the counts of Hainaut. In 1292 John I granted a fief of 20 *m.* of Cologne to Gerard, *avoué* of Cologne. In 1374 Lambert, lord of Oupeye and marshal of the bishop of Liège, was in receipt of a fief of 40 *royaux* from Duke Wenceslas. Gerard van Berk, vicar of the cathedral of Cologne, and Winemar Frambach van Birgel, marshal of Juliers, were also in receipt of *fiefs-rentes* from Wenceslas.[65] In 1355 John, lord of Châtillon, councilor of the French king and master of the royal household, promised to do homage and fealty as quickly as possible to Margaret, countess of Hainaut, for a fief of 300 *livrées de terre.*[66] Another diplomatic function of the *fief-rente* shown by the evidence of Hainaut was to re-establish amicable relations between two lords who had been at war. In 1333, for example, an agreement was concluded between Count William I of Hainaut and Count Louis de Nevers of Flanders, recent opponents in war, whereby William granted Louis a fief of 1,000 *l.* to insure future

---

[64] Other influential men holding *fiefs-rentes* of Guy were Louis de Beaujeu, constable of France, 100 *l.*; Ralph d'Estrées, marshal of France, 100 *l.*; John de Harecourt, marshal of France, 100 *l.*; Humbert de Beaujeu, constable of France, 200 *l.*; the archbishop of Rouen, 100 *l.*; the marshal of Champagne, Hugh des Conflans, 80 *l.*; and John, lord of Choisuel and constable of Burgundy, 140 *l.* (De Saint-Genois, *Monuments,* II, 676, 680–81, 682, 699, 702, 714, 721, 729, 750, 762, 775, 809, 820, 828; A.E.G., De Saint Genois, *Inv. Fl.,* no. 493; *Inv. analytique et chronologique des archives de la chambre des comptes à Lille,* Lille, 1865, no. 1729). See Appendix, nos. 6, 8. In 1310 John, bishop of Potenza and lord of Bevre, gave 50 *l.* "in feodum" to the knight Siger de Gand "ex causa boni et discreti concilii" (A.E.G., De Saint Genois, *Inv. Fl.,* no. 1217).

[65] A.G.R., Verkooren, *Inv. Brab.,* nos. 150, 3070, 4814, 5291, 5497, 5606, 5775, 5808; A.G.R., Verkooren, *Inv. Lux.,* no. 1214.

[66] Devillers, *Cart. de Hainaut,* II, no. 415. See also De Reiffenberg, *Monuments,* I, no. 110, p. 487; Didier, *Revue du Nord,* XVII, 271.

peace between them;[67] in 1347 Louis de Male, count of Flanders, promised faithfully to abide by this agreement entered into by his father and William I. [68]

Specific diplomatic obligations accompanied many grants of *fiefs-rentes*. In 1295 Count Guy of Flanders gave a certain Jakemon, *échevin* and citizen of Liège, a heritable fief of 20 *l.* on condition that he and his heirs would faithfully serve and counsel Guy and his successors whenever called upon to do so. In 1299 Guy granted Everhard, count of Catsenellenbogen, a heritable fief of 100 *l.* in addition to a sum of 2,000 *l.* for which Everhard took in fief one of his allods worth 200 *l.* yearly; Everhard promised that he and his heirs would expedite affairs of the count at the imperial court.[69] Also in 1299 Everhard von Stein, chancellor of King Albert of Germany, received letters from Count Guy promising him a fief of 50 *l.* until he could be provided with a suitable ecclesiastical benefice; Everhard promised to render council and aid favorable to Guy in his negotiations at Albert's court.[70] The foregoing evidence has shown that in the Low Countries, and especially in Flanders, the *fief-rente* procured diplomatic services and helped to secure other political objectives. Easily granted to men living considerable distances from Flanders, it was admirably suited for acquiring diplomatic agents

[67] "Et pour nourir et pardurer pais à tousjours, entre nous contes deseure nommés et nos hoirs, nous contes de Flandres deseure dis avons promis et enconvent ke nous et nostre hoir conte de Flandres serons et deverons estre homme à no dit cousin et à ses hoirs contes de Haynnau, et en leur foy et homaige de mil livrées de terre au tournois, lesquelles mil libvrées de terre nous contes de Haynnau dessus nommés devons assener bien et souffissanment à no dit cousin le conte de Flandres, . . . sour les villes et appartenanches de Blaton et de Fygnies" (Devillers, *Cart. de Hainaut*, in *Monuments*, III, no. 274, p. 310).

[68] Devillers, *Cart. de Hainaut*, I, no. 184. See also Didier, *Revue du Nord*, XVII, 270.

[69] De Saint-Genois, *Monuments*, II, 848 ; Brouwers, *L'administration et les finances du comté de Namur du XIIIᵉ au XVᵉ siècle. Cens et rentes du comté de Namur au XIIIᵉ siècle* (Namur, 1926), II, i, no. 16; A. Kluit, *Historia Critica Comitatus Hollandiae et Zeelandiae* (Middelburg, 1777), Codex Diplomaticus, I, i, nos. 380–81; A.D.N., B. 1266/4138–4269; B. 1266/4140–4270.

[70] Winkelmann, *Acta Imperii*, II, no. 1080 : ". . . promisit nobis et liberis nostris consilium favorem et auxilium impendere in nostris negotiis et specialiter in hiis, que apud predictum dominum regem aut in sua curia habebimus expedire."

and for persuading men to work for pro-Flemish interests. Anyone familiar with the struggle in progress between Guy and Philip IV of France realizes the importance of pro-Flemish support within France and the value of agents working to gain imperial support. But beyond Flanders, and possibly Brabant and Hainaut, it would be dangerous to insist upon the diplomatic importance of the *fief-rente*; the evidence for the rest of the Low Countries is too scant to permit such an assertion.

For France it will be sufficient for the moment to summarize only that evidence presented by Sczaniecki where the diplomatic use of the *fief-rente* is not in doubt. He points out that some *fiefs-rentes* were awarded to foreign princes or lords in return for performing certain diplomatic services for the grantors. Receiving a fief of 100 *l.* in 1185, Jacob of Avesnes, councilor of Count Philip of Flanders, promised Philip Augustus to work for favorable conditions of peace with Count Philip. In 1393 Charles VI granted a fief of 1,000 *l.* to Count Adolf of Cleve who promised to intervene and mediate in the relations of Charles with the archbishop of Cologne and the duke of Guelders.[71] Closely associated with concessions of *fiefs-rentes* to foreign lords were those to officers such as chamberlains and councilors residing at foreign courts and the papal court. These fiefs, Sczaniecki believes, secured for the grantors essential political information; lacking permanent resident ambassadors, princes had to rely upon such men for foreign intelligence. We therefore find the king of France granting a fief of 200 *l.* in 1317 to Arnold de Trian, nephew of Pope John XXII and grand marshal of justice at the papal court. In 1382 the duke of Milan, John Galéas Visconti, conceded a fief of 1,000 gold florins to Guy de La Trémoille, chamber-

---

[71] Sczaniecki, *Essai,* pp. 32–33. These references are found in Gislebert de Mons, *Chronicon,* p. 186; Lacomblet, *Urkundenbuch,* III, no. 1006. Expanding his investigations beyond France, Sczaniecki cites the *fief-rente* of Everhard, count of Catsenellenbogen, mentioned above, and a fief of 1,000 *l.* granted in 1339 by Edward III of England to Count William of Juliers who was to negotiate for the royal interests at the imperial court (*Essai,* pp. 33, 93–94). Sczaniecki draws attention to the fact that such *fiefs-rentes* were similar to the ubiquitous non-feudal pensions of the sixteenth and seventeenth centuries and suggests with all good reason that the *fief-rente* was undoubtedly the antecedent not only of these but of the many non-feudal *rentes* and pensions in the fourteenth and fifteenth centuries (*Essai,* pp. 94–95). See also Clason, *Pensionsverhältnisse,* pp. 44 ff.

lain of the duke of Burgundy. In 1274 John de Vergy, seneschal of Burgundy, held a fief of 90 *l.* from the count of Champagne.[72] Lastly, Sczaniecki emphasizes the value of the *fief-rente* in helping the French kings to knit their immediate and sub-vassals more tightly to them as well as to extend their influence beyond the borders of the royal domain by numbering among their grantees influential lords of the Low Countries, the Rhineland, the Dauphiné, and southwestern France.

The English records best delineate the diplomatic character of the *fief-rente*. This is not to say that the English kings used it for this end more than the French kings, but rather that the English sources, more abundant and detailed, enable one to examine more satisfactorily the diplomatic services and objectives thus attained. It was common for foreign prelates and ecclesiastics to receive *fiefs-rentes* from the kings for their services as proctors as well as for their pro-English efforts in the lands over which they exerted some influence. *Fiefs-rentes* were also granted to the relatives and representatives of the Pope who were to use their position to exert pressure on the Pope in favor of English interests. Starting with the evidence out of the reign of John, we find that a fief of 30 *m.* was granted in 1200 to "magistro Philippo nuntio domini Papae et notario." In 1214 Count Richard, brother of the Pope, was in receipt of a fief of 100 *m.*; John, a cardinal of Rome, was paid an unspecified sum for his fief. In 1215 Master Ranulph, acolyte of the Pope, was granted a fief of 10 *m.*; in the same year a fief of 20 *m.* was given to Reiner, papal notary.[73] The evidence from Henry III's reign is more abundant. Nicholas, the Pope's nephew and chamberlain, received a fief of 40 *m.* from 1228 until 1253 when his nephew re-

---

[72] For these and other references see Sczaniecki, *Essai,* pp. 95–96. For the texts see De La Trémoille, *Guy de La Trémoille,* p. 168; Du Chesne, *Histoire généalogique de la maison de Vergy* (Paris, 1625), p. 202. One text omitted by Sczaniecki is that bearing upon the concession of a fief of 60 *l.* by the count of Champagne in 1229 to the influential Flemish lord Arnold d'Audenarde (Chantereau le Febvre, *Traité des fiefs,* Preuves, p. 196). Sczaniecki takes into consideration grants of *fiefs-rentes* to simple knights as well as to certain Genoese for supplying maritime service. It is difficult to see how this type of service could be regarded as political or diplomatic; it was actually military service that was secured (*Essai,* pp. 96–97). For much of his evidence Sczaniecki resorts to the English records which will be subsequently discussed.

[73] *Rot. Chart.,* p. 61; *Rot. Claus.,* I, 180; *Rot. Pat.,* p. 158 b.

ceived it. In 1254 John de Ambilione, chaplain and chancellor of the Pope, was granted a fief of 20 m. and 200 m. for his expenses; he had been entrusted with expediting certain negotiations at the papal court. In 1267 Master Angelus, canon of Cambrai and the "king's advocate in the court of Rome," was in receipt of a fief of 40 m. In 1267 Berard of Naples, papal notary and procurator of Henry III, received a fief of 50 m.; by 1279 it was increased to 80 m. and in 1290 he was still in receipt of it.[74] A document from the reign of Edward I dated 1289 states that Bertram de Goth, canon of Agen and later bishop of Comminges and Pope Clement V, was granted a fief of 100 l. of black money of Tours plus any amount of money required to further the royal affairs in Gascony. In the same year Arnold de la Case, canon of Bordeaux, was conceded a fief of 100 l. "pro servicio suo nobis in partibus Vasconie impendendo in causis et negociis nostris."[75]

In the late thirteenth century it is difficult to distinguish between the feudal and non-feudal incomes granted to ecclesiastics, for the kings began to designate these incomes as "pensions" rather than "fiefs." Such pensions have been considered fiefs only if the performance of homage was expressly stipulated at the time they were granted. There is less chance for error in the fourteenth century when ecclesiastics were more commonly granted non-feudal incomes for their work, and by the fifteenth century the word "pension" in almost all cases designates a non-feudal income.[76]

[74] Nicholas: *C.L.R. 1226–40*, pp. 78, 128, 271, 329, 381; *C.P.R. 1247–58*, p. 564. Ambilione: *R.G.*, I, no. 2367. Angelus: *C.P.R. 1266–72*, pp. 118, 123, 216, 232, 250. Berard: *C.P.R. 1266–72*, p. 119; *C.P.R. 1272–81*, p. 337; *Foedera*, I, ii, 579; J. Stevenson, *Documents Illustrative of the History of Scotland, 1286–1306* (Edinburgh, 1870), I, 177. See also *C.P.R. 1266–72*, pp. 117, 121, 169–70, 190, 215; *Foedera*, I, ii, 421.

[75] *R.G.*, III, nos. 1065, 1138, 1809, 1829. See also P.R.O., E. 101/369/11, Wardrobe Book, fol. 184^v; E. 101/375/8, fol. 2^v; *Foedera*, I, ii, 578, 582, 634, 649.

[76] The following are examples of non-feudal pensions. In 1319 Bertram, cardinal deacon of Saint Mary in Aquiro, was granted a pension of 50 m. "in consideration of his good service to the kings at the court of Rome." In 1348 John de la Cour, canon of Tournai, received 100 gold crowns from Edward III as part payment of the arrears of his pension ("Dip. Doc. Exch.," in *L.I.*, no. 49, p. 14). In 1442 Adam Moleyns, dean of Salisbury, was commissioned by Henry VI to go to Rome and engage someone of eminence to represent him at the papal court. Adam reported that Francis, cardinal priest of Saint Clement and vice-chancellor at the papal court, had undertaken to act as the

Not having resident ambassadors at foreign courts until the early sixteenth century, the English kings secured through the *fief-rente* vital information and a representation of their interests from men who resided near the princely courts or had access to sources of information.[77] For this service influential men with special training in law and matters of diplomacy were usually preferred; also desirable were foreign merchants and others whose work brought them into contact with sources of information from all over western Europe. One such foreign agent was Peter Saracen, a Roman citizen, to whom John granted a fief of 20 m. in 1212.[78] In 1231 it was increased to 40 l. yearly, a sum which Peter continued to receive annually until his death; in 1251 we find his son John receiving the fief.[79] In 1253 Nicholas, another son of Peter, did homage for the fief of 40 l.[80] Scattered references show that Peter was the representative of John and Henry III at the papal court and we can thus strongly suspect that his sons also served in this capacity. In 1227 the keepers of the bishopric of Durham were ordered to pay 100 l. out of the issues of the bishopric to Peter "who is staying in the Roman court for the king's affairs." In 1233 Compaignus and his fellows, merchants of Florence, were paid 600 l. which Peter had "received from them as a loan in the Roman court for the expedition of the king's affairs there." Diplomatic reports from Peter and other envoys are found among the royal letters of Henry III. In 1225 Peter wrote to Henry that he had seen the papal legate at Saint-Omer and would soon send a report of the interview. Later in

king's proctor for a pension of 100 m. of Florence (P.R.O., Dip. Doc. Exch., E. 30/465; "Cal. Dip. Doc.," in *D.K.R.*, XLVIII, app., 602). See also *Foedera*, I, ii, 69, 94; II, i, 348, 357, 492–93, 759, 854.

[77] For the resident ambassadors see B. Behrens, "Origins of the Office of English Resident Ambassador in Rome," *E.H.R.*, XLIX (1934), 640–56, and "The Origin of the Office of English 'Resident' Ambassador," *Trans. Roy. Hist. Soc.*, 4th ser., XVI (1933), 161–95; J. E. Neal, "The Diplomatic Envoy," *History*, New ser., XIII (1929), 204–18. See also J. P. Kirsch, "Andreas Sapiti, englischer Prokurator an der Kurie im 14. Jahrhundert," *Historisches Jahrbuch*, XIV (1893), 582–603; G. Mattingly, "The First Resident Embassies: Medieval Italian Origins of Modern Diplomacy," *Speculum*, XII (1937), 423–39.

[78] *Rot. Chart.*, pp. 187 b, 202 b.

[79] *C.Ch.R. 1226–57*, pp. 142–43; *C.L.R. 1226–40*, pp. 51, 62, 91, 189, 216, 267, 281, 287, 290; *C.L.R. 1245–51*, pp. 95, 132, 236.

[80] *Cl.R. 1251–53*, p. 360. See also *Cl.R. 1256–59*, p. 422.

the year Peter reported that the legate had made some changes in the arrangements agreed upon during the first interview and that these revisions would be forwarded to Henry.[81] In 1213 and 1214 three other Roman citizens accepted fiefs and entered John's service. Peter Hanibal received a fief of 60 *m.* "pro homagio et servicio suo," Octavian Cassolinis received a fief of 40 *m.*, and Nicholas Romanus, a fief of 10 *m.*[82] For his services rendered to Queen Eleanor when she was on the Continent during the civil war between Henry III and Simon de Montfort, Peter Bonin of Bruges received a fief of 20 *l.*[83] In 1289 a burgess of Bordeaux, Bernard Ferradre, was granted a fief of 100 *l.* by Edward I "pro servicio suo nobis in partibus Vasconie impendendo in causis et negociis nostris." [84] In 1339 Katherine, the daughter of William Duc of Brussels, and her son were granted a fief of 100 *l.* "in consideration of their having done homage to the king and of the effective gratitude shown by her in his affairs." [85]

A more important group of men in receipt of *fiefs-rentes* and associated with English diplomatic efforts were those occupying responsible positions in foreign courts, and the relatives of powerful foreign officials and princes. Their status enabled them to supply the kings with confidential reports and to influence their lords toward a pro-English policy. The *fiefs-rentes* granted by Richard I and John to some Guelf princes and their officers not only reflect the long tradition of Guelf-Angevin co-operation but also emphasize the strenuous efforts of this coalition in the late twelfth and early thirteenth century to destroy the Hohenstaufen and Capetians. Through *fiefs-rentes,* even trusted servants of the Hohenstaufen were bound to the English kings. While in Germany in 1194 Richard granted a fief of 20 *l.* to "Johanni Lupo camerario Imperatoris Alemannie"; John continued to pay this fief during his reign.[86] In

---

[81] *C.L.R. 1226–40,* pp. 51, 62, 216, 256, 267; W. W. Shirley, *Royal and Other Historical Letters of Henry III* (London, 1862), I, nos. 221–22.

[82] *Rot. Pat.,* pp. 105, 108, 117; *Rot. Claus.,* I, 139, 140 b, 362, 363 b, 471, 566 b.

[83] *C.P.R. 1258–66,* pp. 496, 583; *C.P.R. 1266–72,* pp. 258, 557.

[84] *R.G.,* III, no. 1143; IV, nos. 1913, 1973.

[85] *C.P.R. 1338–40,* p. 370; *C.Cl.R. 1339–41,* pp. 201, 376, 508; *C.Cl.R. 1343–46,* p. 183; *C.Cl.R. 1346–49,* p. 189; *C.Cl.R. 1349–54,* pp. 412, 431. See also *C.P.R. 1338–40,* p. 371.

[86] *P.R. 8–10 Ric. I,* pp. 119, 76, 77, 161; *Chanc. R. 8 Ric. I,* p. 275; *P.R. 1–3 John,* pp. 153, 163, 120; *P.R. 9 John,* p. 105.

1209 Henry, duke of Saxony, received a sum of 1,000 m. "de dono et de feodo suo."[87] In 1194 when Richard granted *fiefs-rentes* to the large group of Rhenish and Low Country princes, he also gave one of 38 l. to the butler of the archbishop of Cologne.[88] The desire for Flemish support against Philip Augustus is seen in the concessions made by John to such key figures in Flanders as William, uncle of Count Baldwin IX; Gerard, chancellor of Flanders and *prévôt* of Bruges; Wulmino, clerk of the count; the *châtelain* of Bruges; the marshal of Flanders; and the chamberlain of Flanders.[89] But John's activities were not limited to the Low Countries. In 1200 he conceded a fief of 60 l. of Anjou to the trusted councilor and chamberlain of Philip Augustus, Bartholomew de Roye, "pro homagio et servicio suo salva fidelitate domini regis Francie."[90] There is also evidence that Paul, clerk of the king of Norway, held a fief of 100 s.[91] The most notable concessions of Henry III were a grant of 20 m. in 1230 to Prigentius, the seneschal of the duke of Brittany, and another of 40 l. in 1242 to "Petro de Vinea, magne imperialis aule judici."[92] In 1254 Geoffrey and Simon de Joinville received fiefs of 60 m. and 50 m. respectively.[93] John of Avesnes, count of Hainaut, was granted a fief of 200 l.; his brother Baldwin, one of 100 l. Henceforth John was Richard of Cornwall's chief representative in Germany and director of all the diplomatic activities that

---

[87] *Foedera*, I, i, 103. See also *Rot. Claus.*, I, 152 b; *Rot. Mis. (1213)*, p. 238; Kienast, *Deutschen Fürsten*, I, 184. In 1229 Geoffrey, clerk of Duke Otto of Brunswick received payment for a fief of 5 m. (*C.L.R. 1226–40*, p. 123).

[88] *P.R. 6 Ric. I*, p. 76; *P.R. 9 Ric. I*, p. 167; *P.R. 10 Ric. I*, p. 161; *P.R. 1 John*, p. 153; *P.R. 2 John*, p. 120. See also the introductions to *P.R. 6* and *9 Ric. I*, pp. xxxii–xxxiii, xxii–xxiii. A certain Lambert of Cologne also received a fief of 20 l. (*P.R. 6 Ric. I*, p. 76). Sczaniecki states that in 1172 Henry II granted influential lords of Hainaut fiefs for diplomatic reasons (*Essai*, p. 95, n. 68). As we shall see later these fiefs were probably granted for military service.

[89] *Rot. Lib.*, pp. 15, 17; *Rot. Claus.*, I, 100 b.

[90] *Rot. Chart.*, p. 64.

[91] *Rot. Pat.*, p. 118 b.

[92] *Pat. R. 1225–32*, p. 408; *R.G.*, I, nos. 296, 2019; *C.L.R. 1226–40*, pp. 270, 400, 477. In 1242 William de Punctis, clerk of the count of Toulouse, received a fief of 5 m.; William Donnort, chamberlain of the count of Hainaut, held a fief of 20 l. (*R.G.*, I, no. 421; *C.P.R. 1327–30*, p. 454).

[93] *R.G.*, I, nos. 2433, 4143; *Cl.R. 1253–54*, pp. 181, 211, 212, 245.

finally secured the Imperial Crown for Richard.[94] Otto de Grandison, a noble of Savoy who had strong family ties with the nobility of Savoy and Burgundy and long experience at the Roman Curia, was continually entrusted with important missions by Edward I. It is not certain whether a grant of 40 *l.* yearly in 1331 was a fief, but it is definite that his successor, William de Grandison, was in Edward III's service and in receipt of a fief of 100 *m.* William's son, Otto III, also received a *fief-rente* for his loyal service to Edward III, as well as to Richard II.[95] In 1337 Edward III "attendans les bons et profitables services" rendered by Herman Blankart, dean of the cathedral of Aix-la-Chapelle, granted him a fief of 100 *m.*; Herman's influence extended throughout the Empire.[96] Also in 1337 William van Duvenvoorde, chamberlain and councilor of Count William I of Hainaut and Holland, received a heritable fief of 500 *l.*; Diedrich Pytans, chamberlain of the archbishop of Cologne, a fief of 300 florins; and the provost of Arnhem, John Moyllard, a fief of 600 florins.[97] Although the see of Cambrai was pro-Valois, Henry de Jodoigne, canon of the cathedral of Cambrai, worked against any extension of Valois influence. For his pro-English efforts and friend-

---

[94] *C.P.R. 1247–58,* pp. 461, 468, 553; *Cl.R. 1259–61,* p. 224. See also Lucas, "John of Avesnes and Richard of Cornwall," *Speculum,* XXIII (1948), 81–101. In 1276 Baldwin the *châtelain* of Arras received payment of 40 *l.* for the arrears of a fief (*C.P.R. 1272–81,* p. 152).

[95] *C.P.R. 1330–34,* p. 86; "Cal. of Royal Letters and Writs," in *D.K.R.,* VI, app. ii, 108. In the Issue Roll of 1299 appears the following entry: "Liberate eidem per manus magistri Thome Suwerk' clerici thesauri pro tanta pecunia dicti thesauri mutuata in curia Romana per mercatorem de Spina ad instanciam domini Otonis de Grandissono et certorum nunciorum regis anno xxvi^to eisdem nunciis" (P.R.O., E. 403/103, m. 2). In the Wardrobe Book of 24–29 Edward I appears the following entry: "Domino Otoni de Grandisono de expensis suis in partibus Francie ... CVI *l.* V *s.*" (P.R.O., E. 101/354/5, fol. 3^v). See also C. L. Kingsford, "Sir Otho de Grandison (1238?–1328)," *Trans. Roy. Hist. Soc.,* 3d ser., III (1909), 125–95. For William and Otto III see *C.P.R. 1348–50,* p. 370; *C.P.R. 1377–81,* p. 146; *Foedera* (1704–35), VII, 761; *C.P.R. 1391–96,* p. 342. In 1364 Edward III ordered the regent and council of France "paier a nostre chier et foial William de Grantson mille deux centz sessante et sys motons d'or ... que lui sont ariere pur deux anz passez de les cent marcs et sessante livres annueles ... a prendre chescun an a nostre escheqer a toute sa vie." To this order is attached William's receipt for this amount (P.R.O., Dip. Doc. Exch., E. 30/1425).

[96] *Foedera,* II, ii, 973; Lucas, *English Government at Work,* I, 315. See also P.R.O., Patent Rolls, C. 66/202.

[97] *Foedera,* II, ii, 973, 1000.

ship he received a fief of 500 florins from Edward III.[98] In 1397 the archdeacon of Cologne, Hugh von Hernorst, was given a fief of 300 nobles of gold by Richard II.[99] A constant diplomatic agent of Henry V and Henry VI was the influential German knight, Hertong von Clux, who received a fief of 40 *l.* in 1413. As early as 1411 he was empowered to contract a treaty for Henry V with the emperor Sigismund, and in 1439 we find him renewing certain treaties with Sigismund. The following year he was busy negotiating for an alliance with the archbishop of Cologne.[100]

Concerned so far with those functions of the *fief-rente* that arouse no opposition as to their purely political and diplomatic nature, let us now examine the evidence upon which Sczaniecki, Kienast, Mitteis, and Clason have based their political-diplomatic thesis, a thesis which, as we have noted, subordinates the military function of the *fief-rente* and explains its pre-eminence on the basis of its political and diplomatic usefulness. The records do bear out the view that foreign lords, as well as key officers and councilors, were granted *fiefs-rentes* with the obligation that they either further the grantor's interests in their land or supply him strategic political and military information. The records confirm also that the *fief-rente* promoted double vassalage and effected closer feudal bonds. But when one focuses upon the alliances and political parties secured by the *fief-rente*, he cannot rule out the military objectives. Concurring with Kienast, Mitteis, and Clason that the *fief-rente* was a key element in the international relations of western Europe, Sczaniecki cites what he considers some of the better-known treaties, that concluded by Philip IV of France with King Wenceslas II of Bohemia in 1303, that of 1324 between Charles IV and Duke Leopold of Austria, that of 1430 between Charles VII and Duke Frede-

---

[98] *Ibid.*, pp. 969–70.

[99] *Foedera* (1704–35), VIII, 1. In 1364 Count John of Tankarville, viscount of Melun and chamberlain of France, received a fief of 3,000 crowns of gold (*Foedera*, III, 2, 731, 754; *C.Cl.R. 1364–68*, p. 401; *C.P.R. 1361–64*, p. 484).

[100] *Foedera* (1704–35), IX, 44. See also G. Williams, *Official Correspondence of Thomas Bekynton, Secretary to King Henry VI* (London, 1872), I, nos. 65, 118–19; "Cal. French Rolls," in *D.K.R.*, XLVIII, app., 336, T. Carte, *Catalogue des rolles gascons, normans, et français* (London, 1743), I, 260, 290; II, 202, 299. In 1437 Henry VI granted Louis of Luxemburg, chancellor of France, a fief of 1,000 *l.* (*Foedera* (1704–35), X, 666; P.R.O., Dip. Doc. Exch., E. 30/443(11), (12), (13)).

rick of Austria, and that between Philip IV and Count John I of Hainaut in 1297. But here he stops, without inquiring into the reason for these treaties. When one studies them, however, he can see that they were military alliances; in return for *fiefs-rentes* the recipients had to fight for the kings when summoned against any man save certain specified lords. Some of these men were granted military subsidies as added inducement and all were promised the customary wages of war and maintenance during hostilities.[101] The treaties were obviously directed against the kings of England and the counts of Flanders; they were concluded to secure military assistance, not benevolent neutrality, friendship, or other diplomatic and political intangibles. In another treaty cited by Sczaniecki, that between Edward III of England and Duke John III of Brabant in 1339, the terms were again aimed at military goals. One familiar with the bulky collection of texts concerning the efforts of Edward to secure the military support of John against Philip VI of France cannot doubt that the fief of 1,500 *l.* obliged John to fight for Edward. Though Sczaniecki cites evidence to show the counts of Juliers and Cleve performing diplomatic services for the English and French kings, one has but to place these services into the context of all the relevant texts bearing upon these men to see that not only the original concession of their fiefs but other subsequent documents required them to render military service for which they were entitled to war pay and maintenance. Where Sczaniecki considers the fief of 1,000 *l.* granted in 1340 by Edward III of England to Count William of Juliers as obliging him solely to carry out diplomatic missions for Edward, one of which was to negotiate for the royal interest at the imperial court, we shall see from evidence presented later that such service of William and others like him was but subsidiary to their main obligation—military service. In the three Flemish treaties of 1103, 1110, and 1163 the counts promised in

---

[101] *Essai*, p. 93. The treaties cited are found in J. Emler, *Regesta Bohemiae et Moraviae* (Prague, 1855), II, no. 856; Sievers, *Politischen Beziehungen Ludwigs des Bayern zu Frankreich*, p. 23; J. C. Lünig, *Codex Germaniae Diplomaticus* (Frankfurt, 1732), II, 539; Devillers, *Monuments*, III, no. 406. These treaties are discussed in Clason, *Pensionsverhältnisse*, pp. 12–14. The same objection can be raised against other treaties referred to by Sczaniecki (pp. 102–3), including the treaty of 1339 between Edward III of England and Duke John III of Brabant in which John received a fief of 1,500 *l.* (p. 93, n. 59).

one clause that if the king of France planned to invade England, Normandy, or Maine, they would attempt to dissuade him. The treaty of 1103 stated: "Ita quod, si rex Philippus regnum Angliae super regem Henricum invadere voluerit, comes Robertus, si potuerit, regem Philippum remanere faciet, et queret, quocumque modo poterit, consilio et precibus, per fidem, absque malo ingenio, sine datione pecuniae, ut remaneat." [102] This was, however, but one clause out of nineteen; the other eighteen dealt with the military aid to be supplied to the English kings. And did not even this duty have some military and economic value for the kings? If the counts succeeded in their attempt, then the kings would be relieved of expensive military costs. The counts were not primarily diplomats as Sczaniecki would have us believe; rather, the evidence portrays them as military captains who also performed whatever diplomatic service might be asked of them.

Is it not significant that these alliances and diplomatic activities were at their apogee when Philip Augustus and John fought over the Angevin Empire between 1199 and 1214; when, at the end of the thirteenth century, Edward I and Philip IV were similarly engaged in the Low Countries and southwestern France and Count Guy was fighting for the very existence of Flanders against Philip IV; and when, finally, Edward III and Philip VI had entered that climactic struggle, the Hundred Years' War? It can be rightfully said, it seems to me, that much of the diplomatic activity merely reflected the prime occupation of the medieval prince—war. How true this is can be shown best by evidence from the English records. In 1241 Henry III directed Peter of Savoy to look for allies in France and draw them into the English service by grants of *fiefs-rentes*. Both Kienast and Sczaniecki cite this as evidence *par excellence* of *fiefs-rentes* obtaining political alliances. But, in reality, an envoy was empowered to use *fiefs-rentes* for recruiting men to fight for the English kings.[103] In the Gascon Rolls for this period and somewhat

---

[102] Vercauteren, *Actes de Flandre,* nos. 30, 41 ; *Foedera,* I, i, 6–7 ; Delisle, *Recueil des actes Henri II,* I, no. 152.

[103] *Foedera,* I, i, 242 : "Rex omnibus, etc. salutem. Sciatis quod potestatem dedimus dilecto avunculo nostro, Petro de Sabaudia, attrahendi ad obsequium nostrum nobiles viros comitem Cabionensem, et Willielmum de Vienna, et alios, quos viderit nobis necessarios, et offerendi eis, ex parte nostra, feodum annuum pro eorum homagio et servitio, quale idem avunculus noster viderit, tam ipsis nobilibus, quam honori nostro convenire, sive plus sive minus ipsis

later one finds hundreds of French lords and knights who received *fiefs-rentes* from Henry III and Edward I and were obliged to perform military service.[104] In 1212 Reginald de Dammartin, count of Boulogne, became the liege man of John and received a fief of 1,000 *l.*[105] Henceforth he was to engage in the essential task of recruiting knights and securing military allies on the Continent. Numerous references to Reginald in the records for John's reign prove that many of the lords and knights in the Angevin-Guelf coalition against Philip Augustus were secured through the efforts of Reginald.[106] One such lord, for example, was Ferrand, count of Flanders, who through the negotiations of Reginald finally became John's man in the summer of 1213.[107] While in command of the allied contingents at Bouvines, Reginald was captured by Philip Augustus and his service to John came to an end. But through his diplomatic negotiations John had been supplied with a military force so powerful that the total mobilization of Philip's forces was required to defeat it.[108]

The evidence of the fourteenth and fifteenth centuries impresses even more deeply the pattern of diplomatic efforts aimed at military goals. Commonly when important lords in receipt of *fiefs-rentes* acted as agents of the king, their diplomatic efforts were almost wholly concentrated upon one subject—military assistance. Count William of Juliers, who had married Jeanne, the older sister of Edward III's wife, was a trusted confidant and lieutenant of Edward. In 1329 he had been granted a fief of 600 *l.* and in 1340 it was increased to 1,000 *l.*[109] Along with the renowned warrior John

---

duxerit offerendum ; negotium istud totum discretioni ipsius avunculi nostri committentes." See *Essai*, pp. 101–2 ; Kienast, *Deutschen Fürsten*, II, 97, 118.

[104] See Ch. V, p. 211.

[105] *Rot. Chart.*, p. 186 ; *Foedera*, I, i, 77.

[106] *Rot. Pat.*, pp. 93, 99, 101, 114 b ; *Rot. Chart.*, pp. 30, 47, 57 b, 58, 189, 190 b ; *Rot. Claus.*, I, 112, 118, 119, 130–130 b, 133 b.

[107] *Foedera*, I, i, 105 ; *Rot. Chart.*, p. 197 ; *Rot. Claus.*, I, 129 b. See also Malo, *Renaud de Dammartin*, pp. 138, 145–47, 170, 195 ; Dept, *Influences,* pp. 117–23.

[108] Similar work was done for John by his brother, William Longespée, earl of Salisbury, a man of recognized military ability. In addition to his possessions as earl of Salisbury, he also held a *fief-rente*. See *Rot. Claus.*, I, 5 b, 7 b, 28, 51 b, 60, 125 b, 152 b ; *Rot. Praest.*, pp. 176, 181, 185, 196, 209, 213, 228, 231–32 ; *Rot. Chart.*, p. 197 ; Dept, *Influences*, p. 122.

[109] *C.P.R. 1327–30*, p. 438 ; *C.Cl.R. 1339–41*, p. 541. Sczaniecki incorrectly dated the increase as 1339 and referred to it as the original grant.

of Hainaut, lord of Beaumont, he fought in the campaign against the Scots in 1327. Eight years later, after participation in another futile Scottish campaign, he remained at the English court for a few months discussing with his brother-in-law the relations with Philip VI of France and planning the diplomatic campaign that was to secure in three years the adherence of most of the Low Country princes.[110] With his knowledge of local political situations in the Low Countries, William was invaluable as a royal envoy. In 1335 with two other envoys, John de Shoreditch and William Trussel, he negotiated with the count of Guelders and Zutphen, the count of Hainaut, the duke of Brabant, and the archbishop of Cologne, for their participation in an alliance against France.[111] In 1336 William was appointed proctor to make alliances with certain persons whose names would be revealed to him later by two of Edward's envoys. In 1345 William and two other agents were appointed to treat with the Emperor Louis. Also in that year he was named the king's lieutenant and governor of Flanders.[112] There is evidence from the reigns of Richard II and the three Henrys that the counts of Juliers remained faithful allies and servants of the English kings and continued to further their military interests through diplomatic services.[113] Like the counts of Juliers, the dukes of Guelders often acted as envoys and recruited troops.[114] Otto, lord of Cuyk, a minor Brabançon lord on the Meuse whose family had always been friendly with the English kings, had a fief of 250 *l.* He served Edward III continually with men-at-arms and was a valuable diplomatic agent.[115] A concession by Richard II in

---

[110] Jean le Bel, *Chronique,* ed. J. Viard and E. Déprez (Paris, 1904), I, 41 ; *Foedera,* II, ii, 759, 771, 793, 800, 910, 922, 926–28. See also Lucas, *English Government at Work,* I, 314–15, and *Low Countries,* pp. 182–85, 192–94, 205, 218, 466.

[111] *Foedera,* II, ii, 928.

[112] *C.P.R. 1334–38,* p. 346 ; *C.P.R. 1343–45,* p. 508.

[113] *C.P.R. 1396–99,* p. 556 ; *Foedera* (1704–35), VIII, 80 ; F. C. Hingeston, *Royal and Historical Letters during the Reign of Henry IV* (London, 1860), nos. 1, 14, 38 ; Lacomblet, *Urkundenbuch,* III, no. 1075.

[114] *C.P.R. 1374–77,* p. 503 ; *C.P.R. 1385–89,* p. 310 ; E. Perroy, *The Diplomatic Correspondence of Richard II* (Camden Society, London, 1933), 3d ser., XLVIII, nos. 123, 161, 163, 168, 178, 201, 203–4, 216–17, 231 ; Williams, *Official Correspondence of Thomas Bekynton,* I, nos. 80, 95. See also Lucas, *Low Countries,* pp. 315–16, 319, 324.

[115] *C.Cl.R. 1330–33,* pp. 354, 495 ; *C.Cl.R. 1333–37,* pp. 5, 31, 217, 392,

1398 of a fief of 1,000 *l.* to the archbishop of Cologne obliged the archbishop to supply various categories of fighting men. Still in the 1440's the archbishops were in receipt of the fief with the obligation of supplying 300 men.[116] In addition to their primary obligation other evidence shows them active in winning more allies and extending English influence in the Empire.[117]

By virtue of their military prestige some men holding *fiefs-rentes* were able to attract other nobles and fighters into the service of the English kings. To John of Hainaut, lord of Beaumont, who had received a fief of 1,000 *m.* from Edward III, fell the task of recruiting troops for the Scottish campaign of 1327. Going to Condé in Hainaut where a tournament had attracted men from all over the Low Countries, he easily recruited nobles from Juliers, Guelders, Brabant, Namur, Flanders, Hainaut, and other such states. The name of John is found among the witnesses to many treaties that secured military allies for Edward III.[118]

Citing the formation by Philip VI of a pro-French group of nobles in Dauphiné between 1339 and 1343 as an example of how the *fief-rente* created political parties, Sczaniecki then singles out the Low Countries as best demonstrating how the French and English kings built up such parties. For confirmation he refers us to the works of Dept and De Sturler.[119] According to Dept, both John and Philip Augustus created powerful English and French blocks

---

428, 446, 573, 610 ; *Foedera*, II, ii, 773, 895, 914, 1102. See also Lucas, *English Government at Work*, I, 315–16 ; Lucas, *Low Countries*, pp. 112, 354, 380–81 ; De Sturler, *Relations politiques*, pp. 364–65. John, the father of Otto, had received a fief of 200 *l.* of Tours from Edward I (*C.P.R. 1292–1301*, pp. 134, 232). See also De Sturler, *Relations politiques*, pp. 160–62. Further references to the diplomatic service of Otto and to his *fief-rente* are found in P.R.O., Dip. Doc. Exch., E. 30/40 ; E. 30/1211 ; E. 30/1373.

[116] Lacomblet, *Urkundenbuch*, III, no. 1050; *Foedera* (1704–35), VIII, 2–3 ; X, 834–40.

[117] *Foedera* (1704–35), IX, 346, 359 ; X, 626, 834–40; "Cal. Dip. Doc.," in *D.K.R.*, XLV, app. i, 322 ; "Cal. French Rolls, Henry VI," in *D.K.R.*, XLVIII, app., 343 ; Williams, *Official Correspondence of Thomas Bekynton*, I, nos. 56–59, 74–75, 100, 118, 221, 224.

[118] Jean le Bel, *Chronique*, I, 33–34, 39–42 ; *C.P.R. 1327–30*, p. 10 ; *C.Cl.R. 1327–30*, p. 160 ; *C.Cl.R. 1343–46*, p. 175. See also Lucas, *English Government at Work*, I, 313, 326–27, and *Low Countries*, pp. 56–57, 110, 328, 334, 465–66, 468.

[119] *Essai*, p. 103.

in Flanders in the years before Bouvines.[120] De Sturler states that
the three Edwards established a pro-English group in Brabant partly
through the distribution of *fiefs-rentes* to influential lords.[121] Both
Dept and De Sturler point out the military commitments of the
important lords composing these parties and admit that minor
nobles and simple knights contributed to the English military efforts,
but they place greater emphasis on the political value of the parties.[122] They concentrate upon showing how these vassals, proving
to be excellent propagandists, exerted influence upon the counts of
Flanders and the dukes of Brabant to pursue policies favorable to
England. One cannot deny that these parties were effective pressure
groups but, according to my reading of the evidence, they were
more significant as English military beachheads than as political
and diplomatic spheres of influence. The *fiefs-rentes,* good wages,
frequent gifts, and expense money received by them led others to
join the English cause, particularly during John's reign. As principal
intermediaries between John and Flanders the Flemish lords Adam
Keret, *châtelain* of Bruges; Gerard, chancellor of Flanders and
prévôt of Bruges; Simon de Haveret, marshal of Flanders; and
Baldwin, chamberlain of Flanders, were able through their official
rank to influence others of the nobility. William Cresec, another
important Flemish lord, was constantly acting as a messenger and
envoy for John. The diplomatic and administrative work of these
men, though considerable, was directed at only one thing—the formation of English military strength in Flanders. Forming a chain
of command by which John's orders were carried out, in addition to
possessing unlimited recruiting powers, they transmitted messages
to the nobility of Flanders dealing with the performance of homage
and payment of *fiefs-rentes* and wages, received orders from John
to inform the possessors of these fiefs to report fully armed and
prepared for the king's service at a designated mobilization point,
and sometimes collected the fighters and led them to the campaigns.[123] Both Adam and William participated in the Irish cam-

---

[120] Dept, *Influences,* pp. 74–96, 97–133. For a list of Flemish knights who
received *fiefs-rentes* from Philip Augustus see *Pièces justificatives,* no. 3, and
Appendices, no. 1.

[121] De Sturler, *Relations politiques,* pp. 476–77.

[122] *Ibid.,* pp. 89–90, 148, 332–33, 342; Dept, *Influences,* pp. 108–115,
126–29.

[123] Keret: *Rot. Claus.,* I, 45 b, 119 a–b, 130; *Rot. Pat.,* p. 93; *Rot. Chart.,*

paign of 1210 along with many other Flemish knights possessing *fiefs-rentes*, such as Hostis de Curinham, John de Everingham, William de Saint-Omer, Thomas Keret, Peter de Kaev, Arnold Wavrin and his brother Robert, Geoffrey and Henry Bailleul, and Daniel de Courtrai.[124] Though it is impossible to reconstruct the part of Adam and William in this expedition, it seems reasonable to suggest that they collected these men in Flanders and acted as their leaders during the fighting just as they did when the fighting was on the Continent.[125] Men in Holland, Brabant, Hainaut, Normandy, Gascony, and other regions worked similarly as agents for the English kings. What has been said for the reign of John can be repeated with equal force for the reigns of Henry III, Edward I, and Edward III. Only during the years of actual sustained hostilities and intense preparations for grand operations on the Continent did the kings concentrate upon securing allies by *fiefs-rentes*. If these allies were of primarily political and diplomatic worth, it would seem that one would find many references to their participation in non-military affairs rather than repeated entries on their military actions.

The evidence amassed from the English records shows the bulk of the political and diplomatic ventures conducted by men of a different type, most of whom were Englishmen and the king's most trusted and intimate friends. After some training in civil and canon law these envoys, many of humble birth, began their careers as royal clerks and eventually gained the royal favor and confidence by their loyal and efficient service. The kings, more certain of the loyalty of these clerks than of the nobility, often entrusted them with the most sensitive missions. Other diplomatic agents were certain bishops who had gained the royal trust, some noblemen, and a few foreign friends and relatives.[126] During the thirteenth, four-

p. 186. Gerard: *Rot. Pat.*, p. 26 b; *Rot. Chart.*, p. 45. Haveret: *Rot. Claus.*, I, 56; *Rot. Pat.*, p. 12. Baldwin: *Rot. Lib.*, p. 29. Cresec: *Rot. Claus.*, I, 19 b, 603; *Rot. Pat.*, pp. 10, 19 b, 32, 93. Hugh Boves, the famous mercenary captain, was in receipt of a fief and performed many diplomatic missions (*Rot. Claus.*, I, 118, 119, 143 a–b, 159 a–b, 178, 231; *Rot. Pat.*, p. 93).

[124] H. S. Sweetman and G. F. Handcock, *Calendar of Documents Relating to Ireland, 1171–1251* (London, 1875), I, 60–66; *Rot. Praest.*, pp. 172–232.

[125] See Ch. V, pp. 204–5.

[126] Lucas, *English Government at Work*, I, 310–13; G. P. Cuttino, *English Diplomatic Administration, 1259–1339* (London, 1940), pp. 84–99.

teenth, and fifteenth centuries the embassies consisted of two or three envoys whose business and travels kept them away from the court for two or three months. Always given definite instructions and a specific task—such as the negotiation of a marriage, the disposition of some feudal claim, the conclusion of military alliances, or the settlement of commercial disputes—they received daily wages for their work and remuneration for the members of their retinue (*familia*). The rate of pay was usually determined in advance by the king or his council. At the conclusion of their missions the envoys submitted to the king a report of their activities and presented the exchequer with a bill for their wages and expenses.[127] The pertinent documents of the chancery, exchequer, and wardrobe prove beyond doubt that this class of envoys was paid wages and was not in receipt of *fiefs-rentes*; the *fief-rente* was not a major instrument in the English machinery of diplomacy.

3. CONCLUSIONS

To deny the *fief-rente* a place in the political machinations and diplomacy of the feudal lord would be to misread the evidence. Its political uses were multitudinous and its diplomatic role was valu-

---

[127] Lucas, *English Government at Work*, I, 319–20; Cuttino, *Diplomatic Administration*, pp. 117–37; A. Larson, "The Payment of Fourteenth-Century English Envoys," *E.H.R.*, LIV (1939), 403–14. *Foedera* contains many letters of instructions to these royal agents and some of their expense accounts have been published. See *Foedera*, I, ii, 904–5, 935–36, 940, 942, 1008; II, ii, 907, 915, 928, 938, 941, 966, 998–99, 1063; M. C. L. Salt, "List of English Embassies to France, 1272–1307," *E.H.R.*, XLIV (1929), 263–78. For the accounts see L. Mirot and E. Déprez, "Les ambassades anglaises pendant la guerre de cent ans: catalogue chronologique, 1327–1450," *Biblio. de l'École des Chartes*, LIX–LXI (1898–1900), 550–77, 176–214, 20–58; Cuttino, *Diplomatic Administration*, pp. 143–60; Larson, *E.H.R.*, LIV, 407–10. For the nature of these accounts see the two published by De Lettenhove in his edition of Froissart. One is rendered by John de Woume, June to February 1337, and another by John de Thrandestone, 1336–41 (*Oeuvres de Froissart*, Bruxelles, 1874, XVIII, nos. 20, 41). Most accounts, however, remain unpublished but one can get an idea of their bulk by leafing through the "Various Accounts of the Exchequer, Nuncii" contained in the *Lists and Indexes* of the Public Record Office (*L.I.*, no. 35, pp. 186–204). The following accounts in the P.R.O. are particularly informative on diplomatic missions to the Low Countries: E. 101/308/18, 27; E. 101/310/1, 18, 19; E. 101/311/4, 9, 14, 18, 24, 28–29, 31.

able. Beyond such acknowledgment, however, the evidence does not permit one to go. We have seen from the records that there is no constant pattern for the varied political uses in western Europe. The French and English kings were liberal with grants of *fiefs-rentes* to the members of their family; the Low Country and German lords were not. The French kings and Low Country princes created appanages by means of *fiefs-rentes*; the English kings and German lords did not. In the Low Countries and Germany significant amounts of allodial land were converted into fiefs by means of the *fief-rente*; in France this practice was less prominent, and under the English kings, non-existent. Further comparisons would only emphasize the inconstancy of the political uses of the *fief-rente*. As for the diplomatic functions, not only do they vary from area to area but the amount of evidence concerning them is uneven. It is most abundant in the records of England, less so in those of France, far less so in those of the Low Countries, and difficult to find in those of Germany. Careful study of the documents pertaining to alliances and political parties nourished by *fiefs-rentes* shows that Sczaniecki, Mitteis, Kienast, and Clason have recognized the political and diplomatic worth of these alliances and parties but have ignored the military. If one were to collect the evidence pertaining to *fiefs-rentes* from England, France, Germany, and the Low Countries and break it down into categories on the basis of use, he would find that much less than half of it is of a purely political and diplomatic character. Considering the great mass of evidence and the undeniable prominence of the *fief-rente* in the thirteenth and fourteenth centuries, one is amazed that these scholars find this prominence explicable primarily in terms of political and diplomatic usage. In the following chapter we shall see why such a conclusion is not satisfactory.

V

The Military Role of the Fief-Rente

If we rule out the political and diplomatic value of the *fief-rente* as an explanation for its prominence in the thirteenth and fourteenth centuries, there yet remains the view advanced by such scholars as Brussel, Boutaric, and Delbrück that its prominence was due to its effectiveness as a military institution. These scholars, however, gave the *fief-rente* but cursory treatment and failed to buttress their views with convincing evidence; the military aspect of the *fief-rente* has therefore been neglected. Let us now examine the evidence relative to its military functions so as to determine whether the suggestion of Brussel and his adherents can be upheld.

1. THE HOUSEHOLD KNIGHT

Some fifty years ago P. Guilhiermoz presented the scholarly world for the first time with an exhaustive study on the origin, development, and character of the household knight.[1] With antecedents dating back to the late imperial period and to the Merovingians and Carolingians, this knight was a prominent fixture of the *mesnie* or household of every important feudal lord, particularly in the eleventh and twelfth centuries. The larger the number of knights in a lord's household, the greater was his prestige. Forming a select and permanent military clique about the lord, these knights were fiefless and entirely dependent upon him for their nourishment and maintenance. The household knight was at the peak of his importance in the twelfth century and gradually disappeared from the scene in the late twelfth and thirteenth centuries, usually as a result of having

---

[1] P. Guilhiermoz, *Essai sur l'origine de la noblesse en France au moyen âge* (Paris, 1902), pp. 169–71, 242–54. See also A. Dumas, "Encore la question: fidèles ou vassaux?" *Nouvelle Revue Historique de Droit Français et Étranger*, XLIV (1920), 159–229.

been enfeoffed with an estate of land. This is not to say that a type of household knight did not continue to exist but, as we shall see, he was different from his predecessor. It would be logical to suppose that the household knight, without land and supplied as he was with food, clothing, armor, horses, and occasionally *rentes* in nature or money, would be among the first to receive a *fief-rente*. And, in fact, A. Dumas has stated that household knights received "à titre de fief, des pensions en argent ou en nature ... avec lesquelles ils devaient désormais pour voir à leur subsistance." [2] But how widely were they distributed, how numerous were they, and at what period were they the most prominent?

Avowing that numerous household knights in France held *fiefs-rentes* either in kind or money until the early thirteenth century, Sczaniecki fails to provide enough evidence to bear out his conclusion. [3] The only documents cited are those recording the few modest fiefs in kind granted to household knights between 1093 and 1128 by the abbey of Saint-Père de Chartres. To these should be added the twenty-four fiefs listed in another document of Saint-Père drawn up some time between 1130 and 1150. [4] Undoubtedly a long and scrupulous search would uncover more evidence but the fact remains that it is extremely scarce. In the thirteenth century what few household knights remained were remunerated by non-feudal *rentes* or salaries like the functionaries noted in the previous chapter. [5] The only conclusion possible is that the *fief-rente* was seldom granted to the household knight in France.

The German evidence is even less satisfactory. The suggestion of Sczaniecki that perhaps numerous men residing near Goslar who were granted fiefs by Frederick I, Philip of Suabia, and Otto IV in the twelfth and early thirteenth centuries were household knights, seems untenable. Too many of them are known to have been important lords holding land for them to be considered simple members of a household. These fiefs were granted to obtain castle-guard at the imperial castle of Goslar. Responsible for such service, these men could not very well be members of the imperial household

---

[2] *Nouvelle Revue*, XLIV, 222–23.

[3] *Essai*, pp. 23–25, 44–48.

[4] Guérard, *Cartulaire de Saint-Père de Chartres*, I, xxv–xxvi; II, 290, 310, 312–13, 358–59, 371, 384.

[5] Cf. Sczaniecki, *Essai*, pp. 46–48.

moving about with the emperors.[6] *Fiefs-rentes* may indeed have been granted to household knights in Germany, but there is no evidence to this effect.

Only in the Low Countries are there records numerous and specific enough to permit close examination of household knights in receipt of *fiefs-rentes*. Thanks to Gislebert de Mons we know that the counts of Hainaut built up a large entourage of household knights called *commilitones* who were to follow the counts in their wars and to the tournament. They were nourished and maintained, or they were paid salaries in money, or, what was more common, they were granted *fiefs-rentes*. Toward the end of the twelfth century the *fief-rente* seemed to be a means of recruiting men for the comital household. In 1184–85, for example, Count Baldwin V secured as *commilitones* the Flemish lord Baldwin Caron for a fief of 600 *l.*, Baldwin de Villeneuve for a fief of 300 *l.*, Robert de Beaurin for a fief of 20 *l.*, and Gosuin de Wavrin for a fief of 60 *l.*[7] Gislebert relates also that Baldwin secured many valorous French knights for his household by similar grants.[8] There is no more evidence on the household knight until the late thirteenth and fourteenth centuries and by this time he was quite different; the interval of over one hundred years had wrought a transformation. No longer can it be assumed that he was a continuous resident of the household or that the *fief-rente* was his only benefice. He seemed frequently to be a highly qualified warrior serving as an officer on his lord's military staff. When needed he was always at his lord's side and completely provided for; when not, he often lived elsewhere, usually on a landed benefice. His *fief-rente* helped to maintain him and to create the nexus requiring the household service. The knight in continuous residence and completely dependent upon his lord for support was a figure of the past.

We therefore find Count Guy of Flanders confirming in 1285 a fief of 60 *l.* granted by his mother Margaret with his consent to the knight Baldwin de Castiel in recompense of his service. Whenever

[6] *Ibid.*, p. 4. For the document see Bode, *Urkundenbuch der Stadt Goslar*, I, no. 606.

[7] Gislebert de Mons, *Chronicon*, pp. 175, 180. See also W. Meyer, *Das Werk des Kanzlers Gislebert von Mons* (Jena, 1888), pp. 42, 55; Didier, *Revue du Nord*, XVII, 169.

[8] *Chronicon*, p. 175: "Quosdam eciam milites de regno Francorum probos magnique nominis, . . . infeodavit feodis annuatim habendis."

Baldwin found it convenient he was permitted to live in Guy's *hôtel* and was given the customary wages and robes of a knight of the household and enough oats for three horses. At Baldwin's request Guy agreed to take into his household Jakemon de Castiel, Baldwin's son, who was to enjoy the same rights as his father except that, as a squire, he was to receive the wages and robes customarily given to squires of the *hôtel*; upon becoming a knight Jakemon was to receive the standard maintenance. These letters of Guy refer to the *fief-rente* granted by Margaret in 1276 and to letters of 1279 granting the wages, robes, and oats. In the letters of 1279 we also learn that Baldwin was master of Margaret's household.[9] But we must jump to the fourteenth century in order to get some documents that furnish all the details of a household contract. In 1338 Louis de Nevers, count of Flanders, agreed to retain with him in his "maisnage" the knight John "dit Trament de Noyelles." Louis then set forth the conditions of the contract: as befits a good knight John is to serve loyally in all wars, tournaments, jousts, and matters pertaining to the count. In the same way John is to serve the son of Louis after the count's death. All losses connected with horses while participating in tournament or war are to be recompensed, and the daily wages going to and returning from a tournament will be at the rate of 12 *gros tournois*. While living in the household John will have three horses maintained for him. When he serves during war his wages will be those received by other knights. These terms are to be valid only between John and the count and his successor. Louis then states that he has given John and his heirs a yearly income of 60 *l.* to be held "en fief et en hommage"; Louis and his successors may repurchase the fief at the rate of 10 *deniers* per *denier* with the proviso that John or his heirs must use the money to acquire land or some object to be held in fief. Finally, Louis is to inform the receiver of Flanders to pay henceforth the 60 *l.* annually to John without further order.[10] This document not only emphasizes the military duties of the household knight but shows that he was not always a resident of the count's *hôtel*. It shows, furthermore, that the *fief-rente* could be repurchased and then re-

---

[9] De Saint-Genois, *Monuments,* II, 734; Gaillard, *B.C.R.H.,* VI (1854), nos. 690, 692. See also no. 696 of Gaillard and p. 680 of De Saint-Genois.

[10] A.G.R., *Trés. Fl.,* Sér. I, no. 2083; A.D.N., B. 4065/145.583. See Appendix, no. 24.

placed by an ordinary fief. In this event the obligations would surely continue, but one cannot help wondering whether the status of John as a household knight would be altered. The numerous instances from the *Cartulaire de Louis de Male,* as well as from the Flemish archives, are similar to the one above; it is sufficient merely to emphasize that all point to the military service of the household knight as his most important obligation.[11] Grants emanating from the counts of Hainaut in the fourteenth century lead to the same conclusion.[12] After the middle of the fourteenth century one seldom finds *fiefs-rentes* granted to household knights; it is certain that the custom had practically stopped.

Insufficient evidence on the household knight in England makes him even more obscure there than on the Continent. F. M. Stenton, who has studied this knight with infinite patience, admits that "the household knight is an elusive person. As he held no land, he naturally does not appear in the records from which our knowledge

---

[11] For example, in 1349 Louis de Male granted a fief of 50 *l.* to the knight Hector de Bailleul for his good services to be rendered in war, tournament, joust, and other duties pertaining to the count. He was to be retained in the household and receive the same maintenance as "nos autres chevaliers bacheliers." Hector promised to serve the count loyally in all things "et guardera et sauvera nostre honnour et prouffit en tous cas à son loyal povoir" (De Limburg-Stirum, *Cart. de Louis de Male,* I, no. 38). See also I, no. 55 and II, no. 698; De Saint-Genois, *Monuments,* II, 355. In 1323 Louis de Nevers granted to the knight Reginald Zenart de Lando de Plaisance a fief of 100 *l.* plus robes and maintenance (A.D.N., B. 4064/145.557). In 1338 Louis stated that "nous avons retenons de nostre hostel et mesnage nostre ame et feal chevalier messire Jehan de Saint Quentin a delivrance de trois chevals toutes les fois que nous le manderons et que il sera entour nous et li avons ottroie et ottroions nos robes teles et toutefois que nous liverons a nos autres chevaliers bachelers. Item toutes les fois que il nous servira a la guerre et au tournoy mouture selonc son estat. Item pour ce que il nous serve bien et loyaument en temps avenir et en guerredon daucuns services que il nous a fais en temps passe nous li avons donne et ottroie donnons et ottroions a sa vie tant seulement quarante livres" (B. 4065/145.584).

[12] For example, in 1322 Count William I of Hainaut granted to "Wistasse dou Rues et Fastreit sen frère, chevaliers, à cascun tout le cours de se vie, en acroissement des fiés qu'il tiènent de nous, nos draps à cescun d'iaus deus, pour lui et pour un compaignon, tels que nous les donrons à nos autres chevaliers; et le repaire, l'aler et le venir, et bouce à court en no hostel, cescun à quatre chevaus, toutes les fois . . . il leur plaira à yestre en no hostel". (Devillers, *Monuments,* III, no. 177, p. 115, note). See also Gachet, *B.C.R.H.,* IV (1852), 40; Didier, *Revue du Nord,* XVII, 275.

of feudal organization is mainly drawn." [13] We know that after the Conquest many barons, not having provided fully for the knight service owed the king by enfeoffments in land, made up the difference either by maintaining knights in their own household or by hiring them.[14] During the course of the twelfth century, however, more of the household knights were provided for in land, and by the thirteenth century such knights had all but disappeared.[15] Not a record of this period, however, shows the English barons granting *fiefs-rentes* to household knights.[16] As for the royal household, the evidence is not abundant. John relied principally upon *bachelerii de familia nostra*—for the most part unknighted and landless young men who were his personal dependents.[17] Some of them may have held *fiefs-rentes,* for in letters patent of 1200 John ordered Ralph de Mauléon, the seneschal of Poitou, to seize "omnes feudos et terras quos dedimus bachellariis quos retinuimus de familia nostra ... qui homagia et fidelitates et ligentias nobis non fecerunt." In 1216 John decided to retain Thomas Malesmains in the household and granted him a fief of 60 *l.*[18] Although usually providing for his household knights in the form of yearly salaries, Henry III occasionally gave them *fiefs-rentes.* In 1252, for example, he granted to Geoffrey de Burlemund a fief of 40 *l.* "for his homage and service."[19] An entry in the Patent Roll of 1237 indicates that Henry III was

---

[13] Stenton, *English Feudalism,* p. 139.

[14] *Ibid.,* pp. 136–39.

[15] H. M. Chew, *The Ecclesiastical Tenants-in-Chief and Knight-Service* (Oxford, 1932), p. 275; Painter, *Studies in the History of the English Feudal Barony* (Baltimore, 1943), pp. 28–29.

[16] For example, the famous William Marshal was a household knight of both the Young Henry and Henry II but he never received a *fief-rente.* He was richly remunerated and maintained until receiving a fief of land from Henry II. Once in a tournament on the Continent William performed so well that certain princes bid to secure him as a member of their households. The count of Flanders and duke of Burgundy each offered 500 *l.* yearly if he would serve them, but he refused these offers. In any event the money involved was not a *fief-rente* (Painter, *William Marshal,* pp. 33, 36, 49, 59–60).

[17] Powicke, *Loss of Normandy,* pp. 229–30. See also his article "The Angevin Administration of Normandy," *E.H.R.,* XXII (1907), 39–42.

[18] *Rot. Chart.,* p. 59–59 b; *Rot. Pat.,* p. 190 b.

[19] *C.P.R. 1247–58,* pp. 148, 381; *Cl.R. 1259–61,* p. 223; *Cl.R. 1251–53,* p. 163. See also *C.P.R. 1258–66,* pp. 180, 198; *Cl.R. 1242–47,* p. 440.

also paying *fiefs-rentes* to some household knights of Geoffrey Ridel II, lord of Blavia and an important lord of Gascony.[20]

The Wardrobe Accounts for Edward I's reign and for the fourteenth century have helped to clarify the status of the household knight in this period. T. F. Tout has pointed out that there were always a varying number of bannerets and knights of the household, each with a retinue of followers prepared for instant action. They formed the core of the royal army which in time of war was reinforced by a larger levy.[21] Besides guarding the king and serving as his officers in time of war, they also attended to administrative duties. The evidence would seem to show that these men of the household were like their contemporaries in the Low Countries in that many were not permanent residents of the royal household. But unlike the household knight of the Low Countries, they did not hold *fiefs-rentes*. Prior to 1291 Edward I had maintained in his pay sixty bannerets and knights and sixty troopers of the household at daily wages. In 1291 he began the practice of giving a fixed annual salary (fee).[22] During the greater part of the thirteenth century, then, most household knights were maintained by non-feudal salaries, computed either by the day or the year. Around 1290 it became standard procedure to grant a knight a yearly non-feudal fee, supply his additional needs, and pay him daily wages for duty in the field; this system prevailed throughout the fourteenth and fifteenth centuries. Except that no feudal tenure was involved, maintaining the

[20] *Pat. R. 1232–47*, p. 192.

[21] Tout, *Chapters*, II, 135 ff.; IV, 100–1, 114, 123, 413–14. See also J. E. Morris, *The Welsh Wars of Edward I* (Oxford, 1901), p. 203; Johnson, *English Government at Work*, I, 206–7, 217.

[22] Morris, *Welsh Wars*, p. 203. In December 1299, for the Berwick muster, twenty-two bannerets and forty-four knights of the household received half of their yearly fees. The sum total of these fees for the half-year, computed at the customary yearly fee of 20 *m.* for a banneret and 10 *m.* for a knight, was 327 *l.* In addition to their fees the bannerets and knights received winter and summer robes, wages for military service of 3 *s.* and 2 *s.* per day, respectively, and remuneration for horses lost in combat. All the household bannerets and knights with the fees and wages paid to them are listed under this rubric: "Titulus de denariis liberatis diversis militibus de hospicio regis Edwardi filii regis Henrici, nomine annui feodi loco vadiorum eorundem extra guerram" (*Liber Quotidianus Contrarotulatoris Garderobae, Anno Regni Regis Edwardi Primi Vicesimo Octavo*, Society of Antiquaries, London, 1787, pp. 174 ff., 189, 196). See also Stapleton, *Archaeologia*, XXVI (1836), 318–45;

household knight by this method was the same as by the *fief-rente*. We must conclude that the *fief-rente* never played a significant part in the maintenance of the knight of the royal household.

2. CASTLE-GUARD

From an early time in all western Europe castle-guard had been a form of military service owed by certain fiefs. Rather than serving in the field, the holders of these fiefs were obliged to guard the lord's castle for a specified part of the year. It was so arranged that a continuous guard was mounted by knights supplied in this way.[23] Everywhere except in England the *fief-rente* played a prominent role in providing this type of service; it was in Germany, however, that this role was most significant. Where the fief was used to obtain all sorts of service in the rest of western Europe, in Germany its use was restricted. At least three-fourths of all the German evidence pertaining to *fiefs-rentes* is concerned with castle-guard; it alone accounts for the prominence of the *fief-rente* in Germany from the twelfth to the fifteenth century. Granted most frequently to the *ministeriales*, *Burglehen* were also held by a significant number of important lords. Whether in money or kind, these fiefs were generally of modest value; seldom did they exceed 20 *m*. yearly.[24] Granted by all the important German lords, in particular the emperors, *Burglehen* can be found from the twelfth century to the end of the fourteenth. Of the literally hundreds of examples in the records, a few will serve to illustrate the nature of such concessions. In the well-known document of 1244 from the archives of Goslar is a long list of the *ministeriales* and lords who held *fiefs-rentes* in return for

S. Lysons, "Copy of a Roll of the Expenses of King Edward the First at Rhuddlan Castle," *Archaeologia*, XVI (1812), 32–79. Similar information is found in the unpublished Wardrobe Books. In the Book of 1297 on fols. 59ᵛ–69ʳ and 120ᵛ there are listed as paid fees, wages, robes, and restauration of horses (British Museum, Add. MS. 7965).

[23] See Luchaire, *Manuel des institutions françaises*, p. 200; Guilhiermoz, *Essai sur l'origine de la noblesse*, p. 261; Boutaric, *Institutions militaires*, p. 128; Mitteis, *Lehnrecht*, pp. 566, 621; Ganshof, *Étude sur les ministeriales*, pp. 50, 177, 179, 280, and *Feudalism*, pp. 80–81.

[24] See Niese, *Verwaltung des Reichsgutes*, pp. 222 ff.; C. G. Homeyer, *System des Lehnrechts der Sachsischen Rechtsbücher* (Berlin, 1844), pp. 552 ff.; Bosl, *Reichsministerialität*, I, 188–89, 258–59; II, 575; Sczaniecki, *Essai*, pp. 37–43.

providing guard for the emperors at the castle of Goslar. Most of these fiefs had been granted originally by Frederick I but others had been added by Philip of Suabia and Otto IV.[25] In 1276 King Rudolf granted Henry "scultetus de Frankenfurt" and his heirs 5 *m.* of silver "pro castrensi feodo in Redelnheim." In 1280 Emmelrich von Heppenhefte received from the archbishop of Mainz 6 *m.* yearly "nomine castrensis feodi" in return for the following promise: "Promitto eidem domino archiepiscopo, quod in castro predicto faciam residenciam personalem." In 1366 the knight Helfrich von Dorfelden recognized that "Her Ulrich Herre zu Hanauive, mir gegeben hat, und gebet mit diesem Briefe acht Phunt Heller Geldes, guter Werunge, zu Burg-Lehen."[26] Typical of the German lords granting most of such fiefs were the archbishops of Cologne, the bishops of Speyer and Bamberg, the abbots of Fulda, the counts of Tübingen, Salm, and Catsenellenbogen, and the counts palatine of the Rhine.[27] The grants generally required guard and residence at the castle for short periods of time; seldom did they specify year-long residence as did the one grant cited above.

It should be pointed out, however, that castle-guard was also obtained by grants of lump sums. In fact the evidence shows even more castle-guard secured in this manner than by *fiefs-rentes.* A lord would pay a lump sum to a man who promised to provide castle-guard and to take in fief lands worth yearly ten per cent of the lump sum, either lands of his own or lands acquired by purchase. This lump sum technique should not, as has frequently happened, be confused with the *fief-rente*; it was nothing other than the *fief*

---

[25] Bode, *Urkundenbuch der Stadt Goslar,* I, no. 606; introduction, pp. 35–36. See also C. Frey, *Die Schicksale des königlichen Gutes in Deutschland unter den letzten Staufern seit König Philipp* (Berlin, 1881), pp. 265 ff. In a financial record of 1242 are entries relating to *Burglehen* paid by Frederick II: "Item dedit Johanni Bono de feudo castelli VIII marcas. . . . Item Everhardo de Mendorp de feodo castelli VI marcas" (Huillard-Bréholles, *Historia Diplomatica Friderici Secundi,* VI, ii, 832–33).

[26] Sauer, *Nassauisches Urkundenbuch,* I, ii, nos. 906, 967; Lünig, *Corpus Juris Feudalis Germanici,* III, 46.

[27] See Ennen and Eckertz, *Quellen Stadt Köln,* III, nos. 485, 522; IV, nos. 18, 29, 79, 97, 164, 230, 488; V, nos. 215, 257; Winkelmann, *Acta Imperii,* II, no. 302; Goerz, *Mittelrheinische Regesten,* III, nos. 2000, 2073; IV, nos. 387, 433; Gudenus, *Codex Diplomaticus,* V, 875–76, 979–80; Böhmer, *Acta Imperii,* no. 620.

de reprise.[28] Previous discussion of the lump sum has clearly shown the difference between it and the *fief-rente.*[29]

After Germany, castle-guard obtained by the *fief-rente* was most prominent in Champagne, Lorraine, and Bar where it was known as *estage* (*stagium* and *custodia* in Latin). Though it is impossible to tell whether ordinary fiefs or *fiefs-rentes* obtained more castle-guard, the records show a really significant number of *fiefs-rentes* paid for such service.[30] In the *Livre des vassaux de Champagne* (1172–1222) such entries as the following are numerous:

Lucans de Triaus et Gervais de Vianne deivent feire continuel estage eu chastel de Sainte-Meneut . . . chascuns d'icex fera an ce meisme chastel sanblablement VI semaines de garde. Ge adecertes Blanche, contesse, donc à chascun d'icex LX lb. por lor mesons fere.

Li fiuz Pierres de Novelin, liges et III mois de garde. Tient III setiere de blé à Novi . . .

Berthelemius de Chezi, il vit ; liges et III mois garde. Il ot XXX lb. en deniers.

Guilliaumes de Vianne, liges et il ot XXX *l.* et deit VI semaines de garde.[31]

Typical of the many grants for castle-guard found in the documents of Champagne edited by Longnon is the following. In 1259–60 Theobald V, count of Champagne, granted Geoffrey de Varannes a fief of 10 *l.* for which Geoffrey promised "gardam annuatim . . . apud Coyfeium, castrum dicti domini regis Navarre."[32] Ferri III, duke of Lorraine in the late thirteenth century, was responsible for

[28] Cf. the remarks of Sczaniecki, *Essai,* pp. 41–42.

[29] See Ch. II, pp. 71–74. See also K. Schoppich *et al., Hennebergisches Urkundenbuch* (Meiningen, 1842), I, nos. 61, 65, 105 ; II, no. 88 ; Remling, *Urkundenbuch der Bischöfe Speyer,* nos. 427–29, 507, 518, 531 ; Lünig, *Corpus Juris Feudalis Germanici,* III, 659 ; IV, 661–62 ; Mummenhoff, *Regesten der Reichsstadt Aachen,* nos. 291, 293, 408 ; A. Wyss, *Urkundenbuch der Deutschordens-Ballei Hessen. 1207–1299* (Leipzig, 1879), II, i, nos. 530, 543, 578, 723, 737. In vol. I, pt. iii of Sauer, *Nassauisches Urkundenbuch,* there are over fifty such *Burglehen.*

[30] Sczaniecki, *Essai,* pp. 37–43.

[31] Longnon, *Livre des vassaux du comté de Champagne et de Brie, 1172–1222,* nos. 1770–71, 1775–76, 1799–1800, 2461, 2479, 2484, 2488, 2517, 2593, 2596, etc. See also D'Arbois de Jubainville, *Histoire de Champagne,* II, no. 46 ; III, no. 209. Cf. the remarks of Longnon, pp. 89–93.

[32] *Layettes,* IV, no. 4585. See also Longnon, *Documents de Champagne,* I, nos. 904, 907, 910, 941, etc. The count of Champagne also granted men lump sums with which to acquire land to be held in fief and which obliged them

many such grants. The fiefs ranged in value from 40 to 60 *l.* but always secured guard service for six months.[33] In a document of 1301–2 are the names of those owing castle-guard for *fiefs-rentes* to the counts of Bar; the castles involved were Conflans, Châtillon, and La Marche.[34] *Fiefs-rentes* granted by the kings of France for castle-guard seem to have been less numerous. Perhaps this is because already in the early thirteenth century they had begun to pay daily or annual wages to *châtelains* who, along with serjeants, were responsible for the defense of the royal castles.[35] What evidence we have, however, comes from the thirteenth century. In 1215, for example, Philip Augustus granted a fief of 40 *l.* to a certain Simon du Puits of Pontoise with the obligation of continually guarding the royal tower at Néaufle. The roll of the Norman exchequer for 1257 indicates that a certain William de Lamberville held from Louis IX 3 *s.* 11 *d.* for which he was "homo regis ligius" and owed "custodiam per unum mensem."[36] In France the *fief-rente* can be said to have played an especially important part in castle-guard only in the eastern part around Champagne and Lorraine and then only in the twelfth and thirteenth centuries. Apparently from a relatively early time the French kings preferred to pay non-feudal wages to secure the guard of their castles.

The earliest reference in the Low Countries to castle-guard secured by *fiefs-rentes* is in the charter granted by William Clito to Saint-Omer in 1127.[37] There is not enough evidence to say that

to provide castle-guard. Cf. Sczaniecki, *Essai,* pp. 39–40; he seems to consider such grants *fiefs-rentes.*

[33] For example, in 1286 Ferri granted to Wirion de Condé a fief of 60 *l.* for which six months of guard duty was owed at the castle of Fronard (Sczaniecki, *Essai,* p. 40). There are other examples on the same page.

[34] Kern, *Acta Imperii,* no. 314. The following is a typical entry: "Ce sont les nons de ceus, qui ont repris pour reson de deniers, que le conte leur donoit pour faire gardes au chastel de Chastillon. Poinconnet de Faveney, Jehan Cornete et Guiot de Varannes IIII *l.,* qui leur sont deues, si comme il dient, sus les rentes de Chastillon."

[35] Sczaniecki, *Essai,* p. 42. See particularly Langlois, *Philippe le Hardi,* p. 368; Boutaric, *Saint Louis et Alphonse de Poitiers,* p. 161.

[36] Delisle, *Cart. normand,* no. 233; Léchaudé-d'Anisy, *Scaccarium Normannie sub Regibus Francie,* p. 179.

[37] Giry, *Histoire de la ville de Saint-Omer,* p. 373. Examples for Flanders from the fourteenth century are found in the A.D.N., B. 4324, Compte du domaine de Flandre, 1372–73.

this method of securing castle-guard was as prominent as in Germany, but what we have relating to Namur, Brabant, Luxemburg, Guelders, the Pays d'Outre-Meuse, and Flanders warrants our saying that it was at least as prominent as in Champagne and Lorraine. To secure guard for their castles, the counts of Namur granted out fiefs ranging in value from 10 *l.* to 66 *l.* per annum. These *fiefs de garde* were usually granted to men living in the neighborhood of the castle, that is, to men who possessed lands and who were best able to supply the necessary guard. If the guard was not provided or the contingent to be supplied was deficient, the annual installment of the fief was suspended.[38] For Brabant many instances of *fiefs-rentes* paid for castle-guard appear in the feudal registers.[39] For example, in the *Livre des feudataires* of John III we find that in 1350 John de Merrode held "XX marchas annuatim castelli apud Kerpe." The *Spechtboek* compiled in 1374 refers to this fief as "een bourchleen van XX libras siaers."[40] In Limburg and the Pays d'Outre-Meuse the existence of castle-guard is proved by the inquest of rights made when the duke of Burgundy acquired that region in the late fourteenth century. A reference to "plusieurs fiefs que l'on appelle les fiefs du chastel" appears amidst other entries recognizing the obligations previously assumed by the dukes of Brabant to pay *fiefs-rentes* to men of this region.[41] As we shall see later, castles in this turbulent area were at a premium and were frequently the key to its control. For this reason the dukes of Brabant granted many *fiefs-rentes* to secure castle-guard here. For Guelders a financial account of the duke for 1294 and 1295 contains nineteen entries pertaining

---

[38] For remarks on castle-guard in Namur see Balon, *An. Soc. Arch. Namur,* XL, 15–16. He has included extracts from the *Comptes du domaine, 1355–56,* which relate to the *fiefs de garde* of the *prévôté* of Poilvache. The following is a typical entry: "Item rendu par le compte Philippart de Freyne, cerrier de Poillevache, aux wardains du dit castiel et ailleurs pour leurs fieus que messire leur doit par an en argent, tant en bourse que sur certains fieus, pour cause du dit castiel devens le terme de ces dis comptes: Promiers a Monseigneur Loyt de Juppeleu pour son fieuf de warde, tournois 12 livres" (Annexes, no. 8). There are numerous examples in A.G.R., *C.C.,* nos. 3221, 3226, Comptes des recettes générales de Namur.

[39] The following is a typical entry appearing in the *Spechtboek*: "Jan Hassart hout een bourchleen tot Kerpen van X libras siaers" (fol. 335ᵛ).

[40] Galesloot, *Feudataires de Jean III,* pp. 135, 138–39, 141, 199, 273–74; A.G.R., Galesloot, *Cour féodale,* no. 4, *Spechtboek,* fol. 335ᵛ.

[41] Quicke, *B.C.R.H.,* XCVI, 378.

to payments of *fiefs-rentes* for castle-guard.[42] The counts of Luxemburg relied heavily upon *fiefs-rentes* to provide guard for their castles. A grant by Count Henry VI in 1288 is particularly illuminating. He granted to the knight Werri dit Troussien a fief of 10 *l.* for which Werri became his man and swore to perform "warde chascun an a Thionville demi an." Count Henry stipulated that the fief could be repurchased for 100 *l.* and that Werri should use this sum to acquire a piece of land to be held in fief of him. The land, to be located as near as possible to Thionville, would still carry with it the obligation of castle-guard.[43]

In England castle-guard was established as a military obligation by the Normans but it soon became obsolete. Many barons were relieved of the duty in the twelfth century and those who were not usually commuted their service in money. The kings accepted this money willingly and then hired mercenaries, especially crossbowmen, for garrison duty in the royal castles, a practice which was well established by the second half of the thirteenth century. Although the kings paid for castle-guard, there is no evidence that they granted *fiefs-rentes* to lords who agreed to do the duty themselves or to provide the garrisons.[44] This is understandable when one recalls that in the twelfth and thirteenth centuries sheriffs or royal *châtelains* were in charge of these castles and employed mercenaries to defend

---

[42] Meihuizen, *Rekening Betreffende Gelre,* pp. 7–8, 23–24, 37, 86, 93.

[43] Wampach, *Urkunden,* V, no. 227; Verkooren, *Inv. Lux.,* no. 315. J. Vannérus has shown that the counts of Luxemburg, especially John the Blind, obtained much of their castle-guard by grants of lump sums. Most often the recipients took in fief a part of the income derived from their allods and promised to perform castle-guard at one of the count's castles. This, of course, was a *fief de reprise* (Vannérus, *Mélanges d'histoire offerts à Henri Pirenne,* II, 619–34). According to Balon, the counts of Namur likewise secured some of their castle-guard (*An. Soc. Arch. Namur,* XL, 11–15). It should be pointed out that the princes of the Low Countries also obtained much castle-guard by paying for it as did the French kings. In 1395, for example, Philip the Bold, duke of Burgundy, appointed the knight Arnold de Crainhem, captain and seneschal of the castle, town, and lands of Fauquemont at wages of 400 florins per annum (Quicke, "Documents concernant la politique des ducs de Brabant et de Bourgogne dans le duché de Limbourg ...," *B.C.R.H.,* XCIII, 1929, no. 38, p. 175).

[44] Painter, *Feudal Barony,* pp. 45–47. See also his "Castle-Guard," *American Historical Review,* XL (1935), 450–59; Round, "Castle-Guard," *Archaeological Journal,* LIX (1902), 144–59; Stenton, *English Feudalism,* pp. 190–215; Haskins, *Norman Institutions,* pp. 19–21.

them. The *châtelains* or "keepers" were often paid yearly salaries for their custody of the castles.[45] In the fourteenth century when the indenture system was in full force the kings frequently contracted with warriors to defend a district or a castle with forces adequate to guard it. In 1327, for example, William de la Zouche was appointed "to the custody of the land of Gloumorgan and Morgan. . . . He is to receive for that custody, in time of peace, 200 *m.*, and wages for 30 men-at-arms in his retinue for the siege of Kaerfilly Castle."[46] Admittedly in John's reign many of the royal castles were entrusted to such mercenary captains as Faulkes de Bréauté, Philip Marc, Peter de Maulay, Savaric de Mauléon, William Casingham, and Engelard de Cigogné, all of whom held *fiefs-rentes*. But it should not be assumed that the *fiefs-rentes* had been granted to these men solely to obtain the service of castle-guard; rather, they had been granted for all types of military service. These men served John in any needed capacity; they fought on the Continent, they helped John against the barons in England, and they guarded his castles.[47] We may conclude that the English kings preferred methods other than *fiefs-rentes* for securing castle-guard.

3. STRATEGIC RIGHTS TO CASTLES

It has already been noted that some lords acquired castles by substituting *fiefs-rentes* for them, an arrangement with obvious military

[45] The Pipe Roll of the Norman exchequer for the year 1180 contains this entry: "In liberatione Walteri de Cantilupo 25 *l.* pro custodia castri de Bellomonte de 50 *l.* quas habet per annum" (Stapleton, *Mag. Rot. Scacc. Norm.*, I, 97). In 1244 a writ of *liberate* ordered payment of the yearly salary of one of Henry III's *châtelains*: "Allocate to Waleram Teutonicus, keeper of the castles of Grosmund, Skenefrith, and White Castle, in the issues thereof, 30 *l.* for the twenty-eighth year of his yearly fee of 30 *l.*; and 35 *l.* expenses of himself and his men in maintaining the king's war in the parts of the March from Whitsuntide in the twenty-eighth year till Martinmas" (*C.L.R. 1240–45*, p. 275; *Pat. R. 1232–47*, p. 445). There are many other examples in the *Rotuli Walliae* and *Rotuli Scotiae*.

[46] *C.P.R. 1327–30*, p. 18. See also Devon, *Issues of the Exchequer,* Issue Roll (1391), p. 247; Issue Roll (1402), p. 293; Issue Roll (1403), p. 298; Issue Roll (1441), p. 440.

[47] Ramsay, *Angevin Empire*, pp. 486–501; Painter, *William Marshal*, pp. 182–89; Powicke, *King Henry III and the Lord Edward* (Oxford, 1947), I, 1–41. For Savaric de Mauléon see H. J. Chaytor, *Savaric de Mauléon, Baron and Troubadour* (Cambridge, 1939).

advantages. More often, however, a lord would grant a *fief-rente* to a man who in turn would take his castle in fief and promise either to make it accessible to the lord during hostilities or to hold and defend it against all enemies of the lord. Thus did many lords develop the strategic defense of their lands. In 1217, for example, upon receiving a fief from Blanche of Navarre, regent of Champagne, John de Toul took his castle in liege homage and swore that it would be put at the disposal of the counts of Champagne whenever they so ordered. In 1247 Alphonse of Poitiers granted two fiefs of 100 *l.* to William Maingot, lord of Surgères, who promised to make his castle available to Alphonse during periods of war.[48] In Germany the archbishop of Mainz granted a fief of 10 *m.* in 1291 to Count Herman of Battenberg who took certain of his castles in fief and promised to defend them against the archbishop's enemies. Receiving in 1340 a fief of 4 *m.* from the archbishop of Cologne in augmentation of a previous fief, the knight Adolf von Holdinghausen took his castle Grutpach in fief and promised to defend it. In 1401 Gumprecht, lord of Alpen, received a fief of 50 *écus* from Duke William of Juliers and Guelders and promised the Duke the "Oeffnungsrecht" of his castle and the town of Alpen.[49]

[48] Chantereau le Febvre, *Traité des fiefs*, Preuves, p. 88; *Layettes*, III, no. 3592. For another such grant by Alphonse of Poitiers see *Layettes*, II, no. 2986. For grants by the kings and other French lords see *Layettes*, II, nos. 1653, 2986; III, no. 4550; Longnon, *Livre des vassaux de Champagne*, pp. 93–94. In the well-known treaty of 1346 between Philip VI of France and John of Hainaut, lord of Beaumont, John received a fief of 3,000 *l.* and promised among other things to defend and hold his castles against Philip's enemies (Devillers, *Cart. de Hainaut*, I, nos. 153–54, 170, 186; A.D.N., B. 1177/7531; Zeper, *Jan van Henegouwen*, Bijlage II, nos. 280–81; De Lettenhove, *Oeuvres de Froissart*, XVIII, no. 61; Cooper, *Report of Foedera*, appendices B–D, p. 309). Somewhat different was a grant of Louis IX in 1231 to Arnold d'Audenarde. For a fief of 80 *l.* Arnold promised to build no new fortresses nor to repair any old ones without the royal consent (*Inv. des archives de Lille*, I, no. 553).

[49] Gudenus, *Codex Diplomaticus*, I, 854–56; Lacomblet, *Urkundenbuch*, III, no. 350; IV, no. 4. In 1291 John of Reifferscheid took in fief from the archbishop of Cologne his "castrum Bedebure" as a "ligium castrum." The archbishop then granted John a fief of "octo carratas vini" (Ennen and Eckertz, *Quellen Stadt Köln*, III, no. 353). In 1413 Diedrich of Limburg gave his "slos zu Broiche zu dem hogeborn fursten ind herren hern Adulphe hertzougen zu dem Berge, myme gnedigen hern." Diedrich then promised to serve Duke Adolf faithfully against all enemies; he received a fief of 20 *Gulden* (Lacomblet, *Urkundenbuch*, IV, no. 74).

In the Low Countries we find Hugh de Pierrepont, bishop of Liège, granting in 1204 or 1205 a fief of 100 *l.* to Count Philip I of Namur who did liege homage and swore to aid the bishop against all men save the count of Hainaut. Then in 1209 Philip took in fief from the bishop his castle of Sanson and renounced the fief of 100 *l.* in exchange for another of 50 *m.* In this case the bishop promised to come to the defense of Philip should anyone attack the castle of Sanson, but nevertheless he had acquired a military ally and the addition of a strategic castle.[50] In 1238 Gilles de Rochefort did homage to Count Thomas and Countess Jeanne of Flanders for a fief of 30 *l.* and promised to hold his castle secure for the count and countess against all men save the bishop of Liège and the count of Luxemburg.[51] In 1206 Duke Henry I of Brabant recognized that Count Louis of Looz had taken in fief his castle of Calmont for a fief of 300 *m.* and that Louis had promised to defend it for him.[52] In 1378 Wenceslas, duke of Brabant and Luxemburg, granted a fief of 10 *l.* plus a subsidy of 100 *l.* to Lancelot d'Elz who promised to make his castle accessible whenever necessary.[53] In 1409 Albert de Colditz, an officer in the chamber of King Wenceslas of Germany, became the liege man of Antoine, duke of Brabant, for a fief of 400 florins of Rhine and promised to make his castles available to Antoine.[54] Apparently the English kings seldom granted *fiefs-rentes* to obtain rights to castles; only one instance appears in the records and that devoid of details except that homage was done for a castle.[55]

---

[50] All the transactions described and many more relating to the castle of Sanson are found in Poncelet, *Actes des princes-évêques,* nos. 23, 58, 59; Bormans and Schoolmeesters, *Cart. de l'église Saint-Lambert,* I, nos. 98–101; Walraet, *Actes de Philippe Ier,* nos. 7, 17–18. Cf. Balon, *An. Soc. Arch. Namur,* XL, 11–12.

[51] A.G.R., *Trés. Fl.,* Sér. I, no. 2064.

[52] Van Den Bergh, *Oorkondenboek van Holland,* I, no. 209; Butkens, *Trophées,* Preuves, I, 58; J. Mantelius, *Historiae Lossensis* (Liège, 1717), I, i, 154.

[53] A.G.R., Verkooren, *Inv. Lux.,* no. 1250.

[54] A.G.R., Verkooren, *Inv. Brab.,* unpublished. See also Wampach, *Urkunden,* VII, no. 1084; Van Mieris, *Groot Charterboek,* I, 249, 420; Butkens, *Trophées,* Preuves, I, 85, 86, 128; Bondam, *Charterboek van Gelderland,* I, iii, no. 34; A.G.R., Galesloot, *Cour féodale,* no. 33; Quicke, *B.C.R.H.,* XCIII, nos. 13, 16, 31, pp. 105, 116, 158.

[55] In 1245 Henry III granted a subsidy of 1,000 *l.* to Count Amadeus of Savoy who did homage for the castle of Avyllan and Bard and the towns of

4. THE FIEF-RENTE AND SERVICE IN THE FIELD

The military uses of the *fief-rente* dealt with so far, although by no means negligible, were always subordinate to another—service in the field.[56] One does not derive this conclusion from Sczaniecki for he devotes but relatively few pages to the military service secured by the *fief-rente* in France. Imbued with the conviction that all military service procured by the *fief-rente* was but peripheral to the political and diplomatic, he asserts at one point that "les sources ne nous donnent en général que très peu de renseignements directs concernant le service militaire dû par les concessionnaires des fiefs-rentes." And later, at another point, he contends that "la pénurie des sources" for the large French feudal states, the Low Countries, and Germany restricts one's investigations of the military functions and peculiarities of the *fief-rente* for the most part to England where more abundant records make a detailed study possible.[57] These assertions come as a surprise to one who has examined not only the French but also the German, English, and Low Country evidence. Indeed, there is abundant evidence in all the areas and in none is there a lack of detail on the military obligations of the recipients of *fiefs-rentes*. But justification for contradicting Sczaniecki and proof for the military importance of the *fief-rente* can be obtained only by examining it in relation to the military and feudal changes occurring between the eleventh and fifteenth centuries and

Susa and Saint Maurice in Chablais. In addition to the 1,000 *l*. Amadeus received a heritable fief of 200 *m*. In 1274 Count Philip of Savoy did homage for these castles and towns and continued in receipt of the fief. In 1318 another count of Savoy was still receiving the fief of 200 *m*. "granted to him by the late king [Edward I] for his homage done to him for a certain castle of his in Savoy" (*Pat. R. 1232–47*, p. 469; *C.P.R. 1247–58*, p. 9; *C.L.R. 1245–51*, pp. 20, 40, 115, 168, 227, 308, 379; *C.P.R. 1272–81*, p. 64; *C.Cl.R. 1313–18*, pp. 383, 555). It may be argued that according to English feudal custom the kings had right of entry to the castles of their vassals and thus would not need to grant *fiefs-rentes* to secure this right; this hardly accounts for their not granting *fiefs-rentes* to men of the Continent who were not their vassals. And, moreover, why should the princes of the Continent, many of whom had the right of entry, grant so many *fiefs-rentes* for this purpose?

[56] This statement must be qualified for Germany where, as it has been shown, the military service of castle-guard always predominated.

[57] *Essai*, pp. 34, 56.

by disclosing the tremendous number of records testifying to its military use.

Thanks to the excellent work done by historians of medieval feudal and military institutions, there is no reason to do more than note a few of the basic transformations undergone by such institutions from the eleventh to the fifteenth century.[58] From the eleventh century onward the feudal lords of western Europe began to find the traditional feudal method of supplying military forces inadequate. Less and less were the traditional feudal skirmishes of small bodies of knights the method of combat; ever larger forces were required as wars became more protracted and were fought in more remote areas. More than just the feudal levy was needed for the Norman Conquest, the *reconquista* of Spain, the Crusades, and similar large-scale ventures. To be sure, the lords enfeoffed more and more of their domains to secure additional knights but there was a limit to this process; the domains would be depleted if such

[58] For a discussion in general see C. Oman, *A History of the Art of War in the Middle Ages* (2d ed., London, 1924), vols. I–II; F. Lot, *L'art militaire et les armées au moyen âge* (Paris, 1946), vols. I–II; Delbrück, *Geschichte des Kriegskunst*, vol. III; G. Köhler, *Die Entwicklung des Kriegswesens und der Kriegsführung* (Breslau, 1886), vol. I; E. Daniels, *Geschichte der Kriegswesens* (2d ed., Berlin, 1927), vol. II. For France see Boutaric, *Institutions militaires*, and *La France sous Philippe le Bel*, pp. 366 ff.; E. Audouin, *Essai sur l'armée royale au temps de Philippe-Auguste* (Paris, 1913); A. Vuitry, *Études sur la régime financier de la France* (Paris, 1878), I, 135; E. Berger, *Histoire de Blanche de Castille, reine de France* (Paris, 1895), pp. 299 ff.; E. Fieffé, *Histoire des troupes étrangères au service de la France* (Paris, 1854), I, 6 ff.; H. Géraud, "Les routiers au douzième siècle," and "Mercadier. Les routiers au treizième siècle," *Biblio. de l'École des Chartes*, III (1841–42), 125–47, 417–43. For Germany see H. Conrad, *Geschichte der deutschen Wehrverfassung* (Munich, 1939), vol. I; C. Spannagel, *Zur Geschichte deutschen Heerwesens* (Leipzig, 1885), pp. 71 ff.; J. Mikulla, *Die Söldner in den Heeren Kaiser Friedrichs II.* (Gnesen, 1885); P. Schmitthenner, "Lehnskriegswesen und Söldnertum im Abendlandischen Imperium des Mittelalters," *H.Z.*, CL (1934), 234 ff. For the Low Countries see H. Pirenne, *Histoire de Belgique*, I, 299–301; Smets, *Henri I duc de Brabant*, pp. 239 ff.; Wauters, *Le duc Jean Ier et le Brabant sous le règne de ce prince (1267–1294)* (Bruxelles, 1862), pp. 262, 298–334. For England see the histories and biographies of Norgate and Ramsay; Stenton, *English Feudalism*; Powicke, *Loss of Normandy*, pp. 229 ff.; Morris, *Welsh Wars*; Prince, *English Government at Work*, I, 332–93; J. O. Prestwich, "War and Finance in the Anglo-Norman State," *Trans. Roy. Hist. Soc.*, 5th ser., IV (1954), 19–43.

enfeoffments became too numerous. Fortunately, however, the strain put upon the landed resources of the lord came to be increasingly relieved by the monetary resources put into his hands as a result of the reviving money economy. Thus, wherever the developing money economy filled the coffers of the princes, the feudal levy was augmented by mercenaries. Their role in war from the eleventh to the fifteenth century is so familiar as to make any description of it redundant. Money also made it possible for the lord to pay the knight who fought by virtue of feudal obligation when his service continued beyond the customary forty days. By the late twelfth century some princes, such as the English kings, and by the thirteenth century all princes were not only paying wages for service beyond the forty days but were also paying for the forty days' service. The mode of fighting had become so expensive that it was impossible for the vassal to bear the burden unaided; wages were now essential and, as we shall see later, so too were other forms of remuneration. It is well known that Richard I of England paid wages to the knights fighting in the Norman campaigns and that John, Henry III, and Edward I followed suit. Philip III and Philip IV of France are notable for paying all their vassals wages for military service. A like situation existed in the Low Countries and Germany. Along with these changes occurred that of commuting feudal military service for money (scutage). Found in England as early as the reign of Henry I it was common to all western Europe by the thirteenth century. The princes were only too willing to receive this money and use it to hire mercenaries hardened and skilled by continuous fighting. Such were a few of the changes in the twelfth and thirteenth centuries which were undermining the very *raison d'être* of feudalism and which pointed to a day when it would have no part in the formation of fighting forces.

Probably no institution better than the *fief-rente* epitomizes the transition just described, but in spite of the admittedly limited efforts of such as Brussel, Boutaric, and Delbrück to give it a place in these developments, it has been overlooked by most of the eminent students of military history. Because no one so far has done more than sample the evidence, the *fief-rente* has yet to emerge as a distinct military institution from the massive documentation in which it is buried. Only by careful study of all the pertinent records can we hope to know what actual importance it had in the military developments leading to the disappearance of feudal service. There is no better place to begin than with the records of the French and English kings.

While reconstructing the early chronology of the *fief-rente* it was seen that before 1200 few were granted by the French kings whereas the English kings granted a sizable number, most having as their purpose the acquisition of military assistance.[59] The grant of a fief of 300 *m.* by Duke William the Conqueror of Normandy to Count Baldwin V of Flanders on the eve of the conquest of England stipulated that military assistance should be given; in this case, however, William only secured Baldwin's benevolent neutrality. In the treaties of 1103, 1110, and 1163 concluded between the English kings and Flemish counts, the latter promised in return for their *fiefs-rentes* that if the French kings should invade England or Normandy, they would come to their defense with 1,000 knights; if Maine was invaded, they would help defend it with 500 knights. At the same time that the treaty of 1163 was concluded, Count Thierry and his son approved the agreements made by an unspecified number of their vassals to perform military service for *fiefs-rentes*.[60] When in 1173 Philip of Alsace broke with Henry II to fight in the revolting forces of the Young Henry, he received a fief of 1,000 *l.* The revolt having been suppressed by 1175, Philip again received a *fief-rente* from Henry II in return for military service against Louis VII of France should it be necessary. The counts of Flanders still held this fief when John came to the throne and the Pipe Rolls show that many of their vassals had also come to acquire *fiefs-rentes* for their military service. Meanwhile, as far back as Henry I, the counts of Hainaut had been conceded a fief of 100 *m.* for military purposes. In 1172 when Henry II confirmed this fief he granted fiefs of less value to six vassals of Count Baldwin V for their service. An even more celebrated instance of the value of the *fief-rente* in

---

[59] For the references to the documents cited below see Ch. I, notes 85–86, 90.

[60] "Et pro feodis que predicti barones et castellani habent de rege, sunt homines sui, et debent ei fidelitatem sicut domino." All of them promised to come into Henry's service with varying numbers of knights upon his summons (Delisle, *Actes de Henri II,* I, no. 152; *Foedera,* I, i, 23). For the effectives acquired by the *fiefs-rentes* granted in 1103, 1110, and 1163 see J. Verbruggen, "Le problème des effectifs et de la tactique à la bataille de Bouvines (1214)," *Revue du Nord,* XXXI (1949), 181–93.

securing military allies was in 1194 at Mainz when Richard I thus
secured ten military allies from among the most powerful of the
Rhenish, Low Country, and Italian princes. If, on the other hand,
one looks at the royal records of France he will find that not until
1195 did Philip Augustus grant a *fief-rente* specifically for military
service. He then granted to Richard de Vernone 800 *l.* of Paris "in
feodum et hominagium ligium, per servicium quinque militum." [61]
But the *fief-rente* did not become prominent in the military preparations of the French kings until Philip Augustus and John
fought out their battle between 1199 and 1214.

Following the precedent set by the kings of the twelfth century,
John relied heavily upon the *fief-rente* during his turbulent reign.
It helped him to secure fighters for the defense of Normandy, to
weld the majority of the Rhenish and Low Country princes into a
military alliance against Philip Augustus before Bouvines, and to
fight his own barons in England to a standstill. To the mightiest
princes, to the lowliest knights, indeed to anyone who might prove
useful, John granted *fiefs-rentes*. He faithfully paid the *fief-rente*
of the Flemish counts, both Baldwin IX and Ferrand, and by the
same means secured the military aid of hundreds of other nobles
and knights from the Continent. [62] For example, in 1200 John
granted to Robert, count of Dreux, a fief of 400 *m.* in return for the
service of the count and three additional knights : within fifteen days
after summons the four should be at Verneuil ready to serve for forty
days in any part of France. In 1208 William of Guisnes received a
fief of 30 *l.* on the condition that he and another knight, well
equipped with horses and arms, should serve John. In 1212 Reginald de Dammartin, count of Boulogne, received a fief of 1,000 *l.*

---

[61] *Layettes*, I, no. 441.

[62] Immediately after his coronation John renewed the Flemish alliance
previously contracted between Count Baldwin IX and Richard I (*Foedera*,
I, i, 67 ; *Rot. Chart.*, p. 31 ; Roger of Hoveden, IV, 93–96 ; Dept, *Influences*,
pp.57–88). In 1200 John ordered to be paid "ad opus comitis Flandrie centum marcas quas idem comes habere debet de feudo suo ad scaccarium nostrum" (*Rot. Lib.*, p. 3). In 1201 another writ of *liberate* ordered payment
of the fief, and the Pipe Rolls of the years following indicate payment of the
count's fief (*Rot. Lib.*, pp. 15, 21 ; *P.R. 4 John*, p. 289 ; *P.R. 5 John*, p. 9).
For references to Ferrand's fief see *Foedera*, I, i, 105 ; *C.L.R. 1226–40*, pp.
123, 186, 213 ; *Pat. R. 1225–32*, p. 322 ; *Cl.R. 1227–31*, p. 574 ; Dept, *Influences*, pp. 57 ff.

and was henceforth one of John's most trusted and capable captains. John also recruited men from Poitou, Aquitaine, and Spain.[63]

It was in the Low Countries, however, that John concentrated upon building up a military force against Philip Augustus, particularly after he lost Normandy in 1204 and no longer had a good base of operations in the North. By 1202 Count Philip I of Namur was receiving a fief of 200 m. By 1212, having been lured back into the English service, Duke Walerand of Limburg and Count Theobald of Bar again received their fiefs granted earlier to them by Richard I; their sons, Walerand and Henry, were also awarded *fiefs-rentes*.[64] In a military pact concluded with John in 1213 Count William I of Holland agreed to lead twenty-five knights to England upon John's summons. Should John need more men he was to dispatch a lieutenant to Holland for them, whereupon William would supply a thousand or more men-at-arms. For supplying these fighters William received a fief of 400 m. for which he did liege homage and fealty. At the same time one of William's vassals, Hugh de Fornes, received a fief of 100 m. for which he agreed to lead five knights into John's service for 120 days and, if necessary, to procure up to 1,000 men-at-arms whose wages and expenses would be paid by John. Another knight of Holland, Baldwin de Harlem, received a fief of 10 m. for his personal service.[65] Likewise knights from the Rhine valley, Brabant, and Liège were being recruited, but the *fief-rente* attained its greatest effectiveness in Flanders.[66] Helped

---

[63] *Rot. Chart.*, pp. 58, 186; *Rot. Claus.*, I, 113; *Foedera*, I, i, 77; Malo, *Renaud de Dammartin*, pp. 138, 145–47, 170, 195. Richard, Norman, and Lucas de Hispania held *fiefs-rentes* from John (*Rot. Claus.*, I, 242 b, 269 b, 340, 512, 524, 535, 557 b, 561 b, 591 b, 597). See also Dept, *Influences*, p. 101 for references to Poitou and Aquitaine.

[64] *Foedera*, I, i, 106; *Rot. Claus.*, I, 125 b; *Rot. Mis. (1213)*, pp. 242, 263; *P.R. 2 John*, p. 12.

[65] *Rot. Chart.*, pp. 190 b–191; *Foedera*, I, i, 111–112; *Rot. Mis. (1213)*, p. 257; *Rot. Pat.*, p. 98 b.

[66] In the Mise Roll of 1213 are many payments to knights from all over the Continent. Opposite the marginal notation "Feoda militum de Imperio infeodatorum apud Notingham" appear entries such as the following: "Johanni Creton' militi de Imperio Alemanie de feodo suo ... LX m. ... Renardo de Vendosies militi de Imperio de feodo suo ... XXX m. ... Alelino de Beaveer militi de Imperio de feodo suo ... XV m. ... Walchero sororio Johannis Cretons militis de Imperio de feodo suo ... XV m." (pp. 240–41). The Close Roll of 1213 refers to the passage of knights of Brabant to England: "Inveni

by the fact that the counts held a *fief-rente* and were sympathetic to him, John found Flanders to be his richest recruiting grounds. At various times between 1199 and 1214 it seemed that almost all the important Flemish nobles held *fiefs-rentes*.[67] To be sure, it can rightfully be argued that these men served John's political and diplomatic ends in eventually winning over Flanders to his coalition in 1213, but it is evident from most of the records that John's greatest concern was that of securing their military service. The scrupulousness with which he paid the *fiefs-rentes*, made advances on the installments, granted loans, supplied horses, provided maintenance, and lavished gifts upon these men testifies to the value with which he regarded their services.[68] Needing all the support he could obtain to defend Normandy, John charged William Cresec with recruiting Flemish knights in May 1202 and later empowered Simon d'Havré

passagium Franconio de Arken' cum IIII^{or} militibus de Braibantie sociis suis et XVIII servientibus et Henrico de Bacse cum VIII^{to} militibus de Braibantie sociis suis et VI servientibus et Henrico de Claif' cum I milite de Braibantie socio suo et II servientibus cum hominibus et hernesio suo" (*Rot. Claus.*, I, 139). See also Dept, *Influences*, p. 101.

[67] The following list, though far from complete, is nevertheless long enough to show how well the *fief-rente* had done its work: William Cresec; Simon d'Havré; Gerard de Rodes; William l'Oncle; Baldwin de Comines; Adam Keret, *châtelain* of Bruges; Thomas Keret; Gerard d'Alsace, *prévôt* of Bruges and chancellor of Flanders; Baldwin and Robert de Béthune; Arnold de Landos; Philip and Gilbert d'Aire; Eustace, Walter, Gerard, and Henry de Bailleul; Geldewin de Douai; Rasse de Gavre; Daniel and Walter de Courtrai; William, *châtelain* of Saint-Omer and a *bailli* of Flanders; Arnold d'Audenarde; Gerard and Walter de Sottegem; Alard de Strépy; Renaud de Gand; Esturgeon a knight; John de Gravelines; Wulvin, notary of the count; the *châtelain* of Bourbourg; Robert and Arnold de Wavrin; Walter and Baldwin le Buc; Thomas de Lampernesse; Gilbert de Woumen; Peter de Delettes; the knight Rabon; Thierry de Beveren; Adam and Baldwin de Walincourt; Ghislain, Robert, and Walter de Ghistelles; and Peter de Cresec. Most of these men have been noted by Dept (*Influences*, pp. 54–68, 96–133).

[68] The Close, Mise, and Prest Rolls afford particularly good evidence. The following is a typical entry from the Close Roll of 1212: "Rex W. thesaurario et G. et R. camerariis etc. Liberate de thesauro nostro Willelmo de Sancto Audomaro 100 *l.* de dono nostro de termino Pasche anno regni nostri xiii^{mo} per cartas comitis Bolonie et Hugonis de Boues qui manuceperunt per easdem cartas quod fideliter nobis serviet et deinceps de feodo per annum 60 *m.* Et Simoni fratri comitis Bolonie 100 *m.* de novo feodo etc." (p. 119). Then follow payments to thirty some men for fiefs, *dona*, wages, and other maintenance.

to grant *fiefs-rentes* to all who would come to England.[69] Meanwhile he had enjoined by letters patent all those of Flanders and Hainaut who held fiefs of him to meet him at Rouen for service in the field and threatened to terminate their fiefs if they disobeyed— an action he was indeed forced to take when some of these vassals later joined Philip Augustus.[70] In the last frantic moments before Normandy was lost, John repeatedly called upon these holders of *fiefs-rentes* for military service.[71] After Normandy had fallen to Philip Augustus, some Flemish knights served in Gascony and Poitou; meanwhile, numerous missions to Flanders continued recruiting activities.[72] Although for the next eight years John's influence in Flanders waned, he by no means lost out completely. Many Flemish nobles remained loyal as is testified to by the impressive number who participated in the Irish campaign of 1210.[73] From 1212 to Bouvines, however, John regained the upper hand in Flanders. After Count Ferrand had definitely made his break with Philip Augustus, John's envoys Reginald de Dammartin, Hugh Boves, William Longespée, Adam Keret, and William Cresec, seemed continuously to be on missions in Flanders granting *fiefs-rentes* to recruits; new men were secured and old allies rewon to the English cause. The envoys had full powers to win whatever men they could; any sum of money and any favor was not too high a price.[74] Their efforts were rewarded: the Mise Roll of 1213 refers

---

[69] *Rot. Pat.*, p. 10; *Foedera*, I, i, 41, 86. For *dona* and other payments in recompense of such service see *Rot. Lib.*, pp. 29, 44, 51–52, 71.

[70] *Rot. Pat.*, p. 11 b.

[71] Dept, *Influences*, pp. 64–65.

[72] *Rot. Claus.*, I, 39 b; Dept, *Influences*, p. 64.

[73] Dept lists fourteen Flemish nobles who participated in the expedition and we know there were many more (*Influences*, pp. 108–9).

[74] The following entry is typical: "Rex dilecto sibi Gileberto de Burgell' etc. Sciatis quod quicquid fideles nostri regis comes Bolonie, Hugo de Boves, Adam Keret, Willelmus Cresec vobiscum fecerint de veniendo in servicium nostrum ratum habebimus et stabile et sicut inter ipsos et vos inter convenerit et ipsi nobis per litteras suas patentes mandabit ita faciemus et hoc tenebimus. Et in huius rei testimenta h. l. n. patentes vobis mittimus et per easdem litteras vos in salvum conductum nostrum suscepimus in veniendo ad nos in Angliam ad fidelitatem et homagium nobis faciendum et ibi morando et in revertendo." Then follow the names of twenty-three other knights to be approached (*Rot. Pat.*, p. 93). For Reginald de Dammartin and the activities of the other agents see Dept, *Influences*, pp. 110 ff.; Malo, *Renaud de Dammartin*, pp. 135 ff.

frequently to knights from Flanders and other parts of Europe who had come to England to be enfeoffed with *fiefs-rentes*.[75] When the Battle of Bouvines began, a large element of the Angevin-Guelf force was composed of these knights. From the published records alone, it can be shown that John granted nearly three hundred *fiefs-rentes*. Of them, 88 were granted during his unsuccessful defense of Normandy; 33 between 1205 and 1212, the years of his contest with Innocent III; 115 between 1212 and the Battle of Bouvines, when he was striving to build up a continental coalition against the Capetian-Hohenstaufen alliance; and 58 during the last two years of his life, when he was mainly concerned with the baronial revolt. In other words, we find 33 concessions of *fiefs-rentes* in years of comparative peace, contrasted with 261 in years of war on the Continent and in England. Like a barometer, John's use of the *fief-rente* seems to indicate the intensity of his military efforts.[76]

It is now time to inquire how Philip Augustus competed against the operations of John on the Continent. Certain documents at the outset of the thirteenth century reveal that he had learned the value of the *fief-rente* and granted increasing numbers as his financial resources permitted. An account of royal expenses for 1202–3 lists twenty-seven paid from the royal revenues. A document of 1204 listing the expenses of the *prévôtés* of Normandy includes payment of twenty fiefs. Other *fiefs-rentes* appear in a document of 1204–12 listing the knight service owed by fiefs held of Philip Augustus.[77] As for specific examples, we find that Count Robert of Dreux, who had thrown in his lot with Philip Augustus after the fall of Normandy, received a fief of 500 *l.*; in 1205 Duke Henry I of Brabant, having done homage to Philip against all men save the homage he

---

[75] The Mise Roll of 1213 records eighty knights in receipt of *fiefs-rentes*. The following are typical entries: "Feoda militum Flandrie de novo infeudatorum apud Notingham. Supra feoda 400 *m*." Eight knights were enfeoffed here. A total of 302½ *m*. was granted to five Flemish knights at York, 247½ *m*. to six Flemish knights at Dernington, 100 *l*. to five German knights at Nottingham, and 60 *m*. to two knights at Canterbury (*Rot. Mis.*, pp. 238–40, 262).

[76] These figures were obtained from the Charter, Patent, Close, Norman, Liberate, Mise, English Pipe Rolls; *Foedera*; and the relevant chronicles. See also Verbruggen, *Revue du Nord*, XXXI, 181–93.

[77] Lot and Fawtier, *Premier budget*, pp. 93–94, 121; Delisle, *Cart. normand*, no. 116; *Recueil historiens France*, XXIII, 605–723.

owed to Philip of Suabia, received a fief of 200 m.; and in 1207 Guy d'Auteuil received a fief of 100 l. and henceforth owed the service of one knight.[78] But Philip, like John, granted most of his *fiefs-rentes* to the Flemish nobility; Flanders was the dueling ground of these two contestants. Although after Baldwin IX's departure on the Crusade Philip tried to maintain sway over the Flemish nobles through his influence over the regent of Flanders, Count Philip I of Namur, as well as through his control over Jeanne, the heiress of Flanders, more than this pressure was needed to turn them away from the lure of John's rich treasury; he had to grant them *fiefs-rentes*.[79] The fiefs granted by Philip Augustus were never equal in number to those granted by John, but in 1203 they began to increase in volume as John lost Normandy and continued to lose prestige on the Continent. From 1204 to 1212 the nobles of Flanders, many of whom were won over from John, were the recipients of most of the fiefs granted by Philip. In 1206 Philip empowered Bartholomew de Roye to grant *fiefs-rentes* to men in Flanders. William l'Oncle, for example, received a fief of 30 l.[80] In 1208 thirteen nobles received *fiefs-rentes* and thereafter others joined them.[81] Philip succeeded in holding these men in his camp until 1212 when John again seized the initiative in Flanders and held it until Bouvines. As with John, nothing but the desire of Philip Augustus for military allies in Flanders will satisfactorily explain the upsurge in *fiefs-rentes* from 1203 onward; the grants of John and Philip reflect their feverish drive for military support before Bouvines.

Even in defeat and disgrace John managed to hold on to many men from the Continent. Having broken with his barons in 1214, he called upon men from the Low Countries and southern France to come to his succour. Conspicuous among such men were Thomas and Adam Keret, Robert de Béthune, Baldwin de Haverskerke, Baldwin d'Aire, John and Gerard de Gravelines, and Gerard,

---

[78] Delisle, *Cart. normand*, no. 89; Delisle, *Actes de Philippe-Auguste*, no. 909; Wauters, *Table chronologique*, III, 238; Sczaniecki, *Essai*, p. 35.

[79] For the development of the French influence see the account in Dept, *Influences*, pp. 74–96. See also T. Luykx, *Johanna van Constantinopel* (Antwerpen, 1946), pp. 69–126.

[80] Dept, *Influences*, p. 82.

[81] *Ibid.*, p. 83; Pièces justificatives, no. 3. There were such men as Michel de Hornes, Arnold d'Audenarde, Walter de Sottegem, etc. See also pp. 84–86.

Thierry, and Walter the Younger of Sottegem. They not only went over to England with bands of mercenaries but some, like Gerard and Walter de Sottegem, even assumed important commands; Robert de Béthune, moreover, was a constable in John's army. All continued to receive their *fiefs-rentes* and were granted substantial gifts; some even received land.[82] Only with John's death in 1216 did these men begin to depart from England. The new government of the young Henry III decided against the heavy financial expenditures of John, thereby forfeiting the military support of these men. The last to leave England were Thierry and Gerard de Sottegem and Gerard de Gravelines, who departed in 1218 with their bands of fighters.[83] Meanwhile those Flemish nobles who had remained loyal to Philip Augustus fought for French interests when the future Louis VIII invaded England in 1215. Many led sizable contingents of knights across the Channel to fight their brethren who were in John's army.[84]

The *fief-rente* was as prevalent under Henry III as under his father. It differed only in that it was granted to recipients generally located in southwestern France. The allied fiasco at Bouvines had halted the English kings' employment of the *fief-rente* on a grand scale in the Low Countries and it was toward the end of the century before there was any effort to bring again the nobility of this region within the sphere of English influence. The *fief-rente* now proved its value in the frequent but fruitless Poitevin expeditions of that unmilitary monarch Henry III. The concessions fluctuated with these campaigns, invariably increasing during the years of the first, second, and third attempts to win back the rich lands which the Capetians had steadily won from English hands since Philip Augustus.[85] Henry and his lieutenants constantly resorted to the *fief-rente* to secure the adherence of the unreliable Gascons during the frequent revolts in Gascony. A few of the more notable Gascon

---

[82] Dept, *Influences,* pp. 157–62.

[83] *Ibid.,* pp. 162–65.

[84] *Ibid.,* p. 169.

[85] For a general account of this period see Powicke, *King Henry III and the Lord Edward,* vols. I–II, and *The Thirteenth Century,* pp. 80–128, 644–58; Ramsay, *The Dawn of the Constitution* (London, 1908); N. Denholm-Young, *Richard of Cornwall* (Oxford, 1947); E. C. Lodge, "The Relations between England and Gascony, 1152–1453," *History,* New ser., XIX (1934), 131–39.

lords, as well as others from the regions nearby, who were intermittently in receipt of *fiefs-rentes* from 1216 to the Treaty of Paris in 1259 were William l'Archevêque; Robert de Rancon; Hugh de Lusignan, count of La Marche and Angoulême; Viscount Raymond of Frunzac; Count William of Auvergne; Esquivat de Chabanais; Bozo de Mastac, count of Bigorre; Count Archenbald of Périgord; Viscount Arnald Ottonis of Lomagne; Count Gerard of Armagnac and Fezensac; Gaston de Béarn; Viscount Raymond of Turenne; and Count Bernard of Comminges.[86] These lords and scores of others were prevailed upon to support Henry III in his projects against Louis IX,[87] or at least to remain his faithful allies during times of revolt. If one were to plot upon a map all the *fiefs-rentes* granted by Henry III to men in southwestern France, the area just below Brittany, beginning in Thouars and extending southwest to Provence, would be peppered with *fiefs-rentes.* The same would be true for the area extending due south through Gascony to the Pyrenees. What little success Henry had in fighting his Capetian opponent was due chiefly to these military allies secured by the *fief-rente.*

[86] Archevêque: *Pat. R. 1225–32,* p. 396; *C.L.R. 1226–40,* pp. 124, 158, 172, 187, 211, 236, 430, 473; *C.L.R. 1240–45,* pp. 5, 44, 88, 96. R. de Rancon: *Pat. R. 1225–32,* pp. 147–48; *C.L.R. 1226–40,* pp. 52, 101, 121, 129, 152, 293, 317, 353, 430; *R.G.,* I, nos. 344, 362, 799; *Cl.R. 1242–47,* p. 11. Lusignan: *Pat. R. 1225–32,* p. 436. Thouars: *Pat. R. 1225–32,* pp. 99–100; *Foedera,* I, i, 183. G. de Rancon: *Pat. R. 1225–32,* p. 392; *Cl.R. 1227–31,* p. 423. Berbezille: *Pat. R. 1225–32,* p. 387; *C.L.R. 1226–40,* p. 212. Frunzac: *R.G.,* I, no. 372; *C.P.R. 1247–58,* p. 496; *Cl.R. 1247–51,* p. 5; *C.L.R. 1240–45,* pp. 207, 305. Auvergne: *C.L.R. 1226–40,* pp. 257, 322, 324; *C.L.R. 1240–45,* pp. 31, 42, 87. Chabanais: *R.G.,* I, nos. 221, 342, 895; *C.L.R. 1240–45,* pp. 2, 53, 92, 155, 211, 227. Mastac: *Pat. R. 1232–47,* p. 459; *Foedera,* I, i, 263; *C.L.R. 1240–45,* pp. 2, 47, 73, 76, 108, 269, 300, 321. Périgord: *R.G.,* I, nos. 3769, 4414. Lomagne: *C.P.R. 1247–58,* pp. 67, 297, 346. Armagnac: *R.G.,* I, no. 4063; *C.P.R. 1266–72,* p. 41; *Foedera,* I, i, 307. Béarn: *C.P.R. 1266–72,* pp. 41, 65, 119, 258, 299, 323, 361. Turenne: *C.P.R. 1258–66,* p. 380; *C.P.R. 1266–72,* p. 322; *Foedera,* I, i, 435. Comminges: *R.G.,* I, no. 2466.

[87] For example, in 1226 Philip l'Archevêque and Henry de Argenten were paid their fiefs of 10 *l.* plus wages of 40 *l.* (*Rot. Claus.,* II, 133 b–134). In the same year the knights Nicholas de Boleville and Drogo de Barentin received their fiefs of 10 *l.* for duty "in servicio nostro in Wasconia" (*Ibid.,* p. 129). Elias de Syllak was paid 20 *m.* for his fief in 1242; in 1244 he was granted 30 *m.* for losses sustained by him and his men in the king's service in addition to his fief of 20 *m.* (*C.L.R. 1240–45,* p. 278; *R.G.,* I, no. 353).

Beginning with Philip Augustus and continuing with Louis VIII and Louis IX, the number of *fiefs-rentes* granted by French kings increased rapidly, although never equaling the number granted by Henry III.[88] Louis IX in particular used the *fief-rente* to good advantage in securing allies for his struggle with Henry III in southwestern France, as well as for the other skirmishes which served constantly to expand the borders of the royal domain. One could repeat almost endlessly such concessions as the following. In 1229 the count of Astarac received a fief of 100 *m.* for which he was to supply three knights "in conquesta Albigensi"; when the Agenais was conquered he was to receive 1,000 *l.* of Tours annually for the service of ten knights. In the camp at Ponts-de-Cé in 1230 Louis IX granted a fief of 500 *l.* of Tours to Raymond, viscount of Thouars. In 1231 Gilbert de Malo Buissuno promised the service of three knights for a fief of 600 *l.* of Tours.[89] That there are large clusters of such concessions at the time of the Poitevin campaigns is no accident, but rather an affirmation of the military value of the *fief-rente*.[90] We see also that later in 1248 when Louis IX was preparing for his crusade, he granted a fief of 50 *l.* to the Genoese admiral Hugh Lascari and another of 50 *l.* to the admiral Jacques de Levant. In 1256 Lambert and Simon de Thurey were obliged to serve with six knights for a fief of 1,500 *l.*[91] During the reign of Philip III the scene of action immediately shifts to the Pyrenees where disputes over the succession of Navarre and Castille in 1274 and 1275 and the Aragonese Crusade of 1285 brought the *fief-rente* into play as an essential method for securing the military service of Spanish lords. In 1276, for example, Fernando Ibanez of Castille received a fief of 300 *l.* for which he promised to serve with ten knights plus as many more as Philip III would pay wages to. The same year Juan Nunès promised to serve the king with 300 knights for a fief of 14,000 *l.* of Tours, and Nuno Goncalvetz promised the

---

[88] See, for example, Sczaniecki, *Essai,* pp. 35–36, 59 ; Petit-Dutaillis, *Étude Louis VIII,* no. 444.

[89] Astarac: *Layettes,* II, nos. 1999–2000. Thouars: *Layettes,* II, no. 2055. Malo Buissuno: Sczaniecki, *Essai,* p. 35.

[90] See, for example, *Layettes,* II, nos. 1963, 2035, 2053, 2128, 2135–36.

[91] Sczaniecki, *Essai,* p. 97; Devic and Vaissete, *Histoire de Languedoc,* VII, 973. See also *Layettes,* IV, no. 5325 ; Léchaudé-d'Anisy, *Scaccarium Normannie sub Regibus Francie,* p. 179.

service of 107 knights for a fief of 8,000 *l*. In 1277 Fernando Perez promised a band of sixty knights for a fief of 3,000 *l*.[92]

Because of the almost constant hostilities between Philip IV and Edward I in Gascony and the Low Countries, as well as the expeditions sent into Flanders by Philip IV from 1297 on to force its subjugation, the *fief-rente* became even more prominent in the years around 1300. The nine years of desultory fighting (1294–1303) between Edward and Philip was practically a re-enactment of the events leading up to Bouvines. Edward reverted to the grand strategy of John before Bouvines and vigorously negotiated for military allies in the Low Countries, Germany, and southwestern France in preparation for a two-pronged drive against Philip—one force of foreign allies led by himself to strike in the north from Flanders, and the other consisting of his English barons plus forces from Gascony to attack in the south. In Gascony and the neighboring areas Edward continued to pay the many fiefs granted by his father and proceeded to grant new ones to bolster his forces.[93] Although the fighting was never successful in this theater, hundreds of Gascon nobles remained faithful to Edward. The Gascon, Liberate, and Issue Rolls of 1299, as well as a financial account rendered by two royal officers in Gascony, John de Sandale and Thomas of Cambridge, show that Edward granted *fiefs-rentes* as compensation to over 340 Gascons who had been dispossessed of their lands by Philip because of their loyalty and service to Edward.[94] In the summer of 1294 accredited royal agents traveled from court to court in Germany and the Low Countries in search of military allies. The defensive-offensive alliance concluded in November 1294 between Edward and King Adolf of Nassau induced imperial vassals to join the anti-French coalition.[95] While spending the winter

---

[92] F. F. Michel, *Histoire de la guerre de Navarre en 1276 et 1277* (Paris, 1856), pp. 642–43 ; Langlois, *Philippe le Hardi*, pp. 367–68 ; Sczaniecki, *Essai*, p. 64.

[93] See, for example, *C.P.R. 1272–81*, pp. 108–9, 152 ; *R.G.*, III, nos. 1143, 1232, 1246, 1269, 1296, 1753, 1907, 4614 ; *R.G.*, IV, nos. 1914, 2146, 2151 ; *Foedera*, I, ii, 667, 707. There are more examples in T. Carte, *Catalogue des rolles gascons* (London, 1743), vols. I–II ; Cuttino, *The Gascon Calendar of 1322*.

[94] *R.G.*, III, no. 4528 ff. ; P.R.O., Liberate Roll, C. 62/75, mm. 1, 2, 5 ; Issue Roll, E. 403/103, mm. 4–6 ; Various Accounts, E. 101/157/5, mm. 1–5. See Plates I–II.

[95] *Foedera*, I, ii, 812 ; Bartholomew de Cotton, *Historia Anglicana* (R.S.,

of 1297–98 in Flanders, Edward made lavish donations to a hetero-
geneous group of princes and professional fighters.[96] At Lille,
Edward and Count Guy of Flanders reinforced a previous military
and political *entente* by concluding a new pact for mutual military
assistance. We can be sure that scrupulous payment of the fief of
300 *m.* granted to Guy in 1279 plus payment of huge subsidies
prepared the way for this alliance.[97] In 1295 Walerand, lord of
Montjoie and Fauquemont, was granted a fief of 300 *l.*; and in the
same year another military ally, John, lord of Cuyk, was granted a
fief of 200 *l.* In 1299 a fief of 50 *m.* was granted to John de Bar of
Hainaut.[98] But to comprehend fully the enormous sums paid out in

London, 1865), p. 143. The Wroxham Continuation of *Le livere de reis de
Engletere* states: "This year [1294] the king of England sent envoys to Germany to obtain aid in his war, ... for which cause the king of Germany held
his parliament. ... At which parliament of Dordrecht the following were
present: the king of Germany, archbishop Siegfried of Cologne, the count of
Zealand and Holland, the count of Cleves, the count of Juliers, the duke of
Brabant, the count of Boulogne, the duke of Bavaria, the count of Burgundy,
the count of Savoy, the duke of Austria, the count of Bar, the bishop of
Bamberg(?), the bishop of Lausanne, the count of Vivares, the count of
Salm(?), the knights of Lorraine, the dauphin of Vienne ... who all with
one voice and of free will agreed to go in aid of the king of England" (p.
315). See also Obreen, *Floris V Graaf van Holland*, pp. 146–47; Oppermann, *Holland unter Graf Florens V*, p. 18; *Algemene Geschiedenis der
Nederlanden*, II, 293–97. In an account rendered by Robert de Segre of the
receipts from the wool customs of the staple at Dordrecht for 1294–95 also
appear issues made to many of the men attending the meeting. Large sums
were granted to King Adolf, the archbishop of Cologne, the count of Cleve,
the count of Bar, and others (P.R.O., Various Accounts, E. 101/308/18).
Similar payments were made to the duke of Brabant and John of Cuyk in
1298 at Antwerp (P.R.O., E. 101/619/10).

[96] The Wardrobe Book of 1297 and the Issue and Liberate Rolls have
numerous entries pertaining to such payments (British Museum, Add. MS.
7965, fols. 155ᵛ–156ᵛ, 158ʳ; P.R.O., C. 62/71, mm. 1, 3; C. 62/72, mm. 1;
C. 62/73, mm. 3, 6, 7; C. 62/74, m. 4; E. 403/95, mm. 1–2). See also
Funck-Brentano, *Philippe le Bel en Flandre*, p. 247; De Sturler, *Relations
politiques*, pp. 157–62.

[97] This treaty plus many other agreements concluded between Edward and
Guy are contained in De Limburg-Stirum, *Codex Diplomaticus Flandriae*
(Bruges, 1879), I, nos. 30–38, 45–47. See also *Foedera*, I, ii, 850–51, 862–
63; Rishanger, pp. 378–79; *C.P.R. 1272–81*, pp. 311, 336, 382; *C.Cl.R.
1279–88*, p. 2; "Cal. Dip. Doc.," in *D.K.R.*, XLV, app. ii, 287–89; Palgrave,
Antient Kalendars, I, 147, 150–51. See Appendix, no. 16.

[98] Walerand: *C.P.R. 1292–1301*, p. 134; *Foedera*, I, ii, 820; "Cal. Dip.

the form of fiefs, subsidies, wages, maintenance, and gifts, one must look at the chancery enrollments, the Issue Rolls, and the Wardrobe Account of 1297. The failure of Edward's Low Country campaign cannot be attributed to a lack of financial and military effort but rather to the Scottish campaigns and serious domestic conditions which hindered his continental operations.

The *fiefs-rentes* granted by Philip IV were almost as numerous as those granted by his opponent, and they seemed to pay more satisfactory dividends. Philip managed to hold some of the Low Country states under his influence and to secure from numerous lords military support against both Edward I and Count Guy of Flanders. Like those of Edward, the military preparations of Philip also began in 1294. In that year Philip granted a fief of 500 *l.* to Count Henry VII of Luxemburg who was obliged to provide a contingent of 200 men-at-arms in the war "contre le roi d'Angleterre, ses alies et ses aidans." [99] The same year Humbert, dauphin of Vienne, did liege homage for a fief of 500 *l.* and promised to serve "in guerra contra regem Anglie, eius confederatos et aduitores, quicumque sint" with 200 men well equipped with horses and arms.[100] Hugh of Burgundy promised to fight with sixty men against the king of England for a fief of 300 *l.*[101] Receiving a fief of 2,000 *l.* in 1296 Bouchard, bishop of Metz, promised to fight for Philip against anyone except the emperor.[102] In a long and detailed military treaty of 1296 between Philip and Count Floris V of Holland the latter received a fief of 4,000 *l.* and promised "que nous sommes tenuz de faire guerre a sa requeste a ses anemis aliez au roy d'Engleterre, especiaument a ceus, qui ont receu ses deniers contre le dit roy de France." [103] In 1297 John of Avesnes, count of Hainaut and

Doc.," in *D.K.R.,* XLVIII, app., 573. Cuyk: *C.P.R. 1292–1301,* pp. 134, 232; *Foedera,* I, ii, 820; "Cal. Dip. Doc.," in *D.K.R.,* XLVIII, app., 575. Bar: *C.P.R. 1292–1301,* p. 426. See Appendix, no. 14.

[99] Kern, *Acta Imperii,* no. 90. For an account of the relations between the counts of Luxemburg and Philip IV see E. Welvert, "Philippe le Bel et la maison de Luxembourg," *Biblio. de l'École des Chartes,* XLV (1884), 180–88.

[100] Kern, *Acta Imperii,* no. 307.

[101] Sczaniecki, *Essai,* p. 63. See Appendix, no. 12.

[102] Kern, *Acta Imperii,* no. 114. See also E. Delcambre, "Recueil de documents inédits relatifs aux relations du Hainaut et de la France de 1280 à 1297," *B.C.R.H.,* XCII (1928), no. 43.

[103] Kern, *Acta Imperii,* no. 309; Van Den Bergh, *Oorkondenboek van Holland,* II, nos. 926–27; Van Mieris, *Groot Charterboek,* I, 562–65.

deadly enemy of Count Guy of Flanders, received a fief of 6,000 *l.* from Philip.[104] In a military alliance of 1304 specifically directed against Flanders, Duke John II of Brabant received a fief of 2,500 *l.* from Philip.[105] It is interesting to note that in his struggle with Count Guy of Flanders, Philip secured the adherence of Flemish Leliaerts through *fiefs-rentes.* Thanks to the excellent work done on this period by Funck-Brentano and Verbruggen, it is possible to point to scores of such cases. Verbruggen has compiled a list of forty Leliaerts who received *fiefs-rentes* from Philip between 1298 and 1301, in many cases as compensation for the loss of their Flemish fiefs because of loyalty to Philip.[106] More nobles holding *fiefs-rentes* appear in three lists of Leliaerts; one from the *bailliage* of Cassel, another enumerating those in the service of Philip in 1303, and a third naming the French sympathizers at the time of the Matins of Bruges.[107] If anyone doubts the large part that the shrewd Philip IV assigned to the *fief-rente* in his contests with Edward I and Count Guy, he need only leaf through the pages of the *Registres* edited by Langlois, as well as the *Journaux du trésor,* to be convinced of the groundlessness of his doubts.[108]

Though the records reveal many *fiefs-rentes* granted from Courtrai until Edward III and Philip VI ascended their thrones in 1327–28, the number seems small by comparison with those granted previously or those granted later during the Hundred Years' War.[109] This is not surprising; cursed with weak kings and internal struggle in these twenty-odd years, neither England nor France was engaged in any war of importance. Here again the *fief-rente* reflects the intensity of military activity. By contrast, within the year of Edward III's accession to power his warlike intentions are reflected in the

---

[104] Devillers, *Monuments,* III, nos. 398, 406–7, pp. 552, 560–61.

[105] Kern, *Acta Imperii,* no. 152. See also Jean de Klerk, *Les gestes des ducs de Brabant,* Codex Diplomaticus, I, no. 107. See Appendix, no. 19.

[106] Verbruggen, *De Slag der Gulden Sporen,* pp. 219–20.

[107] *Ibid.,* pp. 220–24. See also Funck-Brentano, *Philippe le Bel en Flandre,* pp. 215–22.

[108] Langlois, *Registres perdus,* nos. 3, 4, 5, 11, 13, 19, 20, 23, 26, 27, 29, 30, 34, 36, 41, 58, 61, 63, 64, 71, 73, 74, 147, 149, 163 ff.; Viard, *Journaux du trésor de Philippe IV,* p. lviii.

[109] For France see Viard, *Journaux du trésor de Charles IV,* p. lxxxi; Fawtier, *Comptes du trésor,* pp. lviii–lxi; P. Lehugeur, *Histoire de Philippe le Long roi de France (1316–1322)* (Paris, 1897).

sharp rise in the number of *fiefs-rentes* granted to men all over western Europe. Applying diplomatic pressure on Germany and the Low Countries at the outset of his reign, Edward constantly increased it and even went in person to the Low Countries and Rhenish Germany in the summer of 1338. After spending the early part of the summer at Antwerp organizing the Low Country princes, he proceeded up the Rhine in August to meet the Emperor Louis of Bavaria and his nobles at Coblenz. There on 5 September in the presence of all the great German princes, the Emperor proclaimed Edward imperial vicar with the assignment of recovering the imperial rights lost to the French kings; all the imperial vassals were bound to support him.[110] Edward spent the days immediately following this impressive ceremony translating the grandiose and rather vague agreement into practical terms, granting *fiefs-rentes*, subsidies, and all sorts of inducements in return for military service. The accounts of the "Nuncii" in the Public Record Office afford good evidence of the tireless efforts of the royal envoys in the Rhine valley and the Low Countries to forge a strong military coalition against Philip VI.[111] The accounts of such foreign merchants as the Bardi and Peruzzi show that on the royal authority they paid out large sums to Low Country and German nobles for their *fiefs-rentes*, subsidies, wages, and other bounties.[112] In the Wardrobe Book of William of Northwell one can observe the role of the wardrobe at Antwerp in 1338 in paying *fiefs-rentes* to the military allies of the Low Countries.[113] In the note below are a few of the more important lords acquired from 1327 to 1340, the year which marks the real end of the Low Country phase of the Hundred Years'

[110] Lucas, *Low Countries,* pp. 284–99; De Lettenhove, *Histoire de Flandre,* p. 297; Pirenne, *Histoire de Belgique,* II, 115–25; *Algemene Geschiedenis der Nederlanden,* III, 42–57; *Geschiedenis van Vlaanderen,* II, 70–79; Van Werveke, *Jacques van Artevelde* (Bruxelles, 1943), pp. 37–67; E. Déprez, *Les préliminaires de la guerre de cent ans* (Paris, 1902), pp. 170 ff.; De Sturler, *Relations politiques,* pp. 322–75; Perroy, *Hundred Years' War,* pp. 95–106.

[111] P.R.O., E. 101/310/1, 8, 19; E. 101/311/4, 9, 14, 18, 29, 32–33. See also De Lettenhove, *Oeuvres de Froissart,* XVIII, 50, 153.

[112] See P.R.O., E. 101/127/32; E. 101/634/28. See also Fryde, *History,* XXXVII (1952), 8–24.

[113] P.R.O., E. 36/203, fols. 328, 332–36, 338, 345, 348, 359–60. See also F. Bock, "An Unknown Register of the Reign of Edward III," *E.H.R.,* XLV (1930), 353–72.

War.[114] It may be argued that this list gives no indication that the recipients performed military service. Let us look, however, at a few of the records pertaining to some of these men. Frequent references to the marquises of Juliers leave no doubt but that their principal obligation was military service. In 1335 Edward paid William 500 *l.* in addition to his fief "pro expensis diversorum hominum ad arma, et aliorum, qui in comitiva ipsius comitis ad nos nuper, in succursum nostrum contra Scotos, hostes nostros, venerunt." Safe conducts were granted to all the men of the marquis who came to defend England against the Scots, and the constable of the Cinque Ports was ordered to provide adequate transportation for the passage of these men.[115] The nature of the *fief-rente* of the dukes of Guelders is clearly defined in an order of Edward III to his treasurer to pay

2,500 florins de Florens, pur les gages du second moys de 1,000 armures de feer, queux il [duke of Guelders] retient en nostre service es parties de France ... 6,000 florins de Florens, pur les gages, de deux moys, de 200 armures de feer, qu'eux il retient in meisme nostre service, outre les 1,000 armures susdites ... 6,666 florins de Florens, et 8 gros des arrerages de son fee de 1,000 *l.* d'esterlings, quel nous lui avons grantez par nos autres lettres patentes, a terme de sa vie, pur son homage fait a nous.[116]

In 1327 John of Hainaut, lord of Beaumont, received payment for all his expenses incurred while coming to the king's aid in the war against the Scots. The next year a writ of *liberate* directed the payment of 7,000 *l.* "in partem solutionis 14,000 *l.*, in quibus eidem Johanni tenemur, pro vadiis suis, et hominum ad arma." [117] In

---

[114] After the name of the grantee is the amount of the fief and the date of concession : John of Hainaut, lord of Beaumont, 1,000 *m.* (1327) ; William, count of Juliers, 600 *l.* (1329) ; Louis of Nevers, count of Flanders, 1,000 *m.* (1330) ; Otto, lord of Cuyk, 250 *l.* (1331) ; Guy II, count of Namur, 400 *m.* (1335) ; Thierry, lord of Montjoie and Fauquemont, 1,200 florins (1337) ; Adolf, count of Marlia, 3,000 florins (1337) ; Henry de Gemenith, 300 florins (1337) ; Everhard of Limburg, 100 florins (1337) ; Reginald, duke of Guelders, 1,000 *l.* (1339) ; John III, duke of Brabant, 1,500 *l.* (1339) ; Robert, count of Varneburg, 1,500 florins (1339). The references to these *fiefs-rentes* were secured from *C.P.R. 1327–30*; *C.Cl.R. 1327–43*; *Foedera*, II, ii, 971–1101.

[115] *Foedera*, II, ii, 922.

[116] *Ibid.*, p. 1108.

[117] *C.P.R. 1327–30*, p. 10; *Foedera*, II, ii, 706, 745. See also pp. 708, 713, 733.

addition to his fief Henry de Gemenith was granted wages for himself and his men-at-arms as long as he served the king.[118] For all the other lords there is similar evidence of military activity.[119]

In the years following 1346 concessions of *fiefs-rentes* begin to decline but until his death in 1377 Edward III continued to grant them for military service. Envoys never ceased recruiting fighters and, as always, the good English money persuaded the knights and lords of the Continent to become vassals of the English king.[120] The excellent pay given by Edward III induced so many knights to seek *fiefs-rentes* from him that frequently he was forced to decline the services of some. Two knights from Germany, John von Rode and Foton von Gustyn, came to England in 1370 for *fiefs-rentes* and enrollment in Edward's retinue for service against the French, but "because it appears to the same lord the king ... that there is sufficient of his own retinue, and of the retinue of other lords, as well English as German, at the present time, the same lord the king granted to the same John and Foton 10 *m.* in aid of their expense to return home." [121]

For reasons chiefly geographical, domestic, and military, the *fief-rente* continued to decline in the remainder of the fourteenth century and eventually disappeared in the fifteenth. The geographical shift in the military operations of the English kings which placed the German and Low Country lords on the perimeter of the main area of military concentration partially explains the drop in concessions. It is common knowledge that the domestic history of

---

[118] *Foedera,* II, ii, 971.

[119] For references to Count Guy II of Namur see *Foedera,* II, ii, 914, 916–17, 920–21 ; E. Niffle-Anciaux, *Guy II comte de Namur* (Bruxelles, 1922), pp. 23–42 ; Balon, *An. Soc. Arch. Namur,* XL, 1–86 ; Prince, *English Government at Work,* I, 347, 354. For Thierry, lord of Montjoie and Fauquemont, see *Foedera,* II, ii, 992.

[120] Tangid de Castro received a fief of 20 *l.* (*C.P.R. 1348–50,* p. 328) ; the knight John de Sore of Hainaut, 300 florins (*C.P.R. 1350–54,* p. 69) ; John, lord of Petersheim, and Thierry de Braunkhorst, fiefs of 50 *m.* (*C.P.R. 1367–70,* p. 293) ; three knights of "Almain"—Gerard and Florence Rolbuk and Henry de Bergynes—, fiefs of 50 *m.* (*C.P.R. 1367–70,* pp. 333, 389, 392) ; John de Claront of Flanders and Diedrich van Hessene of Cleve, fiefs of 25 *m.* (*C.P.R. 1370–74,* p. 69). Galeot de Spinolis of Luchulo received a fief of 300 francs of gold "because he has done homage and fealty to stand with the king in his wars" (*C.P.R. 1370–74,* p. 374).

[121] Devon, *Issue Roll of Thomas de Brantingham,* p. 480.

England from the latter part of Edward III's reign to that of Henry V permitted and warranted no major military undertakings on the Continent; there was consequently less need for the *fief-rente*.[122] When the French wars were resumed on a large scale by Henry V, the military developments of the past one hundred years had rendered the *fief-rente,* in the main, obsolete. Yet despite these forces causing the decline of the *fief-rente,* the important fiefs continued to be paid and even new ones were granted as late as the fifteenth century. For example, the dukes of Guelders and the marquises of Juliers retained their fiefs throughout the reigns of Edward III and Richard II and the early years of Henry IV's reign.[123] In 1352 Edward III had given a fief of 400 florins of Florence to Adolf, count of La Mark; there is intermittent record of this fief until 1439.[124] The new grants were extremely important because usually they were to powerful princes who could provide large contingents of fighters. In 1396 the count palatine of the Rhine and duke of Bavaria, Rupert the Elder, did homage to Richard II for a fief of 1,000 *l.* which the succeeding dukes continued to receive until about the middle of the fifteenth century.[125] That military service was required is evidenced in 1407 when Duke John of Bavaria sent 60

[122] Richard II did, however, recruit knights with *fiefs-rentes.* In 1381, for example, he sent the following letter to Borzewey de Swyner, knight of Germany: "Sciatis quod, de gratia nostra speciali, et pro bono servitio quod, dilectus nobis, Borzewey de Swyner miles, nobis impendit, et impendet in futurum, concessimus eidem Borzewey 500 florenos auri . . . percipiendos singulis annis, ad scaccarium nostrum, ad totam vitam suam . . . faciendo nobis homagium et fidelitatem ex hac causa." Six other German knights received similar letters (*Foedera,* 1704–35, VII, 288).

[123] Guelders: *Foedera* (1704–35), VII, 535, 742; VIII, 66, 191 ;*C.P.R. 1385–89,* p. 310; "Cal. Dip. Doc.," in *D.K.R.,* XLVIII, app., 593. See also Perroy, *The Diplomatic Correspondence of Richard II* (Camden Society, London, 1933), 3d ser., XLVIII. Juliers: *C.P.R. 1345–48,* p. 269; *C.P.R. 1364–67,* pp. 250–51 ; *C.Cl.R. 1364–68,* p. 276 ; "Cal. Dip. Doc.," in *D.K.R.,* XLVIII, app., 587, 594–95. See also Hingeston, *Royal and Other Historical Letters of Henry IV,* I, 1–2, 33 ; Lacomblet, *Urkundenbuch,* III, no. 1063.

[124] *C.P.R. 1350–54,* p. 344; *C.P.R. 1377–81,* p. 147; *Foedera,* III, i, 249; III, ii, 773; *Foedera* (1704–35), X, 700, 745; P.R.O., E. 30/1415; E. 30/1375.

[125] *C.P.R. 1396–99,* pp. 25, 247; *Foedera* (1704–35), IX, 715; X, 95, 126, 310, 379, 633–34, 658; XI, 70; "Cal. Dip. Doc.," in *D.K.R.,* XLIX, app., 44–45; P.R.O., E. 30/1088, 1328, 428 A, 1246 (1–2), 1247, 1372, 1411, 1417.

men-at-arms and 500 archers to England for service with Henry IV.[126] The archbishop of Cologne concluded an alliance with Richard II and received a fief of 1,000 *l.* for which he did homage and fealty and agreed to serve Richard with "numero armigerorum, comitum, baronum, militum, et aliorum militarium ac clientum . . . non tamen ultra numerum 500 lanceatorum." [127] Nowhere is the nature of the *fief-rente* more clearly presented than in a royal letter of instructions (1421) directing three envoys to visit various German princes and procure 500 spears for service in France. Following are the instructions pertaining to Louis, duke of Bavaria, and Diedrich, archbishop of Cologne, who were among the German princes to be approached:

They shall profer duc Lodewic, and also the archbishop of Coloigne (which be vassalls and feed men of the king's) to have thaire fees, over thaire wages, accustumed payed for 2 ycre . . . and if they wol in noe wise assent, they shul trete with hem, profring hem a raisunable some, and encresying, fro some to some, to they come to 2,000 nobles . . . and thus accorded upon the wages, the king wol that the ambassiatours appoint with the said lords for 500 speres . . . to be with the king the first day of May, or atte ferthest within a sevennyght after, and to abide and continue in his service for 5 months suying (30 days accounted for the month) and to be paid for 6 months; the sixth month . . . allowed . . . for comyng to the king, and retournyng home ayein into thair countree.[128]

In 1438 Henry, bishop of Münster, commissioned Ysbrand de Merwyck and John Dowler to seek an alliance with the king and to do homage and receive an "annuity" from him on behalf of the bishop.[129] As a result of the negotiations, the bishop promised in the following year to do homage to Henry VI and to serve him with 100 men for a fief of 400 nobles.[130] Meanwhile dozens of lesser lords

---

[126] *Foedera* (1704–35), VIII, 497.

[127] *Foedera* (1704–35), VIII, 2–3; IX, 346, 359; X, 626; "Cal. Dip. Doc.," in *D.K.R.*, XLV, app. i, 322; "Cal. French Rolls, Henry VI," in *D.K.R.*, XLVIII, app., 343; P.R.O., E. 30/1421; Lacomblet, *Urkundenbuch*, III, no. 1063. In 1440 Diedrich, archbishop of Cologne, received a fief of 600 m. from Henry VI (*Foedera*, 1704–35, X, 834–40).

[128] *Foedera* (1704–35), X, 161–63.

[129] *Foedera* (1704–35), X, 698. Similar instructions were given to Merwyck and Dowler by Gerard of Cleve, count of La Mark (*Foedera*, 1704–35, X, 698).

[130] P.R.O., E. 30/1337; *Foedera* (1704–35), X, 698–700, 741–45.

and knights were granted *fiefs-rentes* for their military service.[131] The last reference to a *fief-rente* granted by the English kings is in 1444; it concerns payment of the arrears for three years to the duke of Bavaria for his fief.[132]

If at any time the French kings surpassed the English in the number of *fiefs-rentes* granted, it was during the Hundred Years' War. Liberal with their money, Philip VI, John the Good, Charles V, and Charles VI granted hundreds of *fiefs-rentes* to lords, both French and foreign, who came into the French service with their bands of men. Two documents drawn up during the early phases of the Hundred Years' War enable us to estimate roughly how many *fiefs-rentes* were granted by Philip VI and John for military service. The first, dating from 1354 or 1355, enumerates all the men who held fiefs from 1337 to 1354 and frequently includes such details as the number of men to be supplied and the wages to be received. This record is headed by the rubric "Ce sont les noms des plusieurs nobles du royaume et dehors qui du comencement de ces presentes guerres sont entre en la foy et hommage du roy." Of the men listed, at least 127, or about 95 per cent, were in receipt of *fiefs-rentes*.[133] The second document drawn up about four years later and headed with a rubric almost identical to that quoted above gives a list of 135 lords within France and beyond its borders who had received *fiefs-rentes* from Philip VI and John to fight against Edward III.[134]

But to be more specific it should be pointed out that many eminent Low Country and German princes were in receipt of *fiefs-rentes* at one time or another during the war. The counts of Hainaut, in receipt of a *fief-rente* since 1297, held their fief with certain interruptions at least until 1435.[135] Having broken with Edward III, John of Hainaut, lord of Beaumont, came to receive a fief of 3,000 *l.* from Philip VI in 1346. He promised to defend the realm of France with one hundred fighters or more, as well as to defend his own

---

[131] Richard II, for example, granted *fiefs-rentes* to such Low Country and German lords as John de Looz, lord of Heinsberg and Lowenberg; Wynand de Holizheim; Thapin Knebil; John de Hutzhoren; John Kamerer de Dalburg; Frederick de Mitra; and Frederick, count of Mor and lord of Bar (*Foedera*, 1704-35, VII, 809; VIII, 4-5, 21-24). See Appendix, no. 30.

[132] "Cal. Dip. Doc.," in *D.K.R.*, XLV, app. i, 327; P.R.O., E. 30/480-82.

[133] A.N., J. 621/90. See Plate IV.

[134] Brussel, *Nouvel examen*, I, 45-52.

[135] See Ch. III, pp. 140-41.

strategic castles and fortresses.[136] The dukes of Brabant had held a
fief-rente since 1304. In 1332, however, a new military alliance was
concluded between Philip VI and John III and his son whereby
John promised the service of 200 men-at-arms against all men save
the king of Germany in return for a fief of 2,000 *l.* Philip confiscated
this fief later when John entered the English service and became a
vassal of Edward III for a *fief-rente.*[137] But at a conference held
at Saint-Quentin in 1347 between Philip VI and John III and his
son Henry, Philip granted Henry a fief of 5,000 *l.* for his good service. In 1364 Duke Wenceslas received a fief of 6,000 gold francs
from Charles V and promised "porter foy, loiaute et service aus
despens de nostre dit seigneur quant requis en serons contre toute
personne excepte contre nostre treschier seigneur et frere l'empereur
de Romme."[138] The counts of Juliers seemed able to keep both the
English and French kings satisfied by their promises of military
support, although the former seemed to receive more benefits from
their money than the latter. In any event, in 1328 Count William
of Juliers received a fief of 600 *l.* from Philip VI of France and
promised his support against all men save the king of Germany and
the duke of Brabant.[139] Down to 1401 the counts received a *fief-
rente* for which they sporadically rendered military service.[140] In
1347 Philip VI granted Count William I of Namur a fief of 1,000 *l.*
"pour consideration des bons et loyauls services que nostre tres chier
et feal cousin, Guillaume, conte de Namur, nous a fais, ou temps
passé en noz guerres, et esperons que il face de bien en mieux, ou
temps a venir." This fief obliged William to defend France against

---

[136] Devillers, *Cart. de Hainaut,* I, nos. 153–54, 170, 186; De Lettenhove,
Oeuvres de Froissart, XVIII, 274–82; Zeper, *Jan van Henegouwen,* pp. 273–
303; Bijlage II, nos. 272, 280 ff.

[137] Jean de Klerk, *Les gestes des ducs de Brabant,* Codex Diplomaticus, I,
156; A.N., J. 524/31¹; Verkooren, *Inv. Brab.,* no. 347. See Appendix, no. 23.

[138] A.N., J. 524/36. An account for the years 1373 to 1380 rendered by a
certain John de Reng to Countess Jeanne and Count Wenceslas notes all the
payments received from certain revenues of the king of France (A.G.R., *C.C.,*
no. 46926). See also Laurent, "Les conventions de Saint-Quentin (juin
1347). Contribution à l'histoire de la première phase de la Guerre de Cent
Ans dans le Pays-Bas," *B.C.R.H.,* XCI (1927), 89–180.

[139] Lacomblet, *Urkundenbuch,* III, no. 239.

[140] A.N., J. 522/6, 7, 8bis, 10ter, 11, 11bis, 11ter, 13, 14, 14bis, 16, 18, 18bis,
19, 26, 27; Lacomblet, *Urkundenbuch,* III, nos. 830, 929, 932.

all the enemies of the king.[141] Beginning in 1304 the bishops of
Liège had been concluding agreements of one form or another to
supply the French kings with military forces.[142] In 1320 the bishop
Adolf de la Mark received a fief of 1,000 *l.* from Philip V and
"recognoit estre tenu et obligie de obeir a nous de venir a nostre
mandement et de estre avec nous pour la defense de nostre royaume
en armes toutes fois que il en sera requis contre toutes manieres de
gens quex que il soient."[143] Military subsidy treaties were concluded
later, and then in 1354 the bishop Engelbert de la Mark received
a fief of 2,000 *l.* and promised to serve loyally against all the enemies
of John the Good; in 1368 the bishops still held this fief under obligation of military service.[144]

Helped by his intimate knowledge of the documents in the *Archives Nationales,* Viard compiled two lists of forty-nine lords who
received *fiefs-rentes* for their military service between 1337 and
1347.[145] Viard's lists, however, are not exhaustive; my investigations
in the *Archives Nationales* disclosed scores of additional such fiefs
granted almost to the end of the fourteenth century. In fact, not
until the reign of Charles VII do such concessions become rare.
Like their English contemporaries, the French kings granted *fiefs-
rentes* to the lowliest of knights; grant after grant are to knights

---

[141] In 1373 Charles V authorized William of Namur, eldest son of Count
William I, to do homage for this fief (Bovesse, *B.C.R.H.,* XIV (1949), nos.
18, 20; A.N., J. 531/9, 9bis, 15, 15bis; Piot, *Inv. Namur,* nos. 1035–36. See
Appendix, no. 26). In 1355 John the Good granted Louis of Namur a fief
of 1,000 *l.* on condition that Louis would serve in all John's wars. In 1368
Charles V granted a fief of 800 *l.* to Robert of Namur, lord of Beaufort, for
his military service (A.N., J. 531/13, 14).

[142] In 1304, for example, the bishop of Liège concluded a military alliance
with Philip IV and promised to supply 200 men-at-arms for three months at
the royal wages (A.N., J. 527/4).

[143] A.N., J. 527/7, 7bis, 11. See Appendix, no. 21.

[144] A.N., J. 527/7, 15, 17, 18; De Lettenhove, *Oeuvres de Froissart,*
XVIII, 42. Some of the lesser lords holding *fiefs-rentes* for military obligations were the counts of La Mark, the dukes of Berg, and the counts of Cleve
(Lacomblet, *Urkundenbuch,* III, nos. 825, 851, 1006; IV, no. 8). In 1337
the bishop of Metz received a fief of 1,400 *l.* for military service (A.N., J.
527/14). In 1382 Charles VI granted Guy de La Trémoille a fief of 300 *l.*
because of his service on the *chevauchée* into Flanders (De La Trémoille,
Guy de La Trémoille, nos. 12, 19–20, 22, 25).

[145] Viard, *Revue des Questions Historiques,* LIX, 352–55, 368–70, 375,
386–88.

from all over France, the Low Countries, and Germany for their personal service.[146] There are many other references to *fiefs-rentes* granted for military service in the financial records of Philip VI.[147] In 1337, for example, Philip granted a fief of 200 *l.* to Walerand, count of Deux-Ponts; Walerand promised the service of twenty men-at-arms and squires. Under the "Redditus ad Vitam" of the *Ordinarium Thesauri* of 1338 and 1339 one finds the entry: "Waleranus comes Duorum Pontium miles ... 106 *l.* 13 *s.* 4 *d.* p. XXIIª Junii."[148] One can similarly crosscheck dozens of other grants and find that the *fiefs-rentes* were paid as well as wages and other expenses and that the recipients performed their military obligations.

In France lords other than the kings granted *fiefs-rentes* for securing military service. Those granting the most were the counts of Champagne and Alphonse of Poitiers. The counts of Champagne began the practice at least as early as the latter part of the twelfth century and continued it until Champagne was absorbed by the Capetians in the late thirteenth century. To cite but one example, a concession of 1200 states that Hugh, count of Vaudémont, became the liege man of Count Theobald III for a fief of 60 *l.* and promised to serve the count against all men except his lord the count of Bar le Duc.[149] The concessions of Alphonse of Poitiers, though less numerous, were like those of the counts of Champagne.[150] The less powerful lords such as the counts of Chartres and Pontieu, and the lords of Bourbon, granted only a few such fiefs.[151] While

---

[146] For example, in 1340 Philip VI granted a fief of 100 *l.* to the knight Godfrey de Vienne who promised his service in all wars (A.N., J. 620/30). In 1355 the knight Lambert du Pe of Liège received a fief of 120 *écus* of gold and promised "servir bien et lealment le dit roy de France monseigneur encontre le roy d'Angleterre" (A.N., J. 626/111).

[147] See, for example, nos. 1342 ff. and 4188 ff. in Viard, *Journaux du trésor de Philippe VI*; Fawtier, *Comptes du trésor,* nos. 1384–1528.

[148] A.N., J. 624/21; Viard, *Journaux du trésor de Philippe VI,* no. 5354. See also nos. 5295, 5298, 5301, 5355, 5356, 5362, 5368, 5371, 5374, 5376, 5379, 5389, 5933, 5936.

[149] Chantereau le Febvre, *Traité des fiefs,* Preuves, p. 17. See also pp. 32, 61, 102, 106, 108, 111, 115, 142, 193; Brussel, *Nouvel examen,* I, 44; Layettes, II, no. 2044; III, no. 4585.

[150] In 1247, for example, Alphonse granted amounts of 100 *l.* and 100 *m.* in fief to William Maingot, lord of Surgères, who promised to serve him against all other men (*Layettes,* III, no. 3592). See also II, nos. 2986, 3471; III, nos. 4086, 4109.

[151] *Layettes,* I, no. 1357; Brunel, *Actes de Pontieu,* no. 180; M. Fazy,

engaged in the Albigensian Crusade, Simon de Montfort granted some *fiefs-rentes* for military service. In 1213 he conceded to Adam Cheverel a fief of 500 *l.* under the obligation of providing the service of two knights; in 1218 he granted a fief of 100 *l.* to Bertrand de Gourdon with the obligation of military service.[152] Though other French lords can be found granting *fiefs-rentes*, the evidence indicates that beyond the kings and such powerful lords as the counts of Champagne few had the financial ability or the military need to grant many; the lesser lords usually belonged to that body of men receiving *fiefs-rentes* from the French kings and other great princes.

The most celebrated vassals obtained by the *fiefs-rentes* of the French and English kings were the princes of the Low Countries. Unlike the French lords, however, they were primarily grantors of *fiefs-rentes* and but secondarily recipients. Each ruled over a miniature feudal state, in some instances but a small reproduction of the French state. They could be almost as independent in their actions as the French and English kings; that their vassalage was more theoretical than real is particularly evident in the case of those princes who owed homage to the emperors. Basically the Low Country princes had the same political and military problems and objectives as did their more powerful brethren. When one adds to this political complexion the economic richness of the Low Countries and the dearth of land, it is easy to understand why all the princes secured military service by means of the *fief-rente*. The evidence is concentrated most heavily in Flanders, Brabant, Namur, and Hainaut, but there is some even for such states as Guelders, Holland, Liège, and Luxemburg. The first ruler of Flanders to grant large numbers of *fiefs-rentes* for military purposes was Count Guy. In 1263 William, count of Juliers, promised to serve and aid Guy against all men save certain named lords in return for a fief of 200 *l.*[153] Such grants steadily increase and, with a sharp crescendo after 1285, become most numerous in the years 1290 to 1302. This rise can be explained only by the tension between Guy and Philip IV which broke out into war in 1297.[154] Standing practically alone against the strongest

---

Catalogue des actes concernant l'histoire du Bourbonnais (Moulins, 1924), no. 808.

[152] Molinier, *Biblio. de l'École des Chartes*, XXXIV, nos. 74, 154; Sczaniecki, *Essai*, p. 35.

[153] A.D.N., B. 497/1352.

[154] See Funck-Brentano, *Philippe le Bel en Flandre*; Nowé, *La bataille des*

military power of western Europe, Guy worked tirelessly at increasing his forces in the period before he was imprisoned by Philip. He granted *fiefs-rentes* not only to men in the area about Flanders but also to German lords and to men of Namur and Luxemburg where, by virtue of his position as marquis of Namur, he wielded much influence. Thus in 1289 Guy granted Gerard, lord of Blankenheim, and his heirs a fief of 40 *l*. Gerard became Guy's man and promised to aid and serve him against all men save the archbishop of Cologne, the duke of Bavaria, the duke of Lorraine, the count of Luxemburg, and the lord of Fauquemont. He agreed to come with his men to the aid of the count and to serve at the count's wages.[155] The *fief-rente* granted to John, lord of Cuyk, in 1293 obligated him to serve Guy against all men except the duke of Brabant, the count of Cleve, and the count of Holland. In 1296 Guy granted John, lord of Harecourt, and his heirs a fief of 300 *l*. and stipulated that because "li dit sire de Harecourt et ses hoirs sont plus lontains de nous que nos autres hommes qui demeurent en nostre contee de Flandres" he would pay them "pour aucun service faite a nous ou a nos hoirs soit de ost ou de chevauchee." In 1296 Walter, lord of Waës, did homage to Guy for a fief of 60 *l*.; he promised to aid Guy and his successors at all times and in all places against all lords except certain named ones.[156] In 1297 Guy granted to William, lord of Hornes, a fief of 100 *l*. and a subsidy of 2,000 *l*. William promised

a servir bien et loialment mi trentisme de boine gent darmes encontre le roi de France et encontre le conte de Haynau toutes les werres durans que il a encontre eaus par ensi ke li chevalier ki avoec mi seront, naront cascuns li chienc chevaus, et cascuns escuiers, trois chevaus. Et de tant nous doit li cuens de Flandres devantdis paiier nos frais raisonnaubles, alans et venans, et demorans avoec lui.[157]

éperons d'or; Pirenne, *Histoire de Belgique,* I, 376–435; *Geschiedenis van Vlaanderen,* II, 39–62; *Algemene Geschiedenis der Nederlanden,* II, 315–37.
  [155] De Saint-Genois, *Monuments,* II, 772–73.
  [156] De Reiffenberg, *Monuments,* I, no. 23, p. 116; A.E.G., De Saint Genois, *Inv. Fl.,* no. 804; De Saint-Genois, *Monuments,* II, 850; Wampach, *Urkunden,* VI, no. 626; Wolters, *Codex Diplomaticus Lossensis,* no. 316. See Appendix, nos. 13, 15.
  [157] A.D.N., B. 498/3919. See Appendix, nos. 17–18. A few of the other men recruited in these years were Walerand, lord of Montjoie and Fauquemont; Henry, lord of Berlaimont; John de Hovedines; Henry, lord of Ligny;

Grants continued to be made in the fourteenth century, but as the century wore on they tapered off and finally disappeared during the Burgundian régime in the fifteenth century.[158]

After Count Guy of Flanders acquired Namur in 1263, the *fief-rente* became prominent in that tiny and relatively backward state. In the eighteenth century De Marne in his *Histoire de Namur* called attention to the great number of *fiefs de bourse* granted by the counts of Namur to obtain military service. He listed twenty-two nobles rendering military service for *fiefs-rentes*.[159] Similar information is found a few years later in C. Galliot's history and, in the nineteenth century, J. Borgnet repeated almost verbatim what De Marne and Galliot had said.[160] More recently, J. Balon in an excellent article on the military organization of fourteenth-century Namur has made a study of the pertinent records and has come to the same conclusions as his predecessors. He has particularly emphasized a treaty concluded between the count of Namur and the duke of Brabant at Maastricht in 1357 wherein sixty men are shown to be holding *fiefs-rentes* from the count and are to fight with him for the duke.[161] My own work with the printed and unprinted records completely substantiates what Balon has so admirably shown. There are many examples of *fiefs-rentes* granted for military service in the collection of documents edited by De Reiffen-

---

Henry, lord of Blamont; Nicolas "dit Famellens dou Hues"; Reginald Zenart de Lando de Plaisance; and Gerard de Juliers, lord of Castre (De Reiffenberg, *Monuments*, I, no. 36, p. 47; no. 37, p. 47; no. 38, p. 50; no. 39, p. 51; no. 49, p. 67; Gaillard, *B.C.R.H.*, VI, 1854, 418, no. 696; A.D.N., B. 1412/3739; B. 4064/145.557). Names of other men who performed military service for *fiefs-rentes* appear in a document of the late thirteenth century recording the knights serving Guy in his wars and receiving his wages (A.D.N., B. 1266/234).

[158] For example, in 1332 Guy of Flanders, lord of Riquebourch, received a fief of 500 *l.*; he promised to serve Count Louis de Nevers against all men "en tous lieus a la guerre et au tournoy" (A.D.N., B. 499/6521, 7597; B. 4060/145.474; A.E.G., De Saint Genois, *Inv. Fl.*, no. 1699).

[159] De Marne, *Histoire de Namur*, pp. 305–6.

[160] C. Galliot, *Histoire générale ecclésiastique et civile de la ville et province de Namur* (Liège, 1788), I, 353–55; Borgnet, *Histoire du comté de Namur*, pp. 104–5.

[161] Balon, *An. Soc. Arch. Namur*, XL, 33–35. From the *Chartrier de Namur* Balon has compiled a list of thirty-three men holding *fiefs-rentes* for military service (pp. 35–36).

berg as well as those edited by Brouwers and Wampach.[162] We shall
cite here but a few of the unpublished texts. In 1315 Count John I
granted a fief of 60 *l.* to the knight Sohier de Courtrai "pour le bon
service kil nous a fait. ... Et promi ce doit li diz messire Soyhiers
servir a nous et a nous hoirs devant touz autres a le were, au tournoy,
et en tous faiz darmez." In 1356 Tilman de Verenne and his son
Louis received a *fief-rente* from Count William I; their military
obligations could be no more clearly stated than in the clause that
follows :

Nous en bonne foy et loyaulment avons enconvent et prometons
a nostre dit treschier signeur le conte de Namur que toute la dite
guerre durant nous li serons aidans et confortanz et le servirons
en tous fais darmes encontre le dit duc de Lucembourc pour son
droit et raison aidier a deframier parmi che que il nous doit jeter
et delivrer de tous frais que pour li et a cause de la dite guerre nous
averiens, et en tel estat et maniere que nous avienrons aveuc
nouz wyt compaingnons darmes bons, souffissament et bien montes,
le quel serviront en la dite guerre.[163]

In Brabant a noticeable rise in the number of *fiefs-rentes* granted
for military service is evident in the late thirteenth century and
comes to a climax in the fourteenth. As late as the first quarter of
the fifteenth century one can still find a considerable number of
men recognizing their obligation to render military service to Duke
Antoine of Brabant or to the dukes of Burgundy because of *fiefs-
rentes* held from these princes. As in Flanders, the *fief-rente* vanished
during the remainder of this century. But turning to a few examples,
we find Thierry of Heinsberg receiving in 1281 a fief of 100 *l.* from
Duke John I of Brabant and promising to serve him as faithfully
as the other vassals of the duke between the Meuse and Rhine. In
1317 Otto van Bueren received from Duke John III a fief of 50 *l.* of
of black money of Tours; he promised to serve John "sesse weken
op sijns selfs kost met vyftigh mannen t'ors als den Hertoge ge-
lieven sal."[164] We would probably not go too far astray to connect

---

[162] See, for example, Brouwers, *Chart. et règ.*, II, nos. 363, 365, 396;
Wampach, *Urkunden*, IV, nos. 541–42; V, nos. 13, 240, 293, 323, 348, 354ª,
480, 494; VI, nos. 597ª, 626, 899.
[163] A.E.N., Piot, *Inv. Namur*, nos. 416, 804. See also nos. 460, 699, 724,
802–3, 819; A.G.R., *Manuscrits divers*, no. 15, Cartulaire de Notre-Dame.
See Appendix, no. 27.
[164] Butkens, *Trophées*, Preuves, I, 114, 150. See also p. 96.

the fief of 1,500 *l.* received by John III from Edward III of England
in 1339, as well as the subsidies, with the military agreements concluded by John with his men for service against Philip VI of France.
Fifty-eight agreements were concluded in 1338 and twenty-six in
1339 whereby for a sum of money each party agreed to supply John
with so many armed men to fight in the forces of Edward III.[165]
Most of the *fiefs-rentes* granted by the dukes of Brabant were to
men in the Pays d'Outre-Meuse; this can surely be explained by
the expansionist tendencies of the dukes of Brabant and, later, of the
dukes of Burgundy in this direction. No doubt political and diplomatic ends were envisaged when granting these *fiefs-rentes,* but the
documents collected by Quicke and Laurent give us enough information about some of the recipients to show that the paramount concern was military service. In 1368 Count Louis de Male of Flanders
had granted Edmond van Engelsdorf, lord of Wildenburg, a fief
of 55 *écus* on the toll of Malines for his military service against all
the enemies of Louis. In 1379 John, lord of Wildenburg, promised
to serve Louis de Male against all men for a fief of 40 francs; in
1386 this agreement was renewed with Philip the Bold, duke of
Burgundy. In 1394 Josset de Halle, *argentier* of the duke of Burgundy, ordered the officers of the *chambre des comptes* at Lille to
determine the status of the *fiefs-rentes* owed to the vassals of the
duke in this area. Many of these fiefs were in arrears. Such was the
case with that of Arnold de Hoemen; Reginald of Fauquemont;
John de Looz, lord of Daalembroek; and William of Juliers, duke
of Berg and count of Ravensberg. In the years 1394–96 nearly all
of them had renounced their fiefs and were in open revolt against

---

[165] For the *fief-rente* and subsidies, see Jean de Klerk, *Les gestes des ducs
de Brabant,* Codex Diplomaticus, I, no. 174; *Foedera,* II, ii, 749, 799, 928,
974, 981, 985, 989, 1103, 1244. For the contracts concluded by John III, see
Wauters, "La formation d'une armée brabançonne du temps du duc Jean III,
de 1338 à 1339," *B.C.R.H.,* I (1891), 192–205. The following is a typical
example: In 1338 the knight Henry de Gronsveld received from John III
18 *l.* and promised to come to the duke "cum dictis IIII[or] armigeris detentis
armatis et equitatis . . . fideliter iuvare contra omnes adversarios eius presenti
guerra iam mota inter reges Anglie ex parte una et Francie ex altera durata-
tur" (A.G.R., Verkooren, *Inv. Brab.,* no. 494). For the second half of the
fourteenth century on almost every page of Verkooren's inventory for Brabant
there is a grant of, or a receipt for, a *fief-rente.* For the years 1360 through
1365 there are 233 such entries.

the duke of Burgundy.[166] For the fifteenth century there are similar examples. In 1402 Duke Philip the Bold of Burgundy granted to Conrad, lord of Schleiden, a fief of 100 francs for his military support. In 1405 Duke Antoine of Brabant conceded to Jacques de Bourbon for the years 1406 to 1409 a sum of 4,000 florins to pay for a fief of 200 *moutons* yearly and for the military expenses incurred by Jacques. In 1411 Antoine augmented the fief of Frambach van Birgel, marshal of Juliers, with another of 100 florins to reward him for supplying the military service of men-at-arms against the duke of Orléans.[167]

The records of Hainaut, particularly abundant for the fourteenth century, serve to emphasize what the documents of Flanders, Namur, and Brabant have so well shown. The *fiefs-rentes* granted in 1307 and 1308 to Renier de Grimaldi, admiral-general of the king of France, and to Enguerrand de Marigny, respectively, were recompense for the military services rendered in the campaigns of Count William I against Flanders. Especially notable was the service of Renier at the naval battle of Zierikzee in 1304.[168] In 1366 Albert of Bavaria, count of Hainaut, granted to the count of Eu for his loyal service a fief of 1,000 *l.* in liege homage. The count of Eu promised to serve Albert at all times against all men save the king of France. In 1410 William of Bavaria, count of Hainaut, granted a fief of 150 *l.* to Gerard de Boussu for his service in the rebellion of the Liègeois.[169] Evidence could be cited for the other states of the

---

[166] Quicke and Laurent, *B.C.R.H.*, XCVII, nos. 1, 4, 6, 9–12, 15, 18, 20, 24, 28–29, 43. For an account of the policies of the dukes of Brabant and Burgundy in the Pays d'Outre-Meuse, see Quicke, *Les Pays-Bas à la veille de l'unification bourguignonne (1356–1384)* (Bruxelles, 1947); Laurent and Quicke, *L'accession de la maison de Bourgogne aux duchés de Brabant et de Limbourg (1383–1407)* (Bruxelles, 1939).

[167] A.G.R., Verkooren, *Inv. Brab.*, unpublished, 11 November 1402; 1405; 1411. See also Galesloot, *Cour féodale*, no. 33.

[168] Gachet, *B.C.R.H.*, IV (1852), 78, 80–81.

[169] Devillers, *Cart. de Hainaut*, II, no. 474; III, no. 995. See also Didier, *Revue du Nord*, XVIII, 271. Didier indicates that political considerations motivated numerous grants of *fiefs-rentes* to German lords by Count William I of Hainaut in the years 1332 to 1336. Undoubtedly military objectives played even a larger role because it was during this period that William, along with the count of Juliers, was one of the principal agents of Edward III of England working to build up a continental military force against Philip VI of France.

Low Countries but the references in the note below should indicate the ease with which cases can be found in the standard collections of documents for Holland, Guelders, Luxemburg, Liège, and some of the minor principalities.[170]

In Germany the *fief-rente* had not the importance for securing military service in the field as it did in the rest of western Europe. It was used primarily, as we have seen, to secure castle-guard. But in spite of the German preference to use it in this way, there are a number of cases where *fiefs-rentes* secured service in the field; indeed such cases are more numerous than those aimed at securing political and diplomatic objectives. Of the *fiefs-rentes* granted for military service, however, only a few issued from the German sovereigns. In 1258 Alphonse of Castille, recently elected king of the Romans, granted to Count Guy of Flanders a fief of 500 *m.* plus a sum of 4,000 *m.* on condition that Guy aid him with military service to secure the crown of Germany.[171] In October 1311 the emperor Henry VII promised to pay before 13 February 1312 the sum of 11,315 florins of gold and 8 *gros tournois* to the heirs of Guy of Flanders "tam pro stipendiis, restauris equorum, expensis aliis in nostro servitio ab eo et sua comitiva factis, quam etiam pro quingentis libris Hallensium hereditarie sibi debitis annuatim." Guy of Flanders was one of the most celebrated and trusted knights accompanying the emperor Henry on his expedition into Italy (1310–1313). He served as marshal of the imperial army and, as such, had an important part in the conduct of the military operations. Eight days before this document made known Henry's debt to Guy, this young prince of Namur had died at Pavia, no doubt as a result of the pestilence he had contracted at the siege of Brescia.[172] In 1313 Henry granted to the knight Thomas de Sept-Fontaines a fief of

---

[170] For example, see Van Den Bergh, *Oorkondenboek van Holland,* I, nos. 232–33, 241, and II, nos. 926–27; Van Mieris, *Groot Charterboek,* III, 50–51, 515, 576; Nijhoff, *Gedenkwaardigheden van Gelderland,* Verzameling van Oorkonden, I, nos. 262, 337; Sloet, *Oorkondenboek van Gelre en Zutfen,* nos. 505, 1140; Wampach, *Urkunden,* I, no. 550; II, nos. 1, 42–43, 408; VI, nos. 554, 676; VII, nos. 1050, 1453. The military service provided by the lords of Cuyk to Low Country princes as well as to the kings of England and France can be found in the *Oorkonden* of J.-J. F. Wap, *Geschiedenis van het Land en der Heeren van Cuyk* (Utrecht, 1858).

[171] Warnkönig, *Histoire de la Flandre,* Pièces justificatives, I, no. 24.

[172] Bovesse, *B.C.R.H.,* XIV, no. 21 and pp. 326–28.

200 florins of gold with the stipulation that Thomas serve him with twenty knights every year for three months.[173]

Some of the powerful princes granted far more fiefs for military service than did the emperors. For example, in 1299 Wicbold, archbishop of Cologne, granted Walerand, lord of Montjoie and Fauquemont, a fief of 200 m. because of his faithful service rendered at the battle of Woeringen. Such grants by the archbishops continued to the third quarter of the fourteenth century.[174] In 1247 Adolf, count of Berg, granted to Gerhard, lord of Wildenburg, a fief of 125 m. on condition that military service be rendered against the count of Spanheim.[175] Though other such grants emanated from the lords, none equal in number the *fiefs-rentes* granted to secure military

---

[173] Wampach, *Urkunden*, VII, no. 1433; Wauters, *Table chronologique*, VIII, 524.

[174] Lacomblet, *Urkundenbuch*, II, no. 1034. In 1291 Everhard von Isenburg received a fief of 6 m. for his service at the battle of Woeringen (Lacomblet, *Urkundenbuch*, II, no. 909). In 1300 the archbishop of Cologne augmented the *fief-rente* of Gerard, lord of Blankenheim, by 300 m. In turn Gerard promised military aid "pro ecclesie et terre sue defensione et alibi extra terram suam, ubicunque necesse habuerit, seu contra quoscunque" (*Ibid.*, III, no. 4). The grant by Archbishop Engelbert III in 1366 to Gather von Hönstein well expresses the military nature of the *fief-rente*: "Uniuersis presentia visuris ego Gatherus de Hoenstein armiger . . . quod quia . . . archiepiscopus Coloniensis michi ratione feodi octo marcas in theolonio suo Lynssensi annuatim soluendas deputauit, recognosco me omnibus et singulis impetitionibus, quas feodi detenti, seu ex quacunque alia occasione siue causa, a toto tempore preterito usque in diem presentem, contra prefatum dominum archiepiscopum seu ecclesiam Coloniensem habui seu habere potui, pure et simpliciter renuntiasse; et nichilominus promisi et promitto bona fide prefato domino archiepiscopo et ecclesie Coloniensi, continue in armis et equis assistere et seruire contra Ropertum comitem de Nassauwe, Philippum de Isenburch, . . . ac cuiuslibet ipsorum adiutores presentes et futuros; necnon per totam guerram, quam ecclesiam Coloniensem fortassis habere contigerit contra opidanos Andernacenses" (*Ibid.*, III, no. 667). See also III, no. 836.

[175] Lacomblet, *Urkundenbuch*, II, no. 315; Goerz, *Mittelrheinische Regesten*, III, no. 551. Having received a *fief-rente* from the archbishop of Mainz in 1252 Bertold, count of Ziegenhain, stated: "Nos ei promisimus, et promittimus fide data et prestito corporali sacramento, quod sibi et ecclesie Moguntine contra ipsorum quoslibet invasores, specialiter marchionem Misnensem et relictam ducis Brabantie, nos et heredes nostri perpetuo fideliter serviemus totis nostris viribus" (Gudenus, *Codex Diplomaticus*, I, 622-24). In 1348 the count and countess of Mark granted Frederick, lord of Bar, a fief of 100 s. "want ons her Vriderich here van Bare heft gelaift tho helpen teghen heren Janne van Cleue" (Lacomblet, *Urkundenbuch*, III, no. 452).

protection by the town of Cologne and other towns of the Rhenish area. Except for details relating to the amount of the fief, the number of men to be supplied, and the duration of the military service, these grants follow a like pattern. On 11 June 1263 Duke Walerand of Limburg, declaring that he had become a citizen of Cologne, promised to protect the citizens of Cologne in his domains and, when necessary, to come to the defense of Cologne with nine knights and fifteen squires; for this he received a fief of 100 m. Nineteen days later Diedrich, count of Catsenellenbogen, received a fief of 40 m. from Cologne for providing the service of the same number of knights and squires. In 1286 Walerand, lord of Montjoie and Fauquemont, declared that he had made a perpetual alliance with the town of Cologne and had promised to come to the defense of the town at the request of the magistrates with ten knights and fifteen squires; Walerand was granted a fief of 100 m. In 1310 Duke John II of Brabant promised to protect the bourgeois of Aix-la-Chapelle in the lands lying between the Meuse and the Rhine. They granted him a fief of 300 l. for this protection.[176] One gets some idea of the number and chronology of such grants when it is known that for Cologne seventeen original concessions, regrants, or confirmations were made in the thirteenth century, and thirty-one in the fourteenth.[177] By totaling up the bands of fighters supplied by the various lords, such as fifty men in this band, thirty-five in another, and so on, it can be seen that in time of need the town of Cologne could call upon a considerable military force for its defense.

5. THE RELATION OF THE FIEF-RENTE TO WAGES, SUBSIDIES, AND MILITARY OBLIGATIONS

It was a fundamental principle of feudalism that the ordinary fief granted by lord to vassal imposed upon the vassal military service, ordinarily that of supplying at his expense knights to serve in the

[176] Ennen and Eckertz, Quellen Stadt Köln, II, nos. 456, 457; III, 265; Wauters, Table chronologique, VIII, 390. Reginald, lord of Montjoie and Fauquemont, held a fief of 300 m. from Aix-la-Chapelle in 1317 (Mummenhoff, Regesten Aachen, II, no. 223).

[177] These grants are published in the Quellen Stadt Köln of Ennen and Eckertz and in the Urkundenbuch of Lacomblet.

field for forty days. Service beyond the forty days was generally paid for and, as we have seen, gradually all feudal service came to be remunerated. From Sczaniecki's discussion of this problem and its relation to the *fief-rente* it is evident that this new fief offered many contrasts to the classic pattern of feudal military service. First, Sczaniecki wholly destroys the misconception held by some scholars that the *fief-rente* was the pay of mercenaries. Such had been the conclusion of Dodu in his work on the institutions of the Latin Kingdom of Jerusalem; regarding the *fief-rente* as an instrument for recruiting and paying fighters, he had labeled it the *fief de soudée*.[178] But even prior to Sczaniecki, La Monte and Cahen had challenged the thesis of Dodu. They had satisfactorily shown that the *fief de soudée*, like the ordinary fief, obliged the vassal to perform military service and that it was not the pay given to mercenaries, who held no fief whatsoever but fought for non-feudal wages.[179] Heartily approving these conclusions, Sczaniecki proceeded to show that they were also valid for France. He found it impossible to equate the *fief-rente* with the pay for military service because he could find no case where the *fief-rente* was commensurate with the amount of pay a mercenary would receive for a year's service and because he could find no instance of a person holding a *fief-rente* and not receiving in addition wages and other remuneration for military service. Noting the standard wages paid for military service by the French kings in the thirteenth and fourteenth centuries, totaling the wages of a man receiving pay for a year's service, and then comparing this total with *fiefs-rentes* granted in the same centuries, Sczaniecki clearly exposed the fallacy of considering the *fief-rente* military pay. In every case the monetary value of the *fief-rente* was far below that of a year's wages.[180]

Sczaniecki's conclusions are equally valid for Germany, the Low Countries, and England. We have already seen in the military evidence reviewed for these areas that from the earliest times the recipients of *fiefs-rentes* were paid wages for their service and were granted other remuneration and maintenance. In the treaty of 1103 concluded between Henry I of England and Count Robert II

---

[178] *Essai*, pp. 48–58; Dodu, *Institutions de Jérusalem*, pp. 182–217.

[179] La Monte, *Feudal Monarchy*, pp. 139–63; Cahen, *Syrie du Nord*, pp. 528–29.

[180] *Essai*, pp. 51–58.

of Flanders much more than a *fief-rente* was involved. Within forty days after Henry's summons for military assistance Robert was to have assembled at Flemish ports 1,000 *milites* for service in England or Normandy; 500 knights for Maine. Henry's ships were to pick them up at Gravelines or Witsand, transport them to England, and, after the campaign, take them back to Flanders. Shipping space was computed on the assumption that every knight would have three horses. As long as Robert and his men served Henry, they were to be completely maintained and to be remunerated for all losses suffered to their horses and equipment. For service in Normandy, Robert was to maintain his men for the first eight days; thereafter Henry was to maintain them and make good their losses. Should Robert and his men serve in Maine, Henry promised to begin their maintenance at the moment they passed into Normandy on their march to Maine and to continue doing so for a month or longer if the campaign so required. The treaties of 1110 and 1163 contained basically the same provisions.[181] The Mise, Prest, Liberate, Patent, Charter, and Close Rolls show that all the knights in possession of *fiefs-rentes* from John received wages, remuneration for armor damaged and horses lost in combat, and *dona* for their miscellaneous expenses in the royal service. The accompanying table drawn up from these records contains a few of the knights who received wages and remuneration in addition to their *fiefs-rentes.* Similar evidence for the reign of Henry III is found in the Gascon Rolls;[182] for the reign of Edward I and later, in the chancery and exchequer enrollments as well as in the Exchequer Accounts and Wardrobe Books.[183]

[181] Vercauteren, *Actes de Flandre,* nos. 30, 41; Delisle, *Actes de Henri II,* I, no. 152.

[182] Amalvin de Bares who held a fief of 50*l.* received payment in 1254 of 10*l.* 10*s.* "pro arreragiis stipendiorum," 50*l.* "de feodo suo," and 45*m.* "pro tribus equis amissis in servicio" (*R.G.,* I, no. 2435). Gerald de Burgo, brother of the viscount of Frunzac, held a fief of 30*m.* for which he received payment in 1246 plus 112*s.* for arrears of wages for service in Gascony (*R.G.,* I, no. 372; *C.L.R. 1245–51,* p. 62). The knight Peter Braunche who held a fief of 20*l.* received 16*l.* 14*s.* for wages in 1250 while in service in Gascony with two other knights (*R.G.,* I, no. 259; *C.L.R. 1245–51,* p. 273).

[183] P.R.O., Liberate Rolls, C. 62/70, m. 3; C. 62/72, m. 1; C. 62/73, mm. 3, 6; C. 62/74, m. 4; C. 62/75, mm. 1–2, 5; Dip. Doc. Exch., E. 30/46, 1508; Wardrobe Books, E. 36/203, fols. 98^{v}–109^{r}, 125^{r}–130^{v}, 328^{r}–360^{r}; Issue Rolls, E. 403/94, m. 2; E. 403/105, mm. 3–6; Warrants for Issues, E.

Some of the wages and remuneration granted by King John

Knight	Fief	Wages		Prests on Wages	Dona	Remuneration for Horses and Armor
Adam Keret	40 *l.*	4 *l.*	16 *s.*			40 *m.*
Thomas Keret	60 *s.*	4 *l.*	16 *s.*	6 *l.* 10 *s.*		20 *m.*
Lamkin de Rollecourt	10 *s.*		24 *s.*	2 *m.*		5 *l.*
Bernard Bailleul	20 *m.*	10 *m.*		4 *m.*	4 *m.*	
William Roillard	25 *l.*			3 *m.*	3 *m.*	
Robert Waverans	15 *l.*	4 *l.*	16 *s.*	1 *m.*		30 *m.*
William de Saint-Omer	8 *m.*	11 *l.*	4 *s.*	10 *l.*	50 *l.*	
William Cresec	40 *l.*			4 *m.*	10 *m.*	
Henry Bailleul	40 *l.*	30 *l.*			100 *m.*	37 1/2 *m.*
Roger de Clifford	60 *m.*			4 *m.*	4 *m.*	
Daniel Betencourt	15 *m.*		72 *s.*			37 *m.*
John Creton	60 *m.*	6 *l.*			15 *m.*	100 *m.*
William Staples	10 *m.*	11 *l.*	4 *s.*		3 *m.*	
Walter Bailleul	35 *l.*			4 *m.*	20 *m.*	200 *m.*
Simon Creton	20 *m.*	6 *l.*			5 *m.*	2 *m.*

In Germany all the *fiefs-rentes* granted by Cologne stipulated that wages and other expenses would be paid for war service. Such a stipulation would invariably appear either in the concession of the *fief-rente* or in a subsidiary military alliance. In 1263, for example, when Duke Walerand of Limburg promised the service of twenty-four men for a fief of 100 *m.* it was stipulated that the "helpin" should be "up iere kost." A later military treaty of the same year further elaborated on the remuneration to be received by Walerand for his military service.[184] The same situation existed in the Low Countries; evidence of payment for military service always appears either in the concessions of *fiefs-rentes* or in other agreements made in connection with them. A good example is a document recording all the wages paid to men fighting for Duke Wenceslas and Duchess Jeanne of Brabant in 1356–57. First there is the rubric "Computationes diversorum stipendiariorum et de aliis diversis debitis, in quibus dux et ducissa et patria Brabantie tenetur, ortos

404/3/20 ; Wardrobe Debentures, E. 404/502/139–45 ; Various Accounts, E. 101/152/14, 157/5, 68/2/45, 68/3/43, 325/2.
[184] Ennen and Eckertz, *Quellen Stadt Köln*, II, nos. 450, 456. See also nos. 449, 451–54, 457, 481 ; III, nos. 265, 418, 424 ff.

ex gwerra inter Brabantiam et Flandriam ..." Then appear such entries as the following: "Debet dux domino Willelmo Quade et domino Karolo de Moriaes per unam litteram 1,486 scilde out. Item eidem per aliam literam supra diversos socios suos 622 scut. vet. Item eisdem per aliam literam supra diversos socios suos de perditione equorum 238 scilde out." William Quade and others appearing in this document held *fiefs-rentes*.[185]

To supplement what Sczaniecki has said about the impossibility of equating a *fief-rente* with a year's pay, certain English evidence can be cited. In the twelfth century whenever military service was bought, knights received 8 *d*. per day; in the early thirteenth century, 2 *s*. per day.[186] Under Edward I in cases where pay was given, the normal wages were 4 *s*. per day for a banneret and 2 *s*. for a knight.[187] In the Hundred Years' War earls were paid 13 *s*. 4 *d*. per day; bannerets, 8 *s*.; knights, 4 *s*.; men-at-arms, 2 *s*.; and mounted archers, 6 *d*.[188] To be considered payment for military service, the *fief-rente* would have to equal the sum of the wages a knight would receive for one year of continuous service. If the Flemish fiefs of 400 *m*. for 500 knights and 400 *m*. for 1,000 knights, granted in 1110 and 1163, are considered pay for the service of these knights, the results are absurd. In the first case the total pay for each knight for one year would be four-fifths of a mark; in the second case, two-fifths of a mark. Actually the total wages of a

---

[185] A.G.R., *C.C.*, nos. 50344–50345, fol. 81ʳ. See also fols. 82ʳ–121ᵛ; Verkooren, *Inv. Brab.*, no. 2043. In 1289, for a fief of 40 *l.*, Gerard, lord of Blankenheim, promised to fight for Count Guy of Flanders. Gerard was to maintain his men only upon the day of departure for service; henceforth Guy was to pay all the wages and military expenses (De Saint-Genois, *Monuments*, II, 773).

[186] Painter, *Feudal Barony*, pp. 33, 40, 172; S. K. Mitchell, *Studies in Taxation under John and Henry III* (New Haven, 1914), p. 309. During the campaigns of Richard and John in Normandy, knights received 6 *s*. of Anjou per day; an *ingeniator* and *balistarius*, 4 *s*. of Anjou; mounted men-at-arms, 2 *s*. 6 *d*. of Anjou; and unmounted men-at-arms, 8 *d*. to 1 *s*. of Anjou (Powicke, *Loss of Normandy*, p. 300).

[187] Morris, *Welsh Wars*, p. 49. See the *Liber Quotidianus* (Society of Antiquaries, London, 1787) for detailed information on the wages of bannerets, knights, men-at-arms, crossbowmen, and other troops.

[188] Prince, "The Strength of English Armies in the Reign of Edward III," *E.H.R.*, XLVI (1931), 364; Ramsay, "Accounts, Edward III–Richard III," *Antiquary*, vols. I, IV, VI, VIII, X, XIV, XVI, XVIII (1880–88). For paid military service throughout western Europe, see Lot, *L'art militaire*, I, 395 ff.

knight serving at 8 *d.* per day for a year would be 12 *l.* 3 *s.* 4 *d.* ; if only for forty days, 1 *l.* 6 *s.* 8 *d.* In the fourteenth century Reginald, duke of Guelders, had a fief of 1,000 *l.* In 1340 he supplied Edward III with 1,200 men-at-arms.[189] If wages were paid for their continuous service for a year, the sum total would be 43,800 *l.* These men, however, served for only two months, but still the wages for this period would be 7,200 *l.* Similar calculations can be made for Germany and the Low Countries.[190] In all western Europe, we may conclude, the *fief-rente* simply obliged the holder to perform military service in person or to supply fighters; in each case the service in the field was paid for at the current rate of wages. The *fief-rente* was never the payment for military service.

Another problem discussed by Sczaniecki was the relation of the *fief-rente* to the "treaty of payment" (*Soldvertrag, traité de solde*) whereby a feudal lord or mercenary captain would contract to supply a designated number of fighters for a stipulated time at a certain wage. Of the numerous methods for drawing up such a contract, in the three most common the contract simply provided for the daily wages of the captain and his men, it provided for wages plus a lump sum subsidy, or it provided for wages plus a non-feudal *rente* or pension. In all the contracts, provision was made for maintenance plus losses of war.[191] Such contracts, being completely non-feudal, obviously have no relation to the *fief-rente.* But from the thirteenth into the fifteenth century agreements were commonly struck involving both the *fief-rente* and the non-feudal contract just noted. We have seen that, whether expressly stated or not, all men holding *fiefs-rentes* received wages for their service, and throughout

---

[189] *Foedera,* II, ii, 1108.

[190] For example, in 1294 when Philip IV of France granted a fief of 500 *l.* *tournois* to Count Henry VII of Luxemburg, it was agreed that the 200 men to be supplied by Henry for military service were to be paid at the rate of 20 *s.* *tournois* per day for a banneret, 10 *s.* *tournois* per day for a knight, and 5 *s.* *tournois* per day for a squire (Kern, *Acta Imperii,* nos. 90, 92). Assuming that the 200 men were equally divided between knights and squires and that they served for forty days, their total wages would be 3,000 *l.* *tournois.* For wages paid by the French kings see Berger, *Histoire de Blanche de Castille,* pp. 299 ff. ; Audouin, *L'armée royale de Philippe-Auguste,* pp. 51 ff., Viard, *Revue des Questions Historiques,* LIX, 377 ff. ; Chénon, *Histoire générale du droit français,* I, 734, 889.

[191] *Essai,* pp. 58–71. See also Delbrück, *Geschichte der Kriegskunst,* III, 327–29 ; Clason, *Pensionsverhältnisse,* pp. 21 ff.

this study we have referred to many cases where a *fief-rente* plus a lump sum subsidy or a *fief-rente* plus a subsidy and wages was granted.[192] Almost all the *fiefs-rentes* granted by the English and French kings from the last quarter of the thirteenth century and into the fifteenth were accompanied by a subsidy and promise of war wages and maintenance.[193] So also were those granted by princes such as the counts of Flanders and dukes of Brabant, as well as other Low Country and German lords.[194] In all these agreements, however, the feudal and non-feudal elements should be sharply differentiated. The *fief-rente* constituted the feudal obligation to perform military service whereas the subsidies, wages, and maintenance constituted payment for the service.

[192] See Ch. II, p. 75.

[193] In 1337 Thierry, lord of Montjoie and Fauquemont, received a fief of 1,200 gold florins and a subsidy of 6,000 florins from Edward III (*Foedera*, II, ii, 992). Duke John III of Brabant held a fief of 1,500 *l.* from Edward III and received in addition subsidies of 10,000 *l.*, 60,000 *l.*, and 100,000 florins (*Foedera*, II, ii, 749, 799, 928, 974, 981, 985, 989, 1103, 1244). In 1294 Philip IV of France granted a fief of 500 *l.* plus a subsidy of 6,000 *l.* to Count Henry VII of Luxemburg (Kern, *Acta Imperii*, nos. 90, 92). In 1296 Philip IV granted a fief of 4,000 *l.* and a subsidy of 25,000 *l.* to Count Floris V of Holland (Kern, *Acta Imperii*, no. 309). In 1337 Philip VI granted a fief of 100 *l.* and a subsidy of 500 *royaux d'or* to John de Quatremars of Cologne (A.N., J. 624/20).

[194] In 1293 Count Guy of Flanders granted a fief of 120 *l.* to John, lord of Cuyk. In addition John received a subsidy and promised to fight for Guy against all men save certain named lords (De Reiffenberg, *Monuments*, I, no. 23, p. 116; De Saint-Genois, *Monuments*, II, 822). In 1296 Count Guy of Flanders granted a fief of 100 *l.* and a subsidy of 2,000 *l.* to William, lord of Hornes, for the service of thirty men against the king of France (De Saint-Genois, *Monuments*, II, 860–61). In the same year Henry, lord of Berlaimont, received a fief of 100 *l.* plus a subsidy of 1,000 *l.*; John de Hovedines, a fief of 100 *l.* plus a subsidy of 2,000 *l.*; Henry, lord of Ligny, a fief of 200 *l.* plus a subsidy of 2,000 *l.* (De Reiffenberg, *Monuments*, I, nos. 37–39, pp. 47–52). In 1292 Count John I of Hainaut granted a fief of 50 *l.* and a subsidy of 1,000 *l.* to Gerard, count of Juliers (Sczaniecki, *Essai*, p. 60). In 1402 Duke Philip the Bold of Burgundy granted a fief of 100 francs and a subsidy of 2,000 francs to Conrad, lord of Schleiden, who promised military service to the duke (A.G.R., Verkooren, *Inv. Brab.*, unpublished, 11 November 1402). When Alphonse of Castille, contender for the Empire, granted a fief of 500 *m.* in 1258 to Count Guy of Flanders for military service, he also gave Guy a subsidy of 4,000 *m.* (Warnkönig, *Histoire de Flandre*, Pièces justificatives, I, no. 24). For examples of wages, subsidies, and remuneration for war losses see Appendix, nos. 12–14, 17, 21, 23–24, 26–27.

But was there a relation between the value of the *fief-rente* and the amount of military service to be supplied? In certain instances such a relation can be established. It is clearly seen in an agreement accompanying the feudal treaty of 1163 between Henry II of England and Count Thierry of Flanders, whereby certain vassals of the count made formal recognition of their *fiefs-rentes* held from Henry; they swore fealty to him and promised to serve him as their lord. The *recognitio* states:

He who is to have 30 *m.* of silver for his fief shall come with ten knights to the king upon his summons just as the count of Flanders ought to come ... and just as he who has 30 *m.* for his fief shall come with ten knights into the service of the king, thus others should come ... with more or less knights, according as they have a greater or smaller number of marks for their fief.[195]

According to these terms the Flemish vassals were obliged to provide one knight for a fief of 3 *m.*; for each additional 3 *m.* they owed another knight. Although not as definite as in the Flemish agreement, a similar relation is also seen in a comparison of the following cases. For a *fief-rente* of 100 *m.* Hugh de Fornes of Holland owed to John the service of five knights for 120 days and, if necessary, the service of up to 1,000 men-at-arms at John's wages and maintenance. Baldwin de Harlem of Holland owed only his personal service for a fief of 10 *m.*[196] The military obligation of Hugh, being much greater than that of Baldwin, consequently merited a more valuable fief. Certain ratios can be seen in some of the French royal grants. For example, Philip III granted fiefs of 300 *l.* for the service of 10 knights or more if needed; 3,000 *l.* for 60 knights; 8,000 *l.* for 107 knights; and 14,000 *l.* for 300 knights. Philip IV granted fiefs of 500 *l.* for 200 men-at-arms and 300 *l.* for 60 men.[197] Beyond these very rough ratios, however, it is difficult to go, either in France, the Low Countries, or Germany.

Most of the records show no relation between the value of the *fief-rente* and the military obligation. Why should a knight like Hugh de Fornes, with military obligations almost equal to those of

[195] Delisle, *Actes de Henri II,* I, no. 152.
[196] *Rot. Pat.,* p. 98 b; *Rot. Mis.,* p. 257.
[197] Michel, *Histoire de la guerre de Navarre,* pp. 642–43; Langlois, *Philippe le Hardi,* pp. 367–68; Sczaniecki, *Essai,* pp. 63–64; Kern, *Acta Imperii,* nos. 90, 92, 307.

Count William I of Holland and the counts of Flanders, receive a *fief-rente* so much smaller than theirs? For that matter, why should the fief of Hugh de Fornes be smaller than that of Robert, count of Dreux, who owed to John only the service of himself and three knights? There is certainly no pattern or uniformity in the following grants made by Philip VI in the years between 1337 and 1347. Nicolas de Seaumes received a fief of 200 *l.* for supplying twenty men-at-arms for one year; Walerand, count of Deux-Ponts, a fief of 500 *l.* for twenty men-at-arms and squires for a year; Peter de Broutelles, a fief of 100 *l.* for the service of himself and three squires for a month; Geoffrey, count of Linanges, a fief of 200 *l.* for twenty men for a year; Henry, count of Vaudémont, a fief of 300 *l.* for thirty men-at-arms; Gerard de Stonehone from Aix-la-Chapelle, a fief of 100 *l.* for his personal service; Robert de Marigny, a fief of 300 *l.* for fifty men-at-arms for two months; and Theobald de Sorboy, a fief of 100 *l.* for fifteen men-at-arms.[198] The *fiefs-rentes* paid by the dukes of Brabant in the fourteenth century present the same discrepancies. For example, in 1365 one encounters the following fluctuation in fiefs paid to men for their personal service. Gilbert van Schimper was paid a fief of 12 *l. petits tournois*; Jacques de Fraipont, 20 *l. noirs tournois*; Arnold van Wachtendonk, 25 *royaux d'or*; Gilles de Berg, 12 *royaux*; Harper van Alsdorp, 20 *m.*; Regnier van Binsfeld, 10 florins; Werner van Rimburg, 30 *royaux*.[199] Many times a man was simply obliged to serve with an indefinite number of knights or men-at-arms, obliged to serve with as many as he could

---

[198] Viard, *Revue des Questions Historiques*, LIX, 352–55, 386–88.

[199] A.G.R., Verkooren, *Inv. Brab.*, nos. 1653–2890. In the grants made, for example, by the town of Cologne it is impossible to arrive at a relation between the value of the fief and the amount of service supplied. In 1263 Count William of Juliers received a fief of 100 *m.* for providing the service of nine knights and fifteen men-at-arms. In 1263 Werner von Rode received a fief of 20 *m.* for the service of himself with the provision that should he bring other knights with him their wages would be paid. In 1263 Count Diedrich of Catsenellenbogen received a fief of 40 *m.* for the service of nine knights and fifteen men-at-arms. In 1293 John, lord of Reifferscheid, received a fief of 15 *m.* for the service of two knights and eight squires. In 1296 Gerhard of Juliers, lord of Kaster, received a fief of 60 *m.* for the service of ten knights and fifteen squires. In 1306 Godfrey, lord of Heinsberg and Blankenheim, received a fief of 50 *m.* for the service of five knights and ten squires (Ennen and Eckertz, *Quellen Stadt Köln*, II, nos. 449, 452, 457; III, nos. 387, 424, 532).

provide, or obliged to serve with as many as were needed. Here again it is impossible to establish a relation between the value of the *fief-rente* and the service required. Because there was customarily no relation between the ordinary fief and the military obligation imposed, it is not unnatural to find the same situation existing with the *fief-rente*.[200]

The evidence suggests several other reasons why no such relation can be established. The difference in feudal rank supplies a partial explanation. For a prince like the count of Flanders it was far more costly to maintain his feudal position than it was for a simple knight and therefore it might be argued that he required a larger fief. Also, a powerful lord could demand more money than a knight for similar obligations. Reflecting on the grants made by the English and French kings to men in the Low Countries, we are conscious that though the princes always received the largest *fiefs-rentes* they did not always render proportionately as much military service as did some of the lesser lords and knights. But there are yet other reasons suggested in the *recognitio* of 1163 made by the Flemish vassals and in such documents as the following letters patent of John of England dated 26 May 1202 that may help to explain the difference:

Rex etc. omnibus baillivis comitis Flandrie de terra Flandrie salutem. Sciatis quod nos mandavimus militibus Flandrie que de nobis terras vel feoda habent quod sicut terras et feoda diligunt veniant ad nos. Ita qui sint ad nos in festo nativitatis Sancti [Johannis] Baptiste instanti et nobis faciunt servicium quod nobis facere debent et nos eis faciemus quod facere debebimus. Et si venire noluerint non debet nobis imputari si nos capiamus ad terras suas et feoda et vobis mandamus quod non permittatis quod ipsi capiant ad gentem nostram et mercatores nostros in potestate vestra propter terras et feoda predicta ex quo illa deservire noluerint. Quia si hoc sustine-

---

[200] Perhaps on the Continent there was a rough relation between the military obligation and the importance and value of the ordinary fief, but this was not the case with fiefs of land held from the English kings (Ganshof, *Feudalism*, pp. 79–80). Didier states: "Les revenus du fief doivent pourvoir à ces dépenses. Le fief lige équivaut au fief de chevalier. Mais, à la différence de ce qui s'observe ailleurs, le rapport entre l'étendue du service armé et l'importance du fief n'a pas été défini par la législation ni par la coutume" (*Droit des fiefs*, pp. 74–75). See also Round, *Feudal England* (London, 1895), pp. 45, 231–35; Stubbs, *Constitutional History*, I, 288; Pollock and Maitland, *History of English Law*, I, 257; Stenton, *English Feudalism*, pp. 164–70; Haskins, *Norman Institutions*, pp. 8, 11, 22; Mitteis, *Lehnrecht und Staatsgewalt*, pp. 601–8.

retis non possemus omittere quin caperemus nos ad ea qua comes Flandrie habet in potestate nostra.[201]

It is evident from the *recognitio* and the letters patent quoted above that the counts of Flanders either formally gave permission to their vassals to receive *fiefs-rentes* from the English kings, or at least did not prohibit the kings from recruiting Flemish knights by means of *fiefs-rentes*. Count Thierry and Philip his son witnessed the *recognitio* and swore that their vassals would adhere to its terms. The letters patent of 1202 show that Count Baldwin IX and his officers were aware of the numerous knights holding *fiefs-rentes* from John. It is logical to conclude, therefore, that the English kings received some co-operation from the Flemish counts and other great continental lords in their efforts to recruit fighters for their wars and paid for it by granting them large *fiefs-rentes*. For providing easy access to their rich recruiting grounds, these princes received more valuable fiefs than lesser lords and knights.

This thesis applies equally well to grants of *fiefs-rentes* by the French kings. If, for example, one looks at the concessions made by Philip Augustus, Philip IV, Philip VI, and the other kings of the fourteenth century, he notes the impressive number of *fiefs-rentes* granted to the Low Country princes and their vassals. Indeed, all the Low Country princes held *fiefs-rentes* from the French kings with the exception of the counts of Flanders, who were generally their enemies. Though many of the Flemish nobility received *fiefs-rentes* at the time of Philip Augustus and Philip IV, at no other time is this the case. On the other hand, there were always numerous lords from the rest of the Low Countries, especially Hainaut, Luxemburg, Namur, Liège, and Brabant, and from the Rhine area, in receipt of *fiefs-rentes* from the French kings.[202] Though the princes of these states constantly fluctuated in their loyalties, more frequently throughout the Middle Ages they sided with the French kings or were their benevolent neutrals. Naturally, then, the French kings granted many more *fiefs-rentes* to the nobles in these states than to those in Flanders. The situation was the same in south-

---

[201] *Rot. Pat.*, p. 11 b.

[202] See Viard, *Revue des Questions Historiques*, LIX, 351–55, 370, 386–88, and *Journaux du trésor de Philippe VI*, Ordinarium Thesauri. For *fiefs-rentes*, subsidies, and wages paid by Philip V to German lords for their military service see Lehugeur, *Philippe le Long*, pp. 225 ff.

western France and such other border regions as Metz, Bar, Lorraine, Burgundy, and Vienne where the princes held large *fiefs-rentes* from the French kings. For example, in Vienne, where the dauphins held a *fief-rente* from Philip VI, a striking number of knights received *fiefs-rentes* from Philip in the 1330's and 1340's.[203] One will never be able to account entirely for the discrepancies between the value of the *fief-rente* and the military obligation, but he can partially account for the lucrative fiefs received by the great princes. Lords over large areas had more than just limited service to offer; if favorably disposed, they could open up their lands to the recruiting agents of the French and English kings and make available for military service hundreds of their vassals.

However one looks at the *fief-rente* and its relation to war wages, subsidies, and military obligations, the following conclusion inevitably emerges. The *fief-rente* was no war wage, no subsidy, or non-feudal pension, nor was there any logical relation between it and the military service required; its chief function was to set up a feudal obligation upon the part of the vassal. But just as the lord imposed feudal obligations upon the vassal, so the vassal secured a guarantee that the lord would fulfil obligations to him. The *fief-rente* enabled the lord to enter into feudal relations with men of all ranks and stations. The amount of service to be supplied was of secondary concern; the obligation once established, the amount of service was merely a matter for agreement, and regardless of how much or how little might be required, remuneration was in the form of war wages and maintenance.

6. THE VALUE OF THE FIEF-RENTE

The recruiting power of the *fief-rente* obviously made it valuable to the feudal princes, but there are still additional and broader reasons for its prominence in the thirteenth and fourteenth centuries. Realizing the inability of the traditional feudalism to meet his expanding military operations, and with his capacity to pay for the required troops ever increasing, the feudal prince employed the

---

[203] Guiffrey, *Histoire de la réunion du Dauphiné à la France*, pp. 12—24, Table chronologique, nos. 8, 10, 22, 23, 24, 29, 31, 33—34, 36, 39, 42, 43, 51, 66, 75, 81, 86, 102, 189, 196, 213. See also Viard, *Revue des Questions Historiques*, LIX, 345—48.

fief-rente to secure the needed fighters in addition to hiring mercenaries. But why did the princes use the *fief-rente* when military service could be secured and paid for without regard to feudal tenure? Why, indeed, would any of the hard-headed princes pay a knight or lord a *fief-rente* yearly in addition to his wages and sustenance? Why not merely hire a mercenary and save the money which the *fief-rente* involved? The answer lies in feudalism itself. This system, so entrenched in western Europe since the middle of the eighth century, completely dominated the political, economic, social, and military institutions. To give a knight wages for his service without binding him by a form of feudal tenure would have been rash in the twelfth and thirteenth centuries. Feudal custom could not be abruptly pushed aside merely because there was more money. Not until money and the institutions it made possible were as common as feudalism had been, would men be completely emancipated from feudal influence. For the medieval lord, homage and fealty were as essential as a deed is today for the conveyance and transfer of a title to a piece of real estate. It was only natural, therefore, that feudal tenure was superimposed upon money, and that the princes considered this annual payment of money worth the guarantee it produced. But specialists in medieval warfare and feudalism have given the *fief-rente* no place in this military development; they argue that feudal service based upon land declined and gave way to non-feudal paid service such as that supplied by mercenaries and other contractual arrangements. In actual fact, however, there was no direct change from feudal to non-feudal service; there was instead a gradual transition beginning at the outset of the twelfth century. The *fief-rente* illustrates this transition because it bridged the old and the new systems. It enabled the princes to buy with money all the vassals they desired; they were limited only by their financial resources and no longer by the land at their disposal. Realizing the advantage of this new type of fief, all the princes by the late twelfth and early thirteenth centuries used it to secure large portions of their feudal armies. Though it may seem paradoxical, the new money economy which eventually destroyed feudalism nevertheless perpetuated it by means of the *fief-rente* at a time when, based upon land, it no longer served its purpose. Military necessity, more money, and a traditional feudalism, already decadent, made the *fief-rente* an important military institution of these centuries.

VI

The Decline of the Fief-Rente: The Arrière-Ban, the Indenture System, and Standing Armies

By the second half of the fifteenth century only traces of the *fief-rente* remained. Sczaniecki found a mere handful in France by the last quarter of the century;[1] in the Low Countries few still existed in 1500; in Germany hardly any can be found after 1450; and in England the *fief-rente* disappeared in the year 1444.[2] The decline of the *fief-rente*, which began in all these areas in the second half of the fourteenth century, cannot be disassociated from that of feudalism in the fourteenth and fifteenth centuries; but, in reflecting that feudalism based upon land had begun to crack up already in the thirteenth century, one realizes that the decline of the *fief-rente* is a problem different from that of the ordinary fief. First, let us

[1] *Essai,* pp. 167–68.

[2] One can follow the decline of the *fief-rente* in the financial records of Flanders, Brabant, and Limburg. For example, the account of the toll at Damme shows seventeen fiefs paid for the year 1364–65. In the 1370's the number declines and by 1433 only one fief was paid (A.G.R., Nélis, *Inv.,* nos. 623–85). In the account rendered by the receiver of Flanders for 1473 but one fief was paid (A.G.R., *C.C.,* no. 2708, fol. 25). The *Comptes et pièces comptables de la recette générale de Flandre* extending from 1247 to the end of the fifteenth century afford other good evidence. They may be consulted in the *Inventaire sommaire des Archives Départementales du Nord,* B. 4033–4120. In the accounts rendered by the receiver general of Brabant for the years 1363–64 and 1364–65 were paid, respectively, twenty-five and thirty-nine fiefs. In the account for 1468–69 only one fief was paid (A.G.R., *C.C.,* nos. 2350–2423). In the account of the receiver of Limburg for the year 1390–91 are dozens of *fiefs-rentes*; in the account for 1500–1501 there are five (A.G.R., *C.C.,* nos. 2436–2451). After 1450 it is difficult to find a *fief-rente* in the Rhenish lands, the area of Germany which saw the most concessions. Only one appears in the *Urkundenbuch* of Lacomblet: In 1467 the duke of Juliers and Berg renewed an alliance with the town of Cologne whereby he continued to receive a fief of 100 *Gulden* (IV, no. 337). A few other cases are in Von der Brügghen, *Die Lehensregister der Propsteilichen Mannkammer des Aachener Marienstifts,* pp. 178, 430. For the English evidence see Ch. V, pp. 217–20.

enumerate the reasons Sczaniecki has given for the decline in France. With the unification of France achieved by the fifteenth century, the French kings ceased to employ the *fief-rente* as an instrument for expanding their control over France. During the fourteenth century numerous *fiefs-rentes* lost their feudal character and simply became pensions; most of those still appearing in the late fourteenth and fifteenth centuries were in reality pensions camouflaged by feudal façade. Large numbers came to be morseled out to so many recipients that they virtually evaporated. When originally granted, many were very lucrative, but as time passed and the annual amount remained unchanged, their value was so lessened by the inflationary spiral of the fourteenth and fifteenth centuries that they ceased to interest the possessors, who eventually forgot about them. Evidence for the fourteenth and fifteenth centuries shows that they became too much of a financial burden for the French kings. Arrears piled up so alarmingly at various times that temporary suspension of payment was ordered. Further prohibitions tended to limit the number of new concessions or stop them completely. Too often, Sczaniecki discovered, *fiefs-rentes,* appearing regularly in the records for periods of a hundred years and longer, suddenly disappear without explanation; the fortunes of such fiefs will never be known. But of all the reasons contributing to the end of the *fief-rente* none were more important, according to Sczaniecki, than its amortization and its replacement by land. Tracing the histories of different fiefs over the course of a hundred to one hundred and fifty years, Sczaniecki showed that it was common for the recipients eventually to turn their fiefs over to the church in the form of alms. The financial records reflect this practice; every year the sums issued for amortized *rentes* increased while those for *fiefs-rentes* decreased. As for the substitution of land, it has been noted previously that Sczaniecki believed this the intended fate of a large proportion of *fiefs-rentes,* a view for which there is some evidence.[3]

But can we apply Sczaniecki's reasons for the decline of the *fief-rente* in France to its decline in the Low Countries, Germany, and England? In Germany and the Low Countries it was used to acquire lordship over feudal and allodial land and thus to expand princely domains; it would, however, be gross exaggeration to give the

---

[3] *Essai,* pp. 168–75.

impression that even where this practice was most prominent as, for example, in Brabant, Limburg, Luxemburg, and Namur, the rulers forged their control over these areas principally by the *fief-rente*.[4] Indeed, by the thirteenth century when *fiefs-rentes* became numerous, all the Low Country states except Brabant had reached the limits of their expansion. The subsequent acquisition of the duchy of Limburg by Duke John I of Brabant was due not to the *fief-rente* but to his victory over the archbishop of Cologne, Reginald of Guelders, and Count Henry VI of Luxemburg at Woeringen in 1288. Never was the *fief-rente* so important in expanding political control over land in Germany and the Low Countries that its decline would be accelerated by the cessation of such a practice. As for the English kings, they had never used it for this purpose; all their lands had been acquired by virtue of conquest, by feudal succession, or by shrewd marriages. With the possible exception of Brabant, there is no evidence outside of France suggesting that the financial burden of the *fief-rente* forced the princes to curtail concessions or to cease payments.[5] During periods of severe financial strain payment of the annual installments was effected by all sorts of expedients, but there is no indication that the lords considered the financial burden serious enough to force economies with the *fief-rente*.[6] The annual payments appear too monotonously in the financial records to give this explanation much weight. That *fiefs-rentes* decreased in value and ceased being important to the possessors may account

---

[4] See Ch. IV, pp. 150–52.

[5] In the inquest of 1389 held by officers of the duke of Burgundy to determine his rights in Limburg, the commissioners reported that more fiefs were being paid than should be and that henceforth none should be paid unless the recipients produced the proper charters with the concessions. These orders indicate that some men were collecting payments for fiefs that did not legally belong to them, but they also show that at this time the payment of *fiefs-rentes* was becoming a strain (Quicke, *B.C.R.H.*, XCVI, 370–73). For similar evidence see Quicke and Laurent, *B.C.R.H.*, XCVII, nos. 9–10, 12, 18. In 1394 Duke Philip the Bold of Burgundy ordered the *Chambre des comptes* at Lille to determine the sum owed to Reginald de Fauquemont, lord of Born, for the arrears of his fief. Attached to this order is a short memo with a record of the arrears. In 1394 Reginald revolted because the arrears had not been paid (no. 11). In the same year William of Juliers, duke of Berg and count of Ravensberg, renounced his homage to Duke Philip because he could not obtain payment of his fief of 1,500 francs (no. 60).

[6] See Ch. III, pp. 116–24.

for the disappearance of some. But this explanation comes from neither the French nor any other evidence; it springs from the observation that if the annual amount of the *fief-rente* remained unchanged in the face of devaluation, it would eventually be worthless. The German, English, and Low Country records indicate that recipients rarely morseled their *fiefs-rentes*. Possession changed hands often and alienation occurred frequently, but the *fief-rente* remained intact. When in the possession of the same family over a long period of time, the amount of the fief never decreased but, in fact, often increased as a result of being augmented.[7] As Sczaniecki observed, hundreds suddenly disappear from the records and we can only guess as to their fate. We have already seen that *fiefs-rentes* granted under heritable, life, and conditional tenures outnumbered those granted with the provision of future substitution of land. Even when fiefs were granted until land could be provided, often lands were never assigned and the tenure became *de facto* either heritable or life.[8] An examination of the *Comptes du trésor* of the French kings shows that while both heritable and life *fiefs-rentes* declined precipitately in the fifteenth century, so too did the amortized *rentes*. In 1329, for example, 4,069 *l*. 11 *s*. 7 *d*. were paid for amortized *rentes*, 9,212 *l*. 11 *s*. 7 *d*. for heritable fiefs, and 2,253 *l*. 16 *s*. 10 *d*. for life and conditional fiefs. In 1384 the payments for amortized *rentes* amounted to 109 *l*. (2,129 *l*. 6 *s*. 2 *d*. were listed as not paid); for heritable fiefs, 480 *l*. (9,264 *l*. not paid); and for life fiefs, 775 *l*. 7 *s*. 4 *d*. (13,848 *l*. 2 *s*. 7½ *d*. not paid). Listed in arrears for amortized *rentes* were 3,208 *l*. 15 *s*. 9½ *d*., and for life and conditional fiefs,

---

[7] For example, in 1263 Count William of Juliers received a fief of 100 *m*. from the town of Cologne. In 1467 the duke of Juliers and Berg was in possession of a fief of 100 *Gulden* (Ennen and Eckertz, *Quellen Stadt Köln,* II, no. 449; Lacomblet, *Urkundenbuch,* IV, no. 337). In the fourteenth century the lords of Gronsveld; Scheiffart de Merode, lord of Heinsbach; Heiligher de Ailsdorp; and the "Banretz de Molenarken" were receiving, respectively, fiefs of 30 florins, 30 *royaux,* 20 *m.*, and 30 florins. In 1500 their descendants were receiving the same amounts (A.G.R., *C.C.,* no. 2436, fols. 17ᵛ–18ʳ; no. 2451, fols. 32ʳ–33ᵛ). To cite but one example from the English records, we find that in 1066 Baldwin V of Flanders received a fief of 300 *m*. In 1103 it was increased to 500 *m.*, and in the last quarter of the century to 1,000 *m*. In the reigns of Jeanne and Margaret it was 500 *m*. During the reign of Guy it was 300 *m*. In 1330, however, when Count Louis de Nevers was granted a *fief-rente* the amount was 1,000 *m*.

[8] See Ch. II, pp. 67–70.

9,480 *l.* 18 *s.* 2 *d.* For the *Saint-Jean* term of 1408 amortized *rentes* totaled 185 *l.* 4 *s.* 11½ *d.*; heritable fiefs, 120 *l.*; life fiefs, 1,653 *l.* 6 *s.* 8 *d.*; and conditional fiefs, 103 *l.* 1 *s.* 4 *d.* In arrears were 1,491 *l.* 6 *s.* 6 *d.* for amortized *rentes* and 20,337 *l.* 7 *s.* 4 *d.* for heritable, life, and conditional fiefs. For the *Saint-Jean* term of 1420 only arrears are noted : 2,036 *l.* 18 *s.* 4 *d.* for amortized *rentes* and 1,267 *l.* 2 *s.* 4 *d.* for life fiefs. For the *Saint-Jean* term of 1477 payments for amortized *rentes* totaled 84 *l.* (5,824 *l.* 1 *s.* 5½ *d.* not paid); the arrears of the amortized *rentes* totaled 85 *l.* Nothing was paid for heritable fiefs although a notation indicates 2,775 *l.* 18 *s.* as not paid. These figures show that not until 1420 and 1477 do amortized *rentes* surpass *fiefs-rentes*;[9] surely one cannot therefore believe that the amortization of *fiefs-rentes* was a major cause for their disappearance in France. And in the Low Countries and Germany evidence for their amortization is scarce; in England, non-existent.

To discredit entirely the reasons given by Sczaniecki for the decline of the *fief-rente* would be incorrect, but not one of them nor all of them satisfactorily account for its decline. One might be tempted momentarily to ascribe the decline to the life and conditional tenures. Such tenures did account for the disappearance of many fiefs, but in the thirteenth and fourteenth centuries when the *fief-rente* was a thriving institution enough new fiefs were continually being granted to more than replace those that had disappeared. Having concluded that the *fief-rente* had little military importance, Sczaniecki does not suggest that the military developments of the fourteenth and fifteenth centuries affected it. If, however, our examination of the evidence has shown anything, it has shown that in all western Europe the *fief-rente* was primarily a military device. Is it not therefore logical to suppose that its decline can be understood only in relation to certain new military developments of these centuries?

The *levée en masse* or *arrière-ban,* the rule that every free ablebodied man owed military service to his lord and should provide himself with weapons according to the worth of his land and chattels, had been known in western Europe since the Carolingians but was never greatly utilized to provide the princes with their fighting forces until the thirteenth century. The knight who fought because

---

[9] Fawtier, *Comptes du trésor,* pp. lxii–lxxi.

of feudal obligation formed the core of the feudal army and, with his tactics, generally dominated the battlefield down into the thirteenth century. When various types of footsoldiers were needed, which was usually in a supporting capacity, they were commonly provided by mercenaries. During the thirteenth century, however, when the pike and longbow came to be used, the princes began increasingly to exercise their traditional right of mobilizing all free men to fight. In the hands of such men, the pike and longbow had proved to be fearsome weapons against the knight and repeatedly destroyed and drove the feudal aristocracy from the field; Courtrai and Falkirk are but two of many such military debacles for the knight.[10] It is therefore not surprising that with the weapons and tactics of the simple footsoldier prevailing over the knight, and with the costs of putting a knight into the field becoming increasingly prohibitive, the princes of western Europe turned to a method based upon the principle that military service had to be performed by men because of their allegiance to the prince; it won more battles and was less expensive, in spite of the fact that the men came to be paid daily wages and were maintained in the field. The commission of array, the English version of the *arrière-ban*, was used regularly by the three Edwards to procure troops for their Welsh and Scottish wars, and occasionally for their continental wars.[11] At the same time the

[10] See particularly Lot, *L'art militaire*, I, 217–331; Verbruggen, *De Krijgs-kunst in West-Europa in de Middeleeuwen (IXe tot Begin XIVe Eeuw)* (Brussel, 1954), pp. 240–334. The basic work for England is Morris, *Welsh Wars*.

[11] The Statute of Winchester in 1285 directed every free man between the ages of fifteen and sixty to provide himself with weapons according to the worth of his lands and chattels. The most scholarly and recent study on the commission of array is by Prince in *The English Government at Work*, I, 332–93. See also B. C. Keeney, "Military Service and the Development of Nationalism in England, 1272–1327," *Speculum*, XXII (1947), 534–49; N. B. Lewis, "The English Forces in Flanders, August–November 1297," *Studies in Medieval History, Powicke*, pp. 310–18; M. R. Powicke, "Distraint of Knighthood and Military Obligation under Henry III," *Speculum*, XXV (1950), 457–470, and "The General Obligation to Cavalry Service under Edward I," *Speculum*, XXVIII (1953), 814–33. The following is a typical commission: "Commission to Thomas le Botiller and William Walsh of Wolvestrop to select 300 foot archers in the forest of Dene, Berkeleyhirnes and elsewhere in the county of Gloucester, and the said William to be their leader to Portsmouth, by Monday after St. Matthew to go thence at the king's wages against the king of France" (*C.P.R. 1324–27*, p. 27). For other

French kings were reorganizing their forces along the same lines. Although the longbow was never effective in French hands, the foot-soldier became more prominent as the insufficiency of feudal service became ever more apparent. The *arrière-ban* was used constantly in the thirteenth century and Philip IV, who fought almost continuously in Gascony and Flanders, relied upon it to provide large parts of his armies.[12] In the Low Countries one need only recall such battles as Courtrai, Mons-en-Pévèle, Cassel, and Roosebeke, to bring to mind the role of the Flemish footsoldier and his pike.[13] But how did this new military development affect the *fief-rente*? In the first place, it greatly slackened the demand for knights provided by *fiefs-rentes*. Secondly, not based upon feudal tenure, it weakened the position of the lord who was retained by a *fief-rente* to supply archers, pikemen, and other types of footsoldiers; the *arrière-ban* obtained these fighters without the expense involved with a *fief-rente*.

There was, however, another military development more responsible for the decline of the *fief-rente* than the *arrière-ban* or commission of array. The princes began to contract non-feudal agreements with lords and captains to provide military service. This system of contract, although varying slightly from region to region, was basically the same in all. It was under the English kings that this contractual method, known as the indenture system, first appeared. It can be found as early as the reign of Edward I (1272–1307), but

---

examples see *C.P.R. 1327–30,* pp. 110 ff., 163; *C.P.R. 1361–64,* pp. 21, 36, 168, 309.

[12] Lot, *L'art militaire,* I, 217–77; Boutaric, *Institutions militaires,* pp. 197–239. The following remark of Boutaric pertains to the reign of Philip IV: "Le système féodal ne permettait pas de faire face à des guerres qui duraient des années entières. La doctrine ancienne du devoir de tout Français de contribuer à la défense de la patrie fut interprétée d'une manière nouvelle: Philippe proclama l'arrière-ban" (p. 227). See also Boutaric, *La France sous Philippe le Bel* (Paris, 1861), pp. 368 ff.; Langlois, *Philippe le Hardi,* pp. 362–63; Fawtier, *Les Capétiens et la France* (Paris, 1942), pp. 187–91; Declareuil, *Histoire du droit français,* p. 755; Chénon, *Histoire du droit français,* I, 746.

[13] For the obligation of all free men to perform *ost* in Flanders see Pirenne, *Histoire de Belgique,* I, 324. For accounts of these battles see Lot, *L'art militaire,* I, 252–69; Verbruggen, *De Slag der Gulden Sporen;* Köhler, *Die Entwicklung des Kriegswesens,* II, 216–82, 574–602. For military developments in Germany see Lot, II, 148 ff.; Delbrück, *Geschichte der Kriegskunst,* III, 329 ff.; Köhler, I, 161–89; III, 97–118.

it is in the reign of Edward III (1327–77) that it became the principal basis of mobilization for the forces that served in the wars against France. Ultimately it replaced all feudal arrangements for the procurement of fighting men from the higher ranks. The prosecution of the French wars on several fronts and over an extended period of time exposed the shortcomings of the old feudal levy: the incoherent arrays, the lack of a proper chain of command, and the frequent insubordination of the vassals. The indenture system made all the fighters from the lowly man-at-arms to the proud earl a contracting stipendiary dependent to some degree upon the crown. It thus produced better discipline and a more efficient military organization. The indenture system was also responsible for the decay of the commission of array under Edward III. Where the commission of array might well serve the military demands of the Scottish and Welsh campaigns, which were sporadic and seasonal and involved no great logistic problems, it proved wholly inadequate for the continental wars which required forces permanently stationed in northern and southwestern France. Edward III needed professional soldiers willing to fight continuously on the Continent; the men provided by the commission of array could not be made to fight indefinitely overseas and, furthermore, too many difficulties were involved in their transportation to and from France. Thus only at the beginning of the Hundred Years' War does one meet the commission of array; it soon fell into desuetude.[14]

We are grateful to Morris, Prince, Lewis, and McFarlane for clarifying the early development of the indenture system and its use by the English kings and lords in the fourteenth and fifteenth centuries.[15] In general, the typical military indenture followed a

[14] For example, the Patent Rolls, in which are enrolled many commissions of array, show that the commissions supplied most of the men who fought in Scotland and Ireland. See especially *C.P.R. 1327–30*, pp. 110 ff., 163; *C.P.R. 1361–64*, pp. 21, 36, 168, 309. See also Morris, *Welsh Wars*, pp. 92 ff. In commenting upon the county levies of foot he wrote: "The custom of requisitioning men for service to their own county was evidently strict" (p. 93).

[15] Morris, *Welsh Wars*, pp. 68–71, 189, 272, 278–79. Prince, *E.H.R.*, XLVI (1931), 353–71; "The Indenture System under Edward III," *Tait Essays*, pp. 283–97; "The Army and Navy," *English Government at Work*, I, 347–55; and "The Payment of Army Wages in Edward III's Reign," *Speculum*, XIX (1944), 137–60. N. B. Lewis, "An Early Indenture of Military Service, 27 July 1287," *Bulletin of the Institute of Historical Research*, XIII (1935–36), 85–89; "An Early Fourteenth Century Contract for Military Service,"

definite pattern. Usually a distinguished captain, often of the feudal aristocracy, would contract with the king or a powerful lord to supply him with a certain number of knights, men-at-arms, archers, or various other fighters for service in the field. The contract was sometimes for life, sometimes for a stipulated number of years or months, and sometimes for the duration of a campaign. The captain, in turn, often had a contract with each of his men. He could also contract for the defense of a castle or a defined area of land with a certain number of men for a definite period of time. An important detail of the contract was the retaining fee. This fee was the only payment normally received by the captain in time of peace and it required him to maintain an armed contingent ready to serve the king at any time. All the essential details were included in these indentures: the period and place of the service, the rate of daily wages, the sustenance, the size of the bonus at the end of service, the compensation for horses lost, payment for transportation, and terms relating to the "advantages of war." [16]

Turning to actual cases, we find an indenture drawn up on 2 July 1297 between Aymer de Valence and Thomas, lord of Berkeley. Thomas agreed to stay in Aymer's "mennage" along with five of his knights during peace and war in England, Scotland, and Wales; he was to receive a retaining fee of 50 l. yearly. In addition to the fee, Aymer promised to supply robes for the knights of Thomas, feed them at his table, and provide a total of nine squires and valets to serve Thomas and his men. During hostilities Thomas was to receive 4 s. daily; the knights, 2 s.; each armed squire with barbed horse, 12 d. Should Thomas serve Aymer other than in the three stipulated areas, his fee would be increased to 100 m. yearly and the transportation overseas would be provided for Thomas, his men,

Bul. Inst. Hist. Res., XX (1943–45), 111–18; "The Organisation of Indentured Retinues in Fourteenth-Century England," Trans. Roy. Hist. Soc., 4th ser., XXVII (1945), 29–39. K. B. McFarlane, "Bastard Feudalism," Bul. Inst. Hist. Res., XX (1943–45), 161–80; "Parliament and 'Bastard Feudalism'," Trans. Roy. Hist. Soc., 4th ser., XXVI (1944), 53–79. See also H. M. Cam, "The Decline and Fall of English Feudalism," History, New ser., XXV (1940), 216–33; R. A. Newhall, Muster and Review: A Problem of English Military Administration 1420–1440 (Cambridge, Mass., 1940), pp. 3–5; Stubbs, Constitutional History of England (5th ed., Oxford, 1898), III, 549–60; C. Oman, A History of the Art of War, II, 62–65, 121–23.

[16] Prince, Tait Essays, pp. 288–89; Lewis, Trans. Roy. Hist. Soc., XXVII, 32.

and their horses. An evaluation of the horses would be made before embarking and, should any be lost, Aymer agreed to pay full compensation within forty days. Certain provisions were also made for Maurice, the son of Thomas, if he should stay with his three knights in his father's retinue. His fee was to be 30 *l.* yearly, to be raised to 60 *m.* if he served overseas.[17] In an indenture of 1371 between John, duke of Lancaster, and the knight Walter Penhergard, the latter was retained by the duke "pour pees et pour guerre a terme de vie." The document then proceeds to state that Walter will receive a fee of 40 *m.* yearly for life. He and a squire suitably armed will serve the duke any place required in peace and war. They will receive the customary wages of war during the service, as well as wages for travel to and from the field of operations. Shipping will be provided for Walter and his men and horses. Should the horses be lost or captured, their loss will be remunerated. As for the profits of war and for prisoners taken by Walter and his men, the duke promised to make reasonable satisfaction.[18] But let us leave the English evidence for the moment and turn to the records of the Continent.

One soon discovers when he studies the works of such as Lot, Bloch, Boutaric, Viollet, Chénon, Langlois, Fawtier, Lehuguer, and Viard that the French kings were also faced with the military

---

[17] P.R.O., Exch. Accts., 68/1. A summary of this indenture appears in J. Bain, *Cal. of Documents Relating to Scotland, 1272–1307* (Edinburgh, 1884), II, no. 905. See also Prince, *Tait Essays,* p. 285. For an indenture drawn up in the tenth regnal year of Edward II see Lewis, *Bul. Inst. Hist. Res.,* XX, 117–18. For indentures concluded by the Black Prince see *Register of Edward the Black Prince* (London, 1931), I, 127–29; II, 45–46, 202, 306, 356–57; IV, 31–32, 83–84, 91, 143–45, 288.

[18] *John of Gaunt's Register, 1371–1375,* ed. S. Armitage-Smith (Camden Society, London, 1911), 3d ser., XX, no. 784. For other examples see nos. 771 ff.; XXI, nos. 859–70. Armitage-Smith has estimated that more than a "hundred knights, banneret or bachelor, and as many squires, entered into a formal compact with the Duke" (*John of Gaunt,* Westminster, 1904, p. 227). Illuminating remarks on the indenture, as well as other examples, are to be found in *John of Gaunt's Register, 1379–1383,* ed. E. C. Lodge and R. Somerville (Camden Society, London, 1937), 3d ser., LVI–LVII; *C.P.R. 1340–43,* pp. 259–69, 278, 330. Indentures for castle-guard are in P.R.O., Exch. Accts., 30/40, 68/2–3, 5–7. In *P.R. 41 Ed. III,* m. 38v, are details pertinent to the retaining fee of 1,000 *m.* held by Thomas de Bello Campo, earl of Warwick, who in 1348 had agreed to stay with Edward III with 100 men-at-arms (P.R.O., E. 372/212; *C.P.R. 1348–50,* p. 145).

inadequacy of feudalism and the *arrière-ban* and had come to use the contractual method to secure adequate forces.[19] In general scholars have expressed doubt that the indenture system with its retaining fees existed on the Continent; this view is correct if one insists upon all the English features.[20] But if one is satisfied with military contracts which varied on certain points from the typical English indenture yet still attained the same objectives, he will find numerous records testifying to the existence of the non-feudal contractual method for securing fighting forces.

In the first phases of the Hundred Years' War up to the Treaty of Brétigny in 1360, the French kings relied upon the feudal levy and the *arrière-ban* to provide their main forces. To secure additional forces during these years, the *fief-rente* especially was used. But, in addition, non-feudal contracts were concluded with lords and captains to acquire even more service. After 1360 the old feudal levy, the *arrière-ban*, and even the *fief-rente* were used less and less as the kings came to employ more extensively the *grandes compagnies*. As under the English indenture system, these bands were organized with a feudal lord or a cutthroat captain at their head. The terms of the agreements were also identical to those of the indenture, the only difference being that there was no retaining fee; the contracting captain would receive instead a subsidy or a lucrative wage along with his men. Thus the contracts were generally of shorter duration, and between periods of hostilities there was no agreement between king and captain as there normally was with the English indenture. Free agents between campaigns, therefore, the leaders and their companions committed the brigandage and excesses which gave them their infamous reputation.[21] But let us examine some of these

---

[19] Lot, *L'art militaire*, I, 395–411; Bloch, *Société féodale*, II, 255–57; Boutaric, *Institutions militaires*, pp. 240–67, and *La France sous Philippe le Bel*, pp. 368–72; Viollet, *Institutions politiques*, II, 435–37; Chénon, *Histoire générale*, I, 888; Langlois, *Philippe le Hardi*, pp. 365–66; Fawtier, *Les Capétiens et la France*, pp. 187–91; Lehuguer, *Philippe le Long*, pp. 313 ff.; Viard, *Revue des Questions Historiques*, LIX, 376–89.

[20] Perroy, "Feudalism or Principalities in Fifteenth Century France," *Bul. Inst. Hist. Res.*, XX (1945), 181.

[21] For the *grandes compagnies* see particularly E. de Fréville, "Des grandes compagnies au quatorzième siècle," *Biblio. de l'École des Chartes*, III (1841), 258–81; V (1843), 232–53; Lot, *L'art militaire*, I, 396 ff.; S. Luce, *Histoire de Bertrand du Guesclin et de son époque* (2d ed., Paris, 1882), pp. 279–

non-feudal contracts. In 1304 Theobald de Bar, bishop of Liège, contracted with Philip IV to provide him with 200 men-at-arms for military service for three months at the royal wages.[22] In 1337 Bishop Adolf de la Mark of Liège concluded a more detailed agreement with Philip VI. Adolf promised a contingent of 500 armed men for service in the war against Edward III of England and the emperor Louis of Bavaria. He received a subsidy of 15,000 $l.$ plus 50 $l.$ for each day's service. His men were to receive daily wages according to the following scale: double banneret, 40 $s.$; simple banneret, 20 $s.$; knight, 10 $s.$; squire, 5 $s.$ The wages were to be paid in advance for each month's service as long as it was required. Should the bishop and his men be taken prisoner, they were to be ransomed. All horses lost were to be restored. Prisoners of war were to be handed over to the king; the horses, armor, and other equipment was to go to the bishop and his men. Should peace be concluded with the enemy, Adolf promised that the 500 men could then be used to fight against other royal enemies according to the same terms.[23] Meanwhile, in 1332 a contract had been concluded between Philip VI and Archbishop Walerand of Cologne, Count Reginald of Guelders, and Count William of Juliers against the duke of Brabant and Robert of Artois, as well as any other enemies of Philip. Should Philip march against the duke of Brabant, each lord promised 1,000 men-at-arms and an additional 100 men if required, all to be paid royal wages. Should service be required in France, each lord promised 600 men-at-arms and up to 100 additional men if necessary. A scale of wages was then stipulated for the different grades of fighters. In this connection it was agreed that should they be engaged in the siege of a town or another fortified point where it would be impossible "prendre fourrages," the wages of squires would be increased from six to seven *sous* per day. Before the campaign two marshals of France were to evaluate all the horses and after the hostilities to remunerate the men properly for all horses lost. Should any of the men be captured, they were to be ransomed. All prisoners were to be handed over to the king. And lastly, the three lords promised to

303; A. Coville, in Lavisse, *Histoire de France,* IV, i, 161–66, 177–81; R. Delachenal, *Histoire de Charles V* (Paris, 1909–31), II, 21–42, 215–322; III, 239–302, 358–64, 440–51.

[22] A.N., J. 527/4.

[23] De Lettenhove, *Oeuvres de Froissart,* XVIII, no. 17.

fulfil the terms of the agreement; they pledged their goods and possessions as security for their good faith and put their seals to the contract.[24] Though not many of these contracts are extant, we know that they became more numerous in the reigns of John the Good and Charles V because of the evidence of muster rolls and receipts given to the treasurers of war. In 1351, for example, the company of the lord of Beaumanoir was composed of four knights including Beaumanoir, eighteen squires, and thirty archers. The lord of Rohan had a band of six knights, fourteen squires, and twenty archers.[25] The kings tended to contract ever more frequently with captains who were little more than brigands. Receipts for wages show that Alain de Taille-Col, called the "abbé de Malepaie," and Lorent Coupe-Gorge contracted to furnish, respectively, twenty-three and five squires.[26] Contracts were also concluded with the most powerful lords of the land. When war was resumed around 1368 against the English by Charles V, the French lords and men-at-arms enrolled themselves under powerful captains who had in turn a contract with the king. The duke of Burgundy agreed to lead 300 men at the royal wages, the duke of Berry provided 800, and the duke of Bourbon, 400. John de Vienne contracted to provide 200 men-at-arms, five knights, and nineteen squires; there was also to be under his command the knight Robert de Bailledart with eleven squires, a band of two knights and nineteen squires under Gilles de Poissi,

---

[24] *Ibid.,* no. 9.

[25] Boutaric, *Institutions militaires,* p. 257 ; H. Morice, *Mémoires pour servir de preuves de l'histoire de Bretagne* (Paris, 1742), I, 1469, 1660. The collection of documents edited by Morice are filled with receipts for payment of wages by the treasurer of war. The following are typical : "Quittance de Jean du Mesle : Saichent tuit, que nous Jehan du Melle Chevalier, confessons avoir eu et receu de Jehan le Flamenc Tresorier des guerres du Roy nostre Sire, la somme de quatre vingt deux frans et demi, en prest sur les gaiges de nous et de neuf Escuiers de nostre compaignie, desservis et à desservir en ces presentes guerres ez parties de la basse Normandie, sous le gouvernement de Mons. le Connestable, etc. Donné à Karenten soubz nostre scel le X. Aoust MCCC. LXXI" (p. 1662). In 1371 the knight Peter Tournemine recognized to have received from the treasurer of war 312 *l.* 10 *s.* "en prest sur les gages de luy Banneret, deux autres Chevaliers et seize Escuiers de sa compagnie, du nombre de cent hommes d'armes ordonnez demourer au siege devant Becherel" (p. 1662). See also pp. 1662 ff.

[26] Boutaric, *Institutions militaires,* p. 257 ; Morice, *Preuves de Bretagne,* I, 1664.

18

and a band of one knight and nineteen squires under the knight John de Girolles.[27]

In spite of the military reforms of John and Charles V, which were actually attempts to put authorized captains in command of companies and thus bring the fighting forces under a chain of command running up to the king himself, helter-skelter contracting continued down into the fifteenth century.[28] The campaigns against the English saw the use of contracted service as did the bitter feud between the Armagnac and Burgundian factions. Even at the end of the century Louis XI and Charles VIII were enrolling bands of Swiss and Germans for military service against Charles the Rash of Burgundy and for service in Italy. It is the opinion of Lot that

redoutées, haïes, les compagnies sont désormais considérées comme indispensables. Rois et princes, encore plus prétendants à un trône ou à une principauté ne rougissent pas de les prendre à leur service. . . . L'incapacité du ban et de l'arrière-ban en France est tellement évidente que l'utilisation des compagnies de routiers s'avère comme un expédient, sans doute fâcheux, mais indispensable. Au siècle suivant, pour continuer à exercer efficacement le métier des armes, qui est sa raison d'être, la noblesse devra imiter l'organisation et la discipline des "compaignons." [29]

Though the French system of military contract differed from the English indenture in that it had no retaining fee, it did essentially the same thing—it produced the needed military forces and in the process gradually supplanted the *fief-rente*. As under the English kings, this development occurred chiefly in the fourteenth and early fifteenth centuries.

In the Low Countries the military developments of the fourteenth and fifteenth centuries paralleled those of France. Again we find non-feudal contracts for military service but, as in France, no evidence of retaining fees. We do know that the counts of Flanders had their retainers in the household who were rewarded with non-feudal pensions and livery.[30] We know, too, that the dukes of

---

[27] Coville, in Lavisse, *Histoire de France,* IV, i, 218.

[28] Boutaric, *Institutions militaires,* pp. 263–67.

[29] Lot, *L'art militaire,* I, 411. See also Boutaric, *Institutions militaires,* pp. 326–29.

[30] In 1291, for example, Count Guy of Flanders took into his service as secretary and councillor Leon Batman, canon of Sainte-Pharaïlde of Ghent, "dont nous sommes patron, avons retenu et retenons à estre nos clers et de

Burgundy and the great lords not only retained household staffs by fees and livery but also organized around their persons bands of retainers to do their bidding just as did the English lords in the fourteenth and fifteenth centuries. That the principal obligations of of the retainers were, however, probably political is indicated in decrees of 1385 and 1397 by the duke of Burgundy ordering that the lords cease giving livery to men not normally in their service. The decrees stated that bands of retainers had unlawfully assembled and done harm to him and his lawful subjects. As in England, these bands, under orders of their lords, hindered the functioning of courts and terrorized the countryside.[31] Military musters from the time of Philip the Good and Charles the Rash suggest that non-feudal pensions were granted to lords and captains for providing companies of men, but there seem to be no extant contracts wherein it is definitely stated that retaining fees or pensions were granted.[32] In any event, however, from the late thirteenth century to the time of Charles the Rash, princes of the Low Countries contracted for military service. In 1297, for example, the knight Colart d'Averey made a contract with Count Guy of Flanders to serve with "dix hommes armez de fer, chevaliers, et escuiers filz de chevaliers, tant comme la guerre qui maintenant est entre noble prince le roi de France et noble homme le conte de Henaut dune part et le dit conte de Flandres et ces hoirs dautre durra." For this service Count Guy promised a sum of 700 l. of which 200 l. was to be paid in advance and the remainder at stipulated times. Guy was to pay the transportation costs to and from the campaign and to pay wages to Colart and his men as long as the war lasted. Horses at the rate of five for a knight and three for a squire were to be maintained; if any were lost remuneration was guaranteed. If peace or a truce should be concluded, Guy was still to be held responsible for payment of

---

no conseil, et pour son service nous li donnons sissante livres paresis de pen-cion cascun an tant com il vivera ... et se li donnons avoec tout ce deus paire de reubes par an, cis faisons teiles comme nous donnons à nos autres clers et wages à trois kevaus quant il serra avoec nous; et, se nous l'envoyens en aucune besoingne pour nous, nous li feriens donner ses despens raisonnavle-ment" (P. Thomas, *Textes historiques sur Lille et le Nord de la France avant 1789*, Lille, 1936, II, 218–19), Cf. Bloch, *Société féodale*, II, 255.

[31] Thomas, *Textes historiques*, II, 284–87. Cf. Bloch, *Société féodale*, II, 255.

[32] Lot, *L'art militaire*, II, 112, n. 2.

the 700 *l.* To vouch for his good faith, Colart had three witnesses who, along with him, put their seals to the contract.[33] Many knights from the Rhine area were recruited in this period by Guy and, though most held *fiefs-rentes,* some were only bound by non-feudal contracts. For example, in 1297 Count John of Spanheim contracted to serve Count Guy with thirty men-at-arms against the king of France and the count of Hainaut as long as war lasted. John was to receive 2,000 *l.* plus wages and maintenance for his men and remuneration for all losses suffered to man and horse. If captured, John and his men were to be ransomed.[34]

It was pointed out previously that Duke John III of Brabant, while in receipt of huge subsidies and a *fief-rente* from Edward III of England in return for service against Philip VI of France, contracted with lords of Brabant for their service.[35] Most already held *fiefs-rentes* from John but it should be noted that the contracts which secured their service for Edward III, as well as that of other men not holding *fiefs-rentes,* were similar in many respects to the English indenture. John's receivers, Herman van Os and John de Meldert, were empowered to conclude contracts with a certain number of lords and to grant them lump sums in return for a specified number of knights and squires fully equipped for service. Some eighty-six of these contracts were concluded with the result that Edward III and John III were supplied with a considerable

[33] A.D.N., B. 498/3960. In the same year the knight Warnier de Daules engaged to serve Count Guy in his war with France with a band of four knights and twenty-one squires completely equipped. The count promised a sum of 1,000 *l.* to Warnier plus the usual wages of war (A.E.G., De Saint Genois, *Inv. Fl.,* no. 914).

[34] Brouwers, *Chart. et règ.,* I, no. 311. For other references to German and Low Country knights recruited by Guy and his sons, see Nowé, *La bataille des éperons d'or,* pp. 49–50; Verbruggen, *De Slag der Gulden Sporen,* p. 232; H. Johnstone (ed.), *Annales Gandenses* (London, 1951), pp. 3–4, 29.

[35] Ch. V, pp. 227–28. See also Wauters, *B.C.R.H.,* I (1891), 192–205. In 1339, for example, the knight Ghevard de Deurne received 36 *l.* from Herman van Os and John de Meldert and promised to serve John III "cum undecim viris probis et honestis bene et honeste cum galeis armatis et detentis equitatis ituris extunc cum predictis viris in armis ubicumque dominus noster, dux predictus, nos ire preceperit ipsum etiam juvare promittens cum eisdem contra omnes eius adversarios et inimicos presente guerra jam mota inter regem Anglie ... et regem Francie ex altera" (A.G.R., Verkooren, *Inv. Brab.,* no. 568).

force for their action at Tournai. In the fifteenth century the dukes of Burgundy were still using every possible method for raising troops—the antiquated feudal levy, the *arrière-ban,* the *fief-rente,* and non-feudal contracts. Even after the military reforms of Charles the Rash in the years 1470–73 aimed at a standing army composed of *compagnies d'ordonnance* after the French model, one still finds that companies of Italian professionals and other nondescript groups augmented the main force and were secured through contracts.[36]

In Germany it is much more difficult to trace the military changes of the fourteenth and fifteenth centuries. Not unified as were England, France, and the Low Country states, Germany saw no military developments common to all the principalities and free cities. Because of the works of Delbrück and Köhler, however, it is possible to review briefly the major changes.[37] The *fief-rente,* as we have seen, was never used extensively in Germany to obtain service in the field; its principal function was providing castle-guard. Consequently new recruiting methods never had the effect upon the *fief-rente* in Germany that they did in the rest of western Europe. According to Köhler, however, by the early fourteenth century the emperors, princes, and towns began to conclude *Soldverträge* with lords and captains for supplying the service of a stipulated number and type of fighter. Noting that the practice of contracting for groups of fighters supplanted the hiring of individual fighters, Köhler traces the use of the *Soldvertrag* by Emperor Charles IV and King Ruprecht, shows how the German towns used it in their wars, and points out how large a role it played in furnishing the German military orders in Prussia and the Baltic area with troops in the late fourteenth and fifteenth centuries.[38] Because the German contracts resembled those of the Low Countries and France, it would only be repetitious to cite examples; it should be noted, however,

---

[36] Lot, *L'art militaire,* II, 116.

[37] Delbrück, *Geschichte der Kriegskunst,* III, 526 ff.; Köhler, *Entwicklung des Kriegswesens,* III, ii, 161–83, 192–93.

[38] *Entwicklung des Kriegswesens,* III, ii, 166–68, 169–76, 179. Particularly interesting is a *Soldvertrag* concluded between the Teutonic Knights and the knight Wisel Czambor in 1390. Czambor promised to supply the Knights with a contingent of 100 men, knights and squires, in return for "500 Schock böhmischer Groschen." Each man was to receive monthly wages of 27 *Gulden* (Köhler, III, ii, 172). See also Lacomblet, *Urkundenbuch,* II, no. 981.

that here, too, the only difference from the English indenture was the lack of a retaining fee. This discussion of contractual military service could be expanded beyond the four areas under consideration to include the *condottieri* and the fascinating history of their bands in the service of the Italian city-states. But enough evidence has been cited to show that by the late fourteenth and early fifteenth centuries contractual service prevailed in Europe.

With the *fief-rente* on the decline and contractual service coming to predominate, one can conclude that the *fief-rente* was largely superseded by this non-feudal method of recruitment. It has already been suggested in the previous chapter that the *fief-rente* was a transitional military institution which helped to bridge the gap between non-paid feudal service and contractual non-feudal paid service, and that as such it has been completely overlooked by historians of military institutions, even by those whose specialty is English military history where this transition clearly shows itself and where the evidence is abundant enough to trace the evolution in detail. Although Prince remarked, while commenting on the role of the wardrobe for the payment of army wages under Edward III, that this part of the household may have, in war finance, "bridged the gulf from feudal unpaid military service based on homage and tenure to contractual military service based on the talent of the soldier and its appropriate remuneration," he still did not look for a military practice which may have linked the one system to the other. We are left to understand from the historians of England and of the Continent that in the late thirteenth century the non-feudal contract suddenly arose replacing a decadent feudalism and proceeded to dominate the recruiting of armies for the next one hundred years.[39] Such a conclusion is untenable, it seems to me, when one considers the close resemblance between the non-feudal military contract and the *fief-rente*. With both there was provision for wages for war service; sustenance, transportation, ransom, and sundry expenses; the profits of war; reimbursement for armor and horses; bonuses; and the number and type of men to be supplied. There was yet another likeness between the English military indenture and the *fief-rente*— both provided for a yearly fee. The contractual service and the *fief-rente* differed in only one respect: the

[39] Prince, *Speculum*, XIX, 160. See also *English Government at Work*, I, 348 ff. For the Continent see above, notes 19 and 37.

military contract was concluded without regard to feudal tenure; the *fief-rente* was not. With the military contract, whether or not a yearly fee was involved, the grantee or contracting captain performed no homage or fealty; the only nexus between grantor and grantee was money and mutual military respect. The similarity between the two systems cannot be ascribed to mere coincidence.[40] Although many military and administrative practices developing independently of the *fief-rente* in the twelfth and thirteenth centuries contributed to the rise and effectiveness of the military contract, it was the *fief-rente* that was its feudal antecedent.[41] For Eng-

[40] The oft-cited treaties of 1103, 1110, and 1163 between the kings of England and the counts of Flanders had all the characteristics of a fourteenth-century indenture. So, too, do the following grants. In 1337 Thierry, lord of Montjoie and Fauquemont, did homage to Edward III for a fief of 1,200 gold florins of Florence to be received during his lifetime. To this fief Edward added a subsidy of 6,000 florins. Thierry promised to supply upon summons one hundred men-at-arms; each was to receive wages of 15 florins per month. Should Thierry or any of his men be captured in battle, Edward promised to ransom them. Two representatives of Edward and two of Thierry would evaluate all losses and injuries relating to horses; upon their recommendations Edward would pay suitable compensation (*Foedera,* II, ii, 992). In France, the Low Countries, and Germany *fiefs-rentes* were granted under similar conditions. In the military treaty concluded between Count Henry VII of Luxemburg and Philip IV of France in 1294 Henry received a fief of 500 *l.* and a subsidy of 6,000 *l.* In return he promised to serve Philip with 200 men-at-arms against Edward I of England. If more men were required Henry would provide them. Philip promised "les gages acoustumes, c'est assavoir vint sols tournois pour le benneres, diz sols pour chevalier, cinc sols pour escuyer, des la que nous mouverons pour son service faire iuques a tant, que nous serons retournes ou porrons estre retournes en nos lieuz, et en prenant retourz de chevauz les comme nobles hommes Hue de Chastillon comte de Blois et mesire Godefroi de Breban diront et ordeneront, et nous tendrons pour paies et tenons des orendroit de ce, qu il en woudront dire et ordener." It was agreed that the terms of payment and restoration of horses should remain in force as long as the war lasted (Kern, *Acta Imperii,* no. 92). It will be recalled that in all military treaties concluded by Cologne not only were *fiefs-rentes* granted but provisions were also made for the number and type of fighters, war wages, restoration of horses and armor, maintenance, and all the other details found in the English and French examples (See Ch. V, p. 235). As for the Low Countries, it should also be remembered that Count Guy and Count Louis de Male of Flanders concluded similar agreements for military service. The grants of *fiefs-rentes* to the household knights of the fourteenth century are particularly good examples (Ch. V, pp. 185–86).

[41] By the thirteenth century it was customary throughout western Europe for the holder of an ordinary fief of land to receive wages for each day's

land this conclusion is beyond doubt; for the Continent it may be questioned because there the retaining fee is lacking. And yet with such striking resemblances between the *fief-rente* and the military contract, it would be strange if the *fief-rente* was not more of an antecedent than other military developments. This opinion is strengthened by what Clason has told us about the *fief-rente* and its relation to non-feudal pensions in the fifteenth century. Indicating that German princes continued to receive *fiefs-rentes* from foreign princes in the fifteenth century, he then pointed out that non-feudal pensions became more numerous and that by the middle of the century had completely superseded the *fief-rente*. He wrote: "Der Umschwung vollzieht sich am Ende des Mittelalters, in der zweiten Hälfte des 15. Jahrhunderts; die deutschen Fürsten werden jetzt nicht mehr die Vasallen der fremden Könige, sondern ihre Pensionäre."[42] Have we not here the same evolution that occurred in England, only at a later date? Clason proceeded to show how, in particular, the French kings of the late fifteenth, sixteenth, and seventeenth centuries used pensions to secure the military services of the German princes and how the princes themselves adopted the same practice.[43] The ancestry of the famous pensions of the Thirty Years' War, we can conclude, goes back principally to the *fief-rente*.

Emerging in response to the growing military requirements from the twelfth century onward, both the *fief-rente* and the contractual military service clearly expressed the tenor of the age in which they flourished. In the twelfth century when the *fief-rente* became prominent, feudalism was the military system of western Europe. It is therefore not surprising that feudal lords, coming into possession of money, should attempt to work it into the fabric of feudalism when using it to acquire additional military service. The *fief-rente*, although made possible by the returning money economy, was nevertheless a product of the feudal mentality, enabling lords to follow the accepted practice of binding men to them by homage and fealty. Because it was a hybrid institution its destiny was tied both to feudalism and the money economy. In the thirteenth century the

service as well as to be promised all the other pecuniary benefits found with both the *fief-rente* and the military contract. See above pp. 200–01.

[42] Clason, *Pensionsverhältnisse*, p. 45.

[43] *Ibid.*, pp. 56–75.

traditional feudalism started to crumble. Growing ever farther apart from the new institutions springing up with the money economy and showing itself ever less effective, it ceased to occupy the dominant position as the political and military system of the state and of the feudal aristocracy. As a result, men were being emancipated from feudal thinking and a decline of the *fief-rente* was inevitable. During the course of the fourteenth century money had so antiquated feudal custom that men no longer saw the necessity of guaranteeing their relations through the bond of a fief and the performance of homage and fealty. Relations were now being formed through contracts based simply upon pecuniary arrangements. In such a milieu there was less and less room for the *fief-rente* and none for the traditional feudalism. In this transitional period of the fourteenth and early part of the fifteenth century the *fief-rente* and the military contract existed side by side with the latter consistently gaining ground at the expense of the former. Finally the *fief-rente* succumbed; only a few are to be found after 1450. Just as the combination of the money economy and new military demands lessened the military value of the old land fief, so contractual military service replaced its stubborn rival, the *fief-rente*. To see in the *fief-rente* a transitional feudal institution would seem to offer an explanation more satisfactory than any other for the rise of contractual military service and its replacement of feudal military service. The *fief-rente*, the antecedent of contractual service, epitomized the transition from the time when feudalism provided the armies of western Europe to when it was but a sentimental memory of such as Froissart and John the Good of France.

Just as the *fief-rente* yielded to the non-feudal contract, so in turn did the latter give way to another conception of military relationship. In a study of English military administration from 1420 to 1440, R. A. Newhall has shown how this contractual system (indenture) began to break down. The violation of a private contract gradually came to be considered an evasion of public duty and a crime against the king rather than a violation of a contract and an offense against the other contracting party. Newhall writes: "Such an attitude of mind is a step towards a modern conception of an army." [44] In Germany pension arrangements seemed to prevail from

---

[44] Newhall, *Muster and Review,* p. 154.

the second half of the fifteenth century into the seventeenth,[45] but in France and the Low Countries the military forces were so revamped as to produce armies not far removed from modern standing armies. Already in the reigns of John the Good and Charles V of France the military disasters suffered at the hands of the English forced military innovations anticipating a royal standing army controlled by a central military staff and paid completely by royal wages. The *Ordonnance* of 1374 was but an amplification of two preceding ones of 1355 and 1357. The royal constable was to appoint a lieutenant, and the royal marshals, four lieutenants who were to review the troops when mustered for mobilization. Under this central staff were to be the captains of the various companies of troops. With his command to be authorized by royal letters, each was to command a company of one hundred men, be responsible for mustering them, lead them to the point of mobilization, and account for the loyalty of his men to the king and for their conduct in the field.[46] After the death of Charles V this military reform was let to lapse during the anarchy of Charles VI's reign and in the face of new military reverses against the English, but under Charles VII military reform was again tackled and the French army again organized into an efficient fighting force. An *Ordonnance* of 1439 once more placed in effect the one of 1374. Then in 1445 came yet new reforms prepared with the advice of the constable, marshals, royal council, some of the captains, and the great princes. Henceforth there were to be fifteen "compagnies de grande ordonnance." Each company was to have one hundred mounted lances, a lance composed of six men: a man-at-arms, who held the lance and commanded the group of six, a sword-bearer, a page, two

---

[45] Clason, *Pensionsverhältnisse*, pp. 45 ff. The remarks of Delbrück, *Geschichte der Kriegskunst*, III, 526–27 are pertinent: "Auch Deutschland ist ja im dreizehnten, vierzehnten und fünfzehnten Jahrhundert erfüllt von Fehden und Bürgerkriegen, aber doch nicht in dem Masse, wie Frankreich und Italien, besonders deshalb nicht, weil die deutschen Städte sich nicht in dem Grade zu selbständigen Staaten ausbilden wie die italienischen, sondern einen mehr wirtschaftlichen, relativ friedlicheren Charakter bewahren. ... Die deutschen Kriegsgesellen, die als Söldner dem Kriege nachgehen, finden daher ihren Erwerb zum grossen Teil ausserhalb Deutschlands, in den französisch-englischen Kriegen und namentlich in Italien."

[46] Boutaric, *Institutions militaires*, pp. 253–56, 262; Coville, in Lavisse, *Histoire de France*, IV, i, 217–20.

archers, and a varlet of war. At times there were not full complements for each company, but to the end of his reign Charles VII
had at least fifteen companies and generally twenty mobilized. The
captains of the companies, who were appointed by the king and
dismissed at will, had all the command functions as previously and
were to sift their men with care to insure that their companies contained only lawful citizens. The companies were to be stationed and
lodged in certain designated towns and to be paid wages and fed
at the expense of the provinces. Severe discipline was introduced to
insure against the lawlessness and brigandage of the *grandes compagnies*. To reinforce these permanent companies in time of stress,
smaller auxiliary companies were recruited. In 1448 and 1451
Charles turned to the reorganization of the infantry; he formed the
francs-archers. According to the *Ordonnances* instituting them, each
group of fifty households had to furnish the king with an archer and
a crossbowman. Chosen by the *prévôts* and *élus* all had to be of good
repute, of effective military age, and robust and skilled with their
weapons. These men were to live at home but were to be inspected
periodically. They were to have suitable armor, to practice their
military skills on every feast day, and to serve the king whenever
summoned. While on active service each received four francs a
month. All were exempt from the royal *taille* and if any were too
poor to provide themselves suitably with armor, they were to be
equipped at the expense of their parish. It has been estimated that
there were 8,000 *francs-archers* at the time of Charles VII. This
organization plus some artillery groups formed the new standing
army of France.[47] In the words of Petit-Dutaillis the "roi avait
maintenant une armée régulière, une cavalerie soldée, une infanterie
recrutée directement dans la plupart des provinces du royaume,
sans intervention des seigneurs. ... En fait, l'armée permanente
était fondée, au profit de la monarchie."[48]

The over-ambitious military projects of Charles the Rash of Burgundy led to his reorganization of the Burgundian army after the
model of the *compagnies d'ordonnance* of his French opponent. In
1470 he demanded from the estates of Flanders an *aide* of 120,000
écus of gold payable over three years for the continuous support of

---

[47] Lot, *L'art militaire*, II, 78–80; Boutaric, *Institutions militaires*, pp. 308–
26; Petit-Dutaillis, in Lavisse, *Histoire de France*, IV, ii, 94–101.

[48] Petit-Dutaillis, in Lavisse, *Histoire de France*, IV, ii, 101.

1,000 lances. It was granted after much delay and in 1471 Charles began his reforms. His intention was to have companies of nine hundred men plus a trumpeteer; six hundred and one were to be mounted and three hundred were to be footsoldiers. Both groups were to contain subdivisions of special troops; for example, the footsoldiers were to be comprised of one hundred crossbowmen, one hundred cannoneers, and one hundred pikemen. Each company was to be subdivided into ten groups of ninety men. Such were the original plans for the standing army of Charles the Rash. We know, however, that these projected companies never contained their full complements of men. In 1473 the *Grande Ordonnance* gave the final organization to these companies. Under its terms each company, under the command of a *conducteur*, was to be divided into four squadrons of twenty-five men. Each squadron, under the command of a chief, was to be subdivided into four groups each consisting of five men-at-arms and one chief. Each company thus contained a commander and one hundred lances with four horses assigned to each lance. Companies of archers were to contain three hundred men divided into squadrons of seventy-five, each to be commanded by a man-at-arms. The footsoldiers were also formed into companies of three hundred with a knight for a captain. The companies were then divided into three squadrons of one hundred men, each commanded by a mounted man-at-arms called a *centenier*. Each squadron was subdivided into three groups, each commanded by a footsoldier. No detail of pay, supply, maintenance, or discipline was neglected. This *Grande Ordonnance* of Charles the Rash was the most specific and complete military reform of the fifteenth century.[49] Although its objectives were never fully realized and although the grand military projects of Charles were demolished on the fields of Morat and Nancy, this *Ordonnance* proves that the concept of a standing army, completely paid and controlled by the territorial prince, was competing for supremacy with contractual service. Except in Germany where lack of a strong centralized government made any extensive military reorganization impossible, the military

---

[49] Lot, *L'art militaire*, II, 114–16; Pirenne, *Histoire de Belgique*, 4th ed., II, 404–7; J. de la Chauvelays, *Mémoire sur la composition des armées de Charles le Téméraire dans les deux Bourgognes* (Mémoires de l'Académie de Dijon, Dijon, 1878), 3d ser., V, 139 ff.; G. Guillaume, *Histoire de l'organisation militaire sous les ducs de Bourgogne* (Bruxelles, 1848), pp. 110 ff.

contract was gradually being superseded in western Europe by the new military relation established directly between ruler and subjects. Private contractual service, like the traditional feudal service and after it the *fief-rente,* had been outmoded by the political, social, economic, and military revolution sparked by the money economy.

The Significance of the Fief-Rente:
Summary and Conclusion

This study of the *fief-rente* in the heartland of feudalism—England and the lands between the Loire and the Rhine—has necessarily been of a comparative nature in that the records of France, England, Germany, and the Low Countries were involved. From the relevant chancery, financial, legal, and military records it has emerged as a prominent institution with a character clearly delineated. Mitteis concluded that it was a completely new institution. Sczaniecki, though recognizing certain deviations from the ordinary fief, nevertheless contended that it was devoid of any originality. It was, according to him, modeled in almost all respects upon the ordinary fief. The traditional type of fief was indeed the model, but the fact that money rather than land was the foundation of the *fief-rente* made of it a new institution. To say that a man held land in fief was customarily to imply heritability; with the *fief-rente* life and provisional tenures prevailed. From region to region the application of the feudal incidents to the *fief-rente* varied; in none can it be asserted that the customary aids were applied. A *fief-rente* could be terminated at a moment's notice; an ordinary fief had to be confiscated with perhaps a war necessary to enforce the sentence. With the *fief-rente* such action was rarely taken. From even these few instances of juridical differences it is obvious that money set the *fief-rente* apart from the ordinary fief in the realm of feudal law. Money also brought to the *fief-rente* a fluidity unknown with the ordinary fief. No matter how great the distance between the lord and the man whose services were required, feudal relations were readily effected by means of the *fief-rente*. It is without exaggeration to say that fully half of the recipients of *fiefs-rentes* never saw their lords. One has but to recall the geographical dispersion of the vassals performing the political, diplomatic, and military services to understand how easily the *fief-rente* inaugurated and stretched the fabric of feudal relations. Practically all the *fiefs-rentes* granted by the English kings were to men on the Continent. The French kings conceded *fiefs-rentes* to men throughout France, the Low Countries, and Germany. In the Low Countries the *fief-rente* knew no boundaries except the English Channel and the North Sea; it criss-crossed the borders of the Low Country states and spilled into Germany and France. The German emperors, princes, and towns likewise crossed over borders, granting *fiefs-rentes* to Low Country nobles. The lord was limited as to the number of vassals he might have only by the amount of money at his disposal; the amount of land and the geographical location of lord and vassal were no longer restricting forces. But not all the advantages of the *fief-rente* fell to the lord. For the vassal it was a new means of augmenting an income which progressively decreased as his revenues from land shrank in value. It also provided employment of all sorts not only to feudal aristocrat but to men of the other estates. Whoever could offer military, political, and diplomatic services was a likely candidate for receiving a *fief-rente*; it would link lord to vassal by feudal bond and often, especially where military service was involved, would bring to the vassal, in addition to his yearly fee, war wages and other financial perquisites. Men performing diplomatic and political services for *fiefs-rentes* frequently received bonuses such as *dona* and were extended other considerations. Just as the pensions of the sixteenth, seventeenth, and eighteenth centuries kept the feudal aristocrat from bankruptcy, so the *fief-rente* in the Middle Ages gave him employment and helped to save him from financial ruin. Between the rigidity of the ordinary land fief and the malleability of the *fief-rente* there was a sharp difference. By introducing a flexibility into feudal tenure and relations, as well as by greatly multiplying the number of men and type of services that could be obtained through feudal custom, the *fief-rente* injected new vigor into feudalism and helped it to withstand for a longer time the ever new demands and situations brought about by the money economy.

The *fief-rente* varied in its use from area to area. The continental princes used it for political purposes much more than the English kings. As a diplomatic tool it was always of greater value to the French and English kings than to the German and Low Country princes. Its use to obtain castle-guard was almost exclusively limited to the Continent and predominated in Germany where this was practically the only type of military service acquired by it. On the Continent alone was it a means to secure strategic rights to castles. But in all western Europe princes granted *fiefs-rentes* to obtain service in the field. Relying most heavily upon the *fief-rente* for this form of service were the French and English kings; not far behind them were the most powerful of the Low Country princes. In spite of the varying political, diplomatic, and military emphasis put upon the *fief-rente* in each area, its pattern was fundamentally the same everywhere; there was not an English, French, German, or Flemish *fief-rente* that was a captive of political barriers. Rather the *fief-rente* was a western European institution whose value lay in its military role. It is difficult to understand the position of Sczaniecki, Mitteis, and Kienast when in no area of western Europe does the political and diplomatic evidence compare in bulk to the military evidence. In the evolution from military service provided by the traditional fief of land to non-feudal contractual service and finally to standing armies, the *fief-rente* had a place; it was the link between traditional feudalism and contractual military service.

But it is not enough to have shown what the *fief-rente* was or that it was prominent. A prominent feudal institution, yes, but even more it was a microcosm of the economic, political, and military evolution in western Europe between the eleventh and the fifteenth century; in it can be discerned the slow decline of feudalism in the face of the onrushing money economy and the replacement of feudalism by the new political, military, and social institutions rooted in a money economy instead of a natural economy. Barely existing in the tenth century when there was little money in circulation, but gradually increasing in numbers during the eleventh and twelfth centuries as the money economy spread and gained in rigor throughout western Europe, the *fief-rente* attained its apogee in the thirteenth and fourteenth centuries—a period when the money economy prevailed but had not yet completely routed feudalism. By the fifteenth century money had so antiquated feudal custom that the *fief-rente* virtually melted away. Money created and destroyed the *fief-rente* but did not alone completely control its fate. The *fief-rente* only flourished where feudalism was strong and knew a long tradition, as in the lands between the Loire and the Rhine, or where it had been successfully transplanted, as in the Latin States of the Crusaders. In an area such as southern Italy and Sicily, which had never completely lost touch with money and where feudalism never became strong, the *fief-rente* failed to establish a beachhead. Born from a combination of feudalism and the money economy, the *fief-rente* depended upon both for its existence. Admittedly there were *fiefs-rentes* in kind, but if limited to this type, it would never have become a significant institution. In western Europe the money economy made possible the practice of granting annual incomes of money, but the tradition of strong feudal custom dictated that for a long period the principles of feudal tenure should be superimposed upon these incomes. When money had completely destroyed the hold of feudalism over men, feudal tenure fell away from these incomes and they became simply a non-feudal *rente,* a pension, an annuity, or a retaining fee. But let us not forget that the very money economy which eventually destroyed the traditional feudalism, and after it the *fief-rente,* paradoxically enabled feudalism to survive by means of the *fief-rente* far beyond the time when based solely upon land it would have ceased to exist. It is true that the traditional feudalism of land was teetering in the thirteenth century and was practically a vestigial system in the fourteenth, but in this same period feudalism, as represented and sustained by the *fief-rente,* was extremely virile. It will not do to have feudalism in its grave by the fourteenth century and to explain all the surviving feudal terminology as so much façade; the terminology pertaining to the *fief-rente* was real and meaningful. In the fourteenth century men did homage and fealty for *fiefs-rentes* and performed their feudal obligations; only in the fifteenth century did this cease. Into the early fifteenth century, at least, the feudalism of money had a vitality that must be recognized. No longer is it acceptable to look upon the decline and fall of feudalism as completed in the fourteenth century.

Appendix

1. Margaret, countess of Flanders and Hainaut, and her son Guy recognize that they have granted to Jakemon Louchard, citizen of Arras, a fief of 200 l., money of Flanders, payable by the toll of Damme. Jakemon is bound to perform court service to Countess Margaret at Douai three times yearly; he may, whenever he so desires, transmit this fief to his children.

May 1273

Archives de l'État à Gand. De Saint Genois, *Inventaire des chartes de Flandre*, no. 175.

Nous Margherite, contesse de Flandres et de Hainau, et je Guis ses fiex, quens de Flandres et marchis de Namur, faisons savoir a tous ke nous a nostre ami Jakemon Louchart, citoiien d'Arras, avons done deus cens livrees de rente par an a la mounoie de Flandres a tenir lui et ses hoirs de nous et de nos hoirs, signeurs de Flandres, iretablement et franchement en fief et en houmage lige a tel service ki chi apres est devises. Chest asavoir kil doit estre trois fois en lan a nos plais a Douay zauf chou kil en soit anchois semons de par nous souffissanment et a tans en la veue et en loye de nos homes ses pers. Et se il u aukuns de ses hoirs apres lui en estoit defaillans pour chascun jour dont il seroit troves en defaute il seroit enkeus envers nous en amende de cinc sols de la mounoie devant dite. Et de ches deus cens libres de la dite mounoie a avoir chascun en apparelliement et sans nul detri et sans nul debat, nous avons assene et assenons le devant dit Jakemon et ses hoirs apres lui a nostre tonlieu dou Dam a prendre et a rechevoir a deus termines en lan. Chest asavoir cent libres al Exaltation Zainte Crois prochaine et cent libres a la Chandeliere siewant apres et ensi a tels termines chascun an perpetuelment. Si mandons et commandons au recheveur de nostre tonlieu devant dit, kicunkes che sera dore en avant, ke il des premiers et des plus apparellies deniers ke il avera recheus des pourfis de nostre

tonlieu devant dit pait au devant dit Jakemon et a ses hoirs apres lui
u a lour certain message, ki lour letres pendans aportera, par les
queles il puist conter les deus cens livres devant dites chascun an
sans nul detri faire estachiement as jours ki devant sunt devise
perpetuelment. Et si sachent tout ke nous avons otroiiet otroions
au devant dit Jakemon Louchart ke il ces deus cens livrees de rente
devant dites puet doner a un u a deus de ses enfans si com il miels
li plaira. Et nous celui ou chiaus de ses enfans a qui u as quels il
les donra et otriera par ses letres u en autre maniere souffissanment
et en son vivant, nous avons encovent et prometons en boine foi ke
nous len recheverons a home u a homes a tenir de nous et de nos
hoirs, signeurs de Flandres, apres nous a un houmage u a deus
houmages liges a tel service et en autel maniere chascun des deus
se deus en ia comme devant est devise. Et si volons ke tout sachent se
il avenoit ke nous fesissiens maniier et rechevoir nostre tonlieu devant
dit par aukune persone sans cense et nous celi persone eussiens tant
fait paiier de che ke il averoit recheu dou devant dit tonlieu ailleurs
devant le jour du paiement u des paiemens ke il deveroit faire au
devant dit Jakemon u a ses hoirs ke il ne li peust paiier si comme
devise est. Nous avons promis et prometons et avons encovent au
dit Jakemon et a ses hoirs ke nous li feriens paiier en ses deniers le
paiement u les paiemens ki eskeus u eskeu seroient sans delai tant
tost apres ke li jours de paiement seroit passes. Et de toutes ches
devises devant escrites a tenir fermement et entierement avons nous
proumis et proumetons en boine foi ke nous jamais ne verrons encontre en tout ne en aukune partie ne par nous ne par autrui. Et a
che faire avons nous obligiet et obligons nous et nos hoirs apres nous,
signeurs de Flandres. En tesmoignage et en confermance de laquel
chose nous avons done ches presentes letres au devant dit Jakemon
Louchart seelees de nos seaus ki furent donees en lan del Incarnation Nostre Signeur Jesu Crist mil deus cens sissante treze, el mois
de may.

2. *Letters of William,* châtelain *of Saint-Omer and lord of Fauquemberghe,*
whereby he grants various of his revenues in Saint-Omer to Lambert Wolveric
to be held heritably in fief. Lambert is obliged to pay William a white lance
yearly; should he fail to do so, he will be assessed 5 s. The relief for the fief
will be two lances.

January 1274

Archives Départementales du Nord à Lille. Série B. 964/1815.

Sachent tout chil ki cheste chartre verront et orront ke iou Willaumes, chevaliers et castelains de Saint Omeir et sires de Faukem-
berghe, ai donei a Lambert Wolveric, fil Jehan Wolveric de Saint
Omeir, a tenir en fief de mi et de mes oirs lui et ses oirs les droitures
ke li sueur me devoient en Saint Omeir devant chou ke iou le donai
alui, chou est a savoir les borgois ki estal tinent en le hale trois
deniers et les forains chinc deniers, a prendre et a leveir a teus iours
et a teus usages com iou les peuch leveir devant ke iou les donai
alui, et quatre livres de parisis par an ke li vile de Saint Omeir me
devoit devant ke iou les donai alui a prendre sour toutes les rentes
ke li devant dite vile a sour le Gher, et douze livres de parisis par
an a prendre sour me mairie dou Bruille et veul ke ki kil soit ki
cheste mairie tenra ne maniera kil soit tenus de paier les douze
livres devant dites et de faire plainne main au devant dit Lambert
Wolveric et a ses oirs, le moitie a le Nativitei Saint Jehan Baptiste
et lautre moitie a le Tous Sains apres en suant, et en si dan en an
et de termine en termine iritaulement. Et si veul ke li mairie devant
dite soit obligie au devant dit Lambert Wolveric, mon homme et
a ses oirs, pour les douze livres faire plaines chascun an, et che fief
devant dit doit il tenir pour tous services par une blanke lanche a
paier devens les iours de le Pentecouste. Et sil avenist ke par *ensone*
u par oublianche ne le paiast ou autres pour lui a le Pentecouste en
apres en devroit il deus, et se il ne les paiast il en seroit en amende
de chinc saus de parisis et en si sen aquiteroit. Et che fief devant
dit ensi com il est nomeis par pieches li promet iou, et ai en covent
a warandir contre tous cheaus ki par locoison de mi u de mes
singneurs u de mes oirs li porroient u voroient demandeir, et se li
ai donei che fief par teil condise kon devera dou fief paier deus
lanches quant relief i eskera pour le relief. Et pour chou ke che soit
ferme chose et estaule et seuve, ai iou cheste chartre seelee de men
seel et donee au devant dit Lambert Wolveric. En lan de grase m et
cc et lxxiii, el mois de jenevir.

3. *Guy, count of Flanders and marquis of Namur, makes known that Michael, lord of Auchy, has exchanged a fief of oats and money, worth 120 l. of Paris yearly and paid by the gavène of Cambrai, for a fief of 12 muids and 3 hoeuds of wheat, 381 hoeuds of oats, and 40 l., money of Flanders, payable by the espier and various revenues of Cassel. Guy promises that if he is ever in default in payment of the fief, he will pay the arrears plus a third of the sum in default.*

9 May 1275

Archives Départementales du Nord à Lille. Série B. 1492/1868.

Nous Guis, cuens de Flandres et marchis de Namur, faisons savoir a tous ke nous a nostre chier foiable Mikiel cevalier, signeur d'Auchi, avons fait escange pour ble, avaine, et deniers kil avoit a nostre gaule de Cambresis a le valeur de cent et vint libres paresis a nostre espier et a nos rentes de Cassiel, les queles Jehans de Cornus rechoit. Cest a savoir ke pour le cange devant dit nous li avons donne et donnons douze muis et trois heus de forment, trois cens quatre vins et un heut davaine, et quarante libres de le monoie de Flandres en deniers cascun an a prendre et a rechevoir al espier et as rentes de Cassiel deseure dites as tiermes ke on nous paie et siut paiier a tenir en fief hiretaulement, lui et son hoir, de nous et de nos hoirs, signeurs de Flandres. Et mandons et commandons a nostre recheveur kiconques le soit kil le forment, lavaine, et les deniers devant nommes pait a mon signeur Mikiel deseure dit et a ses hoirs as tiermes que on les nous devoit paiier sans atendre autre mandement de nous ne de nos hoirs. Et sil avenoit que des coses devant dites il en fust en defaute en tout ou en partie, nous volons kil en ait le tierch denier damende avoec chou ke on li seroit en defaute toutes les fois ke on li en defauroit et tel maniere ke nous lavons de nos autres rentes quant on ne nous paie as tiermes assis et faire le devons venir eus. En tiesmoignage et en seurte de la quel chose nous avons ces letres donnees a mon signeur Mikiel devant dit saielees de nostre saiel ki furent donnees a Lille lan del Incarnation Nostre Signeur Ihesu Crist mil deus cens sissante et quinze, le dioes apries les octaves de mai.

4. Letters by which three arbitrators adjudicate differences over the right of Boisard de Renenghes to receive a fief of 60 razières of wheat from William, châtelain of Saint-Omer and lord of Fauquemberghe. Meeting in Saint-Omer in the house of the châtelain and in the presence of other lords and officials, the three arbitrators decide that William should pay the fief to Boisard and his heirs. William must also pay a fine of 100 m.; 50 m. to be paid to Boisard and 50 m. to the three arbitrators.

February 1276

Archives Départementales du Nord à Lille. Série B. 964/1898.

Nous Bauduins de Renenghes canonies de Tierewane, Wautiers de Renenghes sires de Morebeke, et Phelipes d'Ypre sires de Kienvile chevalier, faisons savoir a tous ke com debas eust este entre noble homme Willaume, castelain de Saint Omeir et seigneur de Faukenberghe chevalier, dune part, et mon seigneur Boisart sen oncle, chevalier, dautre part, dendroit sisante rasieres de blei par an a le mesure de Saint Omeir ke li devantdis Boisars demandoit au castelain com sen boen iretage ; et le quel il tenoit du conte d'Artois et li castelains de debatist par proieres damis et par conseil de bones gens les parties devantdites se misent sour nous del content et del debat devantdit selonc che ke il apert en le mise escrite et seelee de nos seaus et des seaus des parties devantdites ki tele est com il ensieut chi apres. Nous Bauduins de Renenghes canonies de Tierewane, Wautiers de Renenghes sires de Morebeke, et Phelipes d'Ypre sires de Kienvile chevalier, faisons a savoir a tous cheus ki ces presentes letres verront et orront ke comme debas fust entre nobles hommes mon seigneur Willaume, castelain de Saint Omeir et seigneur de Faukenberghe, de une part, et Boisart de Renenghes chevalier, dautre, sour chou ke chis Boisars demandoit a mon seigneur le castelain devantdit, sisante rasieres de ble a le mesure de Saint Omeir par an par le raison de sen assenement en le *pardesin* pour toutes riotes et tous contens eskiewer cil Willaumes castelains et cil Boisars chevalier devantdit sour le debat devantdit et sour toutes autres causes, quereles, contens, et controversieses ki avoient este entre aus deus juskes au iour de hui. Et sour quelconkes li uns pooit demander a lautre fust en le court de Saint Omeir fust ailleurs se misent en nous et promisent par foi fianchie dune part et dautre et sour paine de chent mars desterlins a rendre le moitie a celi ki no dit tenra et lautre moitie la u nous vaurons ke il de haut et de bas tenront et rempliront quelconkes nous dirons et ordene-

rons des choses devantdites soit en iritant soit en deseritant u autre-
ment comment ke che soit ne pour chou ne demourroit mie se
aucuns daus deus perdist le paine ke nos dis ne fust estables. Et est
asavoir ke nous devons aler avant en la besoigne devantdite selonc
chou kil samblera a nous trois u as deus se li tiers ni peust estre
mieus fait ke laisie iamar fust chou ke les parties devantdites u
aucune des parties ni fuissent apelees. Et nous canonies Wautiers
et Phelipes devantdit ki volons oster tous contens et toutes riotes
entre les parties devantdites avons en nous rechut le fais de le com-
promission devantdite selonc le forme ki deseure est dite et espressee.
Et pour chou ke cheste letre ait plus grant vertu nous lavons de nos
seaus seelee avoekes les seaus, le castelain et Boisart par devantdis,
li quele fu faite en lan del Incarnation Nostre Seigneur m cc et
sisante quinze, el mois doctobre. Et nous ki larbitre pris aviemes en
nous apresimes de le verite du debat devantdit ki droit iavoit par
bone gent et loial et quant nous en seumes bien le bone verite nous
aiournames les parties devantdites a Saint Omeir el monstier mon
seigneur Saint Omeir pour oir no dit le iour des Chendres, le quel
iour les parties ivindrent en present pour oir no dit par devant mout
de bones gens che loist asavoir le bailliue de Saint Omeir, mon
seigneur de Warennes, le provost d'Aire, larchediakene de Brebant,
le seigneur de Haveskerke, mon seigneur Robert de Haveskerke,
mon seigneur Gilon de Haveskerke, mon seigneur Jakemon de Renenghes, et le seigneur de Wiske, et autre bone gent se desimes no
dit et disons entel maniere ke li castelains de Saint Omeir et si oir
a mon seigneur Boisart et a ses oirs parmenablement paiechent
chascun an, le iour Saint Jehan, sisante rasieres de blei a le mesure
de Saint Omeir u wit saus de parisis pour le rasiere com sen boen
iretage. Et iou Willaumes, castelains de Saint Omeir devantdis,
conois et sui tenus, iou et mi oir, a tenir et a paier le dit ensi com
il est devantdit et devise. Et sil avenist cose ke iou le fesise et me sire
Boisars devantdis en eust cous u damages, en quelconkes maniere
ke che fust par me defaute, iou li seroie tenus de rendre tous cous
et tous damages a sen simple dit sans autre prueve; et si porroit
douner a quelconkes iustiche ke lui plairoit le quint denier dont il
seroit en defaute pour mi destraindre de lui faire paier sans le
princhepal iretage amenrir. Et quant a toutes ces coses fermement
tenir oblege iou especiaument mes oirs et tous mes biens, moebles
et non moebles, present et chaus ki sont avenir, et les mech en

abandon envers tous seigneurs et envers toutes iustiches ke li devantdis me sire Boisars u si oir les puist prendre et faire prendre, lever et faire lever, par quelle iustiche ke lui plaira tant kil soit tous parpaies des couvenenches devantdites. Et si ai renonchie comme croisies a tous privileges de crois, prise et a prendre, et a tous autres privileges a toutes grases dapostoile, de roi, u dautre prinche, et a toutes les coses ke on porroit faire dire ne proposer au destourbier le devantdit mon seigneur Boisart u de ses oirs. En tesmoignage de toutes ces coses desus dites nous arbitre, nous Florens de Warenne provos d'Aire, archediakene de Brebant, Jehans sires de Haveskerke, Robers de Haveskerke, Giles de Haveskerke, Jakemes de Renenghes, et ie Wis sires de Wiske chevalier, et nous castelains de Saint Omeir, et Boisars de Renenghes, parties devantdites, avons a che dit pendu nos seaus et prions au baillieu de Saint Omeir kil imeche le seel de le baillie. Che fu fait en lan del Incarnation Nostre Seigneur mil deus chens sisante et quinte, el mois de fevrier.

5. Guy, count of Flanders and marquis of Namur, declares that he has granted to John de Harecourt, the younger, a heritable fief of 100 l. of Tours payable by the renenghe of Flanders. For this fief John has done homage and fealty save that rendered to his other liege lords.

10 July 1280

Archives de l'État à Gand. De Saint Genois, *Inventaire des chartes de Flandre*, no. 263.

Nous Guis, cuens de Flandres et marchis de Namur, faisons savoir a tous cheaus ki ces presentes lettres verront et orront ke nous dounons a noble houme mon segneur Jehan de Harecourt, le jouene, cent livres de tournois de rente a lui et a son hoir hiretaulement a paier chascun an a nostre renenghe en Flandres au mois apres le jour de le Nativitei Saint Jehan Baptiste. Et ceste rente doit il et si hoir tenir de nous et de nos hoirs, contes de Flandres, en fief et en houmage perpetuelment. Et il nous en a fait feautei et houmage et nous len avons rechut a nostre houme feauble sauve le feautei de ses autres segneurs liges. Et pour ce ke ce soit ferme chose et estable a tous jours nous avons dounees a lui et a ses hoirs ces presentes lettres saielees de nostre propre saiel. Dounees a Paris lan del Incarnation Nostre Segneur mil deus cens quatre vins, le merkedi apres les octaves Sain Piere et Saint Pol.

6. John de Harecourt, marshal of France, makes known that for 1,000 l. of Tours he has sold back to Guy, count of Flanders, his fief en bourse of 100 l. of Tours. He states, however, that he wishes to remain the liege man of Guy for the 1,000 l.

9 February 1286

Archives de l'État à Gand. De Saint Genois, *Inventaire des chartes de Flandre,* no. 393.

Nous Johan de Harecourt chevaliers, mareschaus de France, faesons savoer a touz que come nous soyons hom a haut home et noble mon seigneur Guion, conte de Flandres et marchis de Namur, de cent livrees de terre au tournoys que il nous avoit done en fief de bourse, et nous les ayons vendues pour mil livres de tournoys pour le gre et lotroy de nostre davant dit seigneur, nous des davant dites mil livres demorons et volons demorier hom au dit conte et a ses hoers, contes de Flandres, a autre tel foyaute et a autre tel homage come nous estions davant des dites cent livrees de terre. Et se il avenoit que nous oussons volente de rendre au dit conte u a ses hoers, contes de Flandres, les dites mil livres, nous serions quite de lomage et toutes ces choses et chascunes deles prometons nous et nous obligons au tenir. Par le tesmoing de ces letres saalees de nostre seel. Faytes et donees en lan de grace mil deus cenz quatre vinz et cinc, le samedi empre le jour de le Chandeleur.

7. The knight William de Mortagne, lord of Rumeis, recognizes to have received 120 l. of Paris from Guy, count of Flanders, for his pension of 120 l. payable yearly by the renenghe of Flanders. He also acknowledges receipt of a fief of 80 l. of Paris.

6 July 1289

Archives Générales du Royaume à Bruxelles. *Trésor de Flandre.* Série I. No. 2073.

Je Willaumes de Mortagne chevaliers, sires de Rumeis, fach savoir a tous que ie me tieng plainement a sols et a bien paiiet de cent et vint libres paresis que mes chiers sires Guis, cuens de Flandres et marchis de Namur, me doit a le renenghe, lan quatre vins a noef, pour le raison de me pension de sis vins libres que ie doi avoir a le renenghe cascun an toute me vie. Et me tieng encore plainement a sols et a bien paiiet de quatre vins libres paresis que mes chiers sires devant dis et me dame de Flandres, contesse de Namur, me devient a le Saint Jehan Babtiste, lan quatre vins et noef, les quels ie tient en fief deaus et de Iehan de Namur, leur fil, apprendre cascun an a le Saint Iehan Babtiste en mil libres que Iehans de Namur a par an sour le tonliu dou Dam. Et reconnois que Giars, li recheveres, ma paiiet en ses deniers contans les deus sommes dargent deseure dites, cest a savoir sis vins libres paresis et quatre vin libres paresis einsi et pour che que deseure est dit. Par le tiesmoing de ces lettres saelees de men saiel qui furent faites et donnees en lan mil deus cens quatre vins et noef, le diemenche apres les octaves Saint Piere et Saint Pol apostles.

8. Ralph de Clermont, constable of France, recognizes that Guy, count of Flanders and marquis of Namur, has paid to him at the fair of Lille 220 l. of Tours, a sum due yearly for his fief.

23 August 1289

Archives de l'État à Gand. De Saint Genois, *Inventaire des chartes de Flandre,* no. 493.

Jou Raouls de Clermont, conestables de France et sires de Neele, fais savoir a tous chiaus qui ches presentes lettres verront et orront que iou ai rechut de haut houme et noble mon chier seigneur Guion, conte de Flandres et marquis de Namur, en bone monoie, se ke bien contee et bien nombree, onze vins livres tornois pour le terme de le Feste Saint Jehan Decollate prochaine venant; les quels li dis me sires li cuens me doit cascun en de mon fief que ie tieng de li au terme desusdit en le feste de Lille et de ches onze vins livres de tant com a chest paiement monte cuite iou bonement le dit mon seigneur le conte. En tesmoing de le quele case jou en ai baillie ches presentes lettres seelees de mon propre seel. Qui furent faites en lan de grace mil deus chens quatrevins et nuef, le veille Saint Bertremil lapostre.

9. Letters by which Robin, lord of Kobern, designates an annual income of 5 l., money of Trier, derived from his own lands, to be taken annually in fief from the count of Luxemburg.

20 September 1289

Archives Générales du Royaume à Bruxelles. Verkooren, *Inventaire des chartes du Luxembourg,* no. 323.

Nos Robinus, dominus de Coverna, universis presentes litteras inspecturis et audituris volumus esse notum et presentibus profitemur quod nos ad presentes viri strennui et honesti Rodingeri de Insula militis fideiussorem constituimus et ponimus apud nobilem virum, comitem dominum de Lutzellenburch, super eo quod idem miles ipsi domino comiti bona demonstrabit immobilia et assignabit in villa dicta Ryevinnache annis singulis inperpetuum quinque libras denariorum Trevirensis redituum valencia, que bona seu quinque libras idem miles et sui heredes tenebunt in feudum in perpeptuum a domino comite antedicto. In cuius rei testimonium zigilum nostrum duximus presentibus appendendum. Datum anno Domini m° cc° octogesimo nono, in Vigilia Beati Mathey apostoli.

10. Theobald, count of Bar, presents to Guy, count of Flanders, a memorandum listing all the payments received from Guy for the arrears of a fief of 200 l. Theobald recognizes that his knight Colart Willekant has received in his name all the arrears due him.

17 January 1291

Archives de l'État à Gand. De Saint Genois, *Inventaire des chartes de Flandre*, no. 547.

Li daerains paiements ki fais fu a conte de Bar pour son fief fu fais au Noel lxxxvi, ki monte cc lb. et fu paies par mon seigneur Sohier de Bailluel.

Ensi li doit en pour Paskes lan lxxxvii, cc lb. Item pour ce meisme terme pour se partie dou fief ki fu mon seigneur Renaut de Bar, l lb. Item pour son fief dou Noel apres, cc lb.

Item pour son fief de Paskes lan lxxxviii, cc lb. Item pour se partie dou fief ki fu mon seigneur Renaut de Bar, l lb. Item pour son fief dou Noel apres, cc lb.

Item pour son fief de Paskes lan lxxxix, cc lb. Item pour son fief ki fu mon seigneur Renaut de Bar, l lb. Item pour son fief dou Noel apres, cc lb.

Item pour son fief de Paskes lan lxxxx, cc lb. Item pour son fief ki fu mon seigneur Renaut de Bar, l lb. Item pour son fief de Noel apres, cc lb.

Somme kon doit au conte de Bar pour son fief de iiii ans fineis au Noel lan lxxxx, i^m dccc lb. De ce rabat ou pour les despens ke les gens mon seigneur de Flandres fisent en lost le dit conte de Bar deseure ce kon lor livra si comme il apert par le conte ke me sire Joffrois eu fist dcccc xxvii lb. xii s. iii d. Ensi li doit on encore tout conte et rabatu et dccc lxxii lb. vii s. ix d.

Nous Thiebaus, cuens de Bar, faisons congnissant a tous que nos nos tenons por bien solt et paiet de tous les arrieraiges que nobles homs nostres chiers sires Guys, contes de Flandres et marchis de Namur, nos devoit et estois tenus a nos por raison dou fiei que nos tenons de lui de tout temps trespassei jusques au jor que ces presentes lettres furent faites parmi la some dargent que li dis cuens de Flandres at fait delivrer por nos a mon signor Colart Willekaut, nostre chevalier. Si tesmengnange de la quel chose por ce que ferme soit et estable nos avons fait seeller ces presentes lettres de nostre seel que furent faites lan de grace mil deus cens quatre vins et deux, le mercredi apres les octaves de lapparition.

11. John, lord of Audenarde and Rosoit, and his eldest son Arnold surrender all claim to a heritable fief of 12 charretées of wine held of Count Reginald of Guelders, as well as to all the arrears.

1 August 1292

Archives Générales du Royaume à Bruxelles. *Trésor de Flandre.* Série I. No. 2075.

Nous Jehans, dis sires d'Audenarde sires de Rosoit, faisons savoir a tous ke nous a noble homme Renaut, conte de Ghelre, et a ses hoirs, pour nous et pour nos hoirs quitons a tous jours les douze karetees de vin par an ke nous dou conte de Ghelre devant dit tenimes hiritablement en fief. Et en estiemes en sen hommage le quel fief et tous les arrierages ke li dis quens ou si anciestre nous endoivent dusques au jour dele date de ceste lettre clamons tout quite a tous jours et avons rendut les lettres le conte de Ghelre ke nous aviemes del hommage devant dit. Et pour plus grande seurte nous prions a nostre chier fil et apparant hoir, Ernoul, ke ceste quitance il voille loer et greer. Et nous Ernous, aisnes fieus de noble homme Jehan dit signeur d'Audenarde, signeur de Rosoit, le quitance devant dite loons, et greons, et approvons, et avons en couvent pour nous et pour nos hoirs ke jamais ni venrons encontre par nous ne par autrui. En tiesmoingnage des queles choses devant dites nous Jehans, dis sires d'Audenarde, et nous Ernous, ses fieus devant dit, avons ces presentes lettres saielees de nos saiaus ki furent faites lan del Incarnation Nostre Signeur mil deus cens quatre vins et douze, le jour Saint Piere entrant aoust.

12. The knight Hugh of Burgundy does liege homage to Philip IV of France for a heritable fief of 300 l. of Tours payable by the Temple at Paris. Hugh promises to serve against all men save the count of Burgundy. If Philip should fight against the king of England, Hugh promises to supply 60 armed men, well mounted, who will serve at the royal wages and receive remuneration for all horses lost.

July 1294

Archives Nationales à Paris. *Trésor des chartes.* Hommages. Série J. 622ª/33.

Universis presentes litteras inspecturis, Hugo de Burgundia miles, salutem. Notum facimus universis tam presentibus quam futuris quod cum excellentissimus princeps et dominus noster Philippus, Dei gratia, rex Francie illustris nobis et heredibus nostris in hereditatem perpetuam dederit et concesserit in feodum trecentas libras turonensium annui redditus percipiendas a nobis et heredibus nostris anno quolibet Parisius apud Templum ad Festum Purificationis Beate Marie Virginis infuturum. Nos eidem domino regi fidelitatem et ligium homagium ante omnes homines excepto comite Burgundie prestitimus pro eisdem, nostri que heredes eidem et successoribus suis homagium simile facere tenebuntur. Promisimus que eidem quod si ipsum vel successores suos cum rege Anglie vel aliis quibuscumque, predicto comite dumtaxat excepto, guerram habere contigerit, nos cum gentibus, castris, et fortaliciis nostris, toto posse nostro bona fide cum sexaginta equitibus armatis *adminus,* iuvabimus, et serviemus eidem. Idem vero dominus noster rex nobis et gentibus nostris quas extra loca nostra pro negociis suis nobiscum ducemus prestare tenebitur stipendia et restaurationes equorum prout gentibus regni sui consuevit prestare. Que ut stabilia perseverent presentibus litteris nostrum fecimus apponi sigillum. Datum apud Abbatiam Monialis propre Pontiseram anno Domini millesimo ducentesimo nonagesimo quarto, mense julio.

13. Guy, count of Flanders and marquis of Namur, grants to John, lord of Harecourt, a heritable fief of 300 livrées de terre, money of Paris, payable by the receiver of Flanders; John owes in return the military service of ost and chevauchée. Because he lives farther from Guy than the other vassals, he shall receive costs of transportation whenever summoned to perform military service.

8 February 1296

Archives de l'État à Gand. De Saint Genois, *Inventaire des chartes de Flandre,* no. 804.

A touz ceus qui ces presentes lettres verront et orront Jehan, seigneur de Harecourt, chevalier salut. Sachent tuit que comme tres haut homme et noble mon chier seigneur Guis, cuens de Flandres et marchis de Namur, ait donne a moi et a mes hoirs trois cenz livrees de terre a parisis chascun an a heritage a touz iours mes en la fourme et en la maniere qui ensuit. Guis, cuens de Flandres et marchis de Namur, a touz ceus qui ces presentes lettres verront et orront salut. Sachent tuit que nous avons donne et encore donnons a noble homme nostre ame et foiable Jehan, seigneur de Harecourt chevalier, trois cens livrees de terre a parisis a heritage pour lui et pour ses hoirs a touz iours mes a tenir en fief de nous et de nos hoirs, contes de Flandres, et voulons que il prengne et recoive par la main de nostre receveur de Flandres qui que il soit la moitie des trois cenz livrees de terre desus diz a cest Noel prochainnement venant, et lautre moitie a la Nativite Saint Jehan Baptiste prochainnement ensuiant, et ensi a touz iours mes chascun an de ore en avant. Et commandons a nostre receveur de Flandres qui que il soit que il face et acomplisse les diz paiemenz au dit sire de Harecourt et a ses hoirs as diz termes chascun an de ore en avant sanz attendre autre commandement de nous ne de nos hoirs. Et pour ce que li dit sire de Harecourt et ses hoirs sont plus lontains de nous que nos autres hommes qui demeurent en nostre contee de Flandres, nous voulons et otroions que se nous ou nos hoirs li dit sire de Harecourt ou ses hoirs mandions ou semonnions pour aucun service faite a nous ou a nos hoirs, soit de ost ou de chevauchiee ou dautre chose quele que ele soit, que li dit sire de Harecourt ne si hoir ni soient de riens tenuz a venir a leur couz, ne a leur fraiz, ne a leur despens, mais du tout as noz et au nos hoirs contes de Flandres. Et pour toutes les choses desus dites et chascune de iceles faire et acomplir obligeons nous au dit sire de Harecourt et a ses hoirs, nous et nos hoirs, contes de Flandres, et touz les biens de nous et de nos hoirs et especialment nostre contee de Flandres. En tesmoing des queles choses nous avons fait seeler ces presentes lettres de nostre seel qui furent faites et donnees a Montargis, le joedi dapres les Cendres, en lan de l'Incarnation Nostre Seigneur mil deus cenz quatre vinz et quinze. Ge devant dit Jehan, seigneur de Harecourt, promet en bonne foi pour moi et pour mes hoirs a tenir fermes et estables et a garder et a complir toutes les choses desus dites au dit mon chier seigneur si comme il sont devisees. En tesmoing des queles choses ge devant dit Jehan, seigneur de Harecourt, chevalier, ai fait seeler ces presentes lettres de mon seel qui furent faites et donnees a Harecourt, lendemain de la Feste Saint Luc Evangeliste, en lan de l'Incarnation Nostre Seigneur mil deus cenz quatre vinz et seize.

14. Two writs of liberate *by Edward I of England directing the treasurer and chamberlains of the exchequer to pay the fiefs of* 200 l. *and* 300 l. *of black money of Tours owed, respectively, to John, lord of Cuyk, and Waler- and, lord of Montjoie and Fauquemont. A third writ directs the payment of 16,000 m. to Count Henry of Bar in part payment of 30,000 m. for providing the service of 1,000 mounted men-at-arms for a half-year in the war against Philip IV of France. A fourth writ directs payment of 20,000 l. sterling to Duke John II of Brabant in part payment of 160,000 l. of black money of Tours for supplying 2,000 men-at-arms to fight against the king of France.*

20–28 April 1295

Public Record Office at London. Liberate Roll. C. 62/71, m. 3.

Rex, thesaurario et camerariis suis, salutem. Liberate de thesauro nostri dilecto et fideli nostro Johanni, domino de Cuk, ad valorem ducentarum librarum turonensium nigrorum in sterlingis, videlicet unam medietatem de termino Sancti Michaelis proximo futuris et aliam medietatem de termino Pasche proximo sequenti, de annuo feodo suo ducentarum librarum turonensium nigrorum quorum valorem in sterlingis eidem Johanni concessimus percipiendas ad scaccarium nostrum ad totam vitam ipsius Johannis ad terminos supradictos. Teste rege apud Lammays xxviii die aprilis. Per ipsum regem.

Rex, eisdem, salutem. Liberate de thesauro nostro Waltero de Butencourt, valletto nobilis viri Henrici comitis de Baar, sexdecim milia marcarum ad opus eiusdem comitis in partem solucionis triginta milium marcarum, quas eidem comiti debemus pro obsequio suo nobis faciendo cum mille hominibus equitibus ferro armatis per dimidium annum contra regem Francorum prout inter nos et eundem comitem plenius est convenentum. Teste rege apud Lammays xx die aprilis. Per billam de garderoba.

Rex, eisdem, salutem. Liberate de thesauro nostro dilecto et fideli nostro Walramo, domino de Montioie et de Faukemount, ad valorem trescentarum librarum turonensium nigrorum in sterlingis, videlicet unam medietatem de termino Sancti Michaelis proximo futuris et aliam medietatem de termino Pasche proximo sequenti, de annuo feodo suo trescentarum librarum turonensium nigrorum quorum valorem sterlingis eidem Walramo concessimus percipiendas ad scaccarium nostrum ad totam vitam ipsius Walrami ad terminos supradictos. Teste rege apud Lammays xxviii die aprilis.

Rex, eisdem, salutem. Liberate de thesauro nostro dilecto et fideli nostro Johanni, duci Brabancie, viginti milia librarum sterlingorum in partem solucionis centum et sexaginta milium librarum turonensium nigrorum, quas ei debemus pro servicio quod nobis facere tenetur cum duobus milibus hominum peditum ferro armatorum contra regem Francorum prout inter nos et ipsum ducem plenius est convenentum. Teste rege apud Lammays in Angles' xxiiii die aprilis. Per billam scriptam manu Walteri de Langeton', tunc custodis garderobe.

15. Gerard de Juliers, lord of Castre, declares that Guy, count of Flanders and marquis of Namur, has granted him a heritable fief of 100 l. of Tours to be paid by the receiver of the land of Namur. Gerard swears that he and his heirs will loyally serve Guy and his heirs in all their wars. If Gerard or his heirs should desire to renounce their homage, they will forfeit all claim to the fief of 100 l.

23 August 1295

Archives Départementales du Nord à Lille. Série B. 1412/3739.

Jou Gerars de Julers, sires de Castre, fai savoir a tous ke comme haus prinches et mes chiers sires Guys, cuens de Flandres et marchis de Namur, mait dounei a mi pour mi et pour mes hoirs perpetuelment a tenir en fief de lui et de ses hoirs, contes de Namur, a tous jours cent livrees de tiere au tournois a prendre cascun an a son recheveur de le tiere de Namur. Et avoec tout che ki devant dis nobles prinches me sires ki cuens mait dounei par se courtesie pour tiere acater u pour mon pourfit faire en autre maniere de ses deniers juskes a mil livres de tournois, je recounois ke pour les devant dis cent livrees de tiere et pour le courtoisie des deniers des mil libres devant dis, je sui devenus hom a mon signeur le conte devant dit et apartient par devise cis houmages au conte de Namur et apartenir doit a tous jours de mi et de mes hoirs. Et si ai cn couvent et proumech loyalment et en boine foy pour mi et pour mes hoirs a aidier moon signeur le conte devant dit ki ore est et ses hoirs, contes de Namur, a tous jours encontre tous loyalment et en boine foy ensi com hom lieges doit aidier son signeur. Et sour che me sui mis especialment ou dit de haut et noble prinche Jehan, par le grace de Diu, duch de Lothrice de Brabant et de Lembourch, del ayve et dou service ke je et mi hoir ferons et fere deverons especialment des wieres et de toutes autres besongnes au conte de Flandres et a ses hoirs devant dis. Et ai encouvent et proumech en boine foy a tenir fermement et entierement et loyalment le dit de noble prinche le duch devant dit. Et sil avenist ke ja naviegne ke je u mes hoirs ki venroit apres mi vaussissiens renonchier al homage devant dit fere ne le poons sans rendre avoec le renonchement del homage tous les mil libres de tournois devant dis au conte de Namur. En tiesmongnage des quels choses devant dittes jou Gerars de Julers desus noumeis ai dounet en fermeteit ces presentes lettres sayelees de mon sayel ki furent faites en lan de grace mil deus cens quatrevins et quinze, le mardi devant le jour Saint Biertremin lapostle.

16. *Guy, count of Flanders and marquis of Namur, makes known that his envoys Henry de Blamont, John de Cuyk, and Jacques de Donze (receiver of Flanders), have received from the exchequer at London a sum af 6,000 l. sterling in part payment of a subsidy of 300,000 l. of black money of Tours owed him by Edward I of England.*

19 February 1297

Public Record Office at London. Diplomatic Documents of the Exchequer. E. 30/33.

Nous Guys, cuens de Flandres et marchis de Namur, faisons savoir a tous ke pour nous et en nostre non noble homme nostre chier et foiable Henris, sires de Blaumont, et Jehans, sires de Kuc chevalier, et nos foiables clcrs et recheveres de Flandres, Jakemes de Donze, provos del eglyze Nostre Dame de Bruges, ont recheu de treshaut et excellent prinche nostre chier signeur Edward, par le grasse de Diu, roy d'Engleterre, signeur d'Yrlande, et duc d'Aquitaine, par les mains de honorable pere en Diu Watier, eveske de Chestre, son tresorier del eschekier, et des chamberlains de meyme le liu, siis mille livres desterlings pour vint et quatre mille livres de tournois noirs en rabat et descont des trois cens mille livres de le ditte monoie dont li desus nommeis roys de Engleterre est tenus a nous par assignement et par obligacion si comme il appert par ses lettres ke nous sour che avons de lui. En tesmognage de la quele choze nous avons ches presentes lettres de nostre sael fait saeler ki faites furent et donnees lan de grasse mil deus cens quatre vins et seze, le mardi apries le sexagesme.

17. William, lord of Hornes, declares that he has received from Guy, count of Flanders and marquis of Namur, a fief of 100 l. of Tours payable by the receiver of Flanders, as well as a subsidy of 2,000 l. For the fief and the subsidy William promises to serve Guy with 30 men in his wars against the king of France and the count of Hainaut; William and his men will be paid the customary wages of war. William also promises that if he should die his heirs will faithfully adhere to the terms of the contract.

11 April 1297

Archives Départementales du Nord à Lille. Série B. 498/3919.

Jou Williames, sires de Horne chevaliers, fach savoir a tous ke ie sui devenus hom a noble prinche Guion, conte de Flandres et marchis de Namur, et li ai fait hommage de cent livrees de terre au tournois petit, les quels ie doi prendre et rechevoir, iou et mi hoir, singneur de Horne, au recheveur le dit conte, ki conques le soit ou sera pour le tans avenir, au Noel prochainement venant et ensi dan en an perpetuelment; et devons demorer iou et mi hoir, singneur de Horne, homme des cent livrees de terre devantdittes au conte desus-dit et a ses hoirs, contes de Flandres, a tous iours. Encore est a savoir ke mes chiers sires li cuens de Flandres ma donneit deus mil livres de tournois petis a paiier le moitiet al Nativitei Saint Jehan Baptiste prochainement venant, et lautre moitiet au Noel apres suiant. Et pour les deus mil livres ie li ai encouvent a servir bien et loialment mi trentisme de boine gent darmes encontre le roi de France et encontre le conte de Haynau toutes les werres durans que il a encontre eaus par ensi ke li chevalier ki avoec mi seront, naront cascuns le chienc chevaus, et cascuns escuiers, trois chevaus. Et de tant nous doit li cuens de Flandres devantdis paiier nos frais raison-

naubles, alans et venans, et demorans avoec lui. Et sensi estoit ke
iou alaisse de vie a mort par le volentei de Dieu anchois ke li dis
cuens de Flandres mes chiers sires ou si hoir conte de Flandres
fuissent apaisiet au roy de Franche, ou au dit conte de Haynau, ou
a ambedeus, jou oblige mon hoir singneur de Horne et voel ke il
soit obligies a servir le dit conte de Flandres et ses hoirs, contes de
Flandres, es werres devantdittes enle maniere ke ie mi sui obligies.
Encore est a savoir ke se li rois d'Engleterre venoit par decha en
Flandres ou il i envoiast gens darmes enforchiement pour aidier le
conte de Flandres encontre le roi de France et li dis rois d'Engleterre ou se gent me semonsissent daler avoec eaus et en leur aiuwe
sour le dit roi de France aler i, puis se ie vuel sans mesprendre de
riens encontre le conte de Flandres ne encontre ses hoirs devantdis.
Et pour ce ke ce soit ferme choze et estauble jou ai ces presentes
lettres font saieler de mon propre saiel ki furent faites et donnees
en lan de grace mil deus cens quatrevins et seze, le juedi apres Pasques flories.

*18. Letters by which John, lord of Harecourt, renounces his homage and
his fief of 300 l. of Paris held from Guy, count of Flanders and marquis of
Namur, in order to be free to serve Philip IV of France in the war with Guy.*

14 June 1297

Archives Départementales du Nord à Lille. Série B. 498/3957.

A haut homme et noble monseigneur Guis, cuens de Flandres et
marchis de Namur, Jehan, seigneur de Harecourt, salut. Sire comme
ge soie en vostre homage pour la raison de trois cens livrees de terre
a parisis que vous de vostre courtoisie donnastes a moi et a mes
hoirs et comme monseigneur le roi de France ait ou poit dore a
faire aucunes choses encontre vous es queles il couvient que ge le
serve, le quel service ge ne pourroie pas bien faire encontre vous
sauve ma loialte tant comme ge soie en vostre homage, ge vous fais
assavoir que ge vous rent vostre homage et pour ce que ge nai pas
maintenant oveques moi les letres que iai de vous des trois cenz
livrees de terre dessuz diz. Sachenz si tost comme ge les pourrai
avoir que ge les vous envoierai et wuel des maintenant que il soient
de nule vertu et que il ne puissent fere proffit dore enavant a moi
ne a mes hoirs; et vroiement sire il me poise moult que les choses
se portent si entre mon seigneur le roi et vous que il me couviegne

partir de vostre homage. En tesmoing des queles choses iai fait
saeler ces presentes letres de mon sael qui furent fetes et donnees
es paveillons delez Lens en Artois, le vendredi apres les octaves de
Penthecouste en lan de l'Incarnation Nostre Seigneur mil deus cenz
quatre vinz et dis et sept.

*19. Galaadus, lord of Dorendor, makes known that he has received a life
fief of 200 l. of Tours from Philip IV of France for which he has done liege
homage; he promises to serve Philip against all men save his lord the count
of Juliers. But if the count should invade France, then Galaadus promises to
help Philip defend his realm.*

6 February 1302

Archives Nationales à Paris. *Trésor des chartes.* Hommages. Série J.
620/1.

Universis presentes litteras inspecturis, Galaaddus, dominus de
Dorendor miles, salutem in Domino. Notum facimus quod nos excellentissimo principi domino nostro carissimo domino Philippo, Dei
gratia, Francie regi illustri pro ducentis libris turonensium quas
nobis ad vitam nostram concessit capiendas annuatim in thesauro
suo apud Luperam terminis qui secuntur, videlicet in Festo Om-
nium Sanctorum medietatem et in Festo Purificationis Beate Marie
Virginis aliam medietatem, fecimus homagium. Et illas ducentas
libras ad ipso domino rege tenebimus in feodum toto tempore vite
nostre ac ipsi tanquam suus homo ligius serviemus et omnia que ad
fidelitatem et homagium pertinent faciemus contra quascumque
personas preter quam contra nobilem virum, comitem de Julers,
cui primo sumus astricti nisi idem comes regnum Francie invaderet
seu aggrederetur vel eidem regno nocumentum attemptaret prestare,
in quo casu eidem domino regi servire tenebimus et omnia facere
que ad fidelitatem et homagium pertinebunt, que omnia et singula
promittimus inviolabiliter abservare. In cuius rei testimonium sigillum nostrum presentibus litteris duximus apponendi. Datum in
hospitali prope Corbolium die Jovis post Festum Purificationis
Beate Marie Virginis anno Domini millesimo trecentesimo secundo.

20. Louis X, king of France, makes known that his father Philip IV had granted a fief of 4,000 l. to the counts of Hainaut to be paid out of conquests made in Flanders. Louis confirms the grant, but provides for the fief to be paid to Count William I partly from certain revenues from the châtellenie *of* Lille *and partly from other royal revenues. For this fief William and his heirs owe homage and military service against the count of Flanders as long as war lasts.*

December 1315

Archives Départementales du Nord à Lille. Série B. 1170/5070.

Ludowicus, Dei gratia, Francie et Navarre rex. Notum facimus universis presentibus et futuris quod cum carissimus dominus et genitor noster dum viveret dilecto et fideli nostro G., comiti Hanonnie, gratio se concesserit quatuor milia libratas terre reddituales eidem comiti pro se et suis heredibus supra conquestibus Flandrie assidendas prout hoc in litteris dicti domini genitoris nostri confectis super litteras plenius continentur, nos *iturco* iuxta concessionem huiusmodi quam dicto comiti suis exigentibus mentis quibus in nostris obsequiis se nobis reddiderit gratiosum dignum duximus observandum predictum redditum eidem ut convenientius possimus assidere volentes homagia cum emolumentis nostrorum que Hugo de Mande, Gerardus de Potes, Matheus de Valle, et Robertus de Malde, milites, a nobis in castellania Insulensis et ipsius ratione tenebant. Prefato comiti pro se et suis heredibus vel successoribus et causam habituris ab ipso in deductionem dictarum quatuor milium librarum redditualium concedimus et assignamus exnunc imperpetuum per eum obtenenda que a nobis et successoribus nostris, regibus Francie, tenebit in feodum et exnunc nobis prestabit homagium pro eisdem. Cum tamen dictas quatuor mille libras reddituales si et ut tenemur iuxta formam concessionis dicti domini genitoris nostri eidem comiti perfecerimus, si dicta homagia usque ad valorem ipsius redditus non ascendant, extunc totum huiusmodi redditum, videlicet dicta homagia et quicquid ultra ea pro ipso redditu alibi assignabimus, ad unum tenebit homagium quod tunc nobis tenebitur renovare. Per hoc autem quod homagia huiusmodi dicto comiti in deductionem dicti redditus assignamus alibi, nec in plus quam secundum forman dicte concessionis tenemur ad assidendum residuum predicti redditus, nos erga ipsum comitem non intendimus nec volumus obligare. Volumus etiam tenore presentium specialiter retinentes quod dicti milites, quotiens et quamdiu nos et successores nostri, reges Francie, cum Flamingis guerram habebimus, nobis et successoribus nostris predictis ante omnes et omnibus omissis in ipsa guerra contra Flamingos specialiter servire et ad nostrum mandatum in nostrum venire exercitum teneantur, non obstante quod dicto comiti prestiterint homagia supradicta. Damus igitur ballivo nostro Insulensis presentibus litteris in mandatis contra homagia predicta per fidedignos et expertos in talibus vocato procuratore nostro cum ceteris evocandis faciat sine dilatione iuxta patrie consuetudinem estimari. Ipsamque sub valore que fuerint estimata dicto comiti predicto modo deliberet et assignet. Quod ut perpetuo stabile perseveret nostrum presentibus litteris fecimus apponi sigillum. Actum apud Vincensem anno Domini millesimo trecentesimo quintodecimo, mense decembris.

per W. S.

21. Adolf II, bishop of Liège, reproduces letters whereby Philip V of France grants him a fief of 1,000 l. for his liege homage, as well as a subsidy of 10,000 l. Adolf promises to defend the kingdom of France against all men, and especially against the duke of Luxemburg; when summoned, he is to supply 1,000 men-at-arms who will receive the customary wages of war as long as they serve the king of France.

November 1320

Archives Nationales à Paris. *Trésor des chartes*. Liège. Série J. 527/7.

A tous ceus qui ces presentes lettres verront et orront, nous Adolf, par la grace de Dieu, evesques du Liege, salut en Nostre Seigneur. Savoir faisons que nous avons receu et recevons pardevers nous les lettres de tres excellent prince nostre tres chier seigneur Philippe, par la grace de Dieu, roi de France et de Navarre, contenans la fourme qui ensient. Philippe, par la grace de Dieu, rois de France et de Navarre, a touz ceus qui ces presentes lettres verront et orront salut. Savoir faisons que nostre ame et feal Adolf, par la grace de Dieu, evesque du Liege, considerans que plus grant honeur quant en cest munde ne li puet avenir especialment pour plus grant seurte, tuition, et utilite de sa eglise que de estre homme et alie de nous qui summes et aussi ont este touz iours nos devanciers defendeurs de la foi crestienne et champion de Sainte Eglise est et a confesse par ses lettres estre nostre homme et feal pour mile livres de rente que nous li avons donne tant comme il vivera et sera evesque du Liege; les queles il a acceptees et accepte de nous en fie et en homage a prendre en certains lieus es quex nous les li assignerons par noz lettres chascun an tant comme il vivera, sicomme dit est, et en est devenu et devient nostre homme et nous en a fait homage et sairement de feaute et pour diz mile livres en deniers par une fois les queles il avera et recevera de nous. Et parmi ces choses et par la grant affection que il a de nous servir il est et recognoit estre tenu et obligie de obeir a nous de venir a nostre mandement et de estre avec nous pour la defense de nostre royaume en armes toutes fois que il en sera requis contre toutes manieres de gens quex que il soient. C'est a savoir que il se oblige et sera tenu de venir pour la cause desuz dite a ses propres cous et frais a son pooir convenablement et souffisament appareillies en armes dusques au viles de Buillon ou de Couvin, la ou miex plaira a nous ou a nostre gent. Et de iluec en avant il et ses gens seront tenus de venir au gages et en la maniere que nous avons acoustume a donner et a faire az autres hommes et feaus de nostre royaume dusques a deus iournees dedenz nostre royaume, teles comme gens de armes pueent aler sanz fraude et sanz mal engin convenablement et es lieus que nous voudrons. Et est a entendre que puis que il sera venu en certain lieu de nostre commandement se nous le volons mener en autre lieu il i sera tenu a aler quelcunque lieu que ce soit mais que ce ne soit parfonz dedenz nostre royaume outre deus iournees convenables comme desuz est dit et que ce soit es marches et frontieres de la comtee de *Retect*, de la terre de Maiseres, ou des comtees de Chigny, de Lucembourc, ou de Bar. Et sera tenuz, il et ses gens, a demourer es dis lieus ou nous li manderons et a nous servir tant comme il plaira a nous ou a nostre commandement. Item le dit evesque se est obligie a nous servir et a faire guerre a tout son pooir tout le tans de sa vie a ses propres mises et despens contre de roi de Boeme, conte de Lucembourc, comme comte de Lucembourc, ou quicunque seroit comte de Lucembourc, toutes fois quantes fois nous li ferons guerre et voudrons que il la li face et en toutes les manieres que les tans, les cas, et les fais le requerront es marches des dis eveschie et comtee et par tout le dit comtee ainsi comme nous ou nostre commandement li requerrons et ferons guerre ou le dit roi de Boeme, comte de Lucembourc, nous fera guerre par quelcunque maniere que ce soit et encore contre ceus qui au dit roi de Boeme et comte de Lucembourc voudroient aidier contre nous ou qui a nous voudroient nuire ou tenir damage fust ore le roi de Alemaigne, le duc de Brabant, ou le comte de Haynau, sauf tant que le dit evesque retient que ou cas que nous

leur voudrians faire guerre pour autre cause que pour ceste, le dit
evesque ne seroit pas tenu de nous aidier. Cest a savoir contre le
roi de Alemaigne pour ce que il est son seigneur, contre le duc de
Brabant, ne contre le comte de Haynau, pour ce que il sunt ses
hommes. Et se pour ce que le dit evesque averoit fait guerre contre
le dit comte de Lucembourc, celi comte ou aucuns autre, li faisoient
guerre nous le devons tenir en guerre et le dit evesque en bonne foi
aidier contre eus. Item le dit evesque est tenu et ainsi le a promis
toutes fois que nous voudrons et mestier en averons de nous bailliier
et envoier dusques a mile hommes de armes selonc ce que nous voudrons et besoing en averons selonc le cas pour nous aidier et venir
servir en nostre royaume et les doit et sera tenus a faire venir a ses
propres cous et despens touz prests et appareillies dusques a Buillon
ou a Couvin, sicomme miex plaira a nous ou a nostre commandement. Et de iluec en avant par le tans que il demourroient, ou ven-
droient, ou iroient, ou seroient ou service de nous ou de nostre commandement il averont autre gages de nous et samblables comme il
est acoustume a donner au gens de armes de nostre royaume dusques a tant que il fussent retournez pour raler en leur pais du congie
de nous ou de nostre commandement dusques au viles de Buillon ou
de Couvin desuz dites, ou au mains que il fussent issus de nostre
royaume se par les dites viles, ne se en aloient par autant de espace
comme il a du royaume dusques au dites viles, sauf ce que il doivent
aler dedenz le royaume si avant tant seulement et es marches et es
frontieres desuz dites, sicomme il est plus plenement dit en larticle
qui parle desuz du service que il nous doit faire pour cause del
homage. Item de toutes les choses dont le dit evesque entrera en
guerre pour nous, nous ne ferons pais ne trieues que il ne soit mis
enz devement et convenablement, ne il aussi ne se porra apaisier des
dites choses sanz nostre assentement toutes voies combien que nous
eussians pais et eussians mis ens le dit evesque, et la pais ne li pleust,
il porroit tout par li demourer en sa guerre. Et toutes les choses
desuz dites et chascunes diceles le dit evesque promet et a promis et
les a iurees a Saintes Ewangiles touchie le lune a tenir, garder, et
acomplir en bonne foi sanz fraude, sauf son loial essoigne du quel
essoigne il doit estre creus par son loial sairement avec le sairement
de siz chevaliers, les plus souffisans et plus creables que il porra
avoir en sa terre a ce que il ne puist estre note, repute, ou encoulpe
de parivrement par nous ne par autre mais toutes voies se nous le

dit evesque, appele ou non apele, present ou absent, disians par
nostre simple parole en nostre conscience que le dit evesque eust
este defaillant de acomplir les convenances et les choses desus dites,
il veut a se ottrois que nous en soions creu sanz autre prueve et que
il des lors chiete en sentence de excomiement se il, dedenz lan apres
ce que nous averians dit que il estoit defaillant, ne nous avoit paie
les diz mile livres que il averoit receu de nous comme desuz est dit,
et encore autres diz mile livres, les queles il nous promet a paier en
nom de peinne et la dite sentence de excomiement. Il veut consent
et supplie a nostre tres Saint Pere le Pape que des maintenant il
giete contre li pour li lier et comprendre ou cas et en la maniere
desuz dis et en la meilleur fourme et maniere que il porra et devera
estre valable et encore veut et se consent le dit evesque et avec supplie a nostre dit Pere le Pape que il depute cex executeurs, comme
nous plaira soient, du royaume de France ou dautre part, qui del
autorite diceli Pape puissent getter sentence de excomiement contre
la persone dudit evesque ou cas et en la maniere desuz dis et que il
puissent publier et mettre a execution la sentence que le dit nostre
Pere le Pape ou ceus meimes executeurs averoient giete contre sa
persone sicomme il est dit desuz. Et est a savoir que paiees les dites
vint mile livres dedenz la sicomme dit est les dites sentences ne com-
prendront pas le dit evesque et les convenances desus dites seront
nules dune partie et dautre et *pardera* la rente de mile libres en fie
desus dites. Et a une le dit evesque suz Saintes Ewangiles a nous
rendre les dites diz mile libres que il averoit receu de nous et les diz
mile libres de peinne paier ou cas qui desus est dit. Et a renuncie
quant a toutes les choses desus dites et chascunes diceles tenir, garder, faire, et acomplir, et non venir encontre a toutes exceptions,
defenses, et raisons de droit, de fait et de coustume, qui porroient
estre dites ou proposees au contraire en quelcunque maniere que ce
soit. Et nous en autele maniere pour tant comme nous touche prometons loialment faire, tenir, garder, et acomplir toutes les choses
desus dites et chascunes diceles renunciant expressement a dire et a
faire au contraire. A plus grant seurte de toutes ces choses nous
avons ces lettres fait seeler de nostre seel. Donne lan de grace m ccc
et vint ou mois de novembre. Et nous evesque du Liege prometons
par ses presentes lettres faire, tenir, garder, et acomplir entierement
tant comme nous touche toutes les choses contenues es dites lettres
et chascunes diceles sicomme eles sunt escriptes et devisees sanz

venir encontre en quelcunque maniere que ce soit. Et prometons encore de habitualment a iurer les corporelment et en propre persone suz Saintes Ewangiles quant il plaira a nostre dit seigneur le roi ou a celi ou a ceus que il deputera quant a ce dedenz ceste prochain Noel et a li doner noz autres lettres seur toutes les dites choses et dou tans et du lieu que nous averons iure sicomme dit est. En tesmoing des choses desus dites nous avons fait mettre nostre seel en ces presentes lettres qui furent faites lan de grace mil trois cenz et vint, en mois de novembre.

22. *Louis de Nevers, count of Flanders, grants to his sister Isabelle de Lierde, upon her marriage with the knight Simon de Mirabelle "dit de Hale," a fief of 300 livrées de terre as her dowry. This fief is to be paid from the incomes of the lands of Somerghem or, if these incomes are insufficient, from the briefs of the Quatre-Métiers. If Isabelle should die without heirs, the fief will revert back to the counts of Flanders. To insure that the incomes from Somerghem are sufficient to pay the fief, Louis commissions two of his officers to go to Somerghem and evaluate it. After receiving their report that its incomes are equal to 300 l. yearly, Louis then hands over to Isabelle the rights to these incomes.*

9 April 1326

Archives de l'État à Gand. Oostenrijksche Verzameling. Gachard. 9 April 1326.

Nous Loys, cuens de Flandres et de Nevers, faisons savoir a tous que comme nous aviemes doune de nostre boine volenteit a nostre bien amee seur de bas dame, Ysabeal de Lierde, en mariage a dont a faire et ore fait de luy et de monsigneur Symon de Mierabiel, dit de Hale chevalier, trois cens livrees de tierre a tenir lui et ses hoirs issans dou dit mariage et prendre sour nostre ville de Zomerghem et au plus preis et le demorant, se ces choses ne pooient soffire, sour nos briefs de Quatre Mestiers ens queils biens nous le avons fait mettre par nos hommes pour les tenir de nous en foi et en hommage avoeques la signerie et iustice de la dite ville et des lieus plus preis, excepte les hautes iustices, cest a savoir les quatre poins de mourdre, de arsin, de efforchier femmes, de "rieuroof," reservant et retenant a nous le resort et la souvraineteit en tous cas. Et ou cas ou no dite seur morroit sans hoir issant dou dit mariage, les dites trois cens livrees de tierre, la signierie, et la iustice retourneroient a nous entierement, si comme ces choses sont plus plainement contenues en nos autres lettres que elle en a sour ce de nous. Et no dite seur nous a fait monstreir que la dite ville de Zomerghem ne vaut mie tant que nos dis dons en porroit estre parfais ne emplis en souppliant que nous vausissiemes faire prisier par nos gens la dite ville de Zomerghem et sa valeur iustement estimeir et le demorant asseoir selonc nos autres lettres dessus dites. Nous qui a des volons faire nostre devoir et emplir ce que promis avons establissiemes pour ce a faire en lieu de nous et pour nous a oes de no dite seur nos foils et ameis Roegeir Brisetieste, nostre conselleur, et Olivier de le Most, nostre bailliu dou Vieborgh de Gand, qui de nostre especial commant entendirent a la dite besoingne et troverent que la dite ville de Zomerghem valoit et peut valoir cascun an quatre vins livres parisis en une summe et nient plus es choses par eaus prisies et estimees, a savoir est en la maierie de Zomerghem trente chinq livres et onse sols parisis. Item en trois cens et trois sourseans hostes, que on apele "upsecene late," trente livres a siis sols prisie cascan deus sols lan. Item en deus cens quatrevins et trois desseans hostes, que on apele "ofsecene late," cascun prisie douze deniers lan quatorse livres et trois sols. Item pour asseoir a plus pres de la ville de Zomerghem selonc la teneur de nos dites autres lettres, le demorant de trois cens livrees de tierre qui monte deus cens et vint livres ont no dit commissaire regarde par diligent avis et approve par nous le dit plus preis et les ont assis sour trois paires de briefs pris hors de nos briefs de Assenede, des queils on apele les deus briefs de Zomerghem, li queil ii brief de Zomerghem montent et valent cent trente chinc livres diis et sept deniers parisis rabatu la terre Vaghe qui est prisie a douze sols. Et le tierch brief qui on apele de Lovendeghem Brouc et Belsebrouc qui monte sissante wiit livres quatre sols et deus deniers. Et la faute des ccc libres desus dites qui monte seze livres quatorse sols et chinq deniers ont il assis sour les persones qui sensiewent. A savoir est sour Bauduin le Vriese, quarante quatre sols et siis deniers. Item sour signeur Jehan le Sinet, quarante sols et neuf deniers. Item sour les biens lospital Saint Iaqueme de Gand en Warscoet, quarante wiit sols. Item sour Jehan de Bracle en Lovendeghem, vint et chinq sols et neuf deniers. Item sour Jehan Borlivit, fil Henri Borlivits en Lovendeghem, par pluseures pieches, trois livres wiit sols et onse deniers. Item sour monsigneur Jehan de Lovendeghem en Lovendeghem, chinq livres siis sols et siis deniers. Et nous vehu et diligaument examine la prisie desus dite le avons de certaine sciente ratefiie, approve, et conferme, ratefions, approvons, et confermons, et le tenons pour boine iuste et loyale et le mettons et transportons en la main de no dite seur en la fourme, maniere, et condition en nos autres lettres contenues et en ces presentes declarees. Et ostons des maintenant les dis trois briefs et la faute a pres nommee de nos dis briefs de Assenede en la maniere desus dite pour nous, nos hoirs, et successeurs, et tous ciaus qui apres nous cause en porroient avoir. En commandant a celi qui tient nos dis briefs de Assenede a present ou quil le tenra pour le tamps avenir que de ces choses dessus dites il ne sen melle plus ains en laisse goyr paisuilement rechevoir les et avoir no dite seur ensi que dit est. Remembrance en ses dis briefs de Assenede faisant del estement que fait en avons la maniere et le condition dessus dites, si mandons a tous nos iusticiiers et soubgiez a qui il peut ou porra apartenir que des choses dessus dites fachent no dite seur goyr paisuilement comme dou sien sans ymettre debat, ne opposition, ne soffrir a mettre, et sans attendre autre commandement de nous. En tiesmoing de ce nous avons fait mettre nostre seel a ces presentes lettres que furent faites a Gand et dounees lan de grace mil ccc vint et siis, le neufime jour del mois davril.

Par monsigneur le conte et sen conseil presente, monsigneur W. de Anxoene, monsigneur W. de Aerlebeke, monsigneur W. de Buxani, monsigneur Willaume Bloc chevaliers, et Jehan Gheylinc.

23. *An alliance is concluded between John III, duke of Brabant, and Philip VI of France whereby John does liege homage to Philip for a fief of 2,000 l. of Tours payable by the treasury at Paris during John's life; upon the death of John his successor will be permitted to do homage for the fief. John promises to defend France and to aid Philip in his wars against all men save the emperor of Germany with 200 men-at-arms at his own expense for a period of two months each year. For any service beyond the two months Philip will provide the wages and maintenance. John promises, furthermore, to provide the 200 men whenever Philip needs them, as well as additional men should they be required; in this case Philip will be responsible for all wages and maintenance.*

8 July 1332

Archives Nationales à Paris. *Trésor des chartes.* Brabant. Série J. 524/31[1].

Jehans, par la grace de Dieu, dux de Lothrice, de Brebant et de Lembourgh. Savoir faisons a touz, presenz et avenir, que nous consideranz et attendanz la grant amour et affection que noz seigneurs,

les roys de France, et noz predecesseurs, dux de Lothrice, de Brebant et de Lembourgh, ont eu iadix ensemble et avec ce consideranz
et attendanz que par lamour, confederation, et alliance de nostre
treschier et redoute seigneur, monseigneur Philippe a present roy de
France, madame Jehanne de Bourgoigne, a present royne de France
sa compaigne, et monseigneur Jehan leur filz, duc de Normandie,
conte d'Aniou et du Maine, comoinctement et diviseement dune
part et nous Jehan, duc dessus dit, dautre part moult de granz biens,
seurtez, et proffiz, peuent estre ou temps present et avenir au royaume de France et a noz duchies et terres de Lothrice, de Brebant
et de Lembourgh dessus dittes, les quelz royaume, duchies, et terres
sont assez prochaines. Et pour norrir entre nostre dit treschier seigneur monseigneur le roy et ses successeurs, madame la royne de
France a present, et monseigneur Jehan leur filz dessus dit, et nous
Jehan duc dessus dit et noz successeurs bonne paiz et amour, les
quelles y doivent estre et seront touz jours se Diex plaist, et aussi
entre les habitanz du dit royaume et de noz duchies et terres dessus
dittes, avons fait par nostre grant conseil pour le commun et evident
proffit en conseil et meure deliberation sur ce avec nostre dit treschier seigneur monseigneur le roy pour li, pour madame la royne
dessus ditte, et pour monseigneur Jehan leur filz, leurs hoirs et successeurs, roys de France, les traictiez, liens, alliances, pactions,
couvenances, et autres choses qui sensuient. Premierement que nous
tant comme nous vivrons serons homme lige a noz devant dit seigneur monseigneur le roy, qui est a present et du roy de France qui
sera pour le temps, de deux mille livrees de terre de bons petiz tournois, le gros tournois dargent compte pour douze bons petiz tournois,
que il nous a donne et donne a prenre desorendroit au thresor a Paris
iusques atant quelles soient achetees. Et nous doivent estre payes
chascun an ou dit thresor a deux termes, cest assavoir la moitie au
Noel et lautre moitie a la Saint Jehan, et les dittes deux mille livrees
de terre nous a donne et donne noz devant dit seigneur le roy en fie
des quelles nous soumes entre en sa foy et li en avons fait hommage
lige. Pour les quelles deux mille livrees de terre et pour les alliances
qui sensuient, nous soumes et serons tenuz de servir et de aidier monseigneur le roy dessus dit, madame la royne, et monseigneur Jehan
leur filz en la fourme et maniere qui sensuit. Cest assavoir que nous
soumes et serons tenuz a servir et aidier monseigneur le roy, madame
la royne, et monseigneur Jehan leur filz contre touz hommes et toutes

personnes excepte le roy d'Alemaigne et les seigneurs des quelz nous
tenons a present ou cas que nostre dit seigneur le roy, madame la
royne, et monseigneur Jehan leur filz, ou aucun de eulz yroient ou
envoieroient pour eulz courir sus en leurs terres et pays. Et ou cas ou
le roy dessus dit no sire, madame la royne, et monseigneur Jehan leur
filz, ou lun de eulz auroient besoign de defendre le royaume de
France et les terres que nostre dit seigneur le roy, madame la royne,
et monseigneur Jehan leur filz, ou chascun de eulz tiennent et tenront
comoinctement et diviseement, nous devons servir nostre dit seigneur
le roy, madame la royne, et monseigneur Jehan leur filz, et chascun
de eulz a nos cous de deux cenz hommes darmes par deux moys en
lan compte en yceulz des le temps que nous partirons de nostre pays
tout le temps que nous mettrons en aler, demourer, et retourner en
nostre pays. Et se nostre dit seigneur monseigneur le roy, madame la
royne, et monseigneur Jehan leur filz, ou lun de eulz avoient mestier
des diz deux cenz hommes darmes oultre les diz deux moys, nous
serons tenuz de eulz servir aus gages telz comme nostre dit seigneur
le roy dounra a ses autres genz darmes. Item nous soumes et serons
tenuz de faire le dit service de deux cenz hommes darmes a nostre
dit seigneur monseigneur le roy, madame la royne, et monseigneur
Jehan leur filz sil estoit roys, et a chascun de eulz en nostre personne se li roys nostre seigneur, ou madame la royne, ou monseigneur Jehan leur filz y estoient en leurs personnes. Et ou cas que nul
de eulz ne y seroit en sa personne, nous ferons le dit service par
chevetaine souffisant que nous y envoierons; et ne nous pourront
nostre dit seigneur le roy, madame la royne, ne monseigneur Jehan
leur filz ou aucun de eulz mander pour faire le dit service des diz
deux cenz hommes darmes a noz despenz fors que une fois lan. Mais
se le dit nostre seigneur le roy, madame la royne, et monseigneur
Jehan leur filz, ou lun de eulz nous mandoient plusieurs fois en lan
nous y serons tenuz de y venir ou de y envoier aus gages telz comme
nostre seigneur le roy les donrroit aus genz darmes ou royaume de
France. Et sil plaisoit a nostre dit seigneur le roy, a madame la
royne, a monseigneur Jehan leur filz, ou a aucun de eulz de nous
mander que nous avienissions ou envoissions plus grant quantite de
genz darmes de cheval et de pie, nous y serons tenuz de y venir ou
envoier aus dessus diz gages que li rois nostre seigneur donrroit aus
genz darmes ou royaume de France, et si avant que nous pourrons
bonnement de la quantite que nostre dit seigneur le roy, madame la

royne, monseigneur Jehan leur filz, ou lun de eulz nous manderont. Item nous ne souffrerons que les genz de noz pays aillent contre nostre seigneur le roy dessus dit, madame la royne, monseigneur Jehan leur filz, ou aucun de eulz pour quelconque personne que ce soit sil nestoient si allie a eulz pour hommage quil ne le peussent ou ne deussent refuser ou sil nestoient de si petit estat que nous ne les poussiens contraindre. Item nous ne recepterons ne ne souffrerons a recepter en noz terres aucuns des aucuns du dit monseigneur le roy, de madame le royne, de monseigneur Jehan leur filz, ou de aucun de eulz. Et devons faire les services dessus diz tant comme nous vivrons seulement. Et les dittes deux mille livrees de terre que li roys nos nous a donne si comme dit est par dessus nous ne pourrons lessier ne deffaire les dittes alliances tant comme nous vivrons. Et apres nostre decez venront les dites deux mille livrees de terre a Jehan nostre filz ainsne et aus autres dux de Brebant, qui seront pour le temps, en faisant lommage et le service tel comme il appartendra au fie. Et ne seront point lors tenuz de faire le dit service des deux cenz hommes darmes ne des autres genz darmes dessus dittes fors tel service comme au dit fie appartendra. Les quelles choses dessus dittes toutes ensemble et chascune dycelles ainsi comme elles sont dessus devisees, nous pour nous, pour noz hoirs et noz successeurs, dux de Lothrice, de Brebant et de Lembourgh, avons promis et promettons a nostre seigneur le roy dessus dit pour li, pour ses hoirs et successeurs, roys de France, et pour touz ceulz a qui il appartient peut et pourra appartenir en bonne foy et par nostre serement fait sus Sainz Evangiles en la presence du dit no sire le roy et sur lobligation de touz noz biens, meubles et nonmeubles, presenz et avenir, tenir, garder, et accomplir, bien et loyaument, entierement et parfaitement, sanz tout mauvais engien et sanz corrompre en tant comme a nous, a noz hoirs et a noz successeurs peut et pourra touchier et non aler encontre par nous ne par autre taisiblement ne expressement en jugement, ne dehors, ne consentir que aucuns y viengne. En tesmoing des quelles choses nous avons fait mettre nostre seel en ces presentes lettres faites et donnees a Crievecueur en Brie, le huitieme jour de jullet, lan de grace mil trois cenz trente et deux.

24. *Louis de Nevers, count of Flanders, makes known that he has retained John "dit Trament de Noyelles" as one of his household knights and has promised to give him a heritable fief of 60 l. of Paris on various incomes from lands and the toll of Menin with the provision that it can be redeemed. John is to be provided with war wages, maintenance of food and clothing, and horses; he promises in turn to serve Louis loyally in all wars and tournaments.*

25 April 1338

Archives Générales du Royaume à Bruxelles. *Trésor de Flandre*. Série I. No. 2083.

Donne par copie sur le seel monsigneur Jehan du Tramet de Noielle. Nous Loys, contes de Flandres, de Nevers et de Rethel, faisons savoir a tous que nous avons retenu et retenons aveucques nous et de nostre maisnage nostre ame et feal chevallier monsigneur Jehan dit Tramet de Noielle a sa vie en le maniere qui sen sieut. Chest assavoir que il nous doit servir bien et loyaument tant que nous viverons a la guerre et au tournoy, en joustes, et en toutes autres choses appartenans a chevallier a faire dont nous aurons a faire de lui; et apres nostre deces doit il servir Loys nostre fils en celle meisme maniere. Et se doit monter pour la guerre, pour le tournoy, par cele condition que pour le restor de la montee du tournoy nous li renderons tele somme dargent comme a nos autres chevalliers. Et pour sa montee de la guerre se il len mes avenoit nous li renderons le pris de no mareschal. Et quant nous le manderons pour le tournoy nous li devons faire rendre pour ses despens douze gros tournois pour chascun jour, alant, venant et demourant. Item nous plaist il que li dis messire Jehans dis Trames soit en nostre hostel toutes fois quil y sera a delivrance pour trois chevaus et soit delivrez ensi que a bacheler appartient. Item se nous le mandons pour la guerre nous li devons delivrer ensi que a nos autres chevalliers. Et ne poons le dit messire Jehan dit Tramet baillier a nul fors a Loys nostre fils ou a celui qui tenroit nostre lieu. Et pour les choses dessus dites faire a nous et a nostre dit fil apres nostre deces tant que li dis messire Jehans dis Trames vivera et nous servir bien et loyaument, nous li avons donne et donnons et a ses hoirs sexante livres de rente par an au paresis de Flandres a tenir de nous et de nos hoirs hiretablement en fief et en hommage a paiier a deus termes en lan. Chest assavoir lune moitie a le Saint Remy et lautre moitie a Pasques par tele condition que nous et nos hoirs poons et porrons les dites sexante livres de rente ravoir, retenir et rachater dou dit messire Jehan dit Tramet et de ses hoirs quant il plaira a nous et nos hoirs dessus dis en baillant pour le denier diis deniers, les quels deniers li dis messire Jehans dis Trames et si dit hoir doivent et deveront mettre et convertir en accater hiretage tenu de nous dedens lan apres ce que nous ou nos hoirs aurons fait le dit racat, du quel heritage li dis messire Jehans dis Trames et si hoir seront homme a nous et a nos hoirs. Et est assavoir que apres le deces du dit messire Jehan dit Tramet ses hoirs desservira le dit fief ensi que selonc le coustume appartient a deservir fief vers son seigneur, les quelles sexante livres de rente nous li avons assizes et asseons sur toute nostre terre, et biens, rentes, et molins, et tonlieu de Menin, et sour toutes les revenues et appartenances dicelle. Si mandons a nostre recheveur de le dite terre, qui lest ad present et qui le sera pour le temps avenir, que sans autre mandement de nous attendre ne de nos hoirs apres nostre deces il paiete doresenavant audit messire Jehan dit Tramet et a ses hoirs la dite rente par cascun an aus termes dessus devisez sensi ne fust que li dis racas fust fais. En prendant de lui et de ses hoirs lettres de quitance parmi les quelles li dis recheveurs sera de tant quites a ses comptes les quels don et assenement desus dis, nous promettons et avons promis en bone foi audit messire Jehan dit Tramet et a ses hoirs tenir et acomplir par nous et nos hoirs en la maniere que dit est. Et pour ce que ce soit ferme chose et estable nous avons a ces presentes lettres fait mettre nostre seel en tesmoing de verite. Donne a Bruges le vintchiuncisme jour dou mois davril, lan de grace mil trois cens trente wiit.

25. The knight John de Leefdael makes known that he has done homage to the count of Namur for a fief of 30 l. of Tours which the count assigned to him out of the fief of 400 l. of Tours received yearly from the duke of Brabant. The count can redeem the fief of 30 l. for a sum of 300 l. with which John is to acquire land in Namur worth 30 l. yearly to be held in fief from the counts of Namur.

12 September 1342

Archives de l'État à Namur. Piot, *Inventaire des chartes des comtes de Namur,* no. 665.

Nous Jchans de Leuedale chevaliers faisons savoir a tous que comme no treschiers sires, li contes de Namur, soit a nous tenu en trente librees de terre au tournois de rente annuele et perpetuele, le gros tournois pour seze deniers compte ov monoie au vaillant, des

quelz nous li avons fait foit et homaige, et il nous en a home recheu.
Et les quelz trente livrees de terre il a assigne a nous, nos hoirs et
successeurs, a prendre et a rechevoir chascun an sur les quatre cens
librees de terre au tournois, le gros pour seze, que treshaut et tresnobles mon treschiers sires, li dux de Brabant, li doit en la ville de
Louvain et qui li a assigne sur lieus ciertains si comme il apparit
par lettres sur ce faites quil en a. Et voit que nous, no hoir et successeur prendons, aions, et levons les dites trente livrees de terre sur
le paiement qui chascun an li eschiera a Louvain au terme de la
Toussains des devantdites quatre cens livrees de terre quil ia par teil
maniere et condition que toutes fois quil plaira a no devant dit
treschier seigneur, le conte de Namur, ses hoirs et successeurs. Il
leur loist et porront rachater a nous, nos hoirs et successeurs les
dites trente livrees de terre parmi trois cens livres samblable monoie
a une fois a paiier ; des quelz trois cens livres nos, no hoirz et successeurs, a cui li rachas sera fais, devrons achater et acquerre en la
conte de Namur trente librees de teil monoie ov au mains autant
de terre que on eu porra bien assignee avoir, ov se nous ne poviens
niet bonement trouveir a achater la dite terre en la conte de Namur,
assigner en devons pour ce et en ce lieu autant de terre de nostre
propre allues que nous avons plus pres gisans de la conte de Namur,
la quele terre ensi de par nous, nos hoirs et successeurs rachatee et
acquise ov allues pour yceli terre assigne, nous, no hoirs et successeurs devrons tenir perpetuelment en foit et en homaige de no devant dit treschier seigneur le conte, ses hoirs et successeurs. Et sil
avenoit que il si hoir ou successeur fesissent le rachat des dites
trentes librees de terre si comme faire puent largent dou dit rachat
doit estre mis en sauves mains en la conte de Namur jusques au
tant que nous, nos hoirs et successeurs ariens fait et acompli les
convenances dessus dites, cest de la terre acquerre ov del allues
assigner si comme toutes ces choses apparent clerement par lettres
que nous en avons sur ce faites seellees dou seel no devant dit seigneur le conte de Namur. Saichent tout que le dessus dit assignement
avoecques toutes les convenances et conditions chi dessus escriptes
et contenues, nous loons, greons, et consentons, et volons pour nous,
nos hoirs et successeurs quelles soient tenues entierement sans faire
ne dire al encontre. Et de ce nous obligons nous, nos hoirs et succes-
seurz, nos biens, et les biens de nos hoirs et successeurs envers nostre
dit seigneur, ses hoirs et successeurs. Par le tesmoing de ces lettres

seellees de nostre propre seel qui furent faites et donnees en lan de
grasce Nostre Seigneur mil trois cens quarante et deuz, le joedy
douze jours ou mois de septembre.

*26. Philip VI, king of France, makes known that William I, count of
Namur, has promised to serve him in all his wars against the king of England
with 60 men-at-arms and with 60 men armed in hauberks, all of whom will
be paid the customary wages of war. William will have a sum of 400 l. of
Tours per month beyond his wages. The marshals of France will account for
all the men supplied by William, pay their wages, and remunerate them for
all losses sustained in war. All prisoners taken by William and his men except
the king of England, his children, and earls of England, are to be held by the
count for ransom.*

28 May 1347

Archives Nationales à Paris. *Trésor des chartes.* Namur. Série J.
531/9.

Philippe, par la grace de Dieu, rois de France a touz ceulz qui
ces lettres verront, salut. Comme nous aiens retenu en nostre homme
nostre ame et feal le conte de Namur, savoir faisons que il nous a
promis et doit servir en noz presentes guerres et durans ycelles
entre nous et le roy d'Engleterre en la maniere qui sensieut. Cest
assavoir a soissante heaumes et a soissante haubergons, souffissant
montez et armez, a trente solz tournois de gages par jour pour ban-
neres, a quinze solz tournois pour chevaliers, et a sept solz sis deniers
tournois pour escuiers. Et le dit conte aura chascun mois pour son
estat quatre cens livres tournois oultre ses dis gages et aura telz
restors de chevaus comme nous avons fait et devons faire a nostre
ame et feal Jehan de Haynaut, sire de Beaumont. Et est assavoir
que touz les prisonniers que lidis contes ou ses gens prendront seront
a son proffit excepte le roy d'Engleterre, ses enfans, et aucuns contes
d'Engleterre que nous porrons ravoir sil nous plait par paiant pour
chascun conte pris a ycellui conte de Namur ou a ses gens, quatre
mil livres tournois. Et se li dis contes ou ses gens portens damage
noz guerres durans a noz dis anemis, nous sommes tenuz de les en
advoer. Et ou cas que se pour layde que ycellui conte nous fera en
nos dites guerres aucuns noz anemis li voloient courre sus, nous sommes aussint tenuz de li aidier noz dites guerres durans. Si mandons
a noz amez et feaulz les mareschaus et tresoriers de noz guerres que
il recoivent et enregistrent la moustre dudit conte et de ses dites

gens en prisant leurs monteures justement et de leurs gages les
paient ainsi comme il appartendra. En tesmoing de ce nous avons
fait mettre nostre seel a ces presentes lettres. Donne a Arras le
xxviii^e jour de may, lan de grace mil ccc quarante et sept.

> Par le roy
> Verriere

27. *The knight Tilman de Verenne and his son Louis de Verenne recognize
that William I, count of Namur, has granted them a* fief-rente *for life; they
have done homage for it and have promised to serve William against all men
except certain lords whose men they are. They promise especially to serve
against Wenceslas, duke of Brabant, with the provision that all costs of war
will be paid by William. Eight men, well armed and mounted, will serve with
Tilman and Louis; each will receive beyond the normal wages a sum of 60
florins of Florence, 30 florins upon their arrival and 30 florins at the end of
their service.*

7 May 1356

Archives de l'État à Namur. Piot, *Inventaire des chartes des comtes
de Namur*, no. 804.

Nous Thielemans de Verenghes chevaliers et Loeys de Verenghes,
ses fils escuiers, faisons savoir a tous que comme nos treschiers et
tresames sires messire Guillaumes, contes de Namur, nous ait don-
net et ottriiet par ses lettrez sur ce faites certaines rentes par an nos
vies durans pour les quellez nous estons devenu si homme et en
avons ali fait homaige parmi le quel nous le devons et avons enconvent de servir contre tous hommes excepte nous signeurs as quels
nous seriens homme. Et adpresent aucuns discors et guerre soient
entre noble et poissant prince monsigneur Wincelard de Boeme, par le
grace de Dieu, duc de Lucembourc et nostre dit treschier signeur le
conte pour leurs terrez et pays, nous en bonne foy et loyaulment avons
enconvent et prometons a nostre dit treschier signeur le conte de
Namur que toute la dite guerre durant nous li serons aidans et confortanz et le servirons en tous fais darmes encontre le dit duc de
Lucembourc pour son droit et raison aidier a deframier parmi che
que il nous doit jeter et delivrer de tous frais que pour li et a cause
de la dite guerre nous averiens, et en tel estat et maniere que nous
avienrons aveuc nouz wyt compaingnons darmes bons, souffissament
et bien montes, li quel serviront en la dite guerre nostre dit treschier
signeur le conte par lespasse de demian apres ce que nos dis tre-

schiers sires nous en aura semons des quels cascuns de yaus pour li
monter devera avoir a nostre dit treschier signeur le conte la some de
sexante florins de Florence, dont il auront le moitie a leur venue
et lautre dedens la dite demiannee. Et parmi ce ausi nos dis treschiers sires les doit jeter de tous frais que pour li et a cause de la
dite guerre il averont si comme dit est et leur doit delivrer argent
pour leurs frais en leur venir, seiourrier et raler. Et pour ce que
toutes les choses dessus dites soient fermez, staubles et bien tenues
de point en point, nous Thielemans de Verenghes chevaliers dessus-
dis et Loey de Verenghes, ses fils escuiers, avons mis et appendus en
signe de verite nos sayaus a ces presentes lettres. Faites et donnees
a Namur le septime jour dou mois de may, lan de grace mil ccc
chienquante et siis.

*28. Edmond van Endelsdorf, lord of Wildenburg, makes known that Louis
de Male, count of Flanders, has granted him a fief of 50 écus of silver on the
toll of Malines. For this fief Edmond promises to serve Louis and his successors in all their wars.*

26 May 1368

Archives Générales du Royaume à Bruxelles. *Trésor de Flandre.*
Série I. No. 2085.

Ic Emond van Endelsdorp, here van Wildemberch ridder, doe te
wetene allen lieden dat mi miin lieve ende gheduchte here miin here,
de grave van Vlaendren, ghegheven heift vijftech scilden siaers,
elken scilt van vier ende twintech groten tournoise Vlaenderscher
munten, ende die bewijst te heffene up sinen thol van Machline alle
jare in Sinte Jans Daghe Baptiste mids zomers te minen live dies
ic sine opene brieve van hem hebbe. Ende kenne bi desen lettren dat
ic de vorseide ghifte vriendelike ontfaen hebbe. Ende dat ic daerof
manscerp ghedaen hebbe minen here vorseide ende belove mids
desen hem, sinen hoire, ende naercommers, graven iof gravinnen
van Vlaendren, wel ende ghetrauwelike te dienne in orloghen ende
in allen andre zaken als langhe als ic leven sal ieghen alle andre
heren uteghesteken den hertoghe van Guylke, minen gherechten
here, ende aldus hebbict belooft ende ghezekert bi mire trauwen
ende bi mire eeren bi der orconscerp van desen lettren beseghelt met
minen propren seighele. Ghegheven den xxvi dach van meije int
jaer Ons Here m ccc achte ende zeftech.

29. *Count Louis de Male reproduces letters of Louis de Nevers, count of Flanders, whereby the latter permits Duke John III of Brabant to assign to the merchant Andrien Royer a yearly sum of 1,800 l. of Paris in order to repay a debt of 5,400 l. of Paris; this yearly sum is to be taken from the fief-rente John holds from Louis who promises to pay the money to Andrien until the debt is paid in full.*

6 September 1371

Archives Générales du Royaume à Bruxelles. *Trésor de Flandre.* Série I. No. 1270.

Nous Jehans, dux de Lorhayne et marchis, faisons savoir a tous que comme nostre treschier seigneur et cousin, monseigneur le conte de Flandres, a nostre priiere et requeste nous ait donne et consenti unes lettres dont la fourme ci apres sensieut de mot a mot. Nous Loys, contes de Flandres, duc de Brabant, contes de Nevers, de Rethel, et sires de Malines, faisons savoir a tous que comme nostre treschier et feal cousin Jehans, duc de Lorhayne et marchis, doine a Andrieu Roiier marchant une somme de chinq mille et quatre cens livres parisis monnoie de Flandres, la quelle il a assignet de recevoir sur sa rente heritable quil tient de nous en fief sur nostre thonlieu dou Dam. Cest assavoir diiswiit cens livres parisis a deus termes cescun an as termes de le miaoust et de le Chandeler dont le premier payement de noef cens livres parisis sera a le miaoust prochain venant et le secund a le Chandeller premier apres ensi et ansi dan en an et de terme en terme tant et si longement que la ditte somme sera parpaiiet entirement qui astendent a siis termes. Nous lassignament dessus dit approuvons, confirmons, et consentons, et volons quil soit tenu en sa virtu. Et les promettons a faire paiier bien et loyaument audit Andrieu as termes dessus dittes. Si mandons et commandons a nos thonliers dou Dam, qui seront pour le temps, que sans autre mandement il paient audit Andrieu ou au porteur de lassignament bien et devement. Par le tesmoing de ces lettres seellees de nostre seel donnees a Gand le vi jour de septembre, lan de grace mil ccc soissante et onze. Nous avons promis et promettons loyaulment et en bonne foy ou cas que ainsi fust que mon dit seigneur et cousin mesist aucune chose dou sien es dis paiemens ou encourust et euist aucun coust ou domage pour aucune des dis paiemens de la ditte somme de v^m iiii^c libres parisis contenu es dittes lettres de lui rendre, paiier, et delivrer tout ce quil y avoit mis ensamble tous cous et domages plainement et entirement. Et volons et consentons que ce il puist prendre et ravoir sur la ditte rente des diiswiit cens livres parisis que nous tenons de lui en fief sur le dit thonlieu dou Dam comme dit est qui nous seront deus et escheuront apres les dittes trois annees. Et quant a ce nous avons oblegie et obligons devers nostre dit seigneur et cousin la ditte rente des xviii^c libres parisis par an par la maniere dessus ditte sans fraude et malengien. En tesmoing de ce nous avons seelle ces presentes lettres de nostre seel. Donne le vii^e jour dou mois de septembre, lan de grace mil ccc soissante et onze.

30. The knight Borzewey de Swyner recognizes to have received from John Pisto de Ludeo, his attorney and procurator, a sum of 100 m., money of England, in part payment of a fief of 500 florins owed him by Richard II of England.

28 October 1391

Public Record Office at London. Diplomatic Documents of the Exchequer. E. 30/1228.

Noverit universi me Borzewey de Swyner militem recepisse per manus Johannis Pisto de Ludeco, attornati mei et procuratoris generalis, de excellentissimo principe et domino domino Ricardo secundo, Dei gratia rege Anglie et Francie, per manus thesaurarii et camerarorum eiusdem domini regis de scaccario suo centum marcas monete Anglie in partem solucionis cuiusdam annui feodi quingentorum florenorum michi predicto Borzewey per prefatum dominum regem ad terminum vite mee concessos, percipiendos in dicto suo scaccario ad Festa Sancti Michaelis Archangli' et Pasche per equales porciones. De quibus centum marcis predictis sic michi in partem solucionis pro terminis antedictis solutis in valorem tot florenorum quot attingunt ad centum marcas predictas, fateor me bene fore solutum et predictum dominum regem inde fore quietum. In cuius rei testimonium huic presenti acquietancie sigillum meum apposui vicesimo octavo die octobris, anno regni domini regis predicti quintodecimo.

PLATES

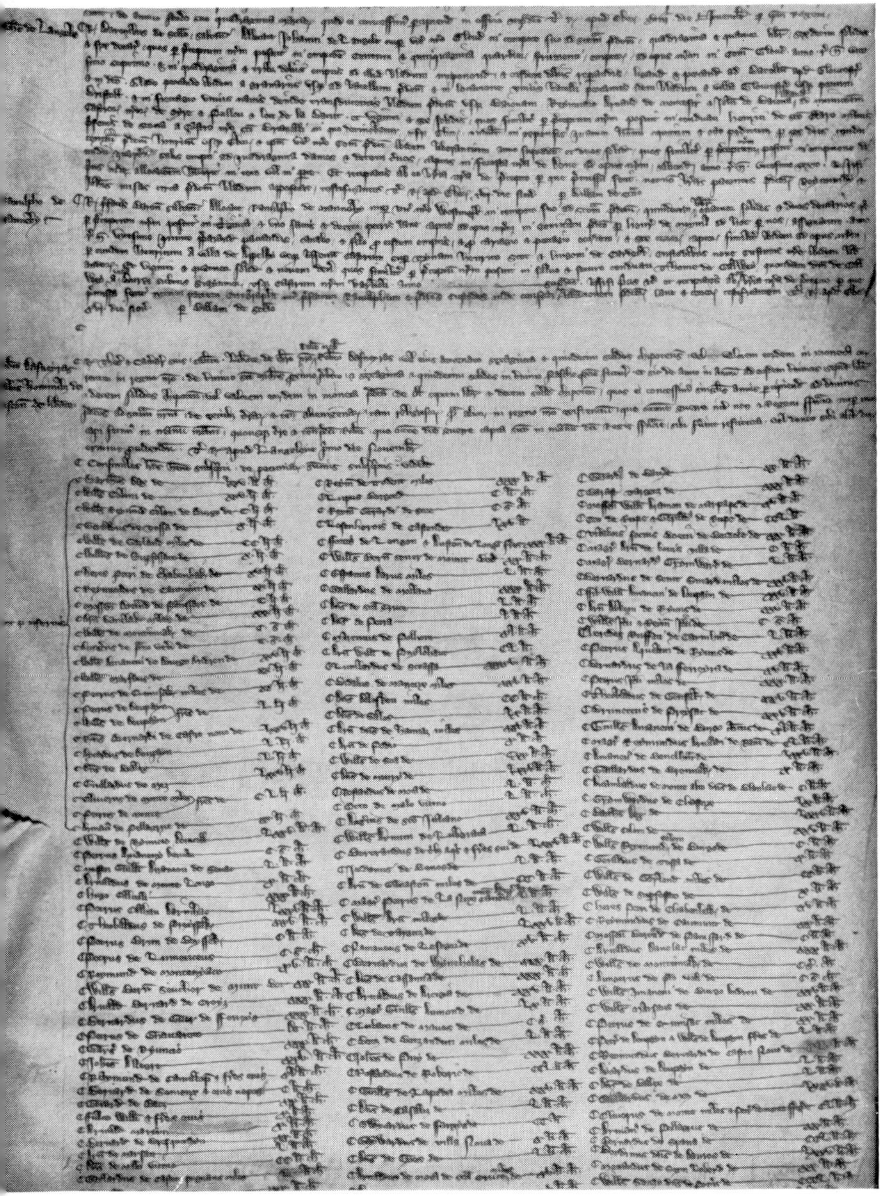

Plate I. Public Record Office. Liberate Roll of 1299. C. 62/75, part of m. 2.

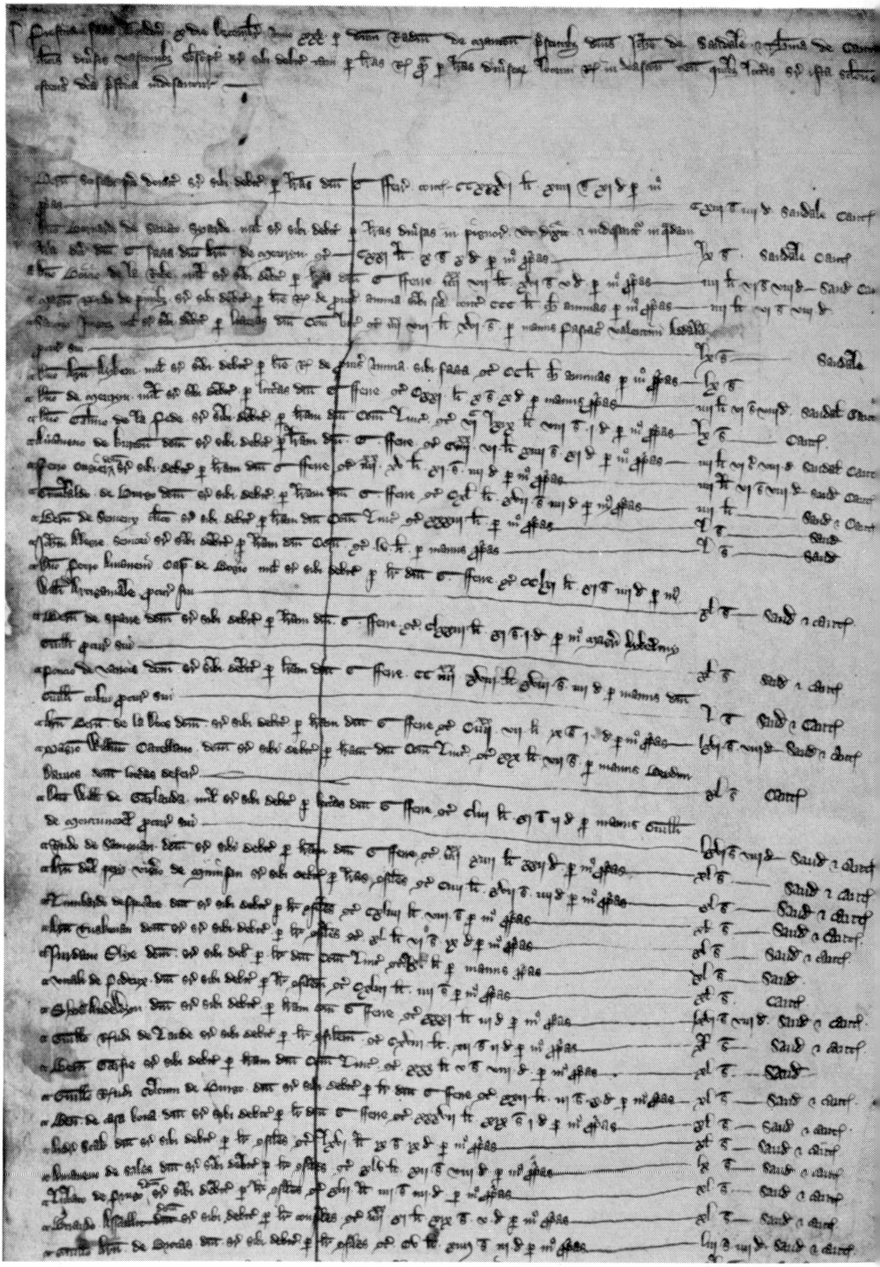

Plate II. Public Record Office. Various Accounts of the Exchequer.
E. 101/157/5. Excerpt from account of John de Sandale and
Thomas of Cambridge (1302).

Plate III. Archives Générales du Royaume à Bruxelles. Nélis, *Comptes en rouleaux*, no. 1. Excerpt from account of Thomas Fin, receiver general of Flanders (1308–09).

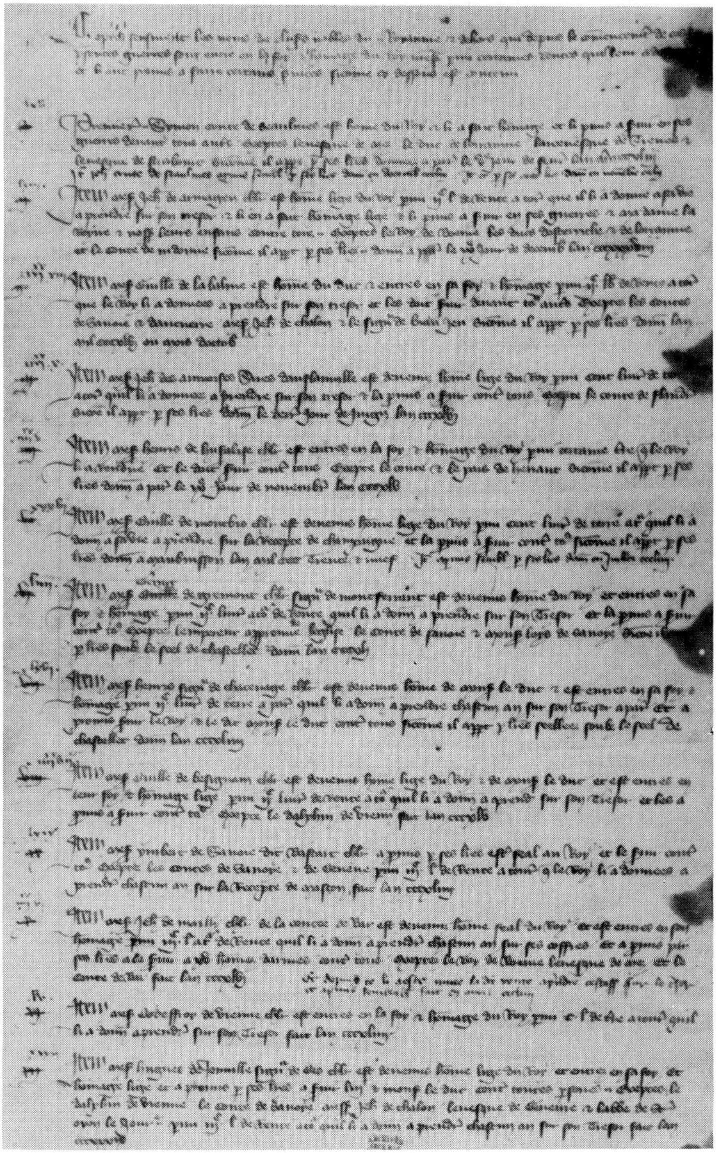

Plate IV. Archives Nationales à Paris. Hommages. Série J. 621/90.
Excerpt from roll recording homage done to French kings from
1337 to 1354.

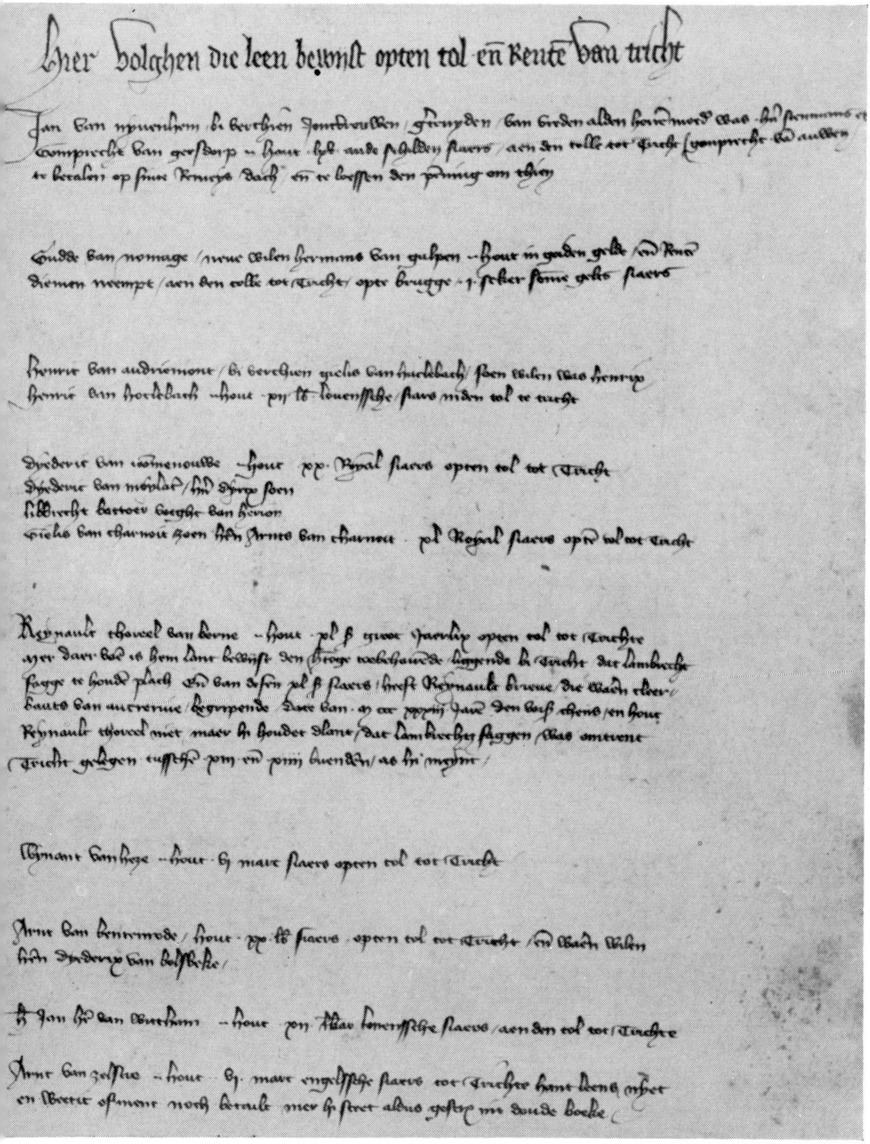
Hier volghen die leen bewijst opten tol en rente van tricht

Plate V. Archives Générales du Royaume à Bruxelles. Galesloot, *Cour féodale de Brabant,* no. 4, fol. 205r. Excerpt from *Spechtboek* (*circa* 1374).

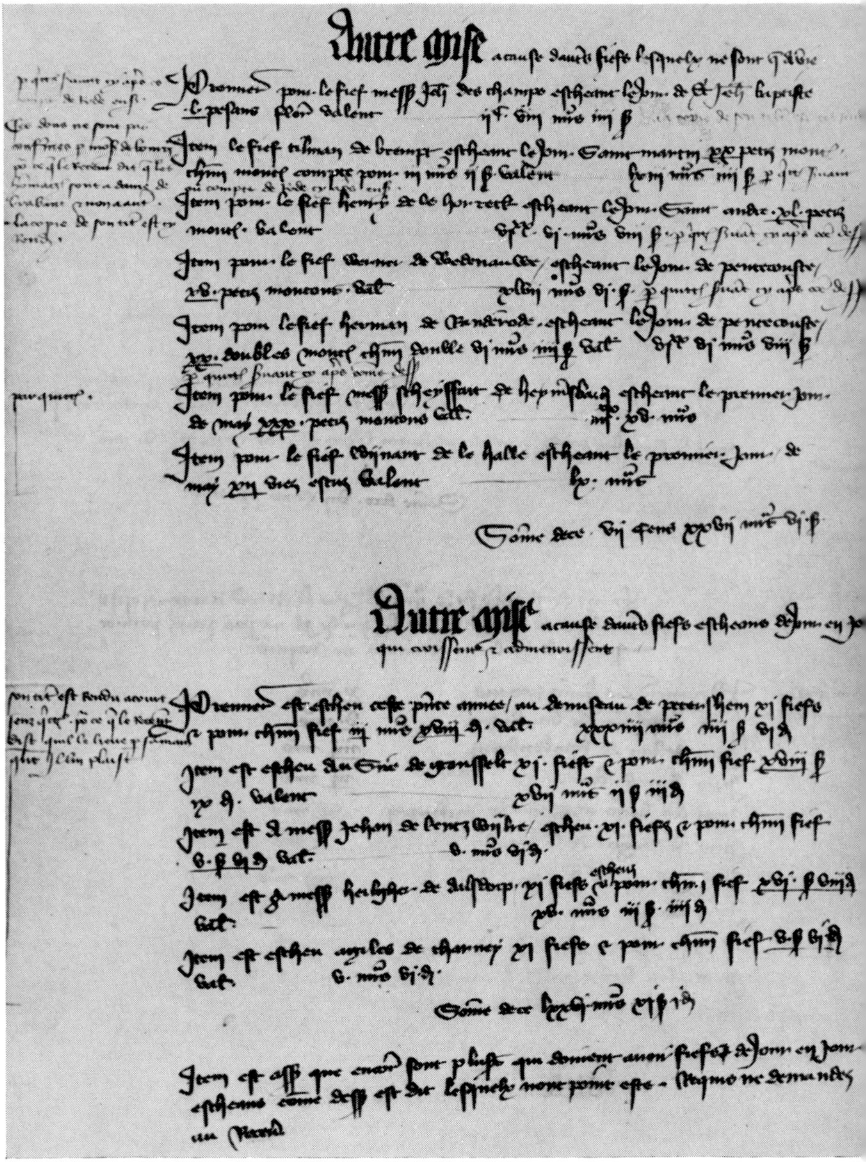

Plate VI. Archives Générales du Royaume à Bruxelles. *Chambre des Comptes*, no. 2436, fol. 76ᵛ. Excerpt from account rendered by Jean Sack de Wijck, receiver general of Limburg (1392–93).

Bibliography of Sources in Manuscript

All the collections of sources used in the present study are included in this bibliography which is arranged by country and by national and provincial archives. The principal published and unpublished inventories are given in parentheses immediately after each collection. In those cases, particularly with the collections of the Public Record Office where only one reference number appears followed by ff., it should be understood that this number represents but the first of a series of records used in this collection.

BELGIUM
Archives Générales du Royaume à Bruxelles

Chartier des duchées de Brabant, de Limbourg et des Pays d'Outre-Meuse.
> (A. Verkooren. *Inventaire des chartes et cartulaires des duchés de Brabant et de Limbourg et des Pays d'Outre-Meuse.* Bruxelles, 1910–22. Première partie. Vols. I–VIII.)
> (A. Verkooren. *Inventaire des chartes et cartulaires des duchés de Brabant et de Limbourg et des Pays d'Outre-Meuse.* Deuxième partie. Unpublished inventory in A.G.R.)
> (A. Verkooren. *Inventaire des chartes et cartulaires des duchés de Brabant et de Limbourg. Années 1383–1403.* Unpublished inventory in A.G.R.)
> (A. Verkooren. *Inventaire des chartes et cartulaires des duchés de Brabant et de Limbourg et des Pays d'Outre-Meuse. Années 1403–1500.* Unpublished inventory in A.G.R.)

Chartier du comté de Luxembourg.
> (A. Verkooren. *Inventaire des chartes et cartulaires du Luxembourg.* Bruxelles, 1914–21. Vols. I–V.)

Trésor des chartes des comtes de Flandre, à Lille. Série I.
> (H. Nélis. *Inventaire des chartes des comtes de Flandre à Lille.* Deuxième section. No. 134.)

Trésor des chartes de la chambre des comptes de Flandre. Série II.
(H. Nélis. *Inventaire des chartes de la chambre des comptes de Flandre*. Deuxième section. No. 96 A.)

Manuscrits divers (Various cartularies and manuscripts). Nos. 1/A, 6, 7, 15, 133.
(H. Nélis and J. Cuvelier. *Manuscrits divers*. Typescript copy in A.G.R.)

Cour féodale de Brabant. Nos. 4, 11, 18, 33, 119–26.
(L. Galesloot. *Inventaire de la cour féodale de Brabant*. Bruxelles, 1870–84. Vols. I–II.)

Chambre des comptes de Brabant et de Flandre.
Cartulaire de Brabant. No. 1.
Cartulaire de Namur. No. 56.
Leenboeck van Overmaeze. No. 572.
Comptes de l'hôtel des souverains. Nos. 1777–80, 1788–89, 1796.
Reliefs des fiefs de la ville de Bruges et du Franc de Bruges. Nos. 1794–1844.
Comptes de la recette générale des finances (Bourgogne). No. 1860.
Comptes des recettes générales des provinces.
    Brabant. Nos. 2350–60, 2376–77, 2382–86, 2395, 2402–3, 2408, 2414, 2420, 2423.
    Limbourg. Nos. 2436–51.
    Luxembourg et Chiny. No. 2628.
    Gueldre et Zutphen. Nos. 2660–61.
    Flandre. Nos. 2702, 2704–9.
    Hainaut. No. 3191.
    Namur. Nos. 3221–26, 3244.
Comptes de domaines.
    Tirlemont. Nos. 4013, 4028.
    Bruxelles. No. 4162.
    Tervueren et Vilvorde. No. 4749.
    Bois-le-Duc. Nos. 5232–39.
    Maestricht. Nos. 5462, 5485–86.
    Fauquemont. No. 5680.
    Daelhem. No. 5725.
    Pays de Rolduc. No. 5767.
    Arlon. No. 5921.
    Chiny et Étale. No. 6116.
    Luxembourg. Nos. 6297–98.
    La ville et district de Gueldre. No. 6675.
Comptes des rennenghes (Flandre). Nos. 7800–7802.

Comptes des domaines.
  Ath. No. 8254.
  Mons. Nos. 9997–98.
  Namur. No. 10929.
Comptes des tonlieux et des winages (Anvers). Nos. 22356–59.
Comptes de l'armée de terre. Solde. Comptes rendus par les trésoriers des guerres (Bourgogne). Nos. 25542–43, 25554–55.
Comptes des châtellenies, pays et métiers du comté de Flandre. Nos. 42521, 42890–901.
Recueil de documents relatifs aux fiefs et aux seigneuries du duché de Luxembourg, de 1200 à 1548. No. 45668.
Registres généraux. Officiers comptables. Domaines. État du revenu du duché de Luxembourg, 1311. No. 45721.
Maison des souverains. Fragment de dépenses particulières du duc de Gueldre de 1346 et 1347. No. 46920.
Maison des souverains. Compte, rendu par Jean de Reng à Jeanne et Wenceslas de Brabant, des revenus grevés sur la France, du 1er octobre 1373 au 22 juillet 1380. No. 46926.
Comptes des recettes générales des provinces.
  Brabant. No. 47026.
  Luxembourg. No. 47035.
  Gueldre. No. 47038.
  Flandre. No. 47045.
Comptes de reliefs de fief. Pays d'Outre-Meuse. No. 48887.
Contributions de guerre. Compte des tailles imposées en Brabant à l'occasion de la guerre entre le duc de Brabant et le comte de Flandre, de 1356–1357. Nos. 50344–45.
(L. Gachard, A. Pinchart, H. Nélis. *Inventaire des archives de la Chambre des Comptes.* Bruxelles, 1837–1931.)

Comptes en rouleaux.
Recette générale de Flandre. Nos. 1–7.
Domaines du bailliage de Menin. Nos. 117–40.
Domaines de Termonde. Nos. 208–220.
Compte de la recette des gros briefs de Flandre. Nos. 267–76.
Comptes de censiers du tonlieu de Damme. Nos. 622–85.
Tonlieu de Rupelmonde. Nos. 691–711.
Winage de Rupelmonde. Nos. 712–13.
Tonlieu de Termonde. Nos. 714–64.
Reliefs des fiefs du comté d'Alost et de Grammont. Nos. 1745–87.
Reliefs des fiefs de la ville de Bruges et du Franc de Bruges. Nos. 1794–1822.
Reliefs des fiefs de la ville et châtellenie de Courtrai. Nos. 1845–64.

Reliefs des fiefs de la ville de Gand et de la châtellenie du Vieux-Bourg de Gand. Nos. 1896–1930.

Tonlieu de Malines. Nos. 2129–34.

Domaines d'Anvers (Marquisat d'Anvers). Nos. 2190–2218.

Tonlieu d'Anvers, dit Borchrecht. Nos. 2224–2231bis.

Domaines de Yolande, comtesse de Bar, dame de Cassel. Nos. 2368–77.

Hôtel des ducs de Brabant. Nos. 2419–24.

Domaines d'Assche. Nos. 2425–2435ter.

Domaines de Maestricht, Limbourg, Daelhem, Rolduc. Nos. 2436–58.

Domaine d'Overyssche. Nos. 2459–63.

Domaine d'Overzenne. Nos. 2464–66.

Domaine de Tirlemont. Nos. 2467–98.

Hôtel des ducs de Gueldre. Nos. 2823–24.

(H. Nélis, *Chambre des comptes de Flandre et de Brabant. Inventaire des comptes en rouleaux.* Bruxelles, 1914.)

Archives de l'État à Gand

Charters der Graven van Vlaanderen.

Verzameling Saint Genois.

(J. De Saint Genois. *Inventaire analytique des chartes des comtes de Flandre avant l'avènement des princes de la maison de Bourgogne, autrefois déposées au château de Rupelmonde, et conservées aujourd'hui de la Flandre-Orientale.* Gand, 1843–46.)

Verzameling Gaillard.

(V. Gaillard. "Inventaire analytique des chartes des comtes de Flandre autrefois déposées au château de Rupelmonde, récemment trouvées aux archives de l'ancien Conseil de Flandre," *B.C.R.H.*, 2e Sér., VI–VII, 1854–55.)

Oostenrijksche Verzameling.

(L. Gachard. *Notice historique et descriptive des archives de la ville de Gand.* Bruxelles, 1854.)

Verzameling Diegerick.

(Unpublished inventory in A.E.G.)

Verzameling Verbaere.

(Unpublished inventory in A.E.G.)

Andere Charters.

(Unpublished inventory entitled *Supplément chronologique des chartes des comtes de Flandre*, in A.E.G.)

Kasselrij Aalst.
(Unpublished inventory entitled *Inventaire analytique des archives de la châtellenie d'Alost*, in A.E.G.)

Land en Leenhof van Dendermonde.
(Unpublished inventory entitled *Inventaire analytique des chartes du Pays de Termonde*, in A.E.G.)

Sint-Baafsabdij en Bisdom Gent (Leenhof van Sint-Baafs).
(A. Van Lokeren. *Histoire de l'abbaye de Saint-Bavon*. Gand, 1855.)

ARCHIVES DE L'ÉTAT À NAMUR

Chartrier des comtes de Namur.
(C. Piot. *Inventaire des chartes des comtes de Namur anciennement déposées au château de cette ville*. Bruxelles, 1890.)

Domaines.
Comptes du domaine. Nos. 1–2.
(Unpublished inventory in A.E.N.)

FRANCE

ARCHIVES NATIONALES

Trésor des chartes (Layettes). Série J.
Hainaut. J. 519–20.
Gueldre et Juliers. J. 522.
Brabant. J. 523–24.
Hollande. J. 525.
Frise. J. 526.
Liège. J. 527.
Artois. J. 530.
Namur. J. 531.
Flandre. J. 532–75.
Gueldre. J. 577.
Jean, comte de Sarrebruck. J. 578.
Lorraine. J. 579.
Metz. J. 580.
Bar. J. 581–82.
Verdun. J. 584–85.
Chastel-sur-Moselle. J. 586.
Luxembourg. J. 608.
Empereurs d'Allemagne. J. 610–12.
Hommages. J. 620–26.
Angleterre. J. 628–56.

(Unpublished inventory entitled *Inventaire du trésor des chartes du roy*, Vols. VI–VIII, in A.N.)

(Unpublished inventory by H. de Curzon entitled *Trésor des chartes. Supplément. Inventaire analytique*, in A.N.)

(*État sommaire par séries des documents conservés aux Archives Nationales*. Paris, 1891.)

(M. Delaborde. *Inventaire général sommaire des Archives de l'Empire*. Paris, 1867.)

(*Inventaire sommaire et tableau méthodique des fonds conservés aux Archives Nationales. Première partie. Régime antérieur à 1789*. Paris, 1871.)

ARCHIVES DÉPARTEMENTALES DU NORD À LILLE

Chambre des comptes. Série B.
  Inventaires des archives. B. 113–94.
  Trésor des chartes.
    Traités, Trèves, Négociations. B. 222–340.
    Hommages des princes. B. 495–501.
    Royaumes et pays.
      France. B. 653–61.
      Bourgogne-Duché. B. 667–73.
      Nevers et Réthel. B. 756–70.
      Picardie. B. 771–79.
      Soissons. B. 784–88.
      Bar, Perche, Étampes, Bretagne, Blois, Chartres, Vendôme. B. 789–823.
      Allemagne. B. 824–26.
      Liège. B. 829–37.
      Hôtel des princes. B. 893–94.
      Artois. B. 917–45.
      Saint-Omer. B. 963–74.
      Bapaume. B. 986–92.
      Béthune. B. 1005–26.
      Cambrai. B. 1046–50.
      Cambrésis. B. 1052–57.
      Lille-Ville. B. 1062–84.
      Châtellenie de Lille, Douai, et Orchies. B. 1104–10.
      Hainaut en général. B. 1161–91.
      Valenciennes (prévôté-le-Comte). B. 1208.
      Bouchain et Ostrevant. B. 1215–23.
      Agimont et Givet. B. 1256.
      Flandre en général. B. 1260–85.

Châtellenie et ville de Cassel. B. 1292–1306.
Nieppe. B. 1310.
Gravelines. B. 1321–25.
Bourbourg. B. 1326–30.
Châtellenie et ville de Bailleul. B. 1332–34.
Gand (châtellenie de). B. 1342–43.
Bruges. B. 1345–50.
Damme. B. 1353.
Franc de Bruges. B. 1354–55.
Ypres et sa châtellenie. B. 1359–63.
Furnes. B. 1369–71.
Courtrai. B. 1377–80.
Menin. B. 1382.
Audenarde. B. 1385.
Pays de Waës. B. 1388.
Rupelmonde. B. 1389.
Tournai et Tournaisis. B. 1390–91.
Alost. B. 1396–97.
Termonde. B. 1400.
Beveren. B. 1407.
Quatre Métiers. B. 1410.
Namur. B. 1411–14.
Brabant. B. 1418–21.
Limbourg. B. 1425.
Gueldre. B. 1426–27.
Luxembourg en général. B. 1430–33.
Luxembourg, divers. B. 1435.
Fauquemont. B. 1440.
Marville. B. 1441.
Hollande. B. 1444–49.
Matières généalogiques. B. 1543–44, 1547, 1549–50, 1556–57.
Trésor des chartes. Supplément. Série B.
Hommages des princes. B. 497–501.
Hainaut en général. B. 1166.
Cartulaires. B. 1561–70, 1573–75, 1582–84, 1587, 1591–95.
Registres des chartes. B. 1596, 1599, 1602–9.
Recette générale des finances. B. 1842–1956, 2108–15.
Recette générale de Flandre. Pièces comptables. B. 4033–83, 4100.
Comptes des briefs et espiers. B. 4240–48.
Comptes du domaine de Flandre. B. 4324–39.
Châtellenies de Douai et Orchies. B. 4626–47.
Châtellenie de Cassel. B. 4956–57.
Châtellenie de Menin. B. 5270.

Souverain bailliage de Flandre. B. 5627–28.
Comptes des bailliages de Flandre. B. 5701–15, 6005–12, 6159–96.
Fiefs de Flandre. B. 6611.
Apanage de Bar et Cassel. B. 7812–13.
Recette générale de Hainaut. B. 7860–61.
Comptes du domaine de Hainaut. B. 8255–58, 8284–91.
Grand bailliage de Hainaut. B. 10267–74.
Bailliage des bois du Hainaut. B. 10616.
Cambrésis. B. 13304, 13308–21.
Comptes des baillis d'Artois. B. 13595–96.
Bapaume. B. 14400.
Béthune. B. 14567–68.
(M. A. Desplanque, M. A. Dehaisnes, and J. Finot. *Inventaire sommaire des Archives Départementales antérieures à 1790. Nord. Archives civiles. Série B. Chambre des comptes de Lille.* Lille, 1872–1906. Vols. I–IX.)
(M. Bruchet. *Archives Départementales du Nord. Répertoire Numérique. Série B. Chambre des comptes de Lille.* Lille, 1921. Vol. I.)

ENGLAND
PUBLIC RECORD OFFICE
Chancery Rolls.
Gascon Rolls. C. 61/36, 49–50.
Liberate Rolls. C. 62/70–77, 114–16.
Patent Rolls. C. 66/200–202.
Patent Rolls (Supplementary). C. 67/17–18.
Roman Rolls. C. 70/16.
Treaty Rolls. C. 76/8, 11–17.
(*Lists and Indexes.* London, 1908. No. 27.)
Ancient Correspondence of Chancery and Exchequer. S. C. 1/1–55.
(*Lists and Indexes.* London, 1902. No. 15.)
Diplomatic Documents (Chancery). C. 47/27–32.
(*Lists and Indexes.* London, 1923. No. 49.)
Chancery Miscellanea. C. 47/22–26.
(Unpublished inventory entitled *Chancery Miscellanea,* in P.R.O.)
Diplomatic Documents (Exchequer). E. 30 ff.
(*Lists and Indexes.* London, 1923. No. 49.)
Wardrobe and Household Accounts. E. 36, E. 101 ff.
(Unpublished inventory by E. W. Safford entitled *Descriptive List of Wardrobe Books, Edward I to Edward IV,* in P.R.O.)

Various Accounts and Documents of the Exchequer.
Army, Navy, and Ordnance. E. 101/3/21 ff.
Army, Navy, and Ordnance (Indentures of War). E. 101/68/5,
E. 101/69/1.
Foreign Merchants. E. 101/126/13 ff.
France. E. 101/152/14 ff.
Nuncii. E. 101/308/18 ff.
Praestita. E. 101/325/2 ff.
(*Lists and Indexes.* London, 1912. No. 35.)
(Unpublished inventory entitled *Various Accounts of Exchequer.
Written Lists,* in P.R.O.)
L.T.R. Memoranda Rolls. E. 368/69.
(Unpublished inventory entitled *Lord Treasurer's Remembrancer
List of Chancellors' Rolls, Memoranda Rolls, Originalia Rolls,
and Pipe Rolls,* in P.R.O.)
Enrolled Accounts (Foreign). E. 364/3, E. 372/212.
(*Lord Treasurer's Remembrancer List,* in P.R.O.)
(*Lists and Indexes.* London, 1900. No. 11.)
Enrolled Accounts (France). E. 372/160, E. 372/183, E. 372/185.
(*Lord Treasurer's Remembrancer List,* in P.R.O.)
(*Lists and Indexes.* No. 11.)
Enrolled Accounts. E. 372/178, E. 372/181.
(*Lists and Indexes.* No. 11.)
Issue Rolls. E. 403/61 ff.
(Unpublished inventory entitled *Receipt and Issue Rolls,* in
P.R.O.)
Wardrobe Debentures. E. 404/481, E. 404/500–503.
(Unpublished inventory entitled *Class List of Records of the
Exchequer of Receipt,* in P.R.O.)
Warrants for Issues. E. 404/1–4.
(*Class List of Records of the Exchequer of Receipt,* in P.R.O.)
Transcripts from Lille. P.R.O. 31/8/143.
(Unpublished inventory entitled *Class List of Collections of Tran-
scripts,* in P.R.O.)

BRITISH MUSEUM

Royal Wardrobe and Household Accounts. Add. MS. 7965, Add.
MS. 37495, Stowe 570, 574.
(*Class Catalogue of MSS. No. 12. Public Revenues. State.* Vol. I.)

Index

Harvard Historical Studies

(Early titles now out of print are omitted.)

45. *Richard William Leopold*. Robert Dale Owen. 1940.

46. *Gerald Sandford Graham*. Sea Power and British North America, 1783–1820. 1941.

47. *William Farr Church*. Constitutional Thought in Sixteenth-Century France. 1941.

48. *Jack H. Hexter*. The Reign of King Pym. 1941.

49. *George Hoover Rupp*. A Wavering Friendship: Russia and Austria, 1876–1878. 1941.

51. *Frank Edgar Bailey*. British Policy and the Turkish Reform Movement. 1942.

52. *John Black Sirich*. The Revolutionary Committees in the Departments of France. 1943.

53. *Henry Frederick Schwarz*. The Imperial Privy Council in the Seventeenth Century. 1943.

54. *Aaron Ignatius Abell*. Urban Impact on American Protestantism. 1943.

55. *Holden Furber*. John Company at Work. 1948.

56. *Walter Howe*. The Mining Guild of New Spain and Its Tribunal General. 1949.

57. *John Howes Gleason*. The Genesis of Russophobia in Great Britain. 1950.

58. *Charles Coulston Gillispie*. Genesis and Geology: A Study in the Relations of Scientific Thought, Natural Theology, and Social Opinion in Great Britain, 1790–1850. 1951.

59. *Richard Humphrey*. Georges Sorel, Prophet without Honor: A Study in Anti-Intellectualism. 1951.

60. *Robert G(eorge) L(eeson) Waite*. Vanguard of Nazism: The Free Corps Movement in Postwar Germany 1918–1923. 1952.

61. *Nicholas V(alentine) Riasanovsky*. Russia and the West in the Teaching of the Slavophiles. 1952.

62. *John King Fairbank*. The Opening of the Treaty Ports: Trade and Diplomacy on the China Coast 1842–1854. Vol. I, text.

63. *John King Fairbank*. The Opening of the Treaty Ports . . . Vol. II, reference material. 1953.

64. *Franklin L. Ford*. Robe and Sword: The Regrouping of the French Aristocracy after Louis XIV. 1953.

65. *Carl E. Schorske*. German Social Democracy, 1905–1917. The Development of the Great Schism. 1955.

66. *Wallace Evan Davies*. Patriotism on Parade: The Story of Veterans' and Hereditary Organizations in America, 1783–1900. 1955.

67. *Harold Schwartz*. Samuel Gridley Howe: Social Reformer, 1801–1876. 1956.